T0369444

FROM ADAM TO OMEGA

FROM ADAM TO OMEGA

An Anatomy of UFO Phenomena

A. R. Roberts

iUniverse, Inc.
Bloomington

From Adam to Omega
An Anatomy of UFO Phenomena

iUniverse books may be ordered through booksellers or by contacting:

iUniverse
1663 Liberty Drive
Bloomington, IN 47403
www.iuniverse.com
1-800-Authors (1-800-288-4677)

ISBN: 978-1-4759-0504-5 (sc)
ISBN: 978-1-4759-0506-9 (hc)
ISBN: 978-1-4759-0505-2 (e)

Printed in the United States of America

iUniverse rev. date: 10/23/2012

Contents

PART 3—FUTURE POSSIBILITIES

Preface

I was only seven years old when I saw the magazine lying on the coffee table and stared at the cover. It was an artist's rendering of a gold disc-shaped craft flying over a small red airplane. Intrigued, I picked up the magazine and began reading the story, and that is when I learned of Kenneth Arnold's historic UFO sighting. It said he was flying his private plane over the Cascade Mountains in the state of Washington when he noticed nine crescent-shaped objects flitting through the sky near Mount Rainier. *My God,* I thought. *What the heck could they be?* My first thought was that they might be from Mars or some other planet, and I was filled with a mixture of awe, excitement, and apprehension. *What were they? Where were they from? Were we being invaded?* I didn't know what to think, but the possibilities fascinated me. It was because of Arnold's description of how they flew like saucers being skipped across the water that a newspaper reporter coined the term "flying saucers." However, going to school and playing baseball with my friends soon made me forget about Kenneth Arnold and whatever it was he saw.

It wasn't until a few years later that I learned about the Roswell incident that occurred two weeks after Arnold's sighting. I might attribute it to the fact that the publicity was so short-lived, and that, as a seven-year-old, I was not much into reading newspapers. However, I learned that the US Army had actually issued a press release stating that it had recovered a flying saucer that crashed on a ranch near Roswell, New Mexico, and that the air force quickly shot down the story by claiming it was only a weather balloon. Yet something about the story never made sense to me. The army's press release clearly stated that they had retrieved a crashed flying saucer, so how could they possibly mistake a weather balloon for a flying saucer? But who was I to argue? These incidents apparently aroused the public's interest, because people all over the world suddenly began seeing strange things in the sky—and have been ever since.

In spite of all the studies and investigations that have been conducted over the years, why do UFOs continue to remain an unsolved mystery? Surely after sixty years, we have acquired the technology to know if they are simply unexplained weather phenomena, hallucinations, or spacecraft from another world. We have computers that fit in the palms of our hands and cell phones that allow us to talk to anyone anywhere in the world at any time. We have launched hundreds of satellites into orbit; we have put men on the moon; and we have sent robotic probes to Mars and unmanned spacecraft to the outer planets, yet we are still unable to prove conclusively what UFOs are—and there has to be a reason. It would seem that someone must know the answer by now.

Many researchers suggest that flying craft have been around ever since man first walked upon the earth. They point to the images he painted on rocks and in caves all over the world, and they question why many medieval artists included strange aerial objects in their paintings. Many believe it is evidence that aliens have been coming here for thousands of years; however, proving it is another matter. So what was it that really inspired ancient man to create these images? What message was he trying to convey thousands of years ago on rocks and cave walls? Of course, these objects might represent any number of things, yet it is difficult to ignore their resemblance to many UFOs reported today. But if UFOs really were around in ancient times, it raises many questions regarding academia's established concepts about the history and evolution of the human race.

It is difficult for modern man, with his iPads and nuclear bombs, to conceive the existence of flying machines long before he invented them; therefore, he assumes that such things cannot be. Mainstream scientists sweep these (and other artifacts that do not conform to conventional beliefs) under the carpet; perhaps they think that if they ignore them long enough, they will go away. But they will not. Ignoring the possibility of what this artwork might represent simply because it does not conform to established beliefs negates any opportunity to learn the real facts, so we are left treading water in a sea of uncertainty about what may be clues to a lost chapter in human history.

However, it does bring into question the technological achievements of ancient man. Did a civilization possess aircraft in some long-forgotten age? Museums around the world contain fossils and bones of creatures that lived hundreds of millions of years ago, so surely by now some evidence of a technologically advanced civilization should also have been uncovered. Of course, it is possible that such a civilization, if it did exist, was wiped out by a disaster similar to what killed off the dinosaurs sixty-five million years ago, along with most all other life on the planet. Such an event today would abruptly end life as we know it: civilization, or what was left of it, would be catapulted into a primitive existence, and it would take thousands of years for our current level of technology to again be realized. By then, any devices of a mechanical nature would have long eroded away, and little, if anything, would be left to tell any future civilization how much we had actually achieved. After a millennium or two of climbing back out of a Stone Age existence, scientists of the future unearthing references to aircraft and men going to the moon in the twentieth century might easily consider it all a myth. Therefore, when examining the objects depicted in ancient man's artwork, one has to wonder if they are simply expressions of art that have been totally misperceived, or if they represent a technology manufactured by some unknown earlier civilization—or even by someone not of this world.

Misperceived artistic expression aptly suits mainstream scientists, as it relieves them of the burden of having to defend their status quo perception of human history. Thus the idea of an earlier and technologically advanced civilization is categorically denied on the basis that there is no proof it ever existed. However, this denial is only an assumption based on the preconceived notions promoted by mainstream science, and an assumption is neither fact nor proof. Therefore, if by chance this artwork is a clue to some lost and forgotten civilization—or even extraterrestrial visitors—we are missing the opportunity to learn what was really going on in the distant past.

Most scientists agree that the disappearance of life sixty-five million years ago was the result of a huge asteroid impact in the Yucatán Peninsula. However, it was not the first mass extinction; it happened several times before, and one must wonder how much of our history that we will never know about was completely obliterated—and how much may have survived in the form of myth. Such an example is Troy. The city of Troy had always been considered a myth until it was discovered in 1870 by a maverick archaeologist named Heinrich Schliemann. Naturally, this raises a legitimate question: how many other myths might also be based on fact? Could it be that what looks like aircraft in ancient man's artwork is more of a reality than we think?

Man is an inherently curious species, always seeking answers. UFOs, however, seemed to be beyond anyone's understanding; no one in the government or the military knew what they were. Their speed and maneuverability displayed superior capabilities, and many thought they might be a new secret weapon; however, the most popular belief among the general populace was that they were spacecraft from another planet.

Eventually, the more practical term unidentified flying object, or UFO, was adopted. Not only have UFOs been seen streaking across the skies, but they have been observed hovering, landing, and taking off. They have been tracked by radar and pursued by military aircraft. They have been seen popping up out of oceans and lakes as well as diving into them. They have caused automobile engines to stall and have been associated with various power outages. There have been reports of encounters with aliens both friendly and hostile and people who claim they were abducted. There are stories about alien bodies being recovered where flying saucers have crashed—and allegations that the government is covering up the evidence.

Alien descriptions have ranged from gelatinous blobs to short grey creatures with large bulbous heads and large dark almond-shaped eyes—

even tall blond-haired Adonises. Contactee cults (people who claimed they interacted with extraterrestrials) sprang up in the 1950s and '60s. They said the aliens were benevolent "space brothers" who had come to Earth to solve all our problems, and many claimed they were even given rides in their spaceships. Depending on the contactee, they came from Venus, Mars, Jupiter, Saturn, or some other star system thousands of light-years away—even from other galaxies.

UFOs have been observed in almost every color of the spectrum. They have been reported as silver or metallic craft or objects emitting a bright glow or engulfed in an aura of light, and they frequently display a variety of flashing or pulsating lights. They have been described in a variety of shapes including disc, oval, crescent, wedge, triangular, diamond, and cigar. They have been reported in sizes ranging from eighteen inches long to over three hundred feet in diameter and, in some cases, over a mile in length. They also seem to display stealth technology. There have been times when military and commercial airline pilots observed UFOs, yet they were invisible to radar, and there were times when they were tracked by radar and invisible to the naked eye.

Today, people all over the world are filming these objects with video cameras. One curious feature is that they often appear to morph (change shape). It flies in the face of logic, as do some of their maneuvers—maneuvers that would be fatal to a human being. If they are of extraterrestrial origin, they are utilizing a dimension of technology far beyond our understanding.

Most experts agree that 95 percent of all sightings are explainable. However, a lack of information isn't what leaves the remaining 5 percent in question—it is just the opposite. They include incidents where UFOs have been tracked by radar, left physical traces of their presence at landing sites, and sightings made by highly credible witnesses such as air force and commercial airline pilots. Are these the same objects that ancient man drew on rocks and in caves? Are these the same objects that many medieval artists incorporated into their paintings? If so, what are they? Where do they come from? Why are they here? These bottom-line questions remain unanswered. The only thing most investigators and researchers seem to agree on is that they display a technology highly superior to ours, and that they are *probably* not from Earth. Whatever they are, the evidence tends to suggest they are real.

My interest in UFOs really began in 1955, while serving as a volunteer in the Ground Observer Corp (GOC). For those who have forgotten, or were not yet born, the GOC was an air force program designed to reduce the threat of a surprise air attack from the former Soviet Union. A radar network scattered across northern Canada, known as the Distant Early Warning (DEW) Line, eventually replaced it.

Civilian volunteers, usually recruited by the local Civil Defense Agency, staffed each GOC post, and it was their job to log and report all aircraft to an Air Force filter center. Each volunteer was issued a manual with a dark blue cover containing photographs and information on every known type of aircraft flying at the time: American, foreign, civilian, and military. Once an observer became familiar with the local air traffic, it was easy to tell by the sound if a plane had one or multiple engines.

At the time, I was living in Plattsburgh, New York, a small city twenty-six miles south of the Canadian border, situated on the west side of Lake Champlain. Our post designation was Bravo Quebec 34 Black (Quebec pronounced as "Kaybek"), and it was located on the roof of Physicians Hospital, the highest point in the city. During the day, Vermont's Green Mountains provided a spectacular view on the east side of Lake Champlain, and to the northeast, the domes of the St. Albans Radar Station glistened like pearls in the sunlight. At night, the lights of Burlington cast a warm glow in the southeastern sky, as did the lights of Montreal, sixty miles to the north. Plattsburgh Municipal Airport was located a few miles west of the city, but beyond that, the area was sparsely populated. Although there were a few small villages tucked away in the hills and valleys, the area became a virtual black void at night. However, at the south end of the city, the sky was aglow from lights of the new air force base under construction. It was to be a Strategic Air Command (SAC) base, one of the largest in the world, hosting a fleet of B-47 bombers and KC-97 refueling tankers.

During the spring of 1955, there were numerous sightings by local citizens as well as observers on duty at the post. As is usually the case, the press treated UFOs as a joke, even the reports made by credible Corps members. They often portrayed those patriotic citizens who were devoting their personal time maintaining the security of their country as fools. One article that appeared in the *Albany Times Union* even referred to them as cultists. However, "Tip" Roseberry, the columnist who wrote the article, eventually tempered his skepticism after Jim Roddy, the news director of one of the local radio stations, invited him to visit our post. After spending one night with us, he realized that we were not lunatics, alcoholics, or prone to believing that every light we saw in the night sky was a UFO. Then, in a later article, he admitted that he himself had seen something in the sky that he could not explain.

I joined the Corps in 1954, when I was just fourteen years old. I was the youngest observer on our post and spent at least one night every weekend on duty. It was really the older folks who put in the most time; they were from the old school, many having served in the First and Second World Wars, so their patriotic values were deeply rooted. However, there were many hours and even days when the post was unmanned. There was no pay and no glory, no real incentive for anyone to give up his free time. Those who put in the time did so because they wanted to.

I was an average teenager of that era. I went to church every Sunday and enjoyed hanging out with my friends after school and on weekends. We were well disciplined in moral and ethical behavior, so the most mischief we ever got into was skinny-dipping at the local swimming hole and soaping up car windows on Halloween. We never did anything that was harmful to anyone or destroyed other people's property—we knew we faced the wrath of our parents if we did. But nothing short of bad weather deterred me from spending most Friday nights operating the post, usually from nine at night until three or four in the morning, and there were times when I stayed until after dawn, all with my mother's permission, of course—life was much simpler back then ... and a lot safer. Nevertheless, anyone who had to walk home in the wee hours of the morning after a late watch was instructed to wear his Civil Defense armband, and the police were aware of this fact.

In retrospect, the Plattsburgh sightings were nothing spectacular: strange lights in the night sky that appeared to move in a manner uncommon to normal aircraft. Since most sightings were made at night by local citizens, it is reasonable to assume that many were probably misidentified conventional aircraft, meteors, or even the planet Venus. However, one incident did occur in broad daylight: two fireballs passed over the post about two hours apart. As I recall, the first was green, the second red, and both followed a south-to-north trajectory. The observers on duty said their speed was phenomenal; they passed from horizon to horizon in a matter of seconds in total silence—and there was no sonic boom. From what I heard, the green one was sighted a few minutes earlier over Albany, about 140 miles to the south. Our filter center, also located in Albany, purportedly called the post, alerting the observers to be on the lookout for it. I often wondered what they thought when told that it had already passed over.

There were, however, a few times during my watch when in the sky appeared lights that I was sure were not conventional aircraft. The first incident involved a bright white light that appeared over Lake Champlain. At first, I thought it was a commercial aircraft en route from Burlington to Plattsburgh, which then flew on to Albany and New York City. Then I remembered that that flight occurred about an hour earlier. The light moved to a position over the new air force base and stopped. It then hovered motionless for over an hour above the glow of construction lights, where crews were working around the clock laying the runways. Not wanting to attract additional negative press, I did not report it.

On another night, I observed a bright orange light approaching from the southeast at what seemed to be an unusually low altitude for an aircraft. I watched as it passed directly overhead in total silence and disappeared into the northwest. Had it been a little smaller, I would have passed it off as one of the jet fighters from Ethan Allen Air Force Base across the lake in Burlington, as it did approach from that direction. Not able to identify it by sound, I reported it as a probable single-engine jet.

Within a few minutes, two jet fighters from Burlington came screaming across the lake, also at an unusually low altitude. They were flying full throttle, with afterburners blazing in what seemed like hot pursuit, but their speed did not match that of the silent light that had passed over a few minutes earlier.

About thirty minutes later, the bright orange light (or another one just like it) approached from the northwest, heading in an east-southeasterly direction and swiftly passed by in total silence north of the post. I could hear the sound of jets in the distance, and what I assumed were the same two fighters that passed over earlier were also approaching from the northwest—on the same course as the orange light.

I was certain, however, that the first light was not a jet. At night, the exhaust from the fighter planes looked like little orange balls of light moving across the sky, and the sound of their engines always followed behind. Day or night, if you heard a high-flying jet, you could usually find it by looking ahead of the sound. However, the orange light was twice the size of what normal single-engine jet exhausts looked like, and there was no discernible sound, yet the roar of jet engines was distinct with the two fighter planes.

I hadn't a clue what the orange light was. I was a practical kid and figured it might be some new type of aircraft. All I knew was that it moved faster than the jets, and there was no discernible sound. And there was a question as to whether the two fighters were really in pursuit; there was no way for me to know. The Ethan Allen birds normally flew during the daylight hours, but on occasion, they did conduct night exercises; however, it was usually at higher altitudes. Having spent many nights operating the post, I was fully aware that flying over a populated area at night, and at a low altitude with afterburners engaged, did not conform to normal routine.

Due to local news coverage of a few sightings, the post began to attract visitors. One Friday night shortly after I went on duty, Professor Rusterholtz, the astronomy teacher from what was commonly called Plattsburgh State Teachers College (State University of New York at Plattsburgh—SUNY), came up to the post with two students. Not long after, a loan officer from one of the local banks arrived with another gentleman; both were retired air force men. One had been a bomber pilot and the other a navigator—

unfortunately, I do not remember their names. Then Jim Roddy, the news director of WEAV Radio, and Art Pierce, the station's newscaster, arrived. Dr. Adolph Ditmar, a local dentist, soon followed. A few minutes later, an air force sergeant, whose name I cannot remember, from the Albany filter center arrived—I assumed to find out what was going on in Plattsburgh and provide a rational explanation. Everyone else had come out of simple curiosity.

I remember that it was cool and damp that night. The air was still, with hardly a breeze, and a thick overcast hung low in the sky, the dark grey color casting an eerie reflection of the city lights below. Disappointed by the overcast, everyone just stood around talking. At approximately ten thirty, I was calling in a routine aircraft report, a commercial flight that passed over every night about the same time, en route (I believe) from New York to Montreal. It was above the overcast, and the sound of its jet engines was very distinct. Then I heard someone say, "What's that?" I turned and looked out the door of the post to see a bright white light approaching from the south; it was beneath the overcast and strobing at a tremendous rate. Assuming it was an aircraft, I advised the officer at the filter center that another plane was approaching, and rather than make another call, I asked if he would hold on while I gathered the details. He said he would. I went outside to determine if it was a jet or prop; however, there was no sound. Everyone stood silent for a moment, but we heard absolutely nothing.

The light was extremely bright, and my first impression was that it was zigzagging back and forth. As it got closer, it looked as if it might have been two strobe lights alternately flashing on and off; the pulsation was so rapid that even with binoculars it was impossible to tell. Because of its brilliance, we could not detect any kind of shape or surface behind or above it. Accustomed to observing aircraft at night, I had the distinct impression that it was moving much faster than any conventional airplane. The retired pilot and his navigator friend estimated the overcast to be about six to seven thousand feet. They attempted to time the light between two land points and approximated its speed at around one thousand miles an hour.

When I relayed this information to the officer at the filter center, he sounded skeptical and suggested it might be a star peeking through the clouds. He said that moving clouds sometimes create the illusion that stars are lights moving across the sky. I explained that while I was familiar with that situation, there were no breaks in the overcast at this time—it was low and heavy, and no stars were visible. I also explained that the light approached from the south, passed overhead, and disappeared in the north, so it could not have been a star. Then he suggested that it might be some kind of weather balloon. I acknowledged that possibility, but the fact that it was moving at an estimated one thousand miles an hour meant the wind would have to be blowing that fast, and if that were the case, it is doubtful that I would still be standing there talking to him—and as I already stated, that night there was hardly a breeze. I also explained that a retired air force pilot and a navigator were the ones who'd calculated the speed. At this point, the sergeant came in and took over the phone. He talked in a low voice, and I could not hear what he was saying. Not wanting to appear to be eavesdropping, I went out and joined the others on the roof.

No one could explain what that strobing light was. They knew it was not a balloon, and they were sure it was not a conventional aircraft. And the sergeant … well, he had no particular comment to make one way or the other. At least there were other witnesses—credible and well-respected members of the community. They were not hallucinating, and no one had been drinking; they all saw the same thing at the same time, and that was a fact no one could dispute.

The most memorable incident occurred one evening when Jim Roddy and Art Pierce from the radio station stopped by. They had visited frequently over the weeks, hoping to see something; but except for the night just described, nothing ever happened while they were there. However, on this particular night, they spotted a low-flying light near the new base but lost it in the glare of the construction lights. I was inside the post calling in a routine aircraft report and hadn't seen it. At first, I thought they were just kidding around, but they were adamant that what they saw was not a conventional aircraft. We even searched with binoculars, but the bright glow of the construction lights made it impossible to see. Being professional newsmen, they decided to drive over to the area and investigate. During the course of their visits, we had gotten to know each other pretty well, and so they asked if I wanted to go along. My curiosity was sparked by their sincere belief that something was out there, so I decided to close the post for a few minutes and go with them.

The nearest we could get to the area was a dirt road recently cut through the woods along the north perimeter of the new base. Eventually, it would be an artery connecting Route 9 in the southeast part of the city to Route 22 on the southwest side, and it would run parallel to the fence separating the road from the main runway. Roddy was driving. He had a vintage 1951 or '52 Chevrolet, and it bounced violently in the muddy ruts of the unpaved road. In a few minutes, we were surrounded by trees and not quite sure where we were, so we decided to stop and check the city map. We came to a clearing that, judging from the large Euclid tire tracks, was originally cleared to park the heavy equipment used to fell the trees and open up the road. We pulled in and parked on a dry patch so we would not become mired down.

Since the road was not yet on the map, we exited the car, and Roddy climbed up on its roof, hoping to spot a city light that might give us a clue as to our exact position. Unfortunately, the trees were too high, completely obscuring any view of the city lights, so we decided to proceed farther down the road. Then, just as we were about to reenter the car, we all looked up simultaneously. Directly above our heads was a bright white oval object about thirty to forty feet above the treetops. It was drifting slowly and silently to the east and seemed to be emitting (or dripping) sparks. In what seemed like four or five seconds, it had moved out of sight above the trees.

In discussing it later, our best estimate of its size was approximately thirty-five to forty feet from front to back. I cannot say for sure how accurate that estimate is, but if you take an average-sized watermelon, and hold at arm's length over your head, it will give you a good idea how big it was. I think it was Roddy who said, "Did you see that?" We replied that we had, still looking in the direction where the object had disappeared over the trees. But what happened next was rather odd. We got in the car and headed back to town without ever trying to catch up to the object for another look. It was not until we were almost back to the GOC post that we even began to talk about it.

Years later, I recognized this as a characteristic that is often associated with the abduction phenomenon, although I am sure nothing like that occurred: there was no "missing time," and this was long before anyone had ever heard about abductions. However, I believe we may have been close enough to the object to experience some kind of a side effect. From the moment we looked up and saw the thing, it was as if everything were happening in slow motion … but not really. It is difficult to explain—I can only describe it as *perceptual distortion*.

You would think the instinctive reaction for professional newsmen would be to pursue the object down the road to try to get another look at it. But for some reason, it would seem that the thought of pursuit never entered our minds. Even if it had, the raw condition of the road made it impossible anyway because we could not drive more than five or ten miles per hour without risking damage to the car. In fact, several minutes passed before we even had the presence of mind to talk about it, and in the back of my mind, I guess I had always wondered why. Whenever the incident came to mind, I found myself pondering more about the object than what happened afterward. I realize now that our experience was not unique because it appears that the same, or similar, effects have been experienced by other UFO witnesses.

I distinctly remember that while standing outside the car, we conversed in a normal tone of voice. If it were a plane or a helicopter, even the noise of the construction equipment operating a short distance away behind the trees on the south side of the road was not loud enough to drown out the sound of an engine, and I do not recall hearing any sound at all. Someone later suggested that it might have been a flare, but that was unlikely: I have never heard of a flare thirty-five feet long—or one that could drift along horizontally at such a slow speed.

After fifty years, I still tend to doubt that it was a new secret aircraft. If it were, it would have become obsolete in twenty years, in which case it probably would no longer have been secret. I have not discounted the possibility that it was some kind of weather phenomenon; however, the distortion of perception tends to negate that idea. Ball lightning is the only phenomenon one might compare it with; it often appears as a ball of light darting across the sky, and it is often mistaken for a UFO. However, it usually measures from a few inches to a few feet; I have never heard of it being thirty-five or forty feet long. Whatever it was, we were sure of two things: it was low—almost skimming the treetops—and it was not a conventional aircraft.

Over the years, I have seen a few of Mother Nature's odd quirks. One of the strangest was a sun dog, what looks like a second sun that is created by ice crystals in the atmosphere refracting or reflecting sunlight. It appeared one morning at just about sunrise while I was on duty at the post. Never having seen one before, I wasn't sure what it was at first; it just hung motionless in the eastern sky and seemed to sparkle in every color of the spectrum. Jim Roddy had stopped by on his way to the radio station, observed it through the binoculars, and said it looked like an inverted dessert dish.

Roddy urged me to call it in to the filter center, and so I did. While on the phone, the filter center contacted the St. Albans Radar Station northeast of us across the lake in Vermont in an attempt to verify the sighting, but they painted nothing on their radar. They even tried to patch me directly to the station so we might effect a triangulation, but for some technical reason, the connection could not be made. The filter center then advised me to keep an eye on it and call them back if anything changed. Roddy had to leave for the radio station, and as the sun rose higher, the spectacle gradually faded and eventually disappeared. That is when I became convinced that it was nothing more than a sun dog. It was only a coincidence that I had recently read an article on sun dogs in a science magazine, but never having seen one before, I wasn't sure at first what it was, and I have not seen another since then.

The incident caught the attention of the late Major Donald Keyhoe, who wrote it up as a sighting in one of the books he had written about flying saucers. How he heard of it is something I'll never know, as I was never contacted, and to the best of my knowledge, neither was Roddy, although I suspect he probably told someone involved in the field of UFO research, and that person passed it on. Had I been contacted to verify the story, I would have explained that it was simply a sun dog, nothing more. I did read Keyhoe's first book, but not the ones he wrote later; I only found out about the story from an acquaintance who had the book and showed it to me. I am sure Keyhoe mentioned the incident in good faith, believing it was a legitimate sighting. However, had he or his researchers been a little more thorough, he could have saved his publisher some ink. And this is a good example of why you shouldn't always believe everything you read about UFOs.

There are those who will undoubtedly question the reliability of the events I have described since they occurred over fifty years ago. Fifty years is a long time, in which one may easily confuse times, dates, and details of an event and recall them incorrectly. However, I pride myself with a rather exceptional memory. As a child, I remember that we lived on the first floor of a two-story house at the end of Front Street in Waterford, New York, right on the Hudson River, and the Erie Canal actually began right behind our backyard. There was a lilac tree behind the house, and I would hide behind it when playing hide-and-seek with the neighborhood kids. Its fresh, clean scent always exhilarated me. I remember that the landlord's last name was Castercani. I remember my third birthday party in that house, and that my parents gave me a stuffed panda bear that was so huge it towered over me. I remember my sister graduating from high school when I was four and taking a postgraduate course before going to work for the telephone company in Albany. I even remember the name of her first boyfriend, whom I will not identify here. I remember that my dad worked for General Electric and died from ruptured appendix in 1946, after we had moved to 1026 Cutler Street in Schenectady—the doctor had misdiagnosed his symptoms as acute indigestion. Although I was an adopted child, it is ironic that mine ruptured a year later on a Sunday afternoon. I was doubled over in pain, and after losing my dad, my mother wasn't taking any chances. She called Dr. Gray, our new family physician, and he agreed to see me. We went straight to his office, and after a quick examination, he immediately had me admitted to Ellis Hospital. However, the surgeon, Dr. McMillan (or MacMillan), couldn't operate because I had a cold, so they had to give me a series of penicillin shots for a few days, even waking me up during the night to do it. My operation was performed on Wednesday morning, and I went home the following Sunday.

I remember going to kindergarten at the Hamilton School. I remember that Mrs. Robbins was the teacher, and that I had a crush on Judy Sanders, the prettiest girl in class. My first-grade teacher was Mrs. Mershon (not sure of the correct spelling), and she drove a two-door coupe with a rumble seat. I even remember the names of some of my classmates: Peter Wolfe, Alva Fox, and Janet Steinky, to name a few. (How could one not remember a "fox" and a "wolf" in the same class?) I remember the names of the neighborhood kids that I played with. There was Perry Druzba and a little girl named Cynthia, whom I called "Cinnie," who lived across the street. There were Sid and Tony Dimacio; and farther down the street were Teddy and Johnny (or Jimmy) Klonowski, whose father played baseball for the Schenectady Blue Jays. On the next block was Tommy Zak, whose parents owned the neighborhood butcher shop where we bought our meat. I remember that a year after my dad died, we got our first telephone; the number was 3-9116. I even remember that the mayor's last name was Begley, and I remember the four different addresses where we lived in Schenectady. I could mention a thousand other details, but I think you get the idea. The events that occurred in 1955 were indelibly burned into my brain, and my memory of them is as clear as if they happened yesterday. But don't ask me what I did this morning! Just kidding.

In the years that followed, I read several books on UFOs and was not impressed with the contactee accounts or those making other wild and bizarre claims. However, I kept an open mind, believing that if they were of extraterrestrial origin, it would eventually be confirmed.

As far back as I can remember, the stars and the universe had always fascinated me. By fourteen, I knew all the planets, and I knew about meteors, meteorites, asteroids, comets, nebulae, novae, and galaxies. I had even read *Words in Collision* by Immanuel Velikovsky and was intrigued by his ideas. In fact, that night on the hospital roof, I talked with Professor

Rusterholtz, the astronomy teacher at the college. I remember asking him about the asteroid belt and the seventeen-degree inclination of Pluto's orbit—I was curious as to how and why these things came to be. Because of my age, my knowledge of these details impressed the professor.

Later on, I developed a strong interest in biblical history. Actually, it resulted from my curiosity about ancient Egypt. The great pyramids had always intrigued me—when were they built, who really built them, and how were they built? Almost every book I read promoted the idea that they were created forty-five hundred years ago, during the Egyptian Fourth Dynasty. However, I came across several articles that challenged this idea with evidence that they may possibly be much older—evidence that mainstream Egyptologists seemed unable to refute. I thought that if the pyramids really were built forty-five hundred years ago, that was during the biblical era, so perhaps there was a clue somewhere in the Bible. So I began searching the scriptures. I found numerous references to the Egyptians, yet there was no mention at all of the pyramids; the only possible connection was in Isaiah 19:19, where it refers to an altar and a monument to the Lord in Egypt, but the reference is vague.

It was not until the late 1970s that my interest in UFOs was rekindled by the stories of alien abductions. This was a new spin. At first, I thought it was a new trend in fanaticism, something created by New Age cultists or a revival of the contactee cults from the 1950s and '60s. Yet the more I read, the more convinced I became that they were real, or at least those making these claims believed they were. Contrary to contactee behavior, it appeared that abductees shunned publicity. This impressed me. Why would people who told such fantastic stories of little grey aliens taking them aboard a spacecraft and subjecting them to a series of bizarre tests and examinations not take advantage of the opportunity to capitalize on their experience?

It was not until several years later, when I picked up a newsmagazine containing an article on alien abductions and began reading it, that something clicked in my head. It had a biblical ring to it. It was probably something I'd read previously, which subliminally planted the seed in my mind and suggested a connection, but the idea seemed ridiculous at the time, so I ignored it. Nevertheless, the thought continued to haunt me for over a year. I eventually went to the library to check out books on the subject, and I explored the Bible several times. The more I read, the more familiar I became with details that had initially eluded my attention because they seemed insignificant.

I realize that associating the Bible with UFOs may offend the sensibilities of the devoutly religious. However, the Bible is simply a collection of stories, most of which were passed down in oral tradition for a few thousand years before they were actually written down. And no one really knows how much they may have been altered or exaggerated in the process—or if a few were even derived from earlier Mesopotamian myths. In 1970, a book written by Eric von Däniken, *Chariots of the Gods*, raised the question of whether God and the angels described in the Bible were really extraterrestrials. Although it offended and even shocked some people, when we consider the numerous technological implications contained in the Bible (which we will examine in chapter 12), I feel it is a legitimate question.

After a few years of sorting and comparing notes, I began to recognize a pattern in the chronology of biblical events. Applying only logic and common sense, the sequence in which they played out seemed to suggest that extraterrestrials may have been involved with mankind far longer than one could imagine. Then I thought that if this was true, why had no one ever picked up on it before? If my ideas had any merit, it was mind-boggling—how could it have gone unnoticed? The answer, however, was simple; no one had ever bothered to connect all the dots.

Well, that is not entirely true. A few had played around with the idea, but only on a selective basis. They focused on examples of what appeared to be references to flying craft in the Bible, without exploring why they were here or what they might have been doing; they were just skimming the surface by examining a few isolated events, completely unaware of what they might actually represent.

I decided to examine objectively all the credible information available on UFOs. Using logic and common sense, I studied the basic details of many accounts along with the major biblical events without being influenced by extraterrestrial theories, or the miraculous, mystical, and supernatural beliefs associated with religion. From a strictly logical perspective, my findings seemed almost too incredible to believe, yet the evidence seemed overwhelming.

The Bible tells us that a "pillar of cloud and fire" led Moses and the Hebrews out of Egypt, and that something concealed in a cloud continuously hovered above their camp. It tells us that a chariot of fire took the prophet Elijah up to heaven in a whirlwind, and that a "star" led the Magi to the Christ child. Then there is the first chapter in the book of Ezekiel, which appears to be a vivid account of an encounter he had with five beings that landed in what certainly sounds like a metallic and mechanical flying craft. To any practical-minded person, the technological implications are obvious. Then I thought, *If these stories actually relate to flying machines, then what is the Bible really telling us?*

In spite of the fact that museums are filled with bones and fossils dating back hundreds of millions of years, the Bible suggests that everything began only 6,000 years ago. Since the Bible was around long before modern science, many of those subscribing to organized religion believe it reflects a factual record of history and evolution. What they fail to recognize is that it is not the Bible but organized religion promoting their beliefs. No god created religion; man invented it to perpetuate his own individual ideas of creation and evolution based on ancient (and questionable) interpretations of the scriptures. The Bible is simply a collection of manuscripts expressing the views of their authors about events that occurred centuries before their own time, and until a few centuries before Christ, there was no such thing as a Bible.

Consequently, people have allowed themselves to be told what to believe. From childhood, they have been conditioned to accept a variety of superstitious ideas and beliefs in which there are inconsistencies and conflict, and it is these conflicts that ultimately gave rise to multiple religions and many of our prejudices. So when it comes to man's past, how much of the truth are we missing? To what degree might we have been misinformed?

Anyone who dares suggest a connection between UFOs, God, and the Bible is treading on controversial ground because he is challenging every other man's fundamental beliefs. Those conditioned by these beliefs have surrendered the right to think for themselves; they faithfully continue believing only that which others have told them to believe. But what if they are wrong—like those in Galileo's time who believed the earth was the center of the universe. What if there is a connection? If there is legitimate reason to suspect it, shouldn't we at least examine the issues? If UFOs were as prevalent in ancient times as they are today, isn't it about time we found out why? Shouldn't we be just a little curious as to what was going on back then?

Since the mechanics of technology seem apparent in many cases, the most logical assumption is that physical beings were in control of it, and if so … *who were they?* Who would be using sophisticated technologies 6,000 years ago if not extraterrestrials, and this only adds to the complexity of the UFO mystery: *What were they up to then? What are they doing now? And why?* I think we must address these questions if we expect to find any real answers, and I will do so in chapters 11 through 19.

It is not my intention to demean anyone's personal religious convictions, yet the biblical events raise many questions, some that I feel require a serious reevaluation of our beliefs. To neglect these issues in order to avoid religious acrimony would only defeat the purpose of being objective.

Right from the beginning, the Bible describes what appears to be an intentional effort to create a new race of man spawned from the seeds of individuals whose own births were considered no less than miracles. I think the most logical question is why. Why would a supernatural God want to create a race of mortal beings? And if it really was God, why did he fail so miserably in his first attempt? Trial and error is a trait common among corporeal beings such as man, which tends to suggest that these events (if they really occurred) were orchestrated by physical beings. And when one asks the obvious questions, there are numerous clues suggesting an extraterrestrial connection:

- Were Adam and Eve really the only two people on Earth at the time of their creation?

- Why did God find it necessary to remove something from Adam's body in order to create Eve?

- What was the real purpose of evicting Adam and Eve from the Garden of Eden?

- What was the tree of life?

- What was the flaming sword flashing back and forth, which was installed to protect the tree of life?

- Why did the tree of life need to be protected?

- Why did it take 130 years for Adam and Eve to produce three children?

- Did Adam and his descendants really live for hundreds of years?

- Who was Cain's wife?

- Was Noah's flood really as devastating as the Bible describes?

- Did old and sterile women truly conceive and give birth as the Bible claims?

- Did Samson really have superhuman strength?

- What was the Ark of the Covenant, and what was its real purpose?

- Why did the angels always appear and disappear in a flash of light?

- Did the Lord really descend in a cloud when he visited Moses?

- Beginning with the Exodus, why did the Lord suddenly start concealing himself in a cloud?

- If the Lord really was God (who supposedly created the entire universe), why was he only interested in the Hebrews?

When we put aside the miraculous significance that religion has attached to these stories and examine them with logic and common sense, an entirely different picture emerges from what we have been taught to believe—one of genetic engineering and manipulation in the evolution of the human race—something that may be related to the UFO activity of today.

The scriptures may be an important message to humanity inspired not by a supernatural deity but rather by someone with very human characteristics, and the Bible may possibly be a blueprint of his plan. It not only describes what has been done over the past 6,000 years but also what we can expect to happen over the next millennium or two.

Of course, there is no easy way to prove this theory. There are no pieces of ancient flying craft sitting on museum shelves to prove they existed. Likewise, no one has ever found the original writings of Moses, and without them, Old Testament scripture amounts to nothing more than a set of beliefs based on a few statements in the book of Genesis—a book that has undergone many changes over the millennia.

Some have suggested that the Bible stories had been passed down orally in Aramaic since the time of Moses. Then, a few centuries before Christ, scribes began to record them in Hebrew, where they were later translated into Greek, German, Latin, and eventually English. Over time, they underwent numerous changes in both translation and editing, sometimes to accommodate political agendas. Since the scribes who put these words into writing lived in an age devoid of machines, any stories depicting technology probably would have been construed as miracles or sorcery. However, if the biblical events are accurate—at least in the context that they actually occurred—then it presents the possibility that the alleged miracles were technological demonstrations. If so, *to whom did this technology belong?* And if someone really has been juggling our genes for thousands of years, then we have to ask why, for without motive, the whole idea seems rather preposterous. However, if the Bible is a blueprint of a plan, we would expect the purpose of the plan and the intended outcome is also revealed, and it may well be—in 1 Thessalonians, 1 Corinthians, and in the book of Revelation. It suggests that many people will eventually be taken off the earth—why?

Starting with chapter 11, I will begin examining the details pertaining to these issues. However, understanding the UFO enigma is contingent on many other things besides the Bible. We must look first at ancient artifacts and artwork and realize that the phenomena may not be unique to the twentieth century—that it might possibly have been around for as long as man himself. We must look at the alternative issues that are frequently associated with UFOs, such as the Bermuda Triangle, cattle mutilations, crop circles, and so forth, and learn what facts are relevant and which ones are attributed to mostly supermarket tabloid sensationalism. We must examine the controversy alluding to what the government does or does not know—insofar as evidence that they may be in league with at least one ET race and are behind a campaign of disinformation designed to desensitize us gradually to the facts. We must examine the facts relating to the abductions and the little-known hostile encounters that resulted in the deaths of some witnesses. Once acquainted with these issues, we will then examine the biblical scenario—the sequence of events covering the four millennia between Adam and Christ, where clues alluding to a project of accelerated evolution will then be more recognizable—and we will also see clues that extraterrestrials may even be responsible for our practice of deity worship.

Now, you may think it all sounds ridiculous—I know I would if I were on the other side of the fence. However, as you will see, I ask over 500 questions and the word *why* appears at least 150 times. This is because I do not always accept what is described or reported at face value without first trying to understand the facts or the reason behind why a particular event occurred. A more thorough analysis usually leads to a better understanding and a more logical interpretation of a particular situation or event. This is especially important when it comes to the Bible.

Although it is my intention to present the evidence in an objective manner, we must keep in mind that this is only evidence, and evidence is not necessarily proof. I am not claiming that my ideas are the answer to the UFO mystery, or that they are even correct. What I am presenting is a logical and commonsense evaluation—a theory, nothing more. I am not a UFO fanatic. Had it not been for the experience I had in 1955, which ignited my curiosity, I would never have considered pursuing the subject to the extent that I have. I am a simple person of modest means. I never had the financial resources to travel around the country or the world to talk to witnesses or visit ancient sites relative to the issues discussed, so I had to rely on information provided by credible researchers and reputable investigators.

I have spent years accumulating a video archive. Except for the Bible, the majority of the evidence presented is from the recorded testimonies of highly credible witnesses such as police officers, military officials, astronauts, air force and commercial airline pilots—in their own words.

I have divided this book into three sections. Part 1 builds a strong case for UFO reality by examining prehistoric artwork, ancient texts, and artifacts. It also examines the government's involvement, disinformation, and alien abductions. The evidence suggests the government is involved in a plan to desensitize the public gradually to the UFO issue through a process of disinformation and controversy. This section also examines the alternative issues frequently associated with UFOs, such as animal mutilations, the Bermuda Triangle, crop circles, and so on. You will learn the pertinent facts relating to these issues, thereby providing a clear understanding of their relevance and/or irrelevance to the UFO phenomena.

In part 2, chapter 11 examines the possibility that certain biblical characters were hybrids created as part of a plan designed to genetically accelerate and upgrade man's social, moral, and technological evolution—a plan that began thousands of years earlier. In chapter 12, we examine the numerous technologies (as suggested in scripture) that were involved—and you will be amazed at how many there actually are. Once familiar with these two chapters, you will better understand the rest of part 2, as it examines the sequence of biblical events describing the various stages that were methodically executed to achieve the goal of accelerating our evolution. The last chapter, chapter 20, examines the Bible facts. Many of these facts tend to conflict with my ideas; however, my goal is to be completely fair and objective, so it will be up to you to draw your own conclusions.

Part 3 examines future possibilities such as the doomsday predictions made by modern-day prophets and those in the book of Revelation. It examines the possibility that the earth could suffer a catastrophic asteroid or comet strike in this millennium or the next, one of the same caliber that occurred in the Yucatán sixty-five million years ago. Other information suggests that our progress is currently being stifled because our technology is out of balance with our wisdom, and several cited cases tend to reinforce this idea. We will also see evidence that we may be in the early stages of an indoctrination designed to enlighten us about what is really going on regarding the government and extraterrestrials.

My evaluation is based entirely from a perspective of logic and common sense. Although some of the evidence may seem far-fetched, the fact that it is so numerous lends to its credibility. Nevertheless, there are always two sides to every story, so all I ask is that you set aside for the moment any preconceived ideas or beliefs you may have about UFOs, religion, and God. Just keep an open mind and accept nothing more than the *possibility* that the information presented could be true. Then examine all arguments, if any, that logically dispute the evidence and decide for yourself.

Acknowledgements

A special thanks to

Jim and Hazel Thompson, dear friends who provided encouragement and moral support during my undertaking in writing this book.

Pauline Barnes, my dear friend who provided constructive criticism in dealing with certain subject matter.

Stacy Griffiths, Esq. who assisted in research.

George Nedeff, editorial consultant who guided me through the procedures to properly format this book.

Colin Andrews, author/crop circle researcher for providing me with the correct details regarding the incident of military helicopter harassment during his investigation of a crop formation in the United Kingdom.

Part 1

UFOS AND ALIENS—Past and Present

Chapter 1

DO EXTRATERRESTRIALS REALLY EXIST?

Extraterrestrial life has always been a rather philosophical issue and not high on the list of priorities for scientific study. However, since the UFO issue revolves around possible alien visitors, it is essential to determine if they could exist, and if so, whether they could visit our world. There are people who claim to have witnessed aliens disembarking from a landed UFO and collecting plant and soil samples; there are people who claim to have seen alien bodies from UFO crash sites; and even others who claim they were abducted by aliens. Their stories are compelling, and many of the witnesses appear credible, yet no one has ever been able to present one shred of evidence to support his claims. So are these people hallucinating? Are they mentally unstable? Did they fabricate the stories simply to gain publicity for themselves? Any serious investigator will always consider these questions. But the most important question is whether any of them are telling the truth.

Millions of people have photographed and videotaped what they believe were UFOs in the sky. Most show indistinct points of light or blurred images and are of little or no value. Nevertheless, there is a small percentage in which state-of-the-art analyzing technology was able to rule out conventional aircraft, balloons, flocks of birds, and so forth. So in these cases at least, investigators were able to determine what they are not but not what they are, so there is still no proof that they are extraterrestrial spacecraft. However, the universe is a big place, and who really knows what is out there?

It is almost impossible for one to conceive the size of the universe. However, once you understand how vast it really is, you almost have to consider the possibility that there is other life somewhere out there. The age of the universe is still under debate but is currently believed to be somewhere around 12 to 15 billion years old. Our sun is just one star in a galaxy we call the Milky Way, which, according to various estimates, contains anywhere from 100 billion to 250 billion stars. We know there are at least 100 billion galaxies, which means there are more stars in the universe than there are grains of sand making up all the beaches on Earth. And that is a fact. What are the odds that some of these stars might host planets with intelligent life?

Our solar system is only about 4.5 billion years old. Considering the size and the age of the universe, how can one not consider the possibility, or even the probability, that life evolved elsewhere millions or even billions of years before it did on Earth? Because of the vast distances between stars, scientists question whether travel between them is even possible: utilizing current technology, it would take us thousands of years to reach the nearest one. For this reason, many mainstream scientists believe interstellar travel is impractical. Their argument involves Einstein's theory of relativity—the laws pertaining to the speed of light. Light travels through space at 186,000 miles per second, and technologically, it is an impossible speed to attain because it would take more energy than the entire universe contains to propel a spaceship to that velocity. Even if we could reach light speed, the laws of physics pertaining to time and space dictate that the faster you move through space, the slower the passage of time. In other words, if the trip took twenty-five years traveling at light speed, the voyagers would have aged only twenty-five years, while back on Earth, hundreds of years would have elapsed. This means they would return to find their loved ones long deceased. Such an expedition would be of no benefit to any people alive on Earth when it departed because they would never live long enough to see its return.

Thus is the argument some scientists have proposed for why UFOs cannot be of extraterrestrial origin. They are saying that since interstellar travel is impossible or impractical for us, it is also impossible or impractical for anyone else who may exist out there, implying that any other intelligent life in the universe is restricted by the same limitations we face. However, in order to make such a claim, one would assume they would have to be well informed on the scientific and technological capabilities of such civilizations. Unless the government really is covering up something big, I fail to see how they can even propose such an idea. For all they know, any number of ET races could have long ago developed the technology to bend the fabric of the space-time continuum and visit Earth as routinely as we visit other countries.

As for our own limitations, are we to believe we have reached the pinnacle of scientific discovery, that there is nothing left to learn … nothing left to achieve? How do we know there isn't a completely new dimension of technology waiting to be discovered tomorrow, which will allow us to overcome the challenge of faster-than-light travel?

Almost everything was considered impossible at one time or another. People once said that if man were meant to fly, he would have been born with wings. But on December 17, 1903, Wilbur and Orville Wright proved them wrong. Then it was thought impossible to fly faster than the speed of sound, until October 14, 1947, when Captain Charles "Chuck" Yeager, flying the Bell X-1 aircraft, broke the sound barrier. After this, it was thought impossible for man to go to the moon. And the naysayers were again proven wrong when on July 20, 1969, astronauts Neil Armstrong and Eugene "Buzz" Aldrin climbed down out of their Apollo 11 lunar lander and walked on the surface of the moon. Now that we have met and overcome these challenges, we are told it is impossible to travel faster than light. Since we were able to conquer yesterday's "impossibilities," I see no reason not to believe that interstellar travel is also a challenge we will eventually overcome. In fact, we may have already taken the first step. In 2000, the *Sunday Times* in the United Kingdom published an article about how particle physicists in the United States demonstrated that light pulses can be accelerated up to three hundred times their normal velocity of 186,000 miles per second. This would seem to suggest that nothing is truly impossible.

In 1916, Barnard's Star was discovered by Edward Emerson Barnard. In 1963, astronomer Peter van de Kamp detected irregularities in the star's movement, suggesting a Jupiter-size planet may be in orbit around it. Lacking the technology available today, his discovery remained in dispute.[1] Astronomers have since discovered that Barnard's Star is really a runaway red dwarf star that will pass by our solar system at a distance of about four light-years in the year 11,800. So it wasn't until 1992 that the first discovery of an extrasolar planet was actually confirmed. Since then, over five hundred other planets have been confirmed orbiting other stars in our galaxy. As new technologies are being applied, they are discovering stars with multiple planets, the number of which is constantly growing—and the search has only just begun.

So the odds favoring the existence of planets capable of supporting life are increasing every day, along with the probability that other intelligent life has evolved. Suddenly, we find it not so inconceivable that others from another world could have visited Earth in the distant past … and may still be doing so today. And if they interacted with ancient man, it is entirely possible that they influenced much of our early history.

Something else to consider is that time (at least to some extraterrestrials) could be very different from how we understand it. We perceive time in a linear fashion—with a past, a present, and a future—and we measure its passage with clocks and calendars. Our day is based on the twenty-four-hour cycle of the earth's rotation, and our year is based on the 365 days it takes to make one complete orbit around the sun. However, in comparison to our standards, it is possible that to an extraterrestrial, a day may equal months, years, or even centuries. The concept of a thousand years being as one day is even mentioned in the Bible (2 Peter 3:8 and Psalms 90:4). We tend to judge everything based on our own concepts and standards, but how do we know that an extraterrestrial civilization would measure things the same way? We don't! There is no law that says everything in the universe is, or has to be, restricted to our limitations.

Of course, none of this is proof of extraterrestrial existence or that they have visited Earth. I have simply expressed an opinion based on a logical assessment of established information. However, to claim that interstellar travel is impossible for an extraterrestrial civilization only because it is currently impossible for us is simply an unscientific assumption that reflects a narrow-minded perspective.

Notes

1. Barnard's Star
   Web links:
   www.britannica.com/EBchecked/topic/53637/Barnards-star
   www.solstation.com/stars/barnards.htm

Chapter 2

THE QUESTION OF ORIGIN

Two of the biggest mysteries man has yet to explain are his own origin and UFOs. As for origin, the Bible claims that divine creation was responsible for man, while science suggests he evolved, possibly from the ape. So far, no tangible evidence exists to support either creation or evolution. They are both part of a debate that will undoubtedly continue for generations to come. There is, however, a mountain of credible evidence supporting the existence of UFOs.

One factor inhibiting our ability to comprehend the UFO issue is the intimidation of religious doctrine. For centuries, religion has dictated what we are *allowed* to believe. This is exemplified by what happened to Galileo in the seventeenth century, when the accepted belief was that the sun and stars revolved around the earth—that the earth was the center of the universe. When Galileo invented the first astronomical telescope in 1609, he saw the heavens as no man before him ever did, and he soon confirmed what Copernicus had already proposed, that the earth revolved around the sun, thus diminishing its status as the center of the universe.

This was in total contradiction to what the church believed. At the time, the church was a powerful influence in government matters and when Galileo published his findings, he was labeled a heretic and subjected to religious persecution. In 1633, he was summoned to Rome for an inquisition and sentenced to life imprisonment for suspicion of heresy. To avoid imprisonment, he was forced to recant all of his work, and only then did the church commute his sentence to house arrest.[1] Thus organized religion set the paradigm by which established beliefs are protected—even if they are wrong. Although Galileo was right, the narrow-minded perspective of religious authorities prevented them from even giving him the benefit of the doubt. Simply put, they had been brainwashed into accepting their inaccurate beliefs as the absolute truth, and no one dare question them. And the same prejudicial attitude still prevails three centuries later: any scientist today who challenges established beliefs risks not only the scorn of his peers; it also puts the security of his job in jeopardy. He, too, becomes a victim of what I call the "Galileo Syndrome."

A more recent example is what happened to Virginia Steen-McIntyre. In 1966, archaeologists excavating a site in Hueyatlaco, Mexico, unearthed a collection of stone tools and leaf-shaped spear points, and McIntyre was part of the United States Geological Survey team sent to date the items. She said they used the radiometric date procedure that determines actual age, and that two procedures were implemented: one using uranium atoms and the other using tiny zircon crystals. At first, she suspected the site might be about 20,000 years old, but to her astonishment, all tests dated the artifacts at 250,000 years.[2]

McIntyre admits that she was naive, unaware of the controversy she had created, and had no idea of how it was about to impact her career. Thinking she might be on to something big, she refused to deviate from the facts that had been established. Consequently, the dig was closed down; she lost her teaching job at an American university and has been unable to work in her profession ever since. She was blackballed for refusing to cave in to mainstream ideology.

There seems to be an unwritten law in the scientific community to bury any evidence that conflicts with mainstream beliefs, such as that which suggests intelligent man was around long before scientists are willing to admit. Excellent documentation of this is presented in *Forbidden Archaeology,* a book written by Michael A. Cremo and Richard L. Thompson. There are over eight hundred pages documenting man's presence as well as artifacts that are hundreds of thousands and even millions of years old.

It seems prehistoric man left many clues that things other than birds were flying around in his skies. All over the world, petroglyphs on rocks and in caves depict what look like many UFOs being reported today, and they appear in many medieval paintings as well. Written references can be found in ancient writings from Mesopotamia, China, India, Mexico, and South America, not to mention the Bible. They are simply too numerous to ignore, and it doesn't take a rocket scientist to recognize the technological implications. So *if* these ancient artists and writers were depicting flying craft, then it would appear that UFOs have been around for many thousands of years. If so, then how far back in time do they really go? Were they around at the dawn of humanity? Could they even be responsible for man's existence? Though the idea may sound crazy, it is not inconceivable.

As near as can be determined, man, as he is today, has been traced back about 50,000 years to the period when the Neanderthal and Cro-Magnon man faded from the scene. The Cro-Magnon allegedly resembled modern man in many ways, and some theorize that he may have been a more evolved descendant of the Neanderthal; supposedly, he was more intelligent and more human in appearance. Until recently, it was thought that the Cro-Magnon came after the Neanderthal. Now there is evidence that they coexisted in some regions before the Neanderthal finally exited the picture. Since this was about the time modern man allegedly emerged, the sequence would seem to support evolution.

Creationists acclimated to the mystical beliefs associated with religion believe human life began only 6,000 years ago, with Adam and Eve. However, 6,000 years seems hardly a sufficient amount of time for so many diversified species of man to have evolved, at least from a common origin such as Adam and Eve. When you consider the variety of races that exist among the human species, each with individual physical characteristics such as height, facial features, skin color, hair color, and those both with and without facial hair, one has to wonder where they did come from. Variety prevails in every species of life on Earth, and it is the result of millions of years of evolution. Logically, we might expect that millions of years would have also produced distinctive differences among Homo sapiens. If, as the Bible claims, modern man only arrived on the scene 6,000 years ago, it seems an insufficient amount of time for such distinct diversity to have evolved—even 60,000 years would not seem long enough.

The evolution theory suggests that man may have evolved from the ape somewhere along the way—but when? Evolution constitutes a gradual process of change, not change and continuance. If apes evolved into man, then there should be no more apes around. Separately, man and ape can be traced back millions of years; however, there is no evidence that ape evolved into man, leaving what scientists refer to as the *missing link*. So until such evidence is discovered to support their theories, it seems that man just suddenly appeared on the scene from out of nowhere. If true, could it explain the missing link?

Most DNA is contained in the nucleus of the human cell, and we inherit half from our mother and half from our father. However, a small portion called mitochondrial DNA exists outside the nucleus and contains elements only contributed by the female, and it can be used to trace a person's lineage far back in time. According to author Mark Eastman, research was conducted at the University of California in Berkeley using mitochondrial DNA samples of 147 individuals from different parts of the world, and the results were surprising. The tests indicated that they all descended from the same female ancestor, which they dubbed the mitochondrial Eve.[3] This would seem to imply that everyone alive on Earth today, descended from the same female ancestor.

Based on the mutational rate of mitochondria, it suggests that the mitochondrial Eve lived about 6,000 to 6,500 years ago, a timeline that could fit the Genesis account of creation. The problem, however, is that it still seems unlikely that so many diversified races of man with such a distinct variation of physical characteristics would have evolved in such a short span of time.

But what if the mitochondrial Eve was actually a series of female hybrids created from the same DNA source containing the same mitochondria? What if they were separate projects conducted at different times on different continents that produced the various races of humanity? Would that not logically explain why the DNA of 147 people from around the world has the same mitochondrial signature?

If, and I repeat *if,* the human race is the product of genetic engineering by extraterrestrials, it could logically explain both the mitochondrial Eve and the missing link. It might also explain how, due to earlier experiments, man just appeared from out of nowhere. If aliens actually conducted such tests, it could have been done over many millennia or even eons. Since the DNA of the tested subjects indicates an origin of 6,000 or so years, it might suggest that the last experiment took place at that time, and that civilizations with mitochondria dating to earlier times were wiped out by some global catastrophe or were purposely eliminated for some reason, possibly because they proved nonviable for their intended purpose. The biblical account of the flood might explain this, as would the stories and legends of many other ancient civilizations from around the world describing similar floods.

When scribes first began translating the Bible into the written word, they applied the name "Adam" to the person whom they had been taught to believe was the very first human being. However, the word from which Adam was derived can also mean "all men" or humanity in general. So could Adam actually have represented multiple male hybrids? That would make sense *if* there were multiple mitochondrial Eves.

So could there really be such a simple explanation? To be perfectly honest, I don't know. I am a practical person, not controlled or influenced by supernatural, superstitious, or mystical beliefs, and my reasoning is based solely on logic and common sense. The Bible describes everything that happened after 4000 BC, which the Lord allegedly passed on to Moses during the forty years he spent leading the Hebrews around the desert. If this is true, I would assume that it was for a reason. I cannot believe Moses spent all that time recording everything the Lord dictated, only to keep it a secret: logic suggests that it was meant to be a permanent record. And it seems unlikely that the intention was to create false beliefs—such as Adam and Eve being the first and only people on the earth at that time—because science would ultimately present evidence to the contrary.

If the human race, as it is today, is the result of genetic juggling, we have to ask why an alien race became involved with our evolution.

The last book in the Bible is called Revelation, and in the Roman Catholic version, it is called Apocalypse. If one can believe the prophecies in this book, many people will be removed from the earth and taken to a different place. Before this happens, there will be a period of tribulation: diseases, devastating weather phenomena, the rise of the Antichrist, and the final war known as Armageddon, after which Christ is supposed to return and reign for a thousand years. Then comes Judgment Day—just before the migration to this other place.

Now, if Christ really is going to return, then it seems we will survive the many tribulations that are predicted to occur. However, the description of Christ taking people off the earth after his long reign could signify an evacuation, suggesting that something terrible is going to happen at that time. We only recently learned of the asteroid that slammed into the Yucatán Peninsula 65 million years ago, causing a mass extinction of life. If a similar disaster is going to occur after Christ's millennial reign, could it possibly be the motive behind what is going on? Could it be that extraterrestrials are providing us with our only chance of survival? Let me present a short hypothesis.

Ancient cave drawings suggest that ETs were around when prehistoric man roamed the land. If so, maybe they didn't create man, but rather, recognizing his potential, initiated a project to accelerate his evolution because they knew an impending disaster threatened his existence long before he would ever develop the technology he needed to survive. If, however, they did create man, it would be even more reason to formulate a plan to protect their project, and the feasibility of such a plan might have warranted creating a few "test races."

You can take this for what it's worth, but numerous skeletons have allegedly been discovered in various places around the world, and they appear to have been a diversified race of giants, some as tall as twenty or more feet. Whoever, or whatever, these people were, many supposedly had red hair, double rows of upper and lower teeth, and six fingers and toes. There are many Internet sites describing these discoveries, a few of which may possibly be credible.[4] Some show newspaper clippings with dates, locations, and the names of the archaeologists involved. Some of the bones allegedly date back millions of years, which if true, might suggest that they were one of the first test races. According to many of the articles, these finds were turned over to the Smithsonian and other museums, and in most cases, the museums have either lost them over the years or stored them in their basements, away from public view. If this is true, it seems like just another attempt by the elite mainstream to avoid having to rewrite the history books. But since there is an insufficient amount of credible evidence regarding these giants, the issue is open for debate.

Nevertheless, accelerating evolution would involve the genetic reconstruction of man, and what better way to speed up the process than with hybrids. This may have been accomplished by collecting ova from female subjects and sperm samples from men—a scenario that parallels procedures described in many alien abduction cases, which I will cover in more detail later. Assuming they had the technology, they would make whatever genetic alterations necessary for improvement in the sperm samples and then inseminate the women.

As the children with the modified genes were born, they would pass their seeds on to the next generation. The more hybrids created, the faster the distribution of improved genes. Again, assuming they had the technology, they may have created several hybrid races over the millennia, in which they may have genetically enhanced certain attributes and/or abilities to see what worked and what didn't. During this phase, they may have made a few mistakes, thereby making it necessary on occasion to eliminate a race and replace it with a new one. The red-haired giants with six fingers and toes and double rows of teeth, assuming they actually existed, may possibly have been one of them. Then, several thousand years ago, using

DNA with the most favorable genetic qualities they had preserved from earlier experiments, they may have created special hybrids to breed a new race from the existing population in the region of Mesopotamia. The male hybrid was Adam, and the female was the mitochondrial Eve, and they were created with the same chromosomal package we carry today. They may have conducted this same process at different times in Asia, Europe, Africa, Australia, and North and South America, each time using the same DNA. If this hypothesis is correct, would it not then provide a logical explanation for why the DNA of all the subjects tested at Berkley have the same mitochondrial signature?

Eventually, man would have become genetically compatible with his extraterrestrial creators, allowing them to mate with human females. This is assuming, of course, that we looked like them—were created in their image—as stated in the Bible. However, it seems unlikely that such unions would be permitted. Their superior genes probably would have been diluted in the still-primitive human species; the offspring may have inherited a higher capacity for learning but would not have evolved far enough up the evolutionary scale to acquire the wisdom necessary to deal with it, and it could create serious problems down the line. However, according to the Bible, such sexual unions did occur, and those who were involved got into a lot of trouble. This issue will be covered in more detail later.

There is, of course, no way to prove that extraterrestrials are involved in a project to accelerate the evolution of the human race. However, let's assume for the moment that they are, and that one phase of their project would be to learn which steps would be most advantageous in achieving this goal. Would it not then be necessary to conduct experiments in order to make such a determination? Might they have created one or more races with which to test genetically enhanced abilities—abilities that could explain the amazing achievements of many ancient civilizations that completely baffle us today, such as the great pyramids in Egypt and numerous other megalithic structures around the world?

Remember, this is only hypothetical; there is no evidence to prove this is what happened. However, you have to admit it could make sense. And when we examine some of the amazing architectural accomplishments of ancient man, it seems to make even more sense.

Notes

1.   Galileo
      Web link:
      en.wikipedia.org/wiki/Galileo

2.   Dr. Virginia Steen-McIntyre
      Web link:
      www.earlyworld.de/forbidden_archeology.htm

Chapter 3

ANCIENT MYSTERIES

One of the theories proposed in the field of UFO research is that we are a hybrid species created by extraterrestrials. One proponent of this theory was the late Zecharia Sitchin, an expert in ancient Mesopotamian languages. Although his ideas are disputed in mainstream circles, he claims that Sumerian cuneiform writings identify these extraterrestrials as the Annunaki, who came from a planet called Nibiru, which orbits through our neighborhood every 3,600 years. He proposed that they were the Nephilim—the biblical giants mentioned in Genesis. One tablet he deciphered allegedly describes a number of items that the goddess Ishtar adorned before making a flight to visit her sister in some distant land.

In his book *The Twelfth Planet,* he states that in 1934, archaeologists excavating a site in Mari unearthed a 4,000-year-old life-size statue of Ishtar wearing what appeared to be the same items. A strange box is strapped to her back and appears to be attached to the back of her helmet by a strap; it is further supported by two large shoulder pads. There is also what appears to be a hose attached to the base of the box by a circular clasp.

Two of the items mentioned on the tablet that Sitchin said adorned the goddess were "straps clasping her breasts," which seemed to be what was holding the box in place on her back, and "twin stones on her shoulders," which appeared to be shoulder pads used to support the weight of this box.

So what was this box? Perhaps it was used for carrying personal effects; however, the hose attached to it suggests that it might have been an oxygen pack designed for high-altitude flight in a small craft. Its appearance implies technology, and since the statue is 4,000 years old, one has to wonder.

As early as 1844, it was suspected that there was an invisible star orbiting around Sirius. Its existence wasn't confirmed until 1862, when astronomer Alvan Graham Clark first viewed it through a telescope. It was named "Sirius B," and it orbits Sirius about once every fifty years. Yet it appears that the Dogon, a primitive tribe in Africa, has known about this star for centuries, and they even worship it in their ceremonial practices. Their legends claim they learned of it from beings that descended from the sky in a large craft. Since this star is invisible to the naked eye, they couldn't possibly have known about it centuries before Clark confirmed its existence, unless there is some element of truth to their legend.[1]

In an isolated area of the South Pacific is a tiny island called Rapa Nui, and it is governed by Chile. More commonly known as Easter Island, it has inspired the imaginations of many with its monolithic stone figures called the moai. Like silent sentries, many are spread along the coastline, facing inland, away from the sea. They were carved out of a high mountain quarry, but how they were moved down from the top of the mountain and across the land to their present locations is still somewhat of a mystery. Many lie broken along the route of transport, evidence that moving them was not always successful. Although many theories have been postulated, it seems no one knows for sure who or what these stone giants represent—or what purpose they served. They bear certain similarities to other statues found elsewhere in South America and in Mexico and Central America. Is it possible there was once interaction between these cultures? The only writings left by these people are carved into a few wooden blocks that have managed to survive the ages. It is called Rongorongo, a language that, to this day, no one has successfully been able to decipher.[2] The immense size of the statues has fueled theories of extraterrestrial involvement; however, those lying broken along the route of transport are mute testimony of human fallibility.

Then there is the Nazca plains in Peru, one of the driest places on earth, averaging about half an inch of rainfall in a five-year span. Carved into the side of a hill is a figure that, because of its appearance, some have nicknamed "The Waving Astronaut." Etched into the ground is a variety of images, including a monkey, a spider, a dog, a frog, a phoenix, a hummingbird, and many others. There is also a huge amalgamation of lines that, oddly enough, seem to resemble aircraft runways.[3] Created about two thousand years ago, these images are almost unrecognizable at ground level; only from the air can they best be seen for what they really are. So far, no one has been able to figure out who actually created them or what purpose they served.

About one hundred miles north of Nazca is a trident (often called a candelabra) carved into a cliff in the Bay of Pisco. It measures 595 feet from top to bottom and is visible from twelve miles out at sea.[4]

Hundreds of miles south of Nazca, in Cerro Unitas, Chile, is a figure so large that it stretches over the top of the mountain into which it is carved.[5]

Who created these images, and why? Did ancient Indians who intended only for their gods to see them create them, or were they, as some believe, landing sites for alien spacecraft? The lines in Nazca resembling runways might suggest this, but some of them stretch for miles across the landscape. If aliens needed runways that long, it might lead to speculation that their landing craft did not have very good brakes.

Logically, I have to question why aliens would even need runways. If, in their planetary exploration, it was necessary for them to land on a runway, then how could they build them before they landed? Moreover, if they did have some means to reach the planet's surface in order to build them, then why would they still need to build them? It is illogical.

Another mystery noted by Erich von Däniken in the *Ancient Aliens* documentary series is a Nazca mountaintop that appears to have been landscaped to a completely flat surface. All the neighboring mountains have high craggy ridges, so how did only one mountain obtain a smooth, flat surface? It seems unlikely that it was caused by natural weathering, thus suggesting it was achieved by some technological process. And von Däniken said there is no evidence anywhere around the base of the mountain of the debris that was cleared from the top. How was this accomplished, and for what reason?

There is no proof of an extraterrestrial connection. But when examining other colossal wonders of ancient man scattered around the world, one has to keep an open mind to the possibility.

Some researchers believe that many of the ancient structures could not have been created without extraterrestrial help, because it is virtually impossible for us to duplicate them with the technology we have today. Although there is no proof of alien involvement, some of the evidence is rather compelling, especially in the ruins of Tiahuanaco.

Tiahuanaco

Tiahuanaco is one of the most intriguing mysteries of the ancient world. Its ruins encompass an area of approximately 2.3 square miles, at 12,500 feet above sea level, in the Bolivian Andes. Adorning the walls of a sunken courtyard are carved faces representing what appear to be different races from around the world.[6] Would this not suggest that whoever built the city was familiar with civilizations on a global scale?

There are also ruins of a large pyramid and the remnants of a seaport. One might wonder about the existence of a seaport at such an elevation, but in all probability, it once bordered Lake Titicaca. It is believed that the lake, now fifteen miles away, was formed over twelve thousand years ago, during the last ice age, so its waters may have originally extended to Tiahuanaco. However, this is only speculation.

The city was built to precise astronomical alignment with huge stone blocks, some weighing four hundred tons, that were precisely cut and fitted together without mortar. The fit is so perfect that you cannot stick a pin in the cracks between them. One has to question how ancient Indians achieved that kind of technology.

One part of the Tiahuanaco ruins is a temple complex called Puma Punku, which was built with such precision that it boggles the mind. When some of the blocks were set into place, a liquid molten copper-like alloy was poured into T-shaped grooves carved into the edges. Once hardened, they became metal staples that firmly held the blocks in place.[7] This suggests that something like a portable smelting plant was used in order to move from stone to stone around the complex. Many of the blocks were precisely cut to interlock with one another. Some stones have very narrow grooves running the span of the block, and they are perfectly straight and maintain the exact same depth from end to end; they were cut with a precision that we cannot duplicate today.[8] And these blocks are made of granite and diorite—this could only have been achieved with diamond-tipped tools.

Research at Tiahuanaco was conducted around the turn of the twentieth century by archaeologist Arthur Posnansky. He estimated the site to be about seventeen thousand years old, which would have made it the oldest known city on Earth.[9] He based his calculations on the location of the portal of the sun, the solstice marker.[10] Like many other ancient civilizations, they used stone formations to mark the solstice points for agricultural purposes, and according to Posnansky, the marker corresponded to where "precession" (the wobbling of the earth's axis) would have placed the rising sun about seventeen thousand years ago. However, more modern and precise dating techniques have allegedly narrowed it down to twelve to fifteen thousand years. Posnansky's findings have been disputed in mainstream circles because according to their beliefs, no kind of civilization was supposed to have existed that long ago. One argument proposed is that whoever built the city miscalculated the placement of the solstice marker.

Tiahuanaco was a city built with stone blocks weighing up to four hundred tons and fitted together without mortar and with such precision that you cannot stick a pin in the cracks. An unknown method was used to staple the blocks together with a liquid molten alloy, and the city was built to precise astronomical alignment. Common sense tells us that to think these people miscalculated the placement of the solstice marker is insane. When you consider the precision involved with all other aspects of construction, it seems like just a ridiculous attempt to protect mainstream beliefs, which, in reality, are based only on assumptions.

Since these people knew enough to build a solstice marker, then they were already using the solstice points for agricultural purposes before they built Tiahuanaco. It seems unlikely that it was something they discovered during construction; they had to have known about it in advance. Would it not make sense to consider the possibility that maybe—just maybe—the portal of the sun was erected right where it was supposed to be? But this is another example of how some mainstream scientists are still caught up in the Galileo Syndrome.

Today, Tiahuanaco remains one of history's biggest mysteries. Who were the people that built the city, and where did they go? How did they lift four-hundred-ton stone blocks, and why did they build at such a high and barren altitude, where vegetation is sparse and its growth stunted? It is evidence that people possessed amazing technical abilities thousands of years before mainstream scientists claim it was possible. So to whom do we credit the construction of this site over twelve thousand years ago? Primitive Indians? Aliens? Or maybe a hybrid race with *genetically enhanced abilities*?

Easter Island, Nazca, Cerro Unitas, and Tiahuanaco are just a few mysteries connected to South America. Although the statues on Easter Island bear similarities to some found in other countries, and carved faces of many different races adorning the walls of a courtyard in Tiahuanaco suggest knowledge of civilizations on a global scale, it contradicts mainstream beliefs established long ago. Unchallenged for many years, these beliefs gradually came to be accepted as fact, just as those in the seventeenth century believed the earth was the center of the universe.

Although there is no proof that extraterrestrials were interacting with these people, we cannot dismiss the possibility that these civilizations possessed enhanced physical or mental abilities that allowed them to perform the same tasks for which heavy-duty machinery is needed today. Our most powerful construction equipment is incapable of moving stone blocks of the size found at Tiahuanaco, not to mention those in Baalbek, Lebanon. Some of the blocks in the temple of Jupiter weigh about one thousand tons, and one that is still at the quarry site weighs an estimated thirteen hundred tons.[11] How in the world did they lift and move these monstrosities? Obviously, they had the means to do it, yet it is way beyond our present capability.

The Sphinx

The Sphinx was carved out of a solid piece of limestone bedrock on the Giza Plateau, and large chunks were cut from the surrounding walls and carved into blocks to build the temples in front of the monument. Many are thirty feet long, ten feet high, twelve feet wide, and weigh about two hundred tons (the approximate weight of a diesel locomotive), and they had to be lifted fifty feet into the air to fit them in place.[12]

In 1991, author and Egyptologist John Anthony West uncovered some interesting facts about the Sphinx. He collaborated with Dr. Robert Schoch, an associate professor of science from Boston University, who holds a Ph.D. in geology and geophysics from Yale. Schoch confirmed that the erosion of the Sphinx, and the wall surrounding it, was definitely created by rainwater. Since there has been no significant rainfall in the area for thousands of years, it could only have occurred when the Nile Valley was fertile, which was thousands of years before the First Dynasty. Of course, this really irked mainstream Egyptologists who claim the Sphinx was created 4,500 years ago, around 2550 BC—another unproven theory usually presented as fact.

Dr. Zahi Hawass, secretary general of the Supreme Council of Antiquities, who oversees the Giza Plateau, claims the erosion on the Sphinx was caused by wind and sand. However, West added credibility to Schoch's claim when he took an enlarged picture of the Sphinx to another geologist. He disguised the Sphinx by covering its head and paws with masking tape, revealing only its severely weathered side. When he asked the geologist what caused the erosion evident in the photograph, the geologist said it was obviously created by water. Then West removed the tape, exposing the image of the Sphinx, and the geologist just said *"Oh!"* After realizing the implication of his original impression, he backed off and refused to get involved in the controversy.[13] And that seems to be the typical mainstream reaction.

With all due respect, Hawass is an archaeologist, not a geologist. When it comes to determining if erosion is caused by wind, sand, or rain, I am more inclined to take the word of an accredited geologist and geophysicist.

During the reign of Tutmoses IV, the Sphinx was buried up to its head in sand. Tutmoses's son had it excavated before he became king, but it again fell victim to time and became buried, as is evident in a photograph taken in 1868. What we may never know is how long it was buried before the time of Tutmoses—or how many times, for that matter.

Because his name is mentioned on a granite stele standing in front of the monument, most Egyptologists believe that Chefren built the Sphinx.[14] Again, this is only an assumption because the stele was installed 1,100 years after the Sphinx was allegedly created.[15] And the writing does not say when or why the Sphinx was created, nor does it say that it was created by Chefren. An inventory stele from the time of Cheops (Chefren's predecessor) states that he built a temple to Isis alongside the Sphinx, which if true, means the Sphinx was already there before Chefren's time.[16] Nevertheless, regardless of its age, there is still the mystery of how two-hundred-ton stone blocks were lifted fifty feet in the air to build its temples. So who really built the temples? Primitive Egyptians? Aliens? Or possibly a civilization with *genetically enhanced abilities*?

The Giza Pyramids

The pyramids are another intriguing mystery on the Giza Plateau. We know they were there 4,500 years ago, but the truth is, no one knows for sure when they were really built, who built them, or even why they were built.

The most publicized theory—and again, I emphasize the word *theory* because it is usually presented as if it were a proven fact—is that they were built as tombs for the pharaohs. Since no sarcophagus or mummy was ever found in them, and their walls and ceilings are devoid of any hieroglyphic images, how can it not be any more than a theory?

Two hundred miles south of Giza, near Thebes, is the Valley of the Kings, where Egyptians of later dynasties buried many pharaohs along with their treasures. Although attempts were made to conceal these tombs, thieves still managed to locate and loot the contents of many. However, the hieroglyphs covering the walls in some of these chambers reveal much information about their kings. This is where the tomb of Tutankhamen (King Tut), the boy pharaoh, was discovered with its treasure virtually intact. So we pretty much know from King Tut's tomb and others in the area what one might expect to find in a pharaoh's burial chamber. So if the Giza pyramids were created as tombs, where are the mummies, treasures, and the hieroglyphics?

To spend decades on such a massive and prestigious construction project just to create a chamber to place the body of a dead king, one would expect to find the interior filled with opulent furnishings and valuable treasures, its walls and ceilings lavishly designed and covered with hieroglyphs telling about the king. Yet there is nothing. It is possible that thieves long ago looted any treasures the pyramids may have contained, but they could not steal writings painted on or carved into the walls and ceiling. So where are they?

In the late eighteenth and early nineteenth centuries, when access to the pyramids was less restricted, many tourists left their calling cards in the form of graffiti. This is especially evident in the area above the King's Chamber in the large Khufu pyramid. Painted on some of the stones are hieroglyphs, one that mentions Khufu's name, which Hawass and other mainstream Egyptologists assume to be the handiwork of those who built the pyramids in the Fourth Dynasty. Of course, it is a possibility. On the other hand, how do we know it is not also graffiti created by an early tourist or even some archaeologist in an effort to perpetuate mainstream beliefs?

Carbon-dating tests were conducted on mortar samples found between some stones on the outside of the Great Pyramid—and they dated to around 2550 BC. Since the stones inside the pyramid, like those at Tiahuanaco, are so precisely cut and fitted together without mortar that you cannot stick a pin in the cracks, we have to ask why mortar is found between some stones on the outside. One theory proposed is that 4,500 years ago, the

Khufu pyramid was already an ancient structure and falling into disrepair. It was suggested that mortar was used by the Fourth Dynasty Egyptians to repair existing damage.[17]

It is evident that a few pyramids built later during the Fifth Dynasty were intended as tombs because their walls and ceilings are covered with hieroglyphs and information about the kings for whom they were intended. They were built within 150 years of when the giants in Giza were allegedly constructed, but their workmanship was inferior. Why? Did the country suddenly experience an economic collapse, or did those who built the Giza giants take their construction secrets with them to their graves? Some speculate that the cost of building the Giza pyramids seriously drained Egypt's economy, and that the Fifth Dynasty simply did not have the resources to duplicate what their predecessors had accomplished. Most of the stones in the Giza pyramids weigh about two and a half tons, and there are approximately 2.5 million of them in the large Khufu pyramid. Inside, many weigh about thirty tons, and those above the King's Chamber weigh about seventy tons.[18] Again, even with today's heavy-duty equipment, it is impossible to duplicate the construction.

The pyramids of the Third Dynasty were made out of mud bricks, and many now stand in crumbled ruins. According to existing records, Imhotep designed the step pyramid in Saqqara (said to be the first one ever constructed) for the pharaoh Djoser. The pyramid of Meidum was built during the late third or early Fourth Dynasty and is believed to be the work of Sneferu. The records also seem to suggest that during the Fourth Dynasty, Sneferu built the Bent Pyramid and the Red Pyramid, both located in Dahshur. It is *assumed*, however, that his son Khufu later built the giants in Giza, even though there are no records to indicate it. Yet there are many records associated with the Fifth Dynasty. The pyramids of the Fifth Dynasty were less sturdy than those of the third, and they are mostly piles of rubble. However, in what is left of the interiors, such as the burial chamber in the pyramid of Unas, the walls and ceiling are covered in hieroglyphs, and there are vertical columns inscribed with 283 of the so-called pyramid texts.

Chronologically, the Stone Age people who supposedly inhabited the area around 3000 BC, about 350 years later during the Third Dynasty (2649–2575 BC) spent 76 years building pyramids with mud bricks. Then, during the Fourth Dynasty, which lasted about 110 years (2575–2465 BC), they suddenly acquired the ability to build huge pyramids with stones weighing as much as 70 tons, after which, starting with the Fifth Dynasty (2465–2323 BC), their construction methods declined to a level more primitive than that with which they began. To paraphrase author Graham Hancock, he expresses it in terms of "the Third Dynasty building the Model T Ford, the Fourth Dynasty building the Porsche, and the Fifth Dynasty building the penny-farthing bicycle."[19]

Information recorded during the time of these dynasties reveals something of their culture, their gods, their wars, and their pharaohs. So if the Fourth Dynasty Egyptians really built the monumental wonders, why is there no mention of it, such as exists with the Third Dynasty and the Fifth Dynasty? Although we at least have some clues as to who constructed the third and Fifth Dynasty pyramids, we know next to nothing about the great Giza pyramids. We do know that they were in existence during the Fourth Dynasty, and considering all the other information these people recorded, it is difficult to understand why such a monumental project would not also have been mentioned. Could the reason be that they were not built by the Fourth Dynasty Egyptians—that maybe they were built much earlier, possibly before the First Dynasty? Were the third and fifth dynasties attempting to recreate something without the technology, or perhaps certain abilities, of a civilization that existed in their distant past? Could that civilization have been created by extraterrestrials—perhaps one of the experimental races with a genetically enhanced ability, perhaps of levitation?

The experts claim that it took approximately twenty-two years to build the large Khufu pyramid. If this is true, it means that for twenty-two years, the people worked around the clock to cut, shape, transport, and set each stone block into place on an average of one every eight to ten seconds. That idea seems even more unbelievable than levitation.

Levitation, of course, is a radical idea. However, if extraterrestrials are genetically manipulating the human race, could the civilizations that

29

built Tiahuanaco, Baalbek, and the great pyramids have possessed genes designed to enhance mental abilities? Although the idea may be hard to fathom, could it be that levitation was as commonplace to them as driving a car is to us?

If ETs are accelerating our evolution to prepare us for some future cataclysmic event, then it is only logical that our survival depends more on technology and the development of space travel than on mental powers. Perhaps they realized early on that an enhanced mental ability was a mistake; no progress was being made toward developing the technologies needed for survival. Why invent machines to do heavy lifting if they could do it with their minds? Technology would not have been one of their priorities and it could explain why they were phased out. Like Adam's descendants, a flood or some other disaster might have wiped them out to make room for a new race. The same situation could also have applied to the Mayans and the Incas. Although they were highly advanced cultures in many ways, their barbaric practice of human blood sacrifices to their gods may have been the reason for their termination. Such practices were based on strong superstitious beliefs and were not conducive to the intellectual quality of the races they were attempting to produce. Theoretically, such terminations could explain the legends of great floods as noted by almost every civilization on the planet. There are, however, indications that certain climatic changes may have occurred, forcing the Mayan and Incan civilizations to abandon their cities.

But what about levitation? Conceivably, it could explain many ancient mysteries, but is it actually possible? Could mental power truly move and manipulate large stone blocks weighing hundreds of tons? Looking at Coral Castle in Homestead, Florida, one almost has to consider the possibility.

Between 1920 and 1940, a Latvian immigrant named Edward Leedskalnin built Coral Castle single-handedly. He created his stone estate by working mostly at night to avoid the prying eyes of curious neighbors. He did not use any heavy-duty construction equipment, yet somehow he managed to lift and maneuver stone blocks weighing over thirty tons. Not bad for a little fellow with a fourth-grade education, standing five feet tall and weighing about a hundred pounds. Allegedly, a group of teenagers spied on him one night and claimed that they actually saw him floating these large blocks in the air. Because it was such a fantastic story, it is understandable that no one believed them.

Leedskalnin originally built his complex in Florida City, and for reasons not completely understood, he later moved it to Homestead, where he added to it. For this, he used a flatbed truck. When it arrived in the in the morning, he would dismiss the driver, telling him to return later in the afternoon. Although it cannot be verified, one day the driver allegedly forgot his lunch in the truck and went back to get it. He was stunned when he saw that a few giant blocks had already been loaded onto the truck's bed—all within the thirty minutes he had been gone—a feat that would be hard to duplicate today even with heavy-duty loading equipment. Leedskalnin was nowhere in sight, so the perplexed driver left.[20]

When you visit Coral Castle and actually see what Leedskalnin accomplished, you almost have to believe he had an ability that no one else possessed, unless you wish to consider the builders of Baalbek, Tiahuanaco, and the Giza pyramids. Recorded messages at Coral Castle claim he accomplished his work by using the tools that are on display in his work area, so it could be true. If so, then why did he not let people watch him work? Why did he work mostly at night and in secret? What was it that he did not want people to see?

A modern builder tried his hand at building a smaller version of one of the large pyramids using only the tools that were available 4,500 years ago. The results were pathetic, even when he had to resort to using modern construction equipment.[21] This only adds credibility to the idea that the ancients, and possibly Leedskalnin, possessed an extraordinary ability that completely baffles us today.

In all fairness to mainstream Egyptologists, I must acknowledge the fact that a complex covering an area larger than three football fields has been excavated near the great pyramids. It appears to have been a work camp that accommodated thousands of people—allegedly, those who built the great pyramids. Many of the bones found in grave sites show signs of heavy stress on the spinal column, indicating they had been involved in very stressful physical endeavors. They uncovered the ruins of numerous grain silos and bread-baking ovens, suggesting that many thousands of people were being fed on a daily basis. There is also what appears to be a barracks-style facility, assumed to be where hundreds of seasonal workers may have slept. Additionally, there are ruins of larger living quarters that presumably housed the overseers of the project and their families.

It is obvious that those living in the camp were working on an enormous project for a long time, and logic suggests that it was on one or possibly all three of the great pyramids. Even though this evidence may contradict the idea of levitation, we must acknowledge the possibility that there was nothing extraordinary involved in how the great pyramids were constructed.

One question that does remain is whether they were really intended as tombs. None contained a sarcophagus or a mummy, and there are no hieroglyphic symbols decorating their walls and ceilings to indicate that they were intended as burial chambers for anyone.

Other Pyramids

Pyramids are not unique to Egypt; they exist all over the world. There is a complex of fifteen pyramids located in Cochasquí, in the northern Andes Mountains of Ecuador.[22]

In the town of Ena, on the Japanese Island of Honsu, is a pyramid about six and a half feet high; it was carved out of a single block of grey granite. It is located on the slope of a hill in a forest, almost hidden from view. No one knows who built it, when, or why.[23]

As recently as 1998, six pyramids were discovered on Tenerife, in the Canary Islands.[24]

An infrared satellite image revealed twelve pyramids tucked away in the dense Brazilian jungle. They are laid out side by side in two rows of six.[25]

Several years ago, Thor Heyerdahl was excavating pyramids near Tucume, in northern Peru. It is reported that twenty-six have been discovered there.[26]

In Australia, there is a stepped pyramid about one hundred feet tall, comprised of large granite blocks in the town of Gympie, New South Wales. Allegedly, there is another in the area, also about one hundred feet tall, and near the coast is said to be one twice the size of the one in Gympie. Five more are said to have been found in New Guinea.[27]

In 1957, *Life* magazine published a picture of what has been called the White Pyramid. It was taken by a World War II pilot flying over the Qin Ling Shan Mountains in the Chinese Province of Tibet. In 1994, German researcher Hartwig Hausdorf photographed more Chinese pyramids when he toured the Shensi Province. He said there were over a hundred of them, and one was as large as the great Khufu pyramid in Giza.[28]

Some of the pyramids in Mexico and Central America predate the Giza pyramids, assuming, of course, that the Giza pyramids were built around 2550 BC. Two of the most famous are in Teotihuacan: the Pyramid of the Moon and the Pyramid of the Sun. And although not as tall, the base of the Pyramid of the Sun is as large as the base of the Khufu pyramid. Others include the Tlahuizcalpantecuhtli pyramid, comprised of five terraces and located in Tula; a huge adobe brick pyramid in Cholula; a long stone pyramid in Tzintzuntzan; and the Kukulkan pyramid in Chichen Itza. And there are at least thirty-two other sites in Mexico with large pyramids, not to mention those in Honduras and in Belize, El Salvador. One rather intriguing site is the Mayan pyramid complex in Tikal, Guatemala.[29] Other sites around the world include Germany, Greece, Turkey, Sudan, and the United States. The odds of different civilizations allegedly unknown to each other and separated by vast oceans constructing monuments of such similarity seem unlikely. How can one not suspect global interaction between past civilizations? Is it just a coincidence that the ancient Egyptians and the Apache Indians both worshipped a god called Amon Ra, and that both gods are strikingly similar in appearance.[30]

Somewhere in the history of mankind is an era that has been lost or forgotten. There was an age when men excelled in architectural accomplishments, producing monuments that our technology is incapable of duplicating today. How do we explain stone blocks weighing as much as diesel locomotives being hoisted fifty feet into the air next to the Sphinx when heavy-duty construction equipment did not yet exist? Attributing such feats to extraterrestrials would seem logical since no civilization so technically advanced is known to have existed. Yet these structures exist, and that is a fact. Similar structures exist all over the world; that is a fact. Most are so old that no one knows who built them, when, or why—and that, too, is a fact. How do we explain this, other than that a segment of man's history has been completely obliterated, or that there may have been extraterrestrial influence?

The Orion Connection

One night while Robert Bauval, a construction engineer, was sitting in the desert looking up at the night sky, he suddenly realized that the Giza pyramids were lined up in precisely the same pattern as the three stars in Orion's Belt. The largest pyramid of Khufu (Cheops) and the middle pyramid of Khafre (Chefren), which is slightly smaller, are perfectly aligned with each other. However, the third and smaller pyramid of Menkaure (Mycerinus) is slightly off center. These, plus two other pyramids, one several miles to the north at Abu Ruwash and the other about three miles south at Zawat-Al-Aryan, are laid out in the exact same pattern as the five major stars in the constellation of Orion.[31] Is this a coincidence?

Now, 4,500 years ago, a shaft leading out of the King's Chamber in the Khufu pyramid would have pointed directly to Orion's Belt, and one leading from the Queen's Chamber would have pointed directly at Sirius. This is significant in that the constellation of Orion represented Osiris, the ancient Egyptian's god of resurrection, and Sirius, the star of his consort, Isis. Allegedly, the belief was that their spirits would depart through the shafts to their place in the heavens, a point favoring mainstream beliefs that the pyramids were built around 2550 BC. But since there is no evidence that these chambers were ever used as tombs, what would be the purpose of aligning the shafts to Orion and Sirius?

Compounding the mystery, Bauval discovered that in 10,500 BC, the stars in Orion's Belt would have perfectly matched the layout of the three pyramids as they rose above the horizon exactly due south of their location. Also, at this time, the constellation of Leo (the lion) would have risen above the horizon at a position due east, directly in front of the Sphinx. Since the Sphinx depicts the body of a lion, is this of significance? Is this a clue that the pyramids and the Sphinx were created over 12,000 years ago?

John Anthony West has provided sufficient reason to believe that the Sphinx was originally created with the head of a lion. Possibly due to severe erosion, it was later carved into the head of a pharaoh. The pharaoh's head is disproportionately small and seems out of place, whereas a lion's head would be in correct proportion with the body.[32]

If the pyramids were built in 10,500 BC, what is the relevance to the shafts' alignments to Orion and Sirius in 2550 BC? It would have had no significance 8,000 years earlier. And if they were built in 2550 BC, their alignment to the stars in 10,500 BC would be of no relevance. Could it be that we are only confusing ourselves by reading more into this than there actually is?

Over fifty years ago, noted psychic Edgar Cayce claimed that the Sphinx was created in 10,500 BC, a date he predicted would gain support around 1998. He also said that beneath the Sphinx was a Hall of Records containing information about the civilization who built it and the real history of the human race. He predicted that it would be discovered between 1996 and 1998, and that its contents would be kept secret for many years. He also associated the opening of this chamber to the return of Christ.[33]

Cayce is best known for the healings he achieved by inducing himself into a trance state, where it seems he could tap into some universal knowledge and come up with a remedy or a cure for just about anything. People with various ailments and afflictions wrote to him and even came in person, seeking his help. He was extremely successful in prescribing effective treatments when the best of the medical profession had failed. His case files are all documented and open to the public at his estate in Virginia Beach.

Another of Cayce's claims was that Atlantis would be discovered off the Florida coast in 1968. In 1968, a discovery was made off the Florida coast, near the island of Bimini. It appears to be a road or the top of a rampart comprised of huge stone blocks, but what it really is remains a mystery. Some claim it is only a natural formation of beach rock, while others associate it with Cayce's prediction that Atlantis would be discovered that same year in that general location. So far, there is no evidence to connect it to Atlantis; only a serious scientific investigation will determine if the site is of artificial construction.

Cayce's prediction about the Hall of Records beneath the Sphinx, however, may be right on target. In 1991, seismic readings taken by Thomas Dobecki, a seismologist, revealed the existence of a chamber twenty feet beneath the paws of the Sphinx.[34] This sparked a lot of interest in that it might be the Hall of Records; however, it was never excavated. In March of 1996, under the auspices of Florida State University, Joseph Schor was approved to do a study of the Giza Plateau to look for faults that might cave in and threaten the safety of tourists. Schor brought Dobecki with him to conduct the seismic readings, and a month later, according to the *Egyptian Gazette* of April 14, 1996, Zahi Hawass was quoted as saying that there were hidden tunnels running between the Sphinx and the pyramids.

A statement posted in 1997 by Richard Hoagland on his "Enterprise Mission" website suggested that Schor might possibly have been involved in more than just looking for faults on the plateau. The information purportedly came from a member of Schor's team who approached Hoagland's colleagues, claiming that discoveries made by Schor in the great pyramid were being kept from the public. Photos posted on the site reveal a ladder and a heavy-duty power cable ascending into the area above the King's Chamber, and they show bags of limestone rocks awaiting removal. They had apparently been lowered from above by a rope visibly hanging down from the top of the chamber.[35] Hoagland suggests that it may have been an attempt to drill a tunnel to a hidden passageway leading to the Hall of Records. Although there is no proof of this, the heavy-duty power cable certainly suggests that something was going on above the King's Chamber.

We know the pyramid was closed on April 1, 1998, for over a year to repair cracks and damage caused by moisture from the breath of tourists, and Hawass said they installed a ventilation system. But the system was installed in a ventilation shaft leading to the outside, not in the area above the King's Chamber—it does not explain what was going on above the chamber in 1996 and '97.

The only things known to be near the King's Chamber are the shafts leading up from the Queen's Chamber below. In 1993, Rudolf Gantenbrink used a specially designed robot called Upuaut to explore the southern shaft. It ascended the eight-by-eight-inch shaft for 208 feet—until it reached a stone block the builders had inserted to seal the passage. Two copper fittings were mounted in it, suggesting they may have acted as wedges, making it impossible to remove the block once it had been dropped into place.[36] In the bottom right corner of the block was a small crevice in which Gantenbrink thought he could devise a miniature camera that would be able to penetrate through to the other side. His request, however, was denied.

On Monday, September 16, 2002, the FOX Broadcasting Company broadcast a live National Geographic special from Egypt, in which the world finally got to see what was behind the Gantenbrink door. A team from National Geographic was contracted to do the job, and they brought their own specially designed robot. There were a couple of preliminary test runs to make sure all systems on the robot were working properly, and there was one visit to the door with an instrument to measure its density, which showed it to be three inches thick. Then a drill was mounted on the robot, and it was sent back to the door, where it bored a hole through the slab. Then it appears there was some sort of power malfunction and the robot rolled out of control back down the shaft, fortunately without causing any major damage. After the malfunction was repaired, the robot was sent back to the door with a miniature fiber optic camera attached to it. The camera was inserted through the hole, only to reveal another stone slab blocking the shaft just a few inches away.

Immediately after the program, conspiracy enthusiasts argued that the still image of the door from Gantenbrink's video taken in 1993 shows the copper fitting on the left to be shorter than the one on the right. Apparently, the piece had broken off and rolled a short distance down the shaft, out of view of the camera. In the still from National Geographic's video posted on their website, the copper fitting on the right was the same length as the one on the left, and the severed piece was nowhere in sight.[37] Admittedly, it does look suspicious. But it is possible that the device used to measure the door's thickness may have broken the copper fitting on the right, and that it rolled down the shaft and out of view of the camera. If this is what happened, the fact that it was not mentioned aroused suspicions among conspiracy theorists who wanted to believe that something was being covered up in the National Geographic presentation. The story on National Geographic's website mentioned the test runs and the one to measure the door's thickness, so I see no evidence of a cover-up.

The FOX Network has broadcast other live programs from the Giza Plateau. On March 2, 1999, they presented *Opening the Lost Tombs of Egypt*, hosted by Maury Povitch and ESPN's Suzy Kolber. The highlight of the program was entering the Tomb of Osiris, a chamber located one hundred feet belowground, a short distance behind the Sphinx.

Viewers watched as Kolber and Zahi Hawass descended twenty feet down a ladder, into a small, empty chamber from which another shaft descended forty feet into what Hawass called a burial chamber. It had six rooms, two of which contained a granite sarcophagus. Hawass said that when discovered, the room was filled with sand that had to be removed. In this chamber was yet another shaft that descended forty feet down into the Osiris Tomb, which he said had been filled with water that had to be pumped out. The floor of the tomb was as an island surrounded by a moat, and in the center, submerged in a large water-filled depression, was a huge sarcophagus that Hawass estimated weighed between eleven and twelve tons. The lid of the coffin was about nine feet long and had been lifted out by a chain hoist. When Kolber asked Hawass how the ancient Egyptians managed to lower it one hundred feet down through the different shafts, he said the shafts had first been filled with sand, which the workers removed from the bottom. As the sand was removed, the sarcophagus was gradually lowered into the tomb. He said the workers had removed the sand through the tunnels.[38] Tunnels? What tunnels?

Remember, according to the *Egyptian Gazette*, Hawass said in April 1996 that there were tunnels running between the Sphinx and the pyramids, which he could only have known from the seismic readings taken by Thomas Dobecki a month earlier. As Hawass gingerly walked on the rungs of a ladder across the moat to an opening in the wall, Kolber mentioned that archaeologists agree that there is a network of tunnels below the plateau and also the predictions of Edgar Casey and asked Hawass if there might be a connection to this tomb. Hawass said he believed it was all a myth. Then he said he had not yet explored this tunnel, and that you never know what secrets might lay beneath the sands of Egypt. In closing, Maury Povitch questioned whether the tunnel might lead to a Hall of Records underneath the Sphinx, reminding the viewers that Hawass said there was much yet to be revealed under the Egyptian sands.

Excavation of the Osiris Tomb began in 1998. Edgar Cayce predicted that a Hall of Records would be discovered under the Sphinx between 1996 and 1998, and seismic readings taken in 1991 and 1996 confirmed the existence of a chamber twenty feet below the paws of the Sphinx. Might it be the Hall of Records? Maybe so, maybe not.

Could it be that like the Osiris Tomb, the Hall of Records is also one hundred feet underground—possibly beneath two other chambers, the uppermost being the one twenty feet beneath the paws of the Sphinx? If the Osiris tunnel does lead to the Hall of Records, it means that Cayce was technically right in his prediction since excavation began on the Osiris Tomb in 1998. If what Hawass said about the tunnel in the Osiris Tomb not yet being excavated was true, then where it led had not yet been determined.

However, in a later documentary, Hawass said the Osiris tunnel leads nowhere. He said they had a small boy inch his way through, only to find that it was a dead end. This contradicts what he told Suzy Kolber about how the sand used to lower the sarcophagus into the Osiris tomb was removed through the tunnels. Since the only tunnel seems to be the one in the Osiris chamber, which he now claims leads nowhere, then we have to assume the sand was removed simply by hoisting it out in buckets. But

---

is he telling the truth about this tunnel? Is it part of Cayce's prediction regarding the contents of the Hall of Records being kept secret? And if it does contain information pertaining to the origin of the human race, why would it need to be kept secret? Could the reason be that it reveals the human race is a product of genetic manipulation by extraterrestrials? Such a revelation would throw the religious community into chaos and result in worldwide problems. And since Casey tied his prediction to the return of Christ, it could mean that there are religious implications—something the world is not psychologically prepared to deal with at this time. Of course, this is only speculation based on the possibility that a Hall of Records does exist.

Casey predicted that Atlantis would be discovered off the coast of Florida in 1968. In 1968, the Bimini Road was discovered in that general location. Although there is nothing to prove it is part of Atlantis, there may still be much more to discover in that area. Only time will tell.

Cayce also said that the Sphinx was created in 10,500 BC, a date he claimed would gain support around 1998. No one can deny the fact that the 10,500 BC date associated with Robert Bauval's *Orion Connection* has gained much recognition since 1998. Considering his well-documented track record of the healings he effected in his lifetime, should we not at least consider the possibility that Casey may be right?

There is much evidence, albeit circumstantial, suggesting the pyramids, or at least the Sphinx, may be thousands of years older than what mainstream Egyptologists claim. However, an extraterrestrial connection is something that cannot be proved. Whatever information is sealed in the Hall of Records may provide the answer, assuming, there really is a Hall of Records. All we can do is wait and see.

Meanwhile, we cannot ignore the fact that many of the monolithic structures built by the ancients are beyond the capability of present-day technology. What does this tell us? That these ancient people had an ability that is incomprehensible to us? Was it levitation? Until the scientific community is willing to explore such possibilities, we may never know.

Notes

1. The Dogon
    "Dark Star." *In Search of...* Prod. Tamara Lucier-Green. A&E. 20
    Dec. 1979.

2. Rongorongo
    Link to image:
    www.enotes.com/topic/Rongorongo_text_R

3. Nazca lines and geoglyphs
    "Ancient Aviators." *In Search Of...* Prod. Jeffrey Pill. A&E. 24
    April 1977.
    Links to images:
    www.youtube.com/watch?v=tHwN8_qa2c8 earthobservatory.nasa
    .gov/IOTD/view.php?id=5848

4. Bay of Pisco trident
    Link to image:
    www.flickr.com/photos/11973893@N00/51687427

5. Mountain images in Cerro Unitas, Chile
    "Giants for the Gods." *Arthur C. Clarke's Mysterious World.*
    Discovery. 1980.

6. Faces on wall of Tiahuanaco Courtyard
    Link to image:
    www.crystalinks.com/preinca.html (scroll down to see image)

7. Stapled blocks at Tiahuanaco
    Chariots of the Gods? The Mysteries Continue. Documentary. Dir.
    Robert Asher. ABC. WPBF. West Palm Beach. 1996.
    Link to images:
    subharanjangupta.wordpress.com/page/4/ (scroll down to see images)

8.	Interlocking and grooved stone blocks at Puma Punku
	Links to images:
	www.ufo-contact.com/pumapunku/interlocking-stone-walls-
	megaliths subharanjangupta.wordpress.com/page/4/ (scroll down
	to see images)

9.	Arthur Posnansky
	The Mysterious Origins of Man. Documentary. Prod. Bill Cote.
	NBC. WPTV. West Palm Beach. 25 Feb. 1996.

10.	Tiahuanaco portal of the sun
	Link to image:
	http://www.thule.org/tiahuanaco.html

11.	1,300-ton stone block at Baalbek
	Link to image:
	www.bearfabrique.org/Catastrophism/Baalbek/Baalbek.html

12.	The Sphinx temples
	The Mystery of the Sphinx. Documentary. Dir. Bill Cote. NBC.
	WPTV. West Palm Beach.
	10 Nov. 1993.
	Link to image:
	www.touregypt.net/featurestories/sphinx3.htm

13.	Second opinion on erosion of the Sphinx
	The Mystery of the Sphinx. Documentary. Dir. Bill Cote. NBC.
	WPTV. West Palm Beach. 10 Nov. 1993.

14.	Granite stele in front of Sphinx
	Link to image:
	heartofthebear.com/SphinxMate.html

15. Stele installed 1,100 years after Sphinx was created
"The Sphinx." *Monumental Mysteries*. Prod. Christopher Swayne.
Discovery. 1999.

16. Inventory stele
The Mystery of the Sphinx. Documentary. Dir. Bill Cote. NBC.
WPTV. West Palm Beach. 10 Nov. 1993.

17. Carbon dating of mortar
"Pyramids and Sphinx." *Digging for the Truth*. Exec. Prod. William
Morgan/Jason Williams. THC. 2005.

18. Blocks inside the Khufu Pyramid
"Secrets of the Pyramids and the Sphinx." *Ancient Journeys*. Prod./
Dir. Roel Costra. TLC. 1995.

19. Graham Hancock on pyramids of three dynasties
"Secrets of the Pyramids and the Sphinx." *Ancient Journeys*. Prod./
Dir. Roel Costra. TLC. 1995.

20. Coral Castle
Link to images:
www.coralcastle.com/

21. Modern attempt to build small pyramid with primitive tools
"This Old Pyramid." *NOVA*. Documentary. Prod. D. J. Roller.
PBS. 4 Nov. 1992.

22. Ecuador pyramids
Link to image:
www.crystalinks.com/pyramidecuador.html

23.   Japanese pyramids
        Web link:
        www.crystalinks.com/pryamidjapan.html

24.   Tenerife pyramids
        Link to images:
        www.exotictenerife.com/attractions/pyramids-of-guimar/

25.   Infrared satellite image of Brazil pyramids
        Web link:
        www.crystalinks.com/pyramidbrazil.html

26.   Peruvian pyramids
        Link to images:
        www.crystalinks.com/pyramidperu.html

27.   Australian pyramids
        Links to images:
        www.crystalinks.com/pyramidaustralia.html
        www.rexgilroy.com/uru_chapter16.html

28.   White Pyramid and other Chinese pyramids
        Link to images:
        www.crystalinks.com/pyramidchina.html

29.   Mesoamerican pyramids
        Link to images:
        www.crystalinks.com/pyramidmesoamerica.html

30.   Amon Ra
        "Earth Visitors." *In Search Of...* Prod. Jeffrey Pill. A&E. 31 Jan.
        1980.

31. The Orion connection
    "Secrets of the Pyramids and the Sphinx." *Ancient Journeys*. Prod./
    Dir. Roel Costra. TLC. 1995.

32. Theory that head of the Sphinx was originally a lion
    The Mystery of the Sphinx. Documentary. Dir. Bill Cote. NBC.
    WPTV. West Palm Beach. 10 Nov. 1993.

33. Edgar Cayce's predictions about date of Sphinx and Hall of
    Records
    "Secrets of the Pyramids and the Sphinx." *Ancient Journeys*. Prod./
    Dir. Roel Costra. TLC. 1995.

34. Seismic readings around the Sphinx
    "Secrets of the Pyramids and the Sphinx." *Ancient Journeys*. Prod./
    Dir. Roel Costra. TLC. 1995.

35. Secret tunneling above the King's Chamber?
    Web link:
    www.enterprisemission.com/pyramid.html

36. The Gantenbrink door
    "Robot Journey into the Past." *The Unexplained*. Prod. Rudolf
    Gantenbrink. A&E. 26 May 1995.
    Link to image:
    www.hansrey.com/egypt-mystery.htm

37. *National Geographic*'s photo of Gantenbrink door
    Link to image:
    www.pyramidofman.com/Plugs/index.html

38. The Osiris tomb
    Opening the Lost Tombs. Documentary. Dir. Artie Kempner. FOX.
    WFLX. West Palm Beach. 2 Mar. 1999.

Chapter 4

ANCIENT EVIDENCE

OOParts

OOParts is an acronym for *out-of-place artifacts*. They are items that scientists cannot explain because they do not conform to the era from which they supposedly originated. Since OOParts seem to defy logical explanation, many attribute them to ancient alien visitors, while others suggest they are remnants of a lost civilization that had reached an advanced level of technology. Whether terrestrial or extraterrestrial, some items appear credible and others remain questionable.

In 1968, a discovery was made near Antelope Springs, Utah, of what appears to be a fossilized footprint of a shoe or moccasin. Embedded in the print is a trilobite, an invertebrate that existed 500 to 600 million years ago, during the Cambrian period. Most scientists have dismissed the footprint without having examined it because it contradicts the preconceived notion that humans did not yet exist—it was, after all, hundreds of millions of years before the dinosaurs had even evolved. However, Dr. Hellmut H. Doelling of the Utah Geological Survey examined the footprint and found no irregularities or evidence of fraud.[1]

Mining engineer and geologist John T. Reid discovered another fossilized shoeprint in Nevada, circa 1922. Although the front part was missing, two-thirds of the print had managed to remain intact. Clearly visible around the outline is a well-defined sewn thread stitching where the welt was attached to the sole. Mainstream scientists shrugged it off as simply a fluke of nature. Reid, however, persuaded an analytical chemist and a photographer from the Rockefeller Institute to examine the fossil, and when magnified twenty times, it was clear that the stitching was man-made. Also, they proved beyond a doubt that it was of Triassic fossilization, a period that is currently dated at 213 to 248 million years ago.

According to a story that appeared in the *Morrisonville Times* in Illinois on June 11, 1891, Mrs. S. W. Culp of Morrisonville discovered a gold chain embedded in a lump of coal she was preparing to put in the scuttle. It was made of eight-carat gold, was about ten inches long, and weighed eight pennyweights. The coal had come from either the Taylorville or the Pana mine in southern Illinois, both of which, according to the Illinois State Geological Survey, are 260 to 320 million years old. Again, this was before dinosaurs even existed.

These items appear credible by virtue of the fact that they exist. But how do we explain them? Who was walking around 600 million years ago and stepped on a trilobite? Who around 213 million years ago was wearing the equivalent of shoes? Who lost a gold chain 260 million years ago, which became embedded in a layer coal? Since these items defy rational explanation, it would seem to suggest that man might have been around a lot longer than scientists are willing to believe.

Another discovery that has perplexed many OOPart enthusiasts is the nickel-steel alloy spheroids excavated from the Wonderstone Silver Mine in South Africa. About two hundred that appear to have been manufactured were recovered. They range from one to four inches in diameter and have a strong thin shell with a spongy material inside that disintegrates when exposed to air. One is locked in a display case at the Klerksdorp Museum in South Africa and is said to rotate on its own with no outside influence. The spheres were mined out of a layer of pyrophyllite rock, and radioisotope dating showed them to be 2.8 to 3 billion years old.[2]

In this case, however, there could be a rational explanation. It would take many pages to explain the technical details, but if you Google "Wonderstone spheroids" and then click on the Wikipedia link for the "Klerksdorp sphere," it explains everything. Although the age of 3 billion years is correct, it claims that the spheres actually originated as concretions that formed in volcanic ash and sediment. And they are not all spheres; some are flattened to almost a disc shape. This may be disappointing to those who want to believe they are artifacts left by ancient astronauts, yet it is a good example of how the context of a story can be altered by omitting some details and embellishing others. Let's use a little common sense here—3 billion years ago, the earth was still coming out of its birthing pangs, and from what we know about its geological history, no one could have survived in the chaotic environment that prevailed, let alone breathed the atmosphere as it was back then.

Another of the more dubious items that gained notoriety over the years is an artifact that rock collectors discovered in the Coso Mountains in California. A spark plug–like device, it is embedded in a rock that is allegedly 500,000 years old. Photos and X-rays of the artifact have appeared in books, magazines, and in documentary films. What is not commonly known is that the photos and X-rays were examined by Chad Windham, president of the Spark Plug Collectors of America, who attests to the fact that it is a Champion spark plug from the 1920s.[3]

What remains in dispute is the rock in which it was encased. Allegedly, its crust is embedded with 500,000-year-old fossils, suggesting that that was when it was created. This is still a grey area since over the last forty years, the artifact and its owners have moved on. If it is 500,000 years old, how could a spark plug from the 1920s have become embedded inside unless it was caused by some fluke condition of nature with which we are unfamiliar? However, I call them as I see them, and in this case, the evidence weighs heavily in favor of it being an early twentieth-century spark plug. I only mention this item because of the publicity it has received over the years— and that many people still believe it is something more than what it is.

One of the more credible artifacts is a device that was recovered in 1900 from a ship that sank off the Greek island of Antikythera sometime between 65 BC and 65 AD. In 1971, Derek Price of Yale University obtained permission from the Greek government to x-ray it, and what he discovered was amazing, to say the least.

The X-rays revealed that it was a mechanical device comprised of over twenty gear wheels mounted on wood. It had broken apart in several pieces, but Price was able to reconstruct a working model to the exact specifications of the original. He was amazed to discover that what he had was an analog computer, a device used to track the movement of the sun, moon, and stars. However, it was built over 1,000 years before such precision clockwork had been invented.[4] Although it was constructed during an era with which we are more familiar, there is nothing on record that would lead us to believe that the technology used to create the device existed at the time. Since the precision clockwork involved supposedly did not become known for another thousand years, perhaps it was the creation of an obscure genius whose ideas were way ahead of his time, such as Archimedes, da Vinci, and Copernicus were in their time.

In the early part of the twentieth century, 1,500-year-old artifacts resembling aircraft were discovered in a grave site along the Magdalena River in Colombia, South America. Each displays the basic elements of any conventional airplane, having a fuselage, wings, a tail rudder, and stabilizers. Larger models were constructed using the same identical body styles and equipped with motors to see if they could fly. To everyone's amazement, the models were aerodynamically stable and flew perfectly.[5] How could people 1,500 years ago have understood the aerodynamic principles of flight unless they created the figurines based on something they had actually seen. Many other ancient figurines found around the world bear an uncanny resemblance to space-suited astronauts, which some believe is proof of alien visitation.[6]

However, fossilized shoe prints and artifacts that are hundreds of millions of years old are something else. Many date back to an era when man supposedly did not yet exist in any way, shape, or form. As smart as we think we are today with our computerized cell phones and GPS systems, we are still ignorant of the past because mainstream science is glued to a status quo belief system from which they fear to deviate. Just as in the time of Galileo and, more recently, Virginia Steen-McIntyre, they are ostracized by their peers when they do so.

What we do know is that there were evolutionary stages of prehistoric man that led up to the Neanderthal and Cro-Magnon. We can only postulate from the evidence that some form of intelligent man, whether from our planet or elsewhere, may have walked along the earth with prehistoric man—and maybe even the dinosaurs—eons ago. However, to suggest that hundreds of artifacts and fossils are a fluke of nature is only an assumption and the only way the mainstream can avoid the issue. Heaven forbid should their current beliefs ever prove to be wrong.

Logically, there would seem to be only three possibilities: time travelers from the future, extraterrestrials, or intelligent man. Time travel is pushing the envelope because at our present stage of scientific development, it seems impossible. Faster-than-light travel is a concept we will accept more readily—even extraterrestrial visitors would seem a more likely possibility. Perhaps a spaceship crashed on Earth eons ago and the survivors had the technology that allowed them to survive. They could have been around for untold millennia and produced a sizable population that existed along with prehistoric man. What happened in the interim is anyone's guess. Perhaps they did not survive the cataclysmic disasters that occurred over the eons, or if they did, maybe they had to start over from scratch under very primitive conditions. They could even be our ancestors. Let's face it: anything is possible when it comes to the unknown. So until someone can prove otherwise, the logical assumption is that regardless of how it came about, some form of intelligent man was around much earlier than is currently believed.

Texts

Another aspect of the ancient astronaut theory is the numerous writings alluding to aerial craft in the skies. But here again, we find some of the information to be credible, while in other cases, some of those researching this material did not do their homework. The following are examples of each.

One incident balancing on the fence between reality and fiction is said to have occurred in ancient Egypt, when Pharaoh Tutmoses III purportedly had his scribe document in writing the appearance of strange glowing craft in the desert skies:

> *In the year twenty-two of the third month of winter, a circle of fire appeared in the sky. After some days, it became more numerous and shone with the brightness of the sun, extending to the very limits of the heavens.*
>
> —Records of Tutmoses III, 1480 BC[7]

This story has been presented in many documentaries, but some skeptics claim that there is no evidence that it even exists. However, I have found several references naming the "Tulli Papyrus" as the source. At the end of this chapter, I have listed various websites that offer ideas, both pro and con, as to its validity.

In the fourth century BC, Alexander the Great supposedly had two separate encounters with UFOs. But I find the accounts highly questionable. The first allegedly occurred in 339 BC, when he and his army encountered "gleaming silver shields" in the sky, spitting fire around the rims. It claims they swooped down repeatedly, frightening the horses and war elephants and causing his troops to scatter. The second apparently occurred in 332 BC, when he was attacking the city of Tyre in the eastern Mediterranean region. One of the UFOs fired a beam of light down on the city's walls, and they crumbled into dust, thereby providing Alexander and his army with easy access and victory.[8] This was allegedly recorded by observers on both sides of the conflict.

These accounts have appeared in several documentaries, and although it has been assumed that Alexander's own historian chronicled them, I have not been able to find any documentation to verify it. Therefore, as interesting as these stories may be, there is much to be desired regarding their authenticity.

The most vivid accounts are those from ancient India, describing an incredible flying craft called the Vimana. It is mentioned in numerous Hindu texts, including the Ramayana, and the Mahabharata.

The Ramayana provides a good description of the Vimana, even its source of propulsion. It was a circular craft with different levels within. It had portholes, a rounded or dome-like top, was able to fly at great speed through the skies, and could even hover motionless. It made a loud noise, produced smoke and flames, and had weapons powerful enough to destroy the earth instantly.[9]

In September of 2000, an item appeared in newspapers around the country—an excerpt from a story that allegedly appeared in a January 1992 publication of the *World Island Review*. The article stated that the Indian government had cordoned off a highly radioactive area in Rajasthan, about ten miles west of Jodhpur. It said that scientists had unearthed the remains of a city that had been destroyed about eight to twelve thousand years ago by what they can only compare to a nuclear blast. It destroyed most of the buildings, and they estimate that it killed about half a million people.[10]

I searched all over the Internet and could find no reference to any publication called the *World Island Review*; however, I did find references that the article originally appeared in Pravda and pertained to excavations at Mohenjo-Daro, located on the Indus River in Pakistan, which is just over the border from the Rajasthan region in India. Apparently, there is much evidence of vitrification in that area; sand has been turned into glass, and the stones in some buildings have fused together, suggesting something occurred that produced heat equivalent to that of a nuclear detonation. It also claims that skeletons were found lying facedown in the streets, some holding hands, suggesting that whatever happened was swift and unexpected. Since Vimanas were receiving a lot of attention in 2000 in UFO circles, I suspect someone resurrected the article after recognizing its significance to what is described in the Mahabharata.

Gurkha flying in his swift and powerful Vimana hurled against the three cities of the Vrishnis and Andhakas a single projectile charged with all the powers of the universe. An incandescent column of smoke and fire, as brilliant as ten thousand suns, rose in all its splendor. It was the unknown weapon, the iron thunderbolt, a gigantic messenger of death which reduced to ashes the entire race of the Vrishnis and Andhakas.

Dense arrows of flame, like a great shower, issued forth upon creation, encompassing the enemy . . . A thick gloom swiftly settled upon the Pandava hosts. All points of the compass were lost in darkness. Fierce winds began to blow. Clouds roared upward, showering dust and gravel. Birds coaked madly . . . the very elements seemed disturbed. The sun seemed to waver in the heavens. The earth shook, scorched by the terrible violent heat of this weapon. Elephants burst into flame and ran to and fro in a frenzy . . . over a vast area, other animals crumpled to the ground and died. From all points of the compass the arrows of flame rained continuously and fiercely.

—The Mahabharata

It even describes what appear to be the effects of nuclear radiation:

The corpses were so burned as to be unrecognizable. The hair and nails fell out; pottery broke without apparent cause, and the birds turned white.

After a few hours all foodstuffs were infected.

To escape from this fire the soldiers threw themselves in streams to wash themselves and their equipment . . . .

—The Mahabharata[11]

The Mahabharata is describing a war that allegedly occurred thousands of years ago between two different races of gods. No one knows if it is ancient science fiction or details of an actual event, yet it describes flying machines, missile-like weapons, and nuclear destruction. How could ancient writers describe such technology and its effects so accurately—

unless they actually witnessed it? And if the story is true, could it explain what happened in Mohenjo-Daro?

I could go on and on, as this is only a brief summary of the written accounts, but there is a lot more information to cover.

Artwork

Ancient hunter-gatherers around the world proved their intelligence and skills in the art they created on rocks and on cave walls. However, one of the more fascinating aspects of their artwork is images suggesting that saucerlike craft were flying around in their skies. In the mountains of southern France near the Spanish border is a fifteen-thousand-year-old cave drawing depicting what appears to be a formation of disc-shaped objects hovering over a field of animals. This certainly suggests that UFOs may have been around for a very long time. We might easily dismiss it as the whim of some ancient cave dweller who had nothing else to do on a rainy day, yet similar drawings all around the world suggest a common impetus behind these creations—that extraterrestrials may have been here for as long as man has been around to record their presence.

Another interesting facet of their art is glyphs depicting what appear to be astronauts in space suits, such as the ten-thousand-year-old cave drawing in Val Camonica, Italy, and they appear to be holding strange devices in their hands.[12] There are others drawn by Indians in Utah, circa 52 BC[13] Some have even been found in Peru, in the northern Sahara Desert, and many Aborigine cave paintings have been discovered in Kimberly, Australia.[14]

One rather interesting find in the southwestern United States is a series of petroglyphs of sine wave patterns denoting electromagnetic circuitry.[15] Since these patterns are only produced on an oscilloscope, how would ancient Indians have known about them?

According to one tale of Indian folklore, two objects collided in the sky and one crash-landed somewhere near Mustard Canyon, in the Death Valley region. Allegedly, the local Indians saw men come down (presumably in another ship) and watched as they repaired the damaged craft. If this is true, then the men were using something like an oscilloscope. How else would ancient Indians have knowledge of these particular shapes?

Also depicted are two glyphs of round bowl-shaped objects with dome-like tops, one of which appears to show structural damage.[16] Could they represent both the vehicle that crashed and the one used by the men who came to repair it? Considering these images are thousands of years old, it makes you wonder.

Another item that many are familiar with is the New Kingdom Temple in Abydos, Egypt, with images resembling modern aircraft carved into one of its ceiling beams—one even resembles a helicopter.[17] According to some sources, it was discovered after pieces of another panel covering it with different artwork had broken off and fallen away. However, archaeologists familiar with the site claim it is the result of carving new images over the old ones on the same panel. In this case, I am inclined to side with the archaeologists, as their explanation seems to be quite credible. There are, however, other pieces of ancient art that cannot be explained so easily.

There are two different paintings from the thirteenth century of medieval knights. Each one shows an object in the sky with what looks like ports, and they appear to be enveloped in an aura of light.[18] One seems to be emitting exhaust flames and appears somewhat similar to a UFO that was photographed over Vancouver City Hall in 1937.[19]

There is a sixteenth-century woodcut depicting a sighting made on April 14, 1561, in the sky over Nuremberg.[20] It shows what looks like a giant spear and several cigar-shaped craft discharging globe-like objects. One person in Nuremburg recorded how these cylinders dispersed smaller circular objects, noting that they seemed to engage each other in battle. A person in Basel, Switzerland, painted his impression of a similar sighting that occurred in 1566, in which the sky was filled with black and white globular objects.[21]

It is impossible to list all the cave and rock paintings or all the medieval artwork because they are so numerous. However, I would like to focus on a few that are of a religious nature. In one of the oldest churches in what used to be Soviet Georgia, an icon that depicts the crucifixion of Christ with two strange objects in the background sky was discovered.[22]

Above the altar in the Visoki Decani Monastery in Kosovo hangs a fresco that was painted in 1350. It depicts the crucifixion of Christ with two flying craft in the background. Inside each one is a man who appears to be operating controls.[23]

The Madonna and Child with the infant St. John is a fifteenth-century Italian Renaissance painting hanging in the Palazzo Vecchio in Florence, Italy. It depicts the Blessed Virgin with two infants: Christ and John the Baptist. In the background is a man with his dog, looking up at an object that seems to be hovering in the sky.[24]

In the French Basilica Notre-Dame in Beaune, Burgundy, are two fourteenth-century tapestries depicting scenes from the life of the Blessed Virgin. Hovering in the background sky in each one is a distinct hat-shaped object, similar to many UFOs photographed in the twentieth century.[25]

A wood painting near the castle Conti Dotremond in Belgium depicts a kneeling Moses holding up the tablets of the Ten Commandments. In the sky are several objects emitting exhaust trails, or they could be antennae protruding from the top, and it appears that Moses has antennae protruding from his head.[26] This makes you wonder if the artist is suggesting he was wearing some kind of communication device.

Hanging in the Santa Maggiore Church in Florence, Italy, is a fifteenth-century painting by Masolino Da Panicale, called *Miracle of the Snow*. Jesus and Mary are pictured in the sky above, on what appears to be a lenticular cloud. Many more lenticular clouds are scattered across the sky, resembling a whole fleet of UFOs.[27]

An image called *The Assumption of the Virgin*, painted by an unknown artist in 1490, shows Mary surrounded by angels and cherubim. No fewer than fifteen UFOs appear to be scattered across the sky.[28]

One thought-provoking image hangs in the National Gallery in London. It was painted in 1486 by Carlo Crivelli and titled *The Annunciation with Saint Emidius*. Hovering in the sky is a distinct disc-shaped cloud emitting a laser-like beam down through the wall of a building, onto the top of Mary's head. A close-up view shows a dove in the beam representing the Holy Spirit, and a close-up of the cloud/craft shows the faces of cherubim encircling the underside.[29] Is it meant to denote the craft that angels travel in?

One painting on display in the Fitzwilliam Museum in Cambridge is *The Baptism of Christ*. It was painted in 1710 by Aert De Gelder and depicts a solid-looking disc-shaped object hovering in the sky and emitting four beams of light down on John the Baptist and Christ.[30] Why would an eighteenth-century artist depict Christ's baptism this way? Why is the sky in so many religious paintings dating back to the fourteenth century littered with disc-shaped objects? Did these artists know something that we don't?

One of the strangest paintings hangs in the Church of San Lorenzo, in San Pietro, Italy. It was painted in 1600 by Bonaventura Salimbeni and is titled *Glorification of the Eucharist*. It shows members of the clergy around an altar displaying the Eucharist, and the area above the altar depicts the Holy Trinity: the Father on the right, the Son on the left, and a dove (the Holy Spirit) in the center. Below the dove and between the Father and Son is a large metallic-looking sphere with antennae protruding from the top or being inserted or held in place by the Father and Son. On the sphere's upper section is a spot that seems to be a reflection of a bright light, and on the lower half is what appears to be a protuberance resembling a camera lens. The sphere bears an uncanny resemblance to the Sputnik satellite launched by the Soviet Union in October 1957.[31]

And the list goes on. These petroglyphs, artifacts, texts, and artwork are so numerous that their existence is difficult to ignore, and they come from all over the world. They suggest technology—aerospace technology—something that no known civilization on Earth possessed at the time. Scientists claim the images do not necessarily represent alien spacecraft, and they could be right. However, they make that claim based on the assumption that any extraterrestrial race is restricted by the same limitations we currently face regarding interstellar travel. The idea that aliens could visit Earth is a monkey wrench in their established beliefs, so they sweep it under the carpet. Since this artwork seems to depict a technology that supposedly did not exist, how can one not consider the possibility that it might be extraterrestrial by virtue of the fact that no known civilizations on Earth at that time could have possessed it?

Although these artifacts, texts, and petroglyphs may appear as evidence of ancient alien astronauts, a balanced argument lies in the proper interpretation of these items. For example, is the figure that looks like an astronaut in a space suit really depicting an astronaut, or simply the leader of some ancient clan dressed in his ceremonial tribal costume. Categorically, the evidence is circumstantial. However, to be completely objective, I must acknowledge opposing viewpoints that are worthy of consideration.

Therefore, I wish to bring your attention to a website that provides a logical explanation of the UFOs depicted in medieval religious art.[32] The content is presented entirely in Italian, with some parts available in French and Portuguese, but only parts 1, 2 and 5 are currently available in English. It compares these paintings to literally dozens of others depicting similar scenes painted by other artists. It explains that those items that have been perceived as aerial craft are either clouds or a variation of symbolism pertaining to angelic beings. It explains that such symbolism was common at the time, intended to accent the spiritual nature of the scene. Therefore, many actually represent angels in various forms: clouds, winged angels, or angels within clouds, etc., and many may simply be just clouds. It presents a strong case that those unfamiliar with the style of art common at the time are exploiting works depicting a more definitive UFO shape without having done the proper amount of research.

In *The Glorification of the Eucharist*, the metallic sphere is supposed to represent the earth. The bright spot that appears to be a reflection of light is supposed to be the sun, and what looks like a camera lens is the moon. Upon close examination of the painting, you will see two equatorial lines that circle the sphere, which is supposed to represent the moon's orbit around the earth, and what looks like antennae are actually wands held by the Father and the Son. This certainly seems to be the case, as these details are evident in many other Trinity paintings where the wands are being held away from the sphere. Therefore, these explanations present a compelling argument that the images in medieval religious art have nothing to do with extraterrestrials or spacecraft.

I have already stated that I am a pragmatist. From my perspective, I question the authenticity of supernatural beings such as angels, especially angels with wings, floating about or hovering in the sky. Actually, wings did not appear on angels until around the sixth century BC. This was when the Hebrews were exiled in Babylonia, where they were exposed to and probably absorbed much of the Babylonian culture. Since the Babylonians depicted their gods with wings, a reasonable assumption is that the concept of winged angels was most likely derived from them.[33] I also question why, in one painting, Moses appears to have antennae sticking out of his head, although this may actually be due to a misinterpretation of ancient writings describing his appearance upon his return from the mountain after receiving the second set of Commandment tablets to replace the ones he had destroyed.

The interpretations presented on this site are based on a belief in a supernatural god and angels that travel about in clouds, thereby assuming that the artists were expressing this idea in their work; such reasoning comfortably fits the mysticism associated with many religious beliefs. However, it does not account for similar objects that appear in nonreligious artwork, nor does it account for ancient petroglyphs, cave paintings, or the aerial phenomena described in many ancient texts. Nevertheless, there are two sides to every story, and it is up to each individual to examine the evidence on both sides and decide for himself which one carries the most weight.

Notes

1.	600-million-year-old footprint
	Link to image:
	clearwisdom.net/emh/articles/2000/12/29/3697.html

2.	2.8-billion-year-old spheroids
	Link to images:
	www.ooparts.us/klerksdorp-spheres.htm

3.	The Coso artifact
	"Earth Visitors." *In Search Of* ... Prod. Jeffrey Pill. A&E. 31 Jan. 1980.
	Link to image:
	www.talkorigins.org/faqs/coso.html

4.	Antikythera Computer
	"Ancient Computer?" *Ancient Discoveries.* Prod. Ali McGrath/ Stuart Clarke. THC. 21 Dec. 2003.
	Link to images:
	dogmacero.wordpress.com/2008/08/15/la-maquina-de-antikythera/

5.	Colombian aircraft figurines
	"The Evidence." *Ancient Aliens.* Prod. Kevin Burns. THC. 20 April 2010.
	Link to image:
	www.2atoms.com/weird/ancient/plane.htm

6.	Ancient astronaut figurines
	Link to image:
	aolsearcht9.search.aol.com/aol/image?q=ancient+astronaut+figurines&v_t=wscreen50-bb

7.   Sightings of Tutmoses III
        UFOs and Alien Encounters. Documentary. Prod, Michael Tetrick.
        TLC.
        Web link:
        www.atlantisquest.com/Firecircle.html

8.   Alexander the Great's UFO encounters
        "UFOs: Then and Now? The Innocent Years." *UFO Files.* Dir.
        Joshua Alper. THC. 2000.

9.   The Vimana
        "UFO: The First Encounters." *Ancient Mysteries.* A&E. 1997.

10.   Atomic blast in Mohenjo-Daro
        Web link:
        www.rense.com/general3/8000.htm

11.   Mahabharata's description of atomic war
        "UFO: The First Encounters." *Ancient Mysteries.* A&E. 1997.
        Web link:
        www.s8int.com/atomic1.html

12.   10,000-year-old cave drawing
        Link to image:
        aboutfacts.net/UFO267.html

13.   Utah glyphs
        Link to image:
        themindfulmystic.blogspot.com/2010/06/ancient-aliens-or-tribal-paintings.html

14. Aborigine glyphs from Kimberly, Australia
Link to image:
revelations-2012.com/Ancient_Cave_Art.html (scroll down to see images)

15. Sine wave glyphs
"Earth Visitors." *In Search Of*... Prod. Jeffrey Pill. A&E. 31 Jan. 1980.

16. Glyphs of a crashed ship and another used by the repair crew
Link to image:
www.crystalinks.com/ufohistory.html (scroll down to see images)

17. Abydos temple glyph resembling various types of aircraft
Link to images:
www.crystalinks.com/ancientaircraft.html (scroll down to see image)

18. Medieval knights and aerial craft
Link to image:
lithiumdreamer.tripod.com/ufoart.html (scroll down to see image)

19. UFO over Vancouver City Hall
Link to image:
www.ufobc.ca/History/Early/cityhall_v2.htm

20. 1561 Nuremburg painting
Link to image:
wiki.razing.net/ufologie.net/htm/1561b.htm

21. 1566 Basel, Switzerland, painting
Link to image:
Bibleufo.com/uabasil.jpg

22.   Russian Crucifixion icon
       Link to image:
       www.crystalinks.com/ufohistory.html (scroll down to see image)

23.   1350 Kosovo fresco
       Link to image:
       www.sprezzatura.it/Arte/Arte_UFO_2_eng.htm (scroll down to
       see image)

24.   Fifteenth-century painting of the *Madonna and Child with the
       infant St. John*
       Link to image:
       www.sprezzatura.it/Arte/Arte_UFO_5.htm

25.   Fourteenth-century tapestries showing hat-shaped objects
       Link to image:
       www.sprezzatura.it/Arte/Arte_UFO_8.htm

26.   UFOs in the sky near Moses
       Link to image:
       www.sprezzatura.it/Arte/Arte_UFO_8.htm (scroll down to see image)

27.   Fifteenth-century painting of *Miracle of the Snow*
       Link to image:
       www.sprezzatura.it/Arte/Arte_UFO_6.htm

28.   1490 religious painting of *The Assumption of the Virgin*
       Link to image:
       www.sprezzatura.it/Arte/Arte_UFO_4.htm (scroll down to see image)

29.   1486 painting of *The Annunciation with Saint Emidius*
       Link to image:
       www.sprezzatura.it/Arte/Arte_UFO_1_eng.htm (scroll down to
       see image)

30.   1710 painting of *The Baptism of Christ*
        Link to image: www.sprezzatura.it/Arte/Arte_UFO_3.htm

31.   Painting of *Glorification of the Eucharist*
        Link to image:
        www.sprezzatura.it/Arte/Arte_UFO_1_eng.htm (scroll down to
        see image)

32.   "ART and UFOs? No thanks, only art …" Main page of site with
        links to many images
        Web link: www.sprezzatura.it/Arte/Arte_UFO_1_fr.htm

33.   When angels acquired their wings
        "Biblical Angels." *Mysteries of the Bible.* Prod. William Kronick.
        A&E. 14 Nov. 1996.

Chapter 5

THE ALTERNATIVE PHENOMENA

The UFO mystery is complicated enough without associating it with every other strange phenomenon on the planet. In my research, I have found Bigfoot, animal mutilations, the Bermuda Triangle, crop circles, the Fatima miracle, and even demons frequently associated with UFOs. I have found much of this information to be vague, speculative, and unreliable. Although a couple of these issues could be relevant, I do not believe they are all part of the UFO enigma. Before proceeding further, it is important that we gain a better perspective by separating the wheat from the chaff. Beginning with Bigfoot, I will explain the facts relating to these phenomena and let you decide for yourself.

Bigfoot

Bigfoot is known by many names throughout the world, too many to mention them all. Of the most familiar are Sasquatch, as Indians in the northwestern United States call it, and yeti, or the abominable snowman, as it is called in the Himalayas. An extrapolation of data from a multitude of reports suggests that the average height of the creature is eight to nine feet tall; it is covered with hair and has arms stretching almost to its knees; it walks upright like a man, slightly bent forward like a primate, and is said to exude a most unpleasant odor. Just like a small child, it seems oblivious to approaching vehicles and does not realize the danger of walking out in front of them, because according to a few motorists, the creature just walked out of the woods and they had to slam on the brakes. So except for the occasional sighting, the creature seems quite adept at avoiding detection.

Roger Patterson made the most famous Bigfoot film on October 20, 1967. He and his friend Bob Gimlin had set out on a personal quest to film the creature, but after spending many days in the wilderness with no luck, they used most of the film shooting scenery.

However, that changed at Bluff Creek in the Trinity National Forest, about 160 miles north of San Francisco. Only when their horses suddenly reared did they see it on the opposite side of the creek. Patterson had fallen off his horse, but he jumped up, pulled his camera out of the saddlebag, and started filming. Not knowing if the creature might attack, Gimlin stood ready with his rifle. The footage shows the creature walking away and turning to look back at them. A few seconds later, the camera ran out of film—Patterson had used it all on scenery.[1]

Of all the footage taken over the years of Bigfoot, many are obvious hoaxes; however, most defy critical analysis because the creature can barely be distinguished behind heavy foliage or trees, or it is too far away and the image indiscernible. The Patterson film is the only one showing the creature out in the open in broad daylight and visible from head to toe. What are the odds that two men who set out to film the creature four decades ago would end up producing the best footage ever taken? No one has yet come up with anything even close to being that good, so skeptics assume it is a hoax—someone wearing a gorilla suit.

Calling it a hoax just because Patterson and Gimlin appear to have beaten extraordinary odds is, at best, a weak assumption. I see no one disputing the integrity of a lottery winner who beat extraordinary odds by picking the winning numbers. Personally, I think the film is authentic, but even if it is a hoax, there have been far too many sightings made by credible people to conclude that the creature does not exist.

Plaster casts have been made of many footprints alleged to be that of Bigfoot. After weeding out the fakes and those of large animals such as bears, only a few are believed to be authentic. Of these, many exhibit similar characteristics. One shows the dermal structure of the creature's toe, something practically impossible to fake.[2] It would be like recreating someone's fingerprints, which is highly unlikely. Analysis of hair samples collected from bushes and trees with which these creatures were known to have made contact reveal they are indicative of a primate; however, it is of a species that is currently unknown.[3]

One possibility proposed by the late anthropologist Dr. Grover Krantz is that it could be a descendant of the Gigantopithecus, a species that has been extinct for fifty thousand years.[4] A Gigantopithecus skeleton was discovered in a cave in China in 1989. When alive, the creature stood about eight feet tall and weighed about twelve hundred pounds, and its bone structure closely resembled the many descriptions of Bigfoot. If Bigfoot is a descendant of Gigantopithecus, how could it have gone unnoticed for so long?

Well, the facts show it is not impossible. The African mountain gorilla was only discovered in 1864, and the first one was not captured until 1901. It was not until the early part of the twentieth century that a giant panda was first captured in China. In 1938, fishermen in South Africa netted a coelacanth, a fish thought to have been extinct for fifty thousand years. A species of shark called the megamouth was unknown until 1976, when the twenty-foot carcass of one got caught up in the net of a navy ship searching for lost "dummy" torpedoes off the coast of Hawaii. Then there is the saola, a spindle-horned mammal discovered in 1994 in the jungles of Vietnam; it was thought to have been extinct. Considering that most of these discoveries were made in the twentieth century, we have to wonder how many other species thought to be extinct may still be walking around. If a Bigfoot is ever captured, might we discover that the Gigantopithecus is not extinct after all?

But the question we are dealing with is whether Bigfoot is part of the UFO mystery. The evidence says no, that it is an unknown species of primate. Yes, UFOs and Bigfoot are occasionally sighted in the same area, but such incidents are rare and may only be coincidental. Now I am not denying the possibility of a connection; I am only stating the fact that there is no evidence to support it.

Animal Mutilations

Another mystery usually associated with UFOs is animal mutilations. The first documented case actually occurred in September of 1967 and involved a horse. Since then, cattle mutilations have grown to alarming proportions throughout the West and Southwest regions of the country. And lights frequently reported at night over areas where mutilations occur have added fuel to the belief that UFOs are responsible. However, I am not convinced.

One commonality of the mutilation mystery is the frequent appearance of unmarked black helicopters over the sites.[5] One does not need a Ph.D. from Harvard to know that FAA regulation 14 CFR part 45 requires that all private, corporate, and commercial aircraft must display identification numbers. Military and government aircraft however, are exempt from this law. Therefore, it comes as no surprise that the government has consistently ignored the pleas of local officials to assist in investigating the problem. They shrug it off and blame it on predatory animals, even though there seems to be an alarming amount of evidence suggesting otherwise.

Eyes are sometimes removed. Often the tongue, the lips, and one ear are missing, and there is a perfectly round incision where the rectum, genitalia, or udders have been removed. These areas do not appear to have been ripped apart by the teeth of a predator; they appear to have been surgically removed and the wounds cauterized, suggesting the application of high-intensity heat, possibly by some form of portable laser device, the likes of which no hospital or military installation supposedly has.[6]

There is rarely a trace of blood found around the wounds as one might expect from a predator's attack. In fact, the animals are usually drained of blood.[7] And no evidence of human presence, such as discarded trash, footprints, or cigarette butts, has ever been found around the carcasses.

Skeptics claim the mutilations are caused by a combination of things: predatory animals, birds, insects, and normal decomposition. One skeptical sheriff in the Southwest attempted to prove this was the case by using a dead cow donated by a local rancher. He laid it in an open field for a few days and set up a video camera to record what happened, and he had deputies standing watch around the clock. The video revealed that vulchers, insects, and other animals picked at the carcass, but the results hardly resembled what most mutilations look like. And it does not explain cases where ranchers said the animal was alive less than twenty-four hours before they found it mutilated.

In most cases, it is obvious the animals did not meet their fate at the location where they were found; broken legs and ribs suggest they were *dropped* from above. In one case, a cow was apparently dropped from a great height because not only were its ribs and legs broken, but one horn had been driven right into its skull.[8] This certainly suggests there is more involved than decomposition and predatory creatures.

Because surgical precision seems evident in many cases, it suggests that the mutilations may occur in a laboratory facility equipped with high-tech surgical tools. If someone is using cows to conduct medical experiments (or whatever it is they are doing), why go to the trouble of returning the carcass for the owner to see what had been done to it—why not dispose of it elsewhere?

One possible explanation for this is that if too many cows disappeared, it might suggest cattle rustling. Some ranchers have lost up to fifteen cows in a matter of several weeks. And if it were suspected that the animals had been transported across state lines, jurisdiction of the investigation could conceivably shift to the federal level. If some government agency is involved, it would not be prudent to have federal investigators nosing around, possibly turning up clues as to who they are. By returning the carcasses, there is no proof that the animals had ever been removed from the property. Of course, this is only speculation.

Initially, it was suspected that satanic cults were involved—that they were using animal parts for ritualistic purposes. However, lacking evidence of human presence at mutilation sites seems to negate that idea. Moreover, how many cults have the finances to afford helicopters or powerful surgical lasers, the likes of which supposedly do not exist?

Some researchers argue against military involvement simply because they could raise their own cattle and experiment to their hearts' content, within the confines of their own facilities. Others suspect that pharmaceutical companies are responsible because they are in a race to develop an artificial substitute for human blood. Some companies are experimenting with the hemoglobin in cattle blood for this purpose, and we can only wonder at the profits to be reaped by whoever is first to develop this technology. But again, the same logic applies, in that these companies could raise their own cattle and experiment all they want in their own laboratory facilities, so why would they need to take them from ranchers?

Perhaps the grazing lands in some regions produce results that are more favorable for whatever it is that they are doing. It might explain why most mutilations have occurred in New Mexico and Colorado. However, they have also been reported in California, Nevada, Oregon, Montana, and as far east as Alabama and Florida. Until recently, it was believed they only occurred on US soil; however, a few have now been reported in Europe and in South America.

Puerto Rico has also experienced a rash of animal attacks, allegedly by a creature called the chupacabra. Chupacabra is Spanish for "goat sucker," but it reportedly has killed other animals, including chickens, rabbits, dogs, cats, and horses. In each case, there is no evidence of surgical procedures or cauterization, and there is no mention of unmarked black helicopters. The only parallel to cattle mutilations is that the chupacabra victims are also drained of blood. Except for exsanguination, no other similarities are apparent.

People who have allegedly seen the creature claim that it has glowing red eyes, spines on its back, and some say it even has wings and can fly. It completely sucks the blood out of its prey and leaves wound marks unlike that of any known predator. One animal autopsied by Dr. Carlos Soto, a Canovanas veterinarian, revealed a puncture wound one-half inch in diameter; entire organs had somehow been sucked out through this tiny hole. He also found four other holes in a section of muscle in which there were no punctures in the skin to account for them.[9]

Although many people claim to have witnessed the chupacabra killing animals, cattle mutilations have never been observed in progress—the mutilated carcass is the only evidence that something bizarre has occurred. There are rumors that the chupacabra is a genetic or hybrid experiment that escaped from a secret US military installation on the island during Hurricane Hugo in 1989; however, there has never been any evidence to substantiate it.

So what is going on? Is the US government involved? We don't know about the chupacabra for certain, but it would seem that it is probably connected to the cattle mutilations. Let's look at the facts:

- There are a few people who claim to have seen a cow being abducted by a UFO, yet they have not been able to provide any proof. Even if they are telling the truth, without some piece of supportive evidence, one cannot conclude it to be fact.

- No one has ever witnessed an extraterrestrial mutilating a cow.

- There is evidence suggesting highly sophisticated surgical laser technology.

- Unmarked helicopters have been seen, photographed, and videotaped over areas where mutilations have occurred.

So the preponderance of evidence leans heavily toward human involvement: unmarked helicopters strongly suggest military or government activity.

One theory recently proposed is that the government is conducting secret research on radioactive fallout from the atomic testing of the 1940s and '50s.[10] Since the majority of mutilations have occurred in areas adjacent to or downwind from the test sites, they could be studying the long-term effects of the fallout on cattle native to these areas. It would be most apparent in soft tissue such as in the mouth, tongue, genitalia, and rectum, the parts most frequently removed. But why would it require such covert tactics unless the technologies being applied are highly classified or they are hiding adverse health implications from the public.

In any event, I think looking for a UFO connection is a waste of time and a distraction. If people are encouraged to believe that helicopter lights are UFOs, it shifts the focus of attention away from who is truly responsible. The real mystery revolves around what they are doing, why they are doing it, and the technical applications involved in how they are doing it. The technology seems to be beyond anything we currently possess, and if it does belong to the government, they have managed to keep it secret for four decades, as they did with stealth technology.

Now, it is possible that the black helicopters are using a new form of stealth. A few people who have encountered them claim that they were unaware of their presence until they felt the downdraft from their rotors and looked up.[11] Therefore, until someone manages to produce verifiable video footage of a cow being taken aboard a UFO, there is no proof of a UFO connection—all the evidence points to the government or the military.

The Bermuda Triangle

Another mystery frequently associated with UFOs is the Bermuda Triangle, a.k.a. the Devil's Triangle. In this area between the coast of southern Florida, Bermuda, and Puerto Rico, many ships and planes have disappeared without a trace.

The most famous case occurred on December 5, 1945, when five Navy Avengers known as Flight 19 took off from Fort Lauderdale Naval Air Station on a routine training flight. They were to fly east to the Bahamas for a practice bomb run, then fly north for about two hundred miles before heading back to Fort Lauderdale. But along the way, something happened, making them the most famous statistic of the Bermuda Triangle mystery.

The records show that the flight leader, Lieutenant Charles Taylor, radioed that he was lost. Attempting to get back to Fort Lauderdale, Taylor and his crew made course changes against the advice of Melvin Baker, the radio operator in Port Everglades, who said he was certain he knew their approximate position. As an enlisted man, he could only advise Taylor to maintain a westerly heading.[12] For some reason, Taylor thought he was over either the Florida Keys or the Gulf of Mexico. Baker said if that were true, his radio signal would have been very weak, whereas he was receiving him loud and clear. At one point, Taylor saw islands and thought it was the Keys, but in all likelihood, it was the Bahamas—in one area, they do tend to resemble the Keys. However, if he believed the islands were the Keys, he would have also believed the open water to the west was the Gulf, so he and the other planes reversed course and headed east, farther out into the Atlantic. This seems to be the consensus of many researchers. Baker said his radio signal gradually became weaker and was eventually covered up by a Cuban radio station.

After contact was lost, a massive search and rescue operation was conducted, but no trace was ever found of the planes or their crews. Then the mystery was compounded when at about ten before six that night, a Martin Mariner en route to the squadron's last reported location suddenly disappeared from radar, never to be seen again.

Many wild theories have been proposed as to what is occurring in the Bermuda Triangle: an energy field activated by a power crystal from sunken Atlantis; abduction by UFOs; and a window into a space/time warp that deposits ships and planes in another time or dimension. As interesting as these theories may be, the Bermuda Triangle is not the only place where ships and planes have vanished; it has occurred over every large body of water on the planet, including the Great Lakes. And the number of disappearances that occur in the Bermuda Triangle are not out of proportion from the rest of the world.

Weather is a prime factor in many cases. People who live along the Florida coast are well aware of how the weather can change radically in a matter of minutes. Many disappearances occur during severe storms that suddenly materialize, and there is nothing strange about this.

Another contributing factor is seismic activity on the ocean floor, which can generate large waves. Ships in the area of such activity can be overwhelmed by the sudden appearance of a rogue wave fifty to one hundred feet high, large enough to capsize and sink many large vessels.

However, the Triangle seems to foster other unexplained anomalies. There is the appearance of weird clouds, green mists, spinning compasses, and often the malfunctioning of electronic equipment—something frequently associated with UFO encounters. However, when these incidents occur out over the Atlantic, it is rare that a UFO is reported. One example is an incident that occurred in 1986, when a man and his wife, flying a PBY from Bermuda to Florida, flew into what they described as an eggnog-like substance. Suddenly, two million dollars' worth of sophisticated electronic equipment went dead.[13]

Dr. Richard McIver believes there is an explanation for part of the mystery. He explained that vast pockets of methane gas have been discovered beneath the floor of the Atlantic, produced by decomposing plants and sea life in the ocean bed. Usually, it seeps out through small fissures and, due to the extreme pressure of the water's depth, crystallizes into hydrates. However, seismic activity occasionally causes underwater landslides that open huge fissures, allowing the release of a vast amount of gas bubbles that rise to the surface. When this happens, the bubbles cause the water to lose buoyancy, and a ship that happens to be in the middle of this pocket can sink quickly. Oil rigs in the Caspian Sea have been lost after penetrating large methane pockets, and one incident was even filmed in the North Sea.[14]

McIver went to Texas A&M University, where he conducted a controlled experiment. He had gas lines laid across the bottom of a large water-filled pool that he used to simulate a gas eruption from the seabed, and he used a perfectly ballasted scale model of a tanker for the test. When the gas bubbles rose to the surface, the model submerged, and water seepage contributed to its rapid descent to the bottom. Then he repeated the test using a model that was completely airtight. When the gas bubbles were released, this model also sank below the surface. Had it not been airtight, it, too, would have gone to the bottom from water seepage.[15]

According to oceanographic studies, the floor of the Bermuda Triangle contains one of the richest hydrocarbon gas deposits in the world.[16] Sonar maps have also revealed that landslides of the magnitude necessary to create large fissures occur frequently, and many have occurred over large pockets of methane. So this may be a clue as to the fate of many ships that disappeared in relatively calm seas.

But what about aircraft? How could a gas eruption on the ocean floor cause an airplane to disappear?

McIver explained that when these blowouts occur, the gas rises quickly to the surface and, in doing so, agitates the water, generating negative ions. In turn, these ions produce an electrical current surrounded by an electromagnetic field, and upon reaching the surface, a gas cloud is released into the atmosphere. Methane clouds are lighter than air, so they can rise to extremely high altitudes and may be highly volatile, susceptible to combustion by the hot exhaust of an aircraft flying into them. If an explosion does not occur, since the gas cloud is much lighter than air, the density of the air within the cloud would be greatly reduced, and like water losing buoyancy, it may become difficult, or even impossible, for an aircraft to stay aloft. Conceivably, it could drop into the sea and disappear without a trace. The electromagnetic field surrounding these clouds could also explain why compasses, radios, and other electronic equipment have gone haywire. So it is possible that planes and ships that have experienced these phenomena penetrated large methane clouds. It may also explain the strange "milky mist" or "cloud" that so many have reported.

In an Australian experiment, an explosion was created deep under an old navy warship, and the large bubble it created actually lifted the vessel out of the water, causing it to split in two. Other experiments suggested even more possibilities.

One test involved injecting 1 percent methane directly into an operating vintage aircraft piston engine to see if it would combust, but all it did was cause the engine to stall. This might suggest that if methane were sucked into the air intake, it could cause an aircraft's engine to stall and the plane could literally fall into the sea. However, it did ignite when the methane was released directly in front of the exhaust pipe. The problem is that no one really knows what percentage of methane a cloud may actually contain; it would probably depend on how big the blowout was on the seabed. Therefore, it is conceivable that a spark from a prop engine or a flame from jet exhaust might cause an explosion; and the higher the methane content, the bigger the explosion.

Another impressive experiment was conducted in a 737 flight simulator. When the outside air was changed to methane, it registered a drastic decrease in air pressure, and what surprised everyone was that the lower air pressure fooled the altimeter into thinking the plane was gaining altitude.[17] This was enlightening because a pilot looking at the instruments might nose the aircraft down in a descent. If this was a real life situation, it might prove to be a fatal mistake.

McIver and the other scientists have produced viable scientific data to study. Their ideas are rational, more so than the extraterrestrial, interdimensional, or Atlantean power crystal theories, and may even shed light on the mystery surrounding Flight 19. It is a known fact that the men of Flight 19 became disoriented for unknown reasons. If they were exposed to an electromagnetic field surrounding a methane cloud, it is possible that it caused their instruments to malfunction. There is, however, no indication in the official records that this was the case: Taylor's communication with Melvin Baker is a clear indication that his radio was working. And apparently, the compasses in the planes were functioning normally: how else would they have known which way to turn to head east?. Although it is only conjecture, the planes could have flown into a methane cloud that was in the process of forming, which created a milky mist, causing the pilots to become *temporarily* disorientated. This is suggested by virtue of the fact that they did see islands.

As for the disappearance of the Martin Mariner, confidence is high that it exploded. A ship in the vicinity reported seeing a midair explosion about the same time it disappeared from radar. The Mariner was a virtual flying gas tank, loaded with volatile fuel so that it could remain airborne during long search missions, and their crews often referred to them as flying bombs.[18] Since it was on a course to Flight 19's last known position, perhaps it flew into the same methane cloud that caused their disorientation or else another that formed from the same, or a later seabed eruption in the same area. It may have accumulated a high density of methane and the hot exhaust from the plane's engines could have ignited it, resulting in an explosion that completely disintegrated the aircraft. It is also possible that the explosion resulted from one of the crewmembers lighting a cigarette, igniting gas fumes in the plane. However, considering the high volatility of their environment, one would expect the crew to be more disciplined.

Now let's examine other strange events that have occurred in the Triangle—ones that McIver's theory cannot explain.

According to pilot and author Martin Caiden, a US Air Force Boeing B-50D Superfortress was en route to Bermuda from the Azores when the radar operator suddenly realized the aircraft was not moving. Even though all four engines were operating normally, the plane was literally standing still. He reported this to the pilot, who in turn contacted Bermuda radar. Bermuda radar confirmed that they did show one plane on their radar screen that seemed to be maintaining a stationary position. Although the pilot was able to increase and decrease altitude, it was almost an hour before the plane resumed forward motion. After landing, a check of the fuel tanks revealed that the consumption far exceeded the amount normally used for the flight. Caiden said the incident remains on the books with no explanation.[19]

This mystery cannot be explained—at least for the moment. Perhaps it was the result of some unexplained atmospheric phenomena creating an abnormally strong headwind. I can see something like this happening to a small single-engine plane, but one the size of a B-50 bomber with four large and powerful engines is something else. I haven't a clue.

Lieutenant Commander Frank Flynn, a retired coast guard officer, described one particularly strange incident. One night while on patrol in the Bermuda Triangle, he said they were moving along on a calm sea when a solid green line suddenly appeared on the ship's radarscope. He said that both he and his assistant agreed that the image resembled land, but they were 165 miles offshore and there were no islands in the vicinity. As they approached the target, Flynn said it looked like a huge grey wall. He shined a carbon arc light upward but could not see the top, although the stars were clearly visible directly overhead. As they penetrated the grey mass, he said the crew began to experience throat irritation and slight difficulty breathing. Then, when the engine room reported problems with steam pressure, the captain decided they had better get out of there. However, just as he was about to turn the cutter around, they broke through the other side. Flynn could not explain the phenomenon. He said that in all his years at sea, he had never encountered anything like it before or since.[20]

Another anomaly reported by some pilots is the experience of time distortion, which seems to be associated with a green cloud or mist. One story, if it is true, suggests such a possibility. The exact date is unknown, and it allegedly involved an airliner identified as either Flight 727 or a National Airlines 727 passenger flight. The plane was on its landing approach to Miami International Airport when the pilot requested a time check. Suddenly, the plane disappeared from the radar screen, and all radio contact was lost. Fearing the worst, the air traffic controller alerted the crash crew and notified the coast guard. However, ten minutes later, Flight 727 suddenly reappeared and landed safely as if nothing happened. Unaware of what had occurred, the crew and passengers were surprised to learn that they had landed ten minutes late. The flight was right on schedule when the pilot requested the time check, yet the plane's chronometers were now ten minutes slow, as were all wristwatches worn by the flight crew. After completing her cabin duties, which usually took ten or twelve minutes, the flight attendant said she had gone to the cockpit and was surprised by the fact that the plane's clock showed she had completed her work in about three minutes. The copilot said that right after the time check, a strange green mist surrounded the plane and then disappeared, so they thought nothing of it.[21] When technicians at the airport checked for a glitch in the radar equipment, they could find nothing wrong—all systems were functioning normally.

So there are a few mysteries surrounding the Bermuda Triangle. Underwater seismic activity, gas eruptions, and methane clouds might explain the disappearance of ships and possibly even aircraft. However, the strange grey wall encountered by the coast guard cutter continues to remain a mystery. Since it is the only event of its kind ever reported, there is no data available for comparison. And since the ship and crew did not disappear, it cannot be associated with interdimensional gateways or any of the other far-out theories, and it was not a UFO-related event. Someday we may find a logical explanation.

Something that does confound logic is the green mist. Those who have encountered a green cloud or mist have also tended to report time distortions connected to their experiences. The sudden disappearance and reappearance of a commercial airliner on Miami radar, if the story is true, certainly suggests such a possibility.

None of these inexplicable events involved an unidentified flying object. There have been sightings at sea where UFOs have popped up out of the ocean and flown off into the sky, and vice versa. However, as for them being responsible for the disappearance of ships and planes and all the other anomalies, there is no evidence to support it. The mysteries of the Bermuda Triangle will continue to fascinate many as long as they remain unexplained. Those with fertile imaginations clinging to the more bizarre theories are either unaware of or choose to ignore the facts.

Crop Circles

Using a small plank, a bit of rope, and some string, two English pranksters demonstrated how easy it is to create crop circles. However, most investigators are of the opinion that not all formations are the product of hoaxers. They claim that patterns in which the wheat is intricately interwoven could not have been accomplished by pranksters' methods. So what do these patterns represent—if anything?

During the summer of 1995, one formation that appeared in Winchester, England, caught my attention, and if it was not a hoax, it seemed to present an ominous message. The pattern resembled our inner solar system, with a circle in the center representing the sun. Around it were five rings, denoting the orbital paths of Mercury, Venus, Earth, and Mars, and the outer ring looked like a jumbled mass of debris, which one might assume to be the asteroid belt located between Mars and Jupiter. On each orbital ring was a circle denoting the planets in their proportional sizes to one another. However, there was one ring without a planet, the third one from the sun—Earth.[22] It is now believed that this formation was probably a hoax, but if—and I emphasize *if*—it was not, one might consider it a message telling us that something is going to happen to the earth. And since the asteroid belt was included in the pattern, might it be a clue as to just what it will be?

On August 21, 2001, a rather unconventional formation appeared in a field next to the observatory in Chilbolton, England. Unlike the geometrically designed formations that appear so frequently, this one was created in a dot matrix pattern and bore a strong resemblance to the binary coded message transmitted into space in 1974 by the Arecibo Radio Telescope in Puerto Rico, but with a few differences. One was in the sequence denoting human DNA, indicating we are a carbon-based life-form. The DNA code in the Chilbolton pattern allegedly suggested a silicon-based life-form. Another difference was in the representation of the solar system; the pattern suggested a planetary system that was different from ours. In the Arecibo transmission was also a code defining the human image. The code in the Chilbolton field allegedly defined a being similar to the little greys associated with abductions.[23]

In the field was also a second dot matrix pattern depicting a face, but it is unclear what connection, if any, it had to the other pattern.

Some speculate that the formation was an alien response to the Arecibo transmission; however, the fact that only twenty-seven years had elapsed from the time it was transmitted makes it unlikely. Unless it was picked up by someone in Alpha Centauri, our nearest neighbor, 4.2 light-years away, it could be hundreds or even thousands of years before the Arecibo signal reaches another star system where someone might receive it. So if it was an extraterrestrial reply, it means they were in our backyard in 1974, when it was sent. As for it being a hoax, it is possible, although I find it hard to believe that someone with the intellectual capacity to understand binary coding and DNA sequencing would be mentally reduced to the level of those who created many of the early hoaxes.

In January of 2001, a documentary on the PAX TV Network (now ION Television) presented an account from England in which the British military demonstrated a serious interest in crop formations. The report provided a detailed interview with Colin Andrews, one of England's prominent crop circle researchers, who just happened to be one of the witnesses.

Andrews had gone to investigate a new formation in a field at Alton Barnes, not far from Stonehenge, and with him were seven other scientists, a few who worked for the United States government. Suddenly, a British military helicopter appeared and began harassing them by making very close passes—as if trying to intimidate them into leaving. At first, they had no idea what was going on. They thought the chopper might have been there to photograph the formation, yet it continued making passes as close as forty feet above their heads. Andrews said the downdraft from the rotors was so strong that it was pushing the hedgerow down over their vehicle.

Then a second helicopter appeared and joined the first. This made everyone a little nervous, so they climbed into their vehicle and proceeded to drive away with both helicopters right behind them. They had only driven a short distance when one of the helicopters suddenly moved to the field. A small flashing sphere of light about eighteen inches in diameter had appeared over the crop formation, and the chopper seemed to be confronting it. Then the light suddenly blinked out and reappeared behind the helicopter. The second chopper also moved to the field, and its pilot was able to see this maneuver. Andrews assumed he advised the other pilot because the first chopper then backed up until the light was in front of it. The men stopped and exited their vehicle, continuing to watch when the little orb of light disappeared completely. Andrews said the helicopters hovered over the area for a few more minutes and then left.[24]

The amazing thing is that they videotaped the entire event: the helicopter's harassing maneuvers, following them in their vehicle, and their confronting the little ball of light. Andrews suggested that they might have stumbled into a situation in which the helicopters were already engaged in some sort of activity with the light, but when their presence was detected, the pilots attempted to intimidate them into leaving.

The way the documentary presented the story, I became suspicious that maybe the helicopters purposely herded the men toward the location so they would see what was going on since the aerial harassment ceased at that point. So I contacted Colin, expressing my views, and he was kind enough to provide me with the correct details.

He explained that they had not traveled too far when the little country road they were driving on rose to a slightly higher elevation, providing them with a good view of the field. This is when the first helicopter moved to the field and faced light. Colin feels that the pilots were overtaken by the event, which forced them to cease their harassment and proceed to the field. Apparently, confronting the light took precedence over forcing the witnesses to leave.

So it appears that the men were being harassed—that they were being forced to vacate the area—but why? And the fact that the helicopters appeared to be confronting the little light is extremely interesting.

For some reason, these little balls of light seem to be frequent visitors to crop formations, and they appear to be under intelligent control. So what are they, and what is their attraction to crop circles? Are they some new kind of secret technology? Are they somehow involved in creating the formations? They are reminiscent of the mysterious little balls of light called "foo fighters," which frequently buzzed military aircraft during the First and Second World Wars. As long as people continue to associate these little lights with UFOs, and UFOs with crop formations, it could be a convenient government ploy to propagate disinformation.

In any case, there is too much of a grey area regarding crop formations, so until more knowledge of the phenomenon is acquired, I think we should keep our minds open.

Fatima

On May 13, 1917, Lucia dos Santos, a ten-year-old shepherd girl in Fatima, Portugal, allegedly had a vision of the Virgin Mary. It occurred in the grotto where she and her two cousins, Francisco and Jacinta, were tending their sheep. She claimed that the Virgin spoke to her and said she would reappear on the same date (the thirteenth) of each month. This was apparently the case except for August 13, when the authorities arrested the children and she *allegedly* appeared on August 19. The woman then promised to produce a miracle in October.[25]

Word quickly spread of the girl's vision, and people began flocking into Fatima. Unable to cope with the massive crowds, the police tried to intimidate the children into admitting the whole thing was a hoax, but in spite of the threats made against them, they stuck together, and Lucia refused to change her story.

On October 13, an estimated seventy thousand people gathered at the site. The vision is alleged to have appeared to Lucia, revealing herself as the *Lady of the Rosary*, and given her information regarding the outbreak of World War II, visions of hell, and warnings about Russia. Then people said that the sun came through the clouds and fell spinning toward the earth, emitting multicolored bands of light. Obviously, the sun did not fall out of the sky, and a few people said they saw nothing out of the ordinary. However, a black–and-white photograph taken at the time shows what could possibly be a UFO.[26]

One eyewitness was Dr. José Maria de Almeida Garrett, a professor at the Faculty of Sciences of Coimbra. He said that at three different times, a thin bluish column of smoke rose above the heads of the children and dissipated. He said it had been raining and the sky was overcast, but then the rain stopped, and it appeared that the sun might come out. Then he said thousands of people suddenly became excited, and their attention was turned toward the sun. This is an excerpt of what the professor wrote when describing the event.

The most astonishing thing was to be able to stare at the solar disc for a long time, brilliant with light and heat, without hurting the eyes or damaging the retina.

The sun's disc did not remain immobile, it had a giddy motion, not like the twinkling of a star in all its brilliance for it spun round upon itself in a mad whirl.

I noticed that everything was becoming darkened. I looked first at the nearest objects and then extended my glance further (sic) afield as far as the horizon. I saw everything had assumed an amethyst color. Objects around me, the sky and the atmosphere, were of the same color. Everything both near and far had changed, taking on the color of old yellow damask. Then, suddenly, one heard a clamor, a cry of anguish breaking from all the people. The sun, whirling wildly, seemed all at once to loosen itself from the firmament and, blood red, advance threateningly upon the earth as if to crush us with its huge and fiery weight. The sensation during those moments was truly terrible.[27]

Being able to stare directly at the sun for a long period without causing damage to the eyes can only mean that they weren't actually looking at the sun. And the spinning he described is a characteristic common in many UFO sightings.

Garrett said that everything suddenly turned an amethyst color, all the way to the horizon. Now, if it were a UFO projecting some sort of colored beam over the area, anything in the distance might also appear the same color to those within. It would be the same as looking through a colored filter.

Next he said that the sun (or what he presumed to be the sun) was now blood red, and it appeared to be descending on them. Such an event today would likely be described as a UFO encounter. But in 1917, people had not yet become aware of UFOs. That did not happen until 1947—thirty years later.

Rather intriguing is the thin blue column of smoke that the professor said rose above the children's heads and dissipated three different times. One might tend to associate that description with someone smoking a cigar, cigarette, or possibly lighting a pipe, and you would assume that a well-educated man like the professor would recognize it as such. Since his is the only account of this, it is difficult to apply any other kind of interpretation logically.

Although it cannot be substantiated today, it is said that when the spectacle was over, those who had been kneeling in mud and on the water-soaked ground found their clothes and the ground to be completely dry. If this is true, I might suspect that the colored beam had something to do with it. Such things have been reported in several UFO incidents—wet ground and clothing becoming dry. Moreover, a similar event is even described in the Bible. According to Exodus 14:21, when the water was parted for Moses and the Israelites, it says the seabed had been dried to a hardened surface.

Because of Lucia's resistance to threats and intimidation by the authorities and her prediction that a miracle would occur on that day, the event seems to merit some credibility. As for it being a miracle, that is a matter of interpretation. Most people came to Fatima predisposed to the idea that a miracle would occur, so the falling sun may simply have been a mass hallucination: they expected to see something, and they did—in their minds.

If it was the sun, moisture in the air from the rain combined with a cloud passing in front of it may have created a sunburst effect, which would explain the bands, or rays, of light. However, it would not explain the bands rotating or the sun falling. It may only have been an optical illusion, or they may have misinterpreted the activity of a UFO as a supernatural event. It seems apparent that the people's attention was drawn to something that appeared through a break in the clouds, and that the photographer who was there attempted to photograph it. Any photographer knows that shooting directly into the sun would have resulted in a whitewashed image unless he used a special filter. However, a glowing *red* UFO could appear as a *grey* disc in a black-and-white photograph such as the one taken that day.

Since the woman in the vision identified herself as the *Lady of the Rosary,* I have to question whether it was the Blessed Virgin. Perhaps it was a vision mentally induced into the young girl's mind by those operating the glowing craft that was thought to be the sun. Could the falling sun have been a UFO ... or maybe a hologram projected from a ship concealed in the clouds? If so, it was not the only time a UFO has exhibited this technology.

If the Fatima event was UFO related, it means there were technological aspects related to what happened, which greatly diminishes the idea that a miracle occurred. And its religious significance would suggest that UFOs might somehow be connected to the deity, which in turn raises the question of who the deity really is. Nevertheless, Lucia's mother was convinced that she had fabricated the whole story, and she put her in a convent, where she grew up and later became a cloistered nun.

The other part of the Fatima mystery is the sealed letter that Lucia gave to the pope. It was supposed to be revealed to the world in 1960, but it never happened—why? What reason did the pope have for disappointing millions of people who were eagerly waiting to hear the secret that had been sealed away for forty-three years? Was it a confession by Lucia that the whole thing had been a hoax, or did it reveal an extraterrestrial connection? Whatever it was, the hierarchical silence only served to perpetuate the mystery.

Pope John Paul II decided to reveal the "third Fatima secret," as it has come to be known, on May 13, 2000, the eighty-third anniversary of the event, and it took place at the original site in Fatima where the apparition allegedly appeared. Nearly a million people had gathered, and Sister Lucia, then ninety-three years old, sat near the pope as a Vatican official read the secret to the crowd.

I expected that this would be an important revelation—something that the lady had told Lucia. Instead, the official read what sounded like a vision of prophecy. It described an angel carrying a sword in his left hand. Then, with his right hand, he struck the ground and said, "Penance! Penance! Penance!" A bishop dressed in a white robe (assumed by Lucia to be the pope), followed by other members of the clergy, then walked through a city that was described as being half destroyed. Along the way, they stopped to pray over numerous dead bodies, after which they proceeded up a steep hill, where the bishop knelt in front of a cross. Suddenly, he and the clergy were attacked and killed by soldiers shooting bullets and arrows.[28]

The Vatican's interpretation associated this vision with the assassination attempt on the pope in 1981 by Mehmet Ali Agca, a Turkish terrorist, which made no sense since he was not killed, and it was a lone gunman, not soldiers shooting bullets and arrows.

Father Paul Kramer of the Fatima Center calls this interpretation a "whitewash." He pointed out that on May 12, 1982, a year after the assassination attempt, Lucia sent a letter to the pope (published in the official Vatican booklet on the Secret) in which she stated that the final part of the prophecy (the third secret) had not yet been fulfilled.[29] This means there is more to the secret that the Vatican did not reveal.

Another point of contention is the handwriting analysis of the document made by Speckin Forensic Laboratories; it does not appear to match the handwriting of other documents written by Lucia. And in a letter she wrote on January 9, 1944, to Bishop da Silva, she stated that the third secret was written on a piece of notepaper and sealed in an envelope. The document read to the public, however, was four pages long.[30] Father Kramer also pointed out that when the sealed letter was supposed to be made public in 1960, the Vatican said it was their decision not to reveal the words of Our Lady contained in the text of the Secret. Then he said, "But the text of the third secret released yesterday contains no words of Our Lady at all."[31]

The vision described hardly seems significant enough to have warranted its secrecy for so long. So Father Kramer could be right—it may be a whitewash, and they may be covering up something since it appears there is more to the secret, which they are not revealing. The description of the vision seems more applicable to the problems now facing the church. The half-ruined city might represent the state of the church as it is today, and the dead bodies might represent the many people who have defected or are nonpractitioners. Also, the scandalous cover-up of pedophile priests sexually abusing children has seriously damaged its image. The clergy being killed by soldiers shooting bullets and arrows could represent the many victims of sexual abuse who are now bringing litigation against the church; however, this is one of many possible interpretations. Unfortunately, Sister Lucia died on February 13, 2005, without providing any more information. The facts mentioned by Father Kramer, however, do suggest that the Vatican has not revealed the whole story, and we have to wonder why.

Demons

I try to keep an open mind, but as a pragmatist, I have yet to see any evidence that demons, ghosts, or any other kind of supernatural entity exists. And yes, I have seen many photographs and video footage of alleged spirits, plasma shapes, and so forth, but they prove nothing—they can easily be faked. I know because I was a professional photographer for many years. Such images can also be the result of lens glare, reflections, or light leaking into an improperly closed camera, or they can even be the result of a defect in the camera. So naturally, I tend to disassociate demons with UFOs.

The facts suggest that UFOs are part of the physical universe and may be using technology related to interdimensional physics, a science that is currently beyond our understanding. The effects produced by this technology might appear to some as supernatural, such as how the little greys seem to materialize out of a bright light, as is often described in abduction cases. However, thinking of UFOs as demons, or being piloted by demons, makes absolutely no sense.

Nowhere in the Bible does it suggest that God himself ever made an appearance; it was always the Lord or his angels—and the scriptures suggest they looked very human. When the Lord visited Abraham with two angels just before the destruction of Sodom and Gomorrah, the Bible described them as "three men" (Ge 18:2). The God who wrestled with Jacob and dislocated his hip (Ge 32:22–31) certainly suggests he was a solid physical being. And in all the face-to-face meetings Moses is alleged to have had with the Lord, never once did he indicate that there was anything unusual about his appearance, such as green skin, pointed ears, or big bulging eyes, so we can assume he was a normal-looking individual. The angels, a.k.a. the Nephilim, the guardians of heaven and the sons of heaven, had to be normal-looking men and biologically compatible with

Earth women since they are said to have produced children with them (Ge 6:4). So even lacking a physical description, the image of the Lord and his angels suggests they were male subjects who were very human in appearance.

What about the entity that is said to have tempted Christ in the desert and the one who allegedly tempted Eve in the Garden of Eden? Although he is referred to as the devil or Satan, there is no description of Christ's nemesis. In Genesis, Eve's tempter is described only as a serpent and in ancient Hebrew legends as an upright being. It is only in later writings where the assumption is made that the serpent was the devil. So who was he? Or perhaps the question should be, *What* was he?

In the Bible, Satan is used as a proper noun, so we might assume that Satan is the name of that person or being. The word "devil" is used primarily as a common noun, which might signify a classification or status, so in effect, we would say that the devil is Satan as opposed to saying that the satan is Devil. An analogy would be that the president is George Bush, as opposed to "the george bush is President." Depending on the circumstances, the classification or status could have slight variations in meaning. For example, if George Bush attended a conference in Moscow, a Russian might refer to him as the *American* or the *president*, which would be a reference to either his place of origin (America) or his title/rank (president). If he attended an intergalactic conference on a planet in Zeta Reticuli, someone there might refer to him as the *human* or the *earthman*, in which case the reference would be to his race (human), or again, his place of origin (Earth). So without knowing the context of the situation, it is difficult to ascertain exactly what the devil's classification is.

Now, if the Lord was an extraterrestrial (the possibility of which we will examine later), wouldn't Satan also be an alien? It is a common belief that the devil and the Lord are adversaries; this may or may not be true. The Bible infers that he is a demon or a deposed angel, which might mean he is a radical or dissident. However, describing him as a serpent or upright being is imprecise and provides no clue as to what he looks like. Unlike the Lord and his angels, whom the Bible describes as men, there are no such references associated with Satan. However, if we consider the possibility that he may be an extraterrestrial, we just might come up with an idea of what he looks like.

One similarity reported in most abduction cases is that usually one grey alien is taller than the others are. He seems to be in charge and is said to exhibit a stronger mental influence over an abductee than the short ones do—and the skin of these creatures is frequently described as reptilian in texture. Could it be that Satan is really one of these taller aliens? Could it be one of them who exercised his mental prowess against the willpower of Christ in the desert? Could one of them have been the upright being who tempted Eve in the Garden of Eden? And was it his *reptilian textured skin* that contributed to his being described as a serpent?

Abductees have occasionally encountered both human-looking aliens and greys during abduction, suggesting they are working together. If this is the case, we might speculate that they have always been allied in some way. The Bible suggests there was animosity, so it is possible they were personal enemies; however, since they were here at the same time, it could also mean they were working together.

If there really was any animosity, it may have been related to different cultural values and ideologies. It could be factions within their own species hold conflicting values, much as it is between different races on Earth, and the evil attributed to Satan may simply be a reference to his race rather than him personally. It might be that Satan's race did not adhere to the same moral and ethical standards as the others and were regarded as an evil or antisocial race. However, it does not necessarily mean that Satan himself shared the same views, especially if he was working with the Lord. And it is possible that his physical appearance has contributed to the demonic references attributed to some UFOs.

Of course, this is all hypothetical. So if the Lord really is a being from another world, it is almost certain that Satan is also an alien. And if he is from an unfriendly race, it might explain the hostilities exhibited by some UFOs. There is evidence that some of these craft have acted in a hostile manner that resulted in injury and even the death of some witnesses. This does not appear to be normal behavior in the greater majority of cases; however, as we will see in the next chapter, it does suggest that a faction in the UFO community is unfriendly.

◆◆◆◆◆

So these are the alternative elements of the UFO puzzle. Although mysteries unto themselves, there is no evidence that Bigfoot, animal mutilations, or the Bermuda Triangle have any relevance whatsoever. However, the little balls of light frequently observed over crop formations are something else. They do not constitute proof of an extraterrestrial connection, and they may very well be a secret technology of man. Nevertheless, their affinity to crop formations justifies keeping an open mind to the possibility.

The events that occurred in Fatima appear relevant because of their technological significance. A spinning red sun descending toward a crowd of people and emitting multicolored rotating bands of light suggests it was some kind of intelligently controlled craft or else a holographic image. And the religious significance of the event associates this technology with the deity. However, the idea that UFOs are piloted by demons is sheer lunacy. Let's be logical—why would supernatural entities, be they demon or deity, need flying machines?

Notes

1.   Image from the Patterson film
Link to image:
paranormal.about.com/library/blclassic_patterson_bigfoot.htm

2.   Footprint with dermal structure of creature's toe
"Missing Link." *Sightings* segment. Sci Fi (now Syfy).

3.   Analysis of hair samples
Bigfoot: Real Monster or Urban Myth. Documentary. Dir. David
Priest. PAX (now ION). 5 Oct. 2001.

4.   "Bigfoot." *Ancient Mysteries.* Prod. James Taylor Sr. A&E. 15 May
1997.

5.   Black helicopters over mutilation sites
"Colorado Mutilation." *Sightings.* Sci Fi (now Syfy).
The Cattle Files. Documentary. Prod. Vanessa Frances. TLC. 8
Aug. 2007.

6.   Evidence of a surgical laser
"Mutilation Report." *Encounters* segment. FOX. WFLX. West
Palm Beach.
Links to images:
www.ufonut.com/wordpress/?tag=miller-cattle-mutilation
www.qsl.net/w5www/mutilation.html

7.   Exsanguination
"Mutilation Report." *Encounters segment.* FOX. WFLX. West
Palm Beach.

8.   Broken legs and ribs suggest cattle dropped from the air
The Cattle Files. Documentary. Prod. Vanessa Frances. TLC. 8 Aug. 2007.

9.   The Chupacabra
        The Cattle Files. Documentary. Prod. Vanessa Frances. TLC. 8
        Aug. 2007.

10.   Radiation study theory
        The Cattle Files. Documentary. Prod. Vanessa Frances. TLC. 8
        Aug. 2007.

11.   Silent helicopters
        The Cattle Files. Documentary. Prod. Vanessa Frances. TLC. 8
        Aug. 2007.

12.   Radio communication between Melvin Baker and Flight 19
        Dive to the Bermuda Triangle. Documentary. Prod. Will Aslett.
        Discovery. 2004.

13.   Eggnog like Substance
        "Bermuda Triangle: Secrets Revealed." *Beyond Belief.* Dir. John
        Wilcox. TLC.

14.   Methane Hydrates theory
        "A Logical Explanation." *Science Frontiers.* TLC.

15.   Methane hydrate experiments
        "Squaring the Bermuda Triangle." *Arthur C. Clarke's Mysterious
        Universe.* Discovery.

16.   Hydrocarbon deposits
        Bermuda Triangle. Documentary. Discovery.

17.   737 flight simulator test
        Dive to the Bermuda Triangle. Documentary. Prod. Will Aslett.
        Discovery. 2004.

18.   Disappearance of the Martin Mariner
       "Vanishings: Lost in the Bermuda Triangle." *Incredible But True?*
       Prod. Philip Nugus. THC.

19.   The stationary bomber
       "Bermuda Triangle: Secrets Revealed." *Beyond Belief.* Dir. John
       Wilcox. TLC.

20.   The grey wall
       "The Bermuda Triangle." *In Search Of…* Dir. H. G. Stark. THC.
       27 April 1977.

21.   Disappearance and reappearance of a commercial airliner on
       approach to Miami International Airport
       "What's the Secret of the Bermuda Triangle?" *Encounters with the
       Unexplained.* Dir. David Priest. PAX (now ION). 18 May 2001.

22.   Missing Earth crop circle
       Link to image: cropcircleconnector.com/Sorensen/2001/missing.
       html

23.   The Chilbolton formations
       Link to images:
       claudescommentary.com/special/chilbolton/

24.   Harassing military helicopters
       "Secret Messages from Crop Circles." *Encounters with the
       Unexplained.* Dir. David Priest. PAX (now ION). 19 Sept. 2000.

25.   Miracle at Fatima—children arrested
       "The Miracle at Fatima. *Unsolved Mysteries.* Lifetime.

26. The spinning sun
    Link to image:
    newtheologicalmovement.blogspot.com/2011/05/fatimas-miracle-of-sun-star-of.html

27. Account of Prof. José Maria de Almeida Garrett
    Web link:
    www.fatima.org/essentials/facts/miracle.asp

28. The third secret
    "Fatima Secrets Unveiled." *History's Mysteries.* Dir. Sueann Fincke. THC.

29. The third secret explanation a "whitewash"
    Web link:
    www.rense.com/general2/fat.htm

30. Handwriting analysis of Lucia's documents
    Web link:
    www.tldm.org/news/fatimagate-1.htm

31. No words spoken by the "Lady"
    Web link:
    www.rense.com/general2/fat.htm

Chapter 6

THE HOSTILE FACTOR

Now that we have examined the alternative issues, you should have a clearer understanding of what is relevant and irrelevant in the UFO controversy. Unfortunately, the majority of people only have a limited knowledge of the phenomena. Not having conducted any serious research on their own, they are completely unaware of the real facts. They have been influenced by biased media coverage and what they have read in supermarket tabloids. If they had talked to a seasoned investigator—one who has conducted extensive research into the phenomena—I think he would tell them that from what he has learned, there is a great deal more to it than what you read in the tabloids. So the next five chapters deal with the relevant details and facts.

Most UFO encounters leave witnesses astounded and perplexed, while some are often elated by the experience. However, on occasion, some have been frightened, terrorized, and have even suffered injuries and death. Many people are unaware of this one element of the phenomena. We would all like to think of alien visitors as benevolent beings who came to Earth to help solve the problems of mankind, and although the evidence suggests some may be friendly—or at least apathetic—there are some who are dangerous, and an encounter with them could be hazardous to your health.

I feel that the following six cases are the most relevant, as they describe the hostilities, injuries, and deaths (whether intentional or accidental) that some witnesses experienced. I found the first two in the research edition of *The Unexplained* published by Marshall Cavendish.

1957 – Sao Paulo, Brazil

At two o'clock on the morning of November 4, 1957, a bright glowing object that flew in from the Atlantic Ocean suddenly terrorized two sentries on duty at a coastal fort near Sao Paulo. It approached at a high rate of speed and then stopped directly above the fort before descending to about 150 feet and hovering over one of the gun turrets. At the same time, the electric power went out in the fort. The emergency generator could not be started.

The object was circular in shape; it bathed the ground in an orange light and emitted a humming noise. Suddenly, the humming intensified, and the sentries felt a searing heat burning their bodies. One fell unconscious to the ground while the other, screaming in mortal terror, sought shelter beneath one of the guns. The guard's screams attracted the attention of other soldiers, and they came running to investigate. Those first on the scene observed a large orange light climbing vertically into the sky and taking off at a high rate of speed. The sentries were taken to sick bay and found to have suffered first- and second-degree burns—underneath their uniforms. The fact that their skin was severely burned and their clothing untouched suggests that it was caused by some form of microwave radiation—but why? There was no reason for the attack. It appears to have been an unprovoked act of hostility.

1967 – Pilar de Goias, Brazil

On August 13, 1967, Inacio de Souza and his wife encountered three people wearing tight-fitting yellow clothes on the runway of the ranch where they worked. There was a strange object that resembled an inverted washbasin, which de Souza said was either sitting on the ground or hovering just above it. When the intruders started to approach him, he became frightened; he grabbed his rifle and fired a shot at them. Suddenly, a beam of green light shot out of the craft, striking him in the head and shoulders, and he fell to the ground. As de Souza's wife ran to his aid, the intruders climbed into the craft, which took off vertically at a high rate of speed, emitting a noise that sounded like the humming of bees. De Souza suffered numbness and a tingling of his body and was taken to the hospital, where he was diagnosed with leukemia. He died two months later, on October 11, and his body was covered with yellowish white blotches.

Since de Souza fired the first shot, the green beam that struck him could have been a defensive response by someone from inside the craft. There is no indication that the intruders were acting in a hostile manner when they started to approach him, and there is no evidence that de Souza did not already have leukemia and would have died anyway. Logically, one might assume that if he already had it and was only two months away from death, he would have exhibited symptoms long before then. The question is, did the green beam somehow cause his fatal disease? Unfortunately, that is something we may never know. This case does leave some doubt as to deliberate hostile intentions; nevertheless, it remains a statistic in the deaths of close encounter witnesses.

1973 – Mansfield, Ohio

One rather astonishing case occurred on the evening of October 18, 1973, when four US Army Reserve medics were en route from Columbus to Cleveland, Ohio, in an army helicopter. Over the city of Mansfield, they suddenly encountered a bright red light speeding directly toward them from the east. Attempting to avoid a collision, the pilot, Captain Lawrence J. Coyne, took over the controls from his copilot and put the chopper into a dive. They were descending at a rate of 2,000 feet per minute when suddenly the controls froze and the helicopter began to rise. The object was now hovering directly above them and projecting a cone-shaped beam of green light down around the helicopter. Coyne struggled to regain control but was unsuccessful until the green beam suddenly went out and the object flew off into the night. With the controls set in dive configuration, the helicopter had risen to an altitude of 3,800 feet. Upon landing at Cleveland, both pilots filed a report of the incident.

One of the other reservists aboard the helicopter was John Healy, a Cleveland police detective. Expecting that there would be an official investigation and he would be debriefed, he decided to tape record the details of the incident while they were still fresh in his memory. The next day, he took one of his colleagues with him into an interrogation room at the police station to record his account of the incident. But there never was an investigation or a debriefing—why? After twenty years of remaining silent, Healy finally agreed to an interview.

Although the incident had been investigated by a few UFO researchers and received some local publicity, it was soon forgotten. Two decades later, Jennie Zeidman, an investigator with the Center for UFO Studies (CUFOS) reopened the case and managed to locate Erma DeLon and her son, Charles Cyrus, who was thirteen years old at the time; they had actually witnessed the incident from the ground. Their credibility was confirmed by the fact that they knew details that were never publicized and known only to those who conducted the initial investigation. They confirmed seeing the helicopter and the UFO hovering above it. They confirmed that the object was projecting a green cone-shaped beam down around the helicopter, and that the helicopter was rising in the beam. At that point, they became frightened, so they got into their car and sped away.[1]

This remarkable case suggests two possible scenarios. The first is that whoever was piloting the object did not see the helicopter until the last second, when it began to dive, and thinking its rapid descent was an indication that it was about to crash, and that maybe they were responsible, attempted to rescue it with a kind of tractor beam. The second is that it was an attempted abduction that was aborted at the last minute, possibly because they realized there were witnesses on the ground watching them. When we take into account the level of technology and maneuverability often displayed by UFOs, it is difficult to believe they do not possess the means to detect an aircraft on a collision course. The act of neutralizing the chopper's controls and pulling it up in a beam of green light might suggest they were attempting to pull it aboard their ship.

1976 – Elmwood, Wisconsin

In *Out There,* Howard Blum, the author, cites a case that suggests deliberate hostile behavior. It occurred on the night of April 22, 1976, when police officer George Wheeler was on routine patrol in Elmwood, Wisconsin. He noticed a bright orange glow near the quarry at Tuttle Hill, and thinking it was a fire, he went to investigate. Arriving at the site, he saw a large silver-colored object. "Bigger than a two-story house" is how he described it over his radio. He said it was about 250 feet across, with a dome on top emitting a bright orange light that hurt his eyes. As he was radioing in his description, there was a *whooshing* sound as a beam of blue light hit his police cruiser. The blast completely destroyed the car's electrical system, leaving it sitting in the road in total darkness and Wheeler lying dazed across the front seat.

Working as dispatcher at police headquarters that night was Gail Helmer, the chief's wife. After losing contact with Wheeler, she became concerned and called Paul Frederickson, who lived a short distance east of Tuttle Hill. She asked him if he could see anything from his window, and he went to check. Returning to the phone, he said he saw a flaming object in the sky that looked like an orange half-moon, but when he looked again shortly after, it was gone.

A motorist named David Moots came upon the police car sitting in the middle of the road with no lights and found Wheeler lying across the front seat. He summoned help, and Wheeler was taken to the hospital, but surprisingly, the doctors could find nothing wrong with him. Upon his release three days later, he was suffering severe headaches and having nightmares. He told his wife that he thought he had radiation poisoning. Since he was still in a lot of pain and becoming distraught, his doctor admitted him to a hospital in Eau Claire. He was there for more than eleven days, and the doctors conducted numerous tests. Still, they could find nothing wrong with him, even though Wheeler kept insisting he had steady and unbearable pains in his arms and legs. Six months later, George Wheeler's heart gave out and he died.

We can only speculate on whether Wheeler's death was the result of his encounter, for he may simply have suffered a heart attack like many other middle-aged men. But even if that were true, the unprovoked attack by the object he encountered cannot be dismissed. Firing a beam that destroyed the car's electrical system and leaving him in a dazed condition constitutes a definite act of aggression.

1978 – Melbourne, Australia

About six nineteen on the evening of October 21, 1978, twenty-year-old Frederich Valentich took off from Moorabbin Airport, south of Melbourne, in a single-engine Cessna 182. He flew southwest along the coastline for about forty-five minutes—until he reached Cape Otway, where he turned out over Bass Strait and headed toward King Island. Stephen Robey was the air traffic controller on duty that evening in Melbourne, and everything seemed routine until he received an unusual call from Valentich.

According to the investigation summary report by the Commonwealth of Australia's Department of Transport (figs. 1, 2, and 3), the following is a transcript of the radio communications between Valentich and Robey. The transcript is devoid of punctuation such as quotation marks, commas, periods, and so on, but I have included punctuation here for clarification. It also states that the words in brackets (in this case meaning parentheses) are open to other interpretations.

Valentich:	*Melbourne, this is Delta Sierra Juliet. Is there any known traffic below five thousand?*
Robey:	*Delta Sierra Juliet, no known traffic.*
Valentich:	*Delta Sierra Juliet. I am seems (to) be a large aircraft below five thousand.*
Robey:	*Delta Sierra Juliet, what type of aircraft is it?*
Valentich:	*Delta Sierra Juliet. I cannot affirm. It is four bright ... it seems like landing lights.*
Robey:	*Delta Sierra Juliet ...*

Valentich:	*Melbourne, this is Delta Sierra Juliet. The aircraft just passed over me at least a thousand feet above.*
Robey:	*Delta Sierra Juliet, roger. And it is a large aircraft. Confirm?*
Valentich:	*Er, unknown due to speed it's traveling. Is there any Air Force aircraft in this vicinity?*
Robey:	*Delta Sierra Juliet, no known traffic in the vicinity.*
Valentich:	*Melbourne, it's approaching now from due east towards me.*
Robey:	*Delta Sierra Juliet …*
Valentich:	(open mike for two seconds) *Delta Sierra Juliet. It seems to me that he's … playing some sort of game. He's flying over me … two, three times at a time, at speeds I could not identify.*
Robey:	*Delta Sierra Juliet, roger. What is your actual level?*
Valentich:	*My level is four and a half thousand, four five zero zero.*
Robey:	*Delta Sierra Juliet, and confirm you cannot identify the aircraft?*
Valentich:	*Affirmative.*
Robey:	*Delta Sierra Juliet, roger. Stand by.*
Valentich:	*Melbourne, Delta Sierra Juliet. It's not an aircraft; it is …* (open mike for two seconds)
Robey:	*Delta Sierra Juliet, Melbourne. Can you describe the, er, aircraft?*

Valentich:	*Delta Sierra Juliet. As it's flying past, it's a long shape* (open mike for three seconds)—*(cannot) identify more than that. It has such speed*—(open mike for three seconds)—*before me right now, Melbourne.*
Robey:	*Delta Sierra Juliet, roger. And how large would the, er, object be?*
Valentich:	*Delta Sierra Juliet, Melbourne. It seems like it's stationary. What I'm doing right now is orbiting, and the thing is just orbiting on top of me also. It's got a green light and sort of metallic (like); it's all shiny (on) the outside.*
Robey:	*Delta Sierra Juliet …*
Valentich:	*Delta Sierra Juliet* (open mike for five seconds)—*it just vanished.*
Robey:	*Delta Sierra Juliet …*
Valentich:	*Melbourne, would you know what kind of aircraft I've got? Is it (a type) military aircraft?*
Robey:	*Delta Sierra Juliet, confirm that the, er, aircraft just vanished.*
Valentich:	*Say again?*
Robey:	*Delta Sierra Juliet, is the aircraft still with you?*
Valentich:	*Delta Sierra Juliet … it's, uh, nor—*(open mike for two seconds) … *(now) approaching from the southwest.*
Robey:	*Delta Sierra Juliet …*

Valentich: *Delta Sierra Juliet. The engine is rough idling; I've got it set at twenty-three, twenty-four, and the thing is (coughing).*

Robey: *Delta Sierra Juliet, roger. What are your intentions?*

Valentich: *My intentions are, ah, to go to King Island. Ah, Melbourne, the strange aircraft is hovering on top of me again ...* (two seconds of open mike). *It's hovering, and it's not an aircraft ...*

Robey: *Delta Sierra Juliet ...*

Valentich: *Delta Sierra Juliet. Melbourne ...* (seventeen seconds of open mike)

Robey: *Delta Sierra Juliet, Melbourne ...*

Then there was silence. When contact could not be reestablished, Robey notified the authorities. An intensive search was launched. It lasted four days, but no trace of the young pilot or his plane was ever found.[2]

If Valentich had crashed into the sea, it would seem that at least some trace of wreckage would have been discovered. If by chance he was able to set the plane down on the water intact, then it is possible it sank without leaving any floating debris. But if that were the case, he should have had time to exit the plane with his life jacket. Then again, who knows—he could have been knocked unconscious. According to Robey, the tone of the young pilot's voice convinced him that he was experiencing a real encounter of some kind. However, the idea that a UFO snatched his plane out of the sky is a matter of conjecture. Since no wreckage or body was ever found, it does remain a possibility.

At about the time Valentich disappeared, Roy Manifold, an amateur photographer, was setting up his camera to photograph the sunset over Bass Strait. After the film was developed, he noticed a blemish on the last photo he had taken. The area he photographed was approximately the same location where Valentich would have turned out over the sea, and recalling the incident, he wondered if the image on the film had any connection. An analysis revealed that the blemish was in the negative, which experts said was only a developing error. Others, however, claimed that the image was a metallic object enveloped by an exhaust cloud.[3]

Having been a professional photographer for many years, my personal opinion is that the blemish was probably the result of a chemistry stain on the negative. Professional labs always processed my work, and even with their stringent quality controls, they were not immune to an occasional mishap. There was one occasion when a small drop of chemistry spattered on a negative and the finished print displayed a blemish similar to the one in Manifold's photo. Since I consider myself somewhat of an expert in this field, I am fairly certain that this is what happened to his photograph.

Another witness, who prefers anonymity, claims to have seen an aircraft descending at about a forty-five-degree angle over Bass Strait near sunset, about the same time Valentich disappeared. He said there was a long green light between one to two thousand feet above the plane, rapidly descending toward it. He could not verify what, if anything, happened because both the plane and the green light passed out of his line of sight.[4]

There are a couple of similarities worth noting between this case and the one that occurred two years earlier with the army helicopter over Mansfield, Ohio. First, the object in the Mansfield case charged across the sky on a collision course with the helicopter, just like the object that made aggressive passes at Valentich. Second, the helicopter was pulled up in a green cone-shaped beam. In the Valentich case, a witness claims he saw a long green light descending toward a plane. Unfortunately, there is no way to confirm that it was Valentich's plane. In either case, the act of charging directly toward an aircraft suggests aggressive behavior.

Whether or not Valentich and his plane were abducted is something that cannot be proved. But whatever did happen appears to have resulted from the hostile-like maneuvers of a UFO.

1991 – Space Shuttle Mission STS 48

On September 15, 1991, UFO investigator Don Ratch captured some rather startling footage while videotaping a live broadcast transmitted from the *Discovery* space shuttle. As the shuttle was passing over the night side of the planet, the curve of the earth could be seen against the background of space, and lightning flashes sporadically illuminated clouds three hundred miles below. Then a bright object appeared just below the limb of the horizon, moving to the left along the curve of the earth. Suddenly, it made a sharp right-angle turn and shot off into space. A split second before the object made its turn, there was a flash from the lower portion of the frame, where two streaks of light suddenly appeared, the first zooming across the spot where the object had been only a second before.[5]

It appeared the object might have made an evasive maneuver to avoid whatever was coming at it. The impression is that something was shot at it. NASA, however, claimed it was ice crystals from a wastewater dump being blown about by the shuttle's altitude control system. Although possible, the objects appeared to be too far away from the shuttle to have been affected, and they were moving in slightly different directions.

If it was one craft shooting at another, and if there is a little war going on between some aliens, it is hard to believe that they would come all the way to Earth to fight their battles. In the Bible, Revelation 12:7–9 mentions a war fought in heaven between the Lord's army and the devil's army. Could this incident be of significance? Is there a dissident faction causing problems? Is it possible that the UFO that allegedly crashed in Roswell in 1947 was the result of a confrontation?

Another possibility is that the government was testing a top secret orbital defense system. The fact that it was able to be recorded on videotape by someone watching the live shuttle broadcast could mean it was intentional. Considering the level of security involved with top secret technology, surely someone would have known that the space shuttle would be in viewing range. And if they were broadcasting live, which they frequently do, a viewer on the ground might capture such a test on film or video. So if it was a test, theoretically it could have been a "staged" event that someone wanted the public to see—and if so, why? It was certain that many would perceive it as UFO related, and it would surely be exploited and stir up controversy. So could it have been staged as a form of disinformation?

There is still another possibility: perhaps something, possibly a particle beam weapon, was intentionally fired at the object from a satellite or from somewhere on the ground, which could suggest an entirely different scenario. If it was an aggressive act, it happened at an awkward moment, when the shuttle's camera was transmitting, allowing viewers on the ground to record it. Of course, this is only speculation.

The *Discovery* video received a fair amount of publicity and stirred up a lot of controversy in UFO circles. Most people, however, know nothing of the other events described in this chapter and are completely unaware that they occurred. Only a few incidents in which aggressive and hostile behavior was demonstrated occurred in the last half of the twentieth century. One conclusion we can draw from these accounts is the fact that *not all UFOs may be friendly.*

COMMONWEALTH OF AUSTRALIA — DEPARTMENT OF TRANSPORT	Reference No.
AIRCRAFT ACCIDENT INVESTIGATION SUMMARY REPORT	V116/783/1047

Publication of this report is authorised by the Secretary under the provisions of Air Navigation Regulations 283 (1)

1. LOCATION OF OCCURRENCE

	Height a.m.s.l.	Date	Time (Local)	Zone
Not known	–	21.10.78	Not known	EST

2. THE AIRCRAFT

Make and Model	Registration	Certificate of Airworthiness
Cessna 182L	VH-DSJ	Valid from 14 February 1968

Certificate of Registration issued to	Operator	Degree of damage to aircraft
Cephus Day,	SAS Southern Air Services,	Not known
33 Reserve Road,	Northern Avenue,	Other property damaged
Beaumauris, Victoria	Moorabbin Airport, Victoria	–

Defects discovered

3. THE FLIGHT

Last or intended departure point	Time of departure	Next point of intended landing	Purpose of flight	Class of operation
Moorabbin	1819 hours	King Island	Travel	Private

4. THE CREW

Name	Status	Age	Class of licence	Hours on type	Total hours	Degree of injury
Frederick VALENTICH	Pilot	20	Private	Not known	150 (Approx.)	Presumed Fatal

5. OTHER PERSONS (All passengers and persons injured on ground)

Name	Status	Degree of injury	Name	Status	Degree of injury

6. RELEVANT EVENTS

The pilot obtained a Class Four instrument rating on 11 May 1978 and he was therefore authorised to operate at night in visual meteorological conditions (VMC). On the afternoon of 21 October 1978 he attended the Moorabbin Briefing Office, obtained a meteorological briefing and, at 1723 hours, submitted a flight plan for a night VMC flight from Moorabbin to King Island and return. The cruising altitude nominated in the flight plan was below 5000 feet, with estimated time intervals of 41 minutes to Cape Otway and 28 minutes from Cape Otway to King Island. The total fuel endurance was shown as 300 minutes. The pilot made no arrangements for aerodrome lighting to be illuminated for his arrival at King Island. He advised the briefing officer and the operator's representative that he was uplifting friends at King Island and took four life jackets in the aircraft with him.

The aircraft was refuelled to capacity at 1810 hours and departed Moorabbin at 1819 hours. After departure the pilot established two-way radio communications with Melbourne Flight Service Unit (FSU).

The pilot reported Cape Otway at 1900 hours and the next transmission received from the aircraft was at 1906:14 hours. The following communications between the aircraft and Melbourne FSU were recorded from this time: (Note: The word/words in brackets are open to other interpretations.)

TIME	FROM	TEXT
1906:14	VH-DSJ	MELBOURNE this is DELTA SIERRA JULIET is there any known traffic below five thousand
:23	FSU	DELTA SIERRA JULIET no known traffic
:26	VH-DSJ	DELTA SIERRA JULIET I am seems (to) be a large aircraft below five thousand

Fig. 1 Official report on the Valentich disappearance - page 1

TIME	FROM	TEXT
:46	FSU	D D DELTA SIERRA JULIET what type of aircraft is it
:50	VH-DSJ	DELTA SIERRA JULIET I cannot affirm it is four bright it seems to me like landing lights
1907:04	FSU	DELTA SIERRA JULIET
:32	VH-DSJ	MELBOURNE this (is) DELTA SIERRA JULIET the aircraft has just passed over over me at least a thousand feet above
:43	FSU	DELTA SIERRA JULIET roger and it it is a large aircraft confirm
:47	VH-DSJ	er unknown due to the speed it's travelling is there any airforce aircraft in the vicinity
:57	FSU	DELTA SIERRA JULIET no known aircraft in the vicinity
1908:18	VH-DSJ	MELBOURNE it's approaching now from due east towards me
:28	FSU	DELTA SIERRA JULIET
:42		// open microphone for two seconds //
:49	VH-DSJ	DELTA SIERRA JULIET it seems to me that he's playing some sort of game he's flying over me two three times at a time at speeds I could not identify
1909:02	FSU	DELTA SIERRA JULIET roger what is your actual level
:06	VH-DSJ	my level is four and a half thousand four five zero zero
:11	FSU	DELTA SIERRA JULIET and confirm you cannot identify the aircraft
:14	VH-DSJ	affirmative
:18	FSU	DELTA SIERRA JULIET roger standby
:28	VH-DSJ	MELBOURNE DELTA SIERRA JULIET it's not an aircraft it is // open microphone for two seconds //
:46	FSU	DELTA SIERRA JULIET MELBOURNE can you describe the er aircraft
1909:52	VH-DSJ	DELTA SIERRA JULIET as it's flying past it's a long shape // open microphone for three seconds // (cannot) identify more than (that it has such speed) // open microphone for 3 seconds // before me right now Melbourne
1910:07	FSU	DELTA SIERRA JULIET roger and how large would the er object be
:20	VH-DSJ	DELTA SIERRA JULIET MELBOURNE it seems like it's stationary what I'm doing right now is orbiting and the thing is just orbiting on top of me also it's got a green light and sort of metallic (like) it's all shiny (on) the outside
:43	FSU	DELTA SIERRA JULIET

Fig. 2 Official report on the Valentich disappearance - page 2

TIME	FROM	TEXT
:48	VH-DSJ	DELTA SIERRA JULIET // open microphone for 5 seconds // it's just vanished
:57	FSU	DELTA SIERRA JULIET
1911:03	VH-DSJ	MELBOURNE would you know what kind of aircraft I've got is it (a type) military aircraft
:08	FSU	DELTA SIERRA JULIET confirm the or aircraft just vanished
:14	VH-DSJ	SAY AGAIN
:17	FSU	DELTA SIERRA JULIET is the aircraft still with you
:23	VH-DSJ	DELTA SIERRA JULIET (it's ah nor) // open microphone 2 seconds // (now) approaching from the southwest
:37	FSU	DELTA SIERRA JULIET
:52	VH-DSJ	DELTA SIERRA JULIET the engine is is rough idling I've got it set at twenty three twenty four and the thing is (coughing)
1912:04	FSU	DELTA SIERRA JULIET roger what are your intentions
:09	VH-DSJ	my intentions are ah to go to King Island ah Melbourne that strange aircraft is hovering on top of me again // two seconds open microphone // it is hovering and it's not an aircraft
:22	FSU	DELTA SIERRA JULIET
:28	VH-DSJ	DELTA SIERRA JULIET MELBOURNE // 17 seconds open microphone //
:49	FSU	DELTA SIERRA JULIET MELBOURNE

There is no record of any further transmissions from the aircraft.

The weather in the Cape Otway area was clear with a trace of stratocumulus cloud at 5000 to 7000 feet, scattered cirrus cloud at 30000 feet, excellent visibility and light winds. The end of daylight at Cape Otway was at 1918 hours.

The Alert Phase of SAR procedures was declared at 1912 hours and, at 1933 hours when the aircraft did not arrive at King Island, the Distress Phase was declared and search action was commenced. An intensive air, sea and land search was continued until 25 October 1978, but no trace of the aircraft was found.

7. OPINION AS TO CAUSE

The reason for the disappearance of the aircraft has not been determined.

| Approved for publication | Woodward. | (A. R. Woodward) Delegate of the Secretary | Date 27.4.1982 |

Fig. 3 Official report on the Valentich disappearance - page 3

113

Notes

1. UFO raises army helicopter in green beam
    "UFO Confrontation: Mansfield, Ohio." *Sightings* segment. Sci Fi
    (now Syfy).
    Link to short video:
    www.youtube.com/watch?v=4uxF9tRPIhM

2. The Valentich disappearance
    Web link:
    en.wikipedia.org/wiki/Valentich_disappearance

3. The Manifold photo
    "The Valentich Case." *Unsolved Mysteries* segment. NBC. WPTV.
    West Palm Beach.

4. Anonymous witness
    "The Valentich Case." *Unsolved Mysteries* segment. NBC. WPTV.
    West Palm Beach.

5. *Discovery* space shuttle footage
    Confirmation: The Hard Evidence of Aliens Among Us? Documentary.
    Dir. Starling Price. NBC. WPTV. West Palm Beach. 1999.

Chapter 7

ROSWELL

It's unlikely that many people on Earth have not heard about the Roswell incident. Movies have been made, books have been written, and it has been featured in numerous documentaries, yet it remains a highly controversial issue. Why? Did an extraterrestrial spaceship really crash near Roswell? Were alien bodies recovered? Was it a new top secret aircraft? Or was it a Project Mogul balloon as the air force now claims?

The facts clearly indicate that something came down in the region, and whatever it was, it caused the government great concern, which was obvious by how they attempted to cover it up. So let's examine the details to better understand what really took place.

It was Sunday morning, July 6, 1947, when Mac Brazel walked into the Chaves County sheriff's office in Roswell, New Mexico, carrying a box of strange-looking debris. He'd discovered the material scattered in a swath about three hundred feet wide and a mile long on the Foster ranch in Corona, which is where he worked. After looking at the material, Sheriff George Wilcox suspected it probably had something to do with the military, so he notified the authorities at Roswell Army Airfield.

Major Jesse Marcel, the base intelligence officer, and Sheridan Cavitt, an agent in the Counter Intelligence Corps (CIC) were dispatched to the sheriff's office to check it out. After looking it over, they agreed that it warranted further investigation, so they followed Brazel back to his ranch in Corona.

Corona is a little town seventy-five miles away, on the northern fringe of adjacent Lincoln County, and it was late when they arrived, so they spent the night. In the morning, Brazel took them out to the site, where they spent most of the day (Monday, July 7) examining the debris. Then they loaded what they could into their vehicles and headed back to Roswell. It was well after midnight when they got back, and Marcel decided to stop at his home and show the material to his family before bringing it to the base. Marcel woke his wife and son, and they spread the material out on the kitchen floor. His son Jesse Jr., now a doctor in Montana, vividly recalls handling one piece shaped like an I-Beam and bearing figures resembling hieroglyphics, but he said it was not Egyptian or like any writing he had ever seen.[1]

Tuesday morning, July 8, Marcel brought the material to the base. Colonel William Blanchard, the base commander, had not yet seen what Mac Brazel had turned in because it was still locked up in a room at the sheriff's office. After seeing what Marcel and Cavitt brought back, he had Lieutenant Walter Haut, the base public relations officer, prepare a press release stating that a flying saucer crashed on a nearby ranch, and that it had been retrieved and brought to the base. Haut was instructed to hand deliver it to the local media, and by eleven that morning, the presses were rolling and the radio stations were broadcasting the story.

Now we have to ask why Colonel Blanchard even issued a press release. He must have suspected the material was not of earthly origin by virtue of the fact that he stated in the press release that a flying saucer had crashed. Would it not have been wiser to send troops out to scour the area, collect the debris, and not alert the media? However, according to some reports, Brazel talked to patrons at a local bar or restaurant about what he had found, and if true, once the news spread, it could have resulted in a mob of curiosity seekers stampeding to the Foster ranch, and Blanchard was concerned that any evidence at the site might be compromised by curious civilians.

So claiming that a crashed flying saucer had been retrieved and brought to the base was a strategy he used to keep the public away from the site. People would be less likely to go there if they thought it had already been cleaned up and there was nothing left to see. Nevertheless, when the story hit the wires, all hell broke loose; the switchboard at the base, the phones at the sheriff's office, the two radio stations, and newspapers were inundated with calls from reporters around the world trying to get more information.

Meanwhile, Marcel had flown to Carswell Air Force Base in Fort Worth, Texas, with some of the debris to show Brigadier General Roger Ramey, commander of the Eighth Air Force. Ramey, also under pressure from all the sudden publicity, was ordered by his superiors at the Pentagon to kill the story, which he did by announcing to the press that the material found was only the debris of a weather balloon with an attached radar reflector.

We now know the story was a cover-up. According to Marcel, Ramey had the debris that he had brought to Fort Worth substituted with that of a chopped up balloon and pieces of a radar reflector. After the switch was made, Ramey, in front of reporters, called in Lieutenant Irving Newton, the base weather officer to examine it, and he identified it as a weather balloon, of course, yet he never saw the original debris, and Marcel was ordered to go along with the story. The balloon explanation successfully killed further interest by the media, and the matter was quickly forgotten.

And so it went until 1978, when Stanton Friedman, a nuclear physicist and prominent UFO researcher, learned about Marcel and contacted him. Marcel agreed to an interview. Marcel firmly stated that the debris he collected from the Foster ranch was not from a weather balloon. He described pieces that were extremely lightweight but could not be dented with a hammer or burned with a blowtorch.[2] Some of the debris looked like pieces of tinfoil, which researchers nicknamed "memory metal' because after being crumpled up, it unfolded to its original smooth shape with no sign of ever having been creased. Other witnesses who had also allegedly handled similar pieces described it the same way.

A photograph taken by a reporter of Major Marcel posing with the balloon fragments in Ramey's office was published in almost every newspaper in the world. But Jesse Marcel Jr. said that the material in that photo was not the same material his father had spread out on their kitchen floor in Roswell after bringing it back from the Foster ranch.[3]

These are the established facts: the dates are firm, and there is the testimony of the base intelligence officer—a US Army major *who was there*. The rest of the information, however, is subject to question.

After Friedman resurrected the event in 1978, he and other investigators found more witnesses, and from their testimonies, it suggests that there may have been more than one crash site—possibly as many as three. Now, the idea that two or three UFOs crashed at the same time automatically raises a red flag ... I mean, what are the odds? However, the Roswell incident is unique. It involved numerous military and civilian witnesses, many of whom were still alive to be interviewed thirty years later.

Phyllis McGuire, the sheriff's daughter, had gone to the sheriff's office on the Sunday that Brazel brought in the box of debris. She said her father had sent two deputies out to the Foster ranch to check things out; however, when they returned, they said they were unable to find any debris but did find a large circular area that appeared to have been burned into the ground. This suggests that something might have bounced off the ground and become airborne again, shedding some debris before coming down at another location. Wilcox allegedly sent two more deputies back on Tuesday in an attempt to learn what was going on, but by then the military had cordoned off the area and the deputies were turned away. This was corroborated by civilian witnesses who said the military had sealed off all side roads along the main highway. Many said they saw trucks loaded with boxes leaving the area, escorted by armed military personnel. Military personnel who had been stationed in Roswell, when interviewed thirty years later, said they saw the crash material loaded onto planes and flown away, also with armed escorts.

But it appeared that some witnesses may have been describing a different crash site, one about thirty-five miles north of Roswell. Was there a second crash, or was this where the craft came down after bouncing off the ground and leaving a burned-out gouge on the Foster ranch? If there was a second crash, that fact still hinges on the reliability of witness testimonies.

The day that Colonel Blanchard issued his press release, Frank Joyce, a news reporter at KGFL radio station, claims that he received a call from a military official at the Pentagon, ordering him to stop broadcasting the story. Joyce said he told the official that he was a civilian and couldn't be told by him what to do. Then the person said something to the effect of "You'll see what I can do" and hung up. George Roberts, the station's manager, said he received a call from someone in the government threatening to revoke the station's license *immediately* if he didn't pull the story.[4] And according to his daughter, Sheriff Wilcox had later been "persuaded" by the military to forget the whole affair.[5] Other witnesses who allegedly handled pieces of the debris said military personnel came to their homes and threatened their lives and the lives of their families if they ever talked. If these accounts are true, it would appear that some rather severe tactics were being employed to hush up the incident.

In a recent documentary, Frank Joyce said that he had talked to Mac Brazel on the phone, and Brazel told him he had found the debris of a flying saucer on the ranch, along with dead alien bodies that emitted a terrible odor. Joyce said he thought he was probably some kind of nut and suggested he contact the military. Allegedly, the military sequestered Brazel at the base for a few days and persuaded him to keep quiet about the whole affair. Joyce said that a few days later—after the military released him—Brazel came to the radio station and said "he was supposed to tell him" that he was mistaken about the flying saucer, and that it was really the debris of a weather balloon. As he was leaving, Joyce asked him about all the stories floating around about the "little green men." He said that Brazel looked back and in a quiet voice said, "They weren't green."[6]

Most of the early accounts (if they are accurate) suggest that Brazel's first contact with Joyce occurred on Sunday morning, July 6, while he was at the sheriff's office. Joyce had apparently called the sheriff's office that morning, looking for any news that might be of interest, and the sheriff handed the phone to Brazel.[7] However, it seems that if Brazel did find bodies on the ranch, as Joyce claims he said, would he not have mentioned that fact to Sheriff Wilcox and to Major Marcel and the CIC agent? And would he not have led them to the bodies when they were at the ranch? Marcel was candid with Stanton Friedman and others who interviewed him, and never once did he mention anything about bodies. Why would Brazel tell Joyce but not the sheriff or Major Marcel that he found bodies? It makes no sense. So there is much confusion regarding many testimonies in the Roswell case. But one might logically assume that if it was an alien spaceship that crashed, someone had to be flying it, unless it was a small unmanned reconnaissance craft.

There are other accounts of alien bodies, one of which is attributed to the late "Barney" Barnett, a land surveyor. One day while they were out fishing together, he had related the story to his close friend Vern Maltais.

According to Maltais, Barnett said that one day while he was out in the desert surveying land for possible irrigation, he came upon a disc-shaped craft that had apparently crashed, and the bodies of several small beings were lying on the ground. He said a group of archaeological students had also spotted the wreckage from a distance and come to investigate, arriving only moments after he did. Then the military suddenly appeared and ordered everyone away from the craft. They were advised that this was a highly classified government operation, and that it was their patriotic duty not to mention anything about what they had seen to anyone. They were threatened with arrest and imprisonment if they talked, and then military police escorted them away.[8]

Now it seems that if the military had made death threats to anyone, it would have been to these people who actually saw the crashed disc and the bodies, not just to those who allegedly handled a few pieces of the debris. In relating the incident, Maltais never indicated that anything other than the threat of being arrested for talking had been made to Barnett and the others. But since we don't know the date of the Barnett incident, there is no way to know if it is even connected to the events at Roswell. Some researchers think Barnett's encounter occurred far to the west, out on the Plains of San Augustin. Since Barnett has since passed on, the story can only be considered as hearsay, even though Maltais had nothing to gain from telling it. He said that in all the years he knew Barnett, he had never known him to lie, and that fabricating such a story was completely out of character.

Then there is the story of the late Captain Oliver Henderson. "Pappy," as he was known to his friends, was a pilot stationed at Roswell in 1947. According to his wife, Sappho, after the Roswell event became public, he told her that he had been keeping a secret from her for thirty-four years, but since it no longer seemed to be classified, he felt it was now okay to tell her. He said that the Roswell event was true, telling her that there really were alien bodies, telling her that he had flown them out of Roswell. She said he described them as being smaller than human bodies, with large heads, and told her that they were not of this earth.[9] Mrs. Henderson appeared sincere in the few interviews she gave. Since she was not seeking publicity and had nothing to gain, I am inclined to believe she was telling the truth.

I think we can discount the idea that the Roswell crash involved an experimental aircraft of either United States or foreign design. Whatever aeronautical technologies were being developed during that time would have become obsolete in twenty years and would probably no longer be secret. If it were an experimental aircraft, surely by now the air force would have admitted it to quell the revived Roswell hoopla in the 1990s instead of shooting themselves in the foot with the Project Mogul explanation. Mogul was a project that involved a high-altitude balloon carrying equipment capable of detecting a nuclear explosion in the Soviet Union. At the time, the government suspected the Russians had developed an atomic bomb, and the balloon was part of the intelligence gathering efforts.[10] So what need was there to keep that a secret for fifty years?

In 1994, the air force published a book titled *The Roswell Report*, which was supposed to clear up the mystery, with the emphasis on Project Mogul.[11] The way it was presented, everyone assumed that the balloon and everything it carried was classified. The truth is, the only thing classified was the mission: there was nothing secret about the balloon or any of the components on board. There were quite a number of balloons launched by Project Mogul that came down all over the place, along with instructions on whom to contact in the event they were found. When they were found, probably only one or two army personnel arrived in a truck to pick them up; there was no massive military response, no soldiers cordoning off the area, and there was no armed military escort. So it would appear that the air force cleverly used Mogul to temper the revived interest in Roswell only because the project happened to be classified in 1947; it provided a new and convenient explanation. But since most people did not buy the story, the air force tried again with a new publication that came out in 1997: *The Roswell Report: Case Closed*.[12] Therein, they claimed that the alien bodies people allegedly saw were anthropomorphic dummies used in testing high-altitude parachutes. However, the records show those tests did not occur until 1953, six years later. The air force claims that after three decades, memories became clouded and people simply confused this incident with the Roswell event. Even if that were true, why did most witnesses describe seeing bodies that were about four feet tall when the dummies used in the parachute tests were about six feet?

What the air force really did was cut off its nose to spite its face because it was admitting that the scene in General Ramey's office with the weather balloon was a sham—exactly what researchers had been claiming all along. And the late Brigadier General Thomas DuBose, who was General Ramey's chief of staff in 1947, admitted in two separate filmed interviews, one in 1990 and the other in 1991, that the balloon story was a cover-up.[13] Stanton Friedman also has a sworn affidavit from Dubose, stating the same.[14] The air force believes that the span of three decades most likely clouded the memories of many witnesses, and it is probably true to some extent. When comparing the original testimonies of some witnesses to their more recent interviews, it appears many have embellished their stories, thereby making them less credible. So Roswell researchers are now beginning to question the reliability of testimonies of many witnesses who were originally considered credible.

In 1947, we were experimenting with captured German V-2 rockets and building the first jet fighters. Had one of these crashed, you can bet the military would have swarmed over the site like flies on horse manure. However, their radical behavior suggests they were dealing with something much bigger. Surely it would not take many trucks to transport the debris of a balloon. Surely balloon debris would not require an armed military escort, and surely (if the accounts were true) they would not make death threats to witnesses over a balloon.

If it was an alien spacecraft that crashed, that would logically explain their actions; the fact that we were being visited by extraterrestrials would have raised hell with many religious beliefs at the time. However, I think their immediate concern would have been foreign powers. We would have had our hands on a technology centuries ahead of our time, and it would not have been in our best interest for the Soviet Union or any other unfriendly nation to know about it. And with news media from around the world suddenly focused on Roswell, it would only have been a matter of time before something leaked out. Someone decided to squelch the story, doing so with remarkable speed. And because civilian witnesses were involved, their silence had to be guaranteed. It is possible that this was accomplished by intimidation and death threats. Still, when looking at the complete picture, one cannot deny the established facts:

- Something either crashed or bounced off the ground on the Foster ranch. The debris collected by Mac Brazel, Major Marcel, and the CIC agent confirm this.

- Marcel testified that the debris was not from a weather balloon, and that some pieces were extremely lightweight and could not be dented with a hammer or burned with a blowtorch.

- Marcel's son testified that he handled one piece shaped like an I-Beam and containing strange writing.

- Brigadier General Thomas DuBose admitted the balloon story was a cover-up.

The late Congressman Steven Schiff of New Mexico made a valiant effort to obtain records pertaining to the Roswell incident through the General Accounting Office in order to satisfy the requests of researchers and numerous constituents. Unfortunately, he received the typical bureaucratic runaround. They sent him on a wild goose chase between various departments that had no records or any other information on the event. When he eventually did get a reply, he was told that the records had been destroyed.

The fact remains that some "thing" came down in the Roswell region—possibly two "things"—and it caused someone in the government great concern. If it was an extraterrestrial craft, the government would have wasted no time in trying to unravel its technology, and according to events that occurred thirty years later, they may have met with at least partial success.

Notes

1. Jesse Marcel Jr. handled I beam with strange writing
    "What Really Happened at Roswell?" *Encounters with the Unexplained*. Dir. David Priest. PAX (now ION). 8 Sept. 2000.

2. Marcel states the debris not from weather balloon
    "UFO Coverups". *In Search Of…* Dir. Seth Hill. THC. 20 Sept. 1980.

3. Jesse Marcel Jr. says debris in Ramey's office not what his father showed him at home
    "The Roswell Incident." *Beyond Belief*. Prod. John Purdie. TLC.

4. Radio station ordered not to broadcast story
    "What Really Happened at Roswell?" *Encounters with the Unexplained*. Dir. David Priest. PAX (now ION). 8 Sept. 2000.

5. Sheriff Wilcox persuaded to forget whole affair
    "The Roswell Incident." *Beyond Belief*. Prod. John Purdie. TLC.

6. Did Mac Brazel find alien bodies?
    "The Roswell Incident." *Beyond Belief*. Prod. John Purdie. TLC.

7. Joyce's first phone conversation with Brazel
    The Roswell Crash: Startling New Evidence. Documentary. Prod. Kelly McPherson. Sci Fi (now Syfy). 2002.

8. Barney Barnett's story of finding crash and bodies
    "What Really Happened at Roswell?" *Encounters with the Unexplained*. Dir. David Priest. PAX (now ION). 8 Sept. 2000.

9. Captain "Pappy" Henderson flew alien bodies out of Roswell
   Encounters with the Unexplained. Documentary. Dir. David Priest
   PAX (now ION). 8 Sept. 2000.

10 Project Mogul
   "Roswell: Final Declassification." *History Undercover.* Dir. Pam
   Rorke-Levy. THC. 2002.

11. "The Roswell Report"
   "Roswell: Final Declassification." *History Undercover.* Dir. Pam
   Rorke-Levy. THC. 2002.

12. "The Roswell Report: Case Closed"
   "Roswell: Final Declassification." *History Undercover.* Dir. Pam
   Rorke-Levy. THC. 2002.

13. Brigadier General Thomas DuBose's admission that balloon story
   cover-up
   "What Really Happened at Roswell?" *Encounters with the
   Unexplained.* Dir. David Priest. PAX (now ION). 8 Sept. 2000.

14. DuBose's Affidavit
   "Mystery at Roswell." *Conspiracy Files.* Prod. Loren Michelman.
   Discovery. 2006.

Chapter 8

THE GOVERNMENT AND ALIEN TECHNOLOGY

There were always questions about the government's role in the UFO mystery. Do they know more than they are telling? Have they acquired one or more crashed UFOs? Are they experimenting with alien technology? If we have learned anything from the Roswell incident, it is the fact that something came down in that region, and whatever it was, they covered up the truth with the phony weather balloon story. Because that is now a confirmed fact, we know they lied once, which makes it probable that they have done so on other occasions. If it was in the interest of national security, then we have no case. Yet holes in the Project Mogul explanation garnered suspicion among the seasoned researchers. Therefore, this chapter deals with the question of whether the government is experimenting with alien technology—and even the possibility that contact has been established. Two events that occurred in December of 1980 suggest such possibilities: one was at an air force base in England, and the other was just outside a small town in Texas.

The Rendlesham Forest Incident

It all began on the night of December 25 (morning of December 26), when security police at a US air base in England saw strange lights in Rendlesham Forest, the woods separating the Bentwaters and Woodbridge

Air Force Bases in Suffolk. Allegedly, both civilian and military radar had tracked a bogie that disappeared near the base, so it was possible the lights were from a downed aircraft. When personnel from the Eighty-First Security Patrol Squadron at Bentwaters went to investigate, it turned into one of the most bizarre cases in UFO history. Had it not been for a memo issued by Lieutenant Colonel Charles Halt, the deputy base commander, which was later obtained through the Freedom of Information Act (FOIA), the event might never have gained such notoriety.

Once the memo became public, a myriad of confusing information clouded the incident in a sea of uncertainty. Some witnesses described the events occurring at night, while others referred to the time as morning since it was after midnight, and information in affidavits submitted by witnesses to their superiors contrasted with what seemed like exaggerated accounts later given to the media. This resulted in conflicting dates and difficulty in trying to verify certain facts. But because the deputy base commander was a key witness, it suggests that something did happen—something the air force and the British Ministry of Defence (MoD) took extreme measures to cover up.

Suspecting the lights might be from downed aircraft, security police entered the woods near the east gate of Woodbridge to investigate. Communication soon became difficult due to the limited range of their portable radios, so Airman Edward Cabansag was posted at a location where he was able to relay transmissions back to the base; Sergeant Jim Penniston and Airman John Burroughs then proceeded farther into the woods.

According to Penniston, in a clearing, he encountered an object that was triangular shaped, with white, blue, and red lights. He said the surface was like black opaque glass with symbols etched into it, and that he walked around the object and took thirty-six pictures of it with his camera.[1] However, there was one detail mentioned in an early article on the Internet by journalist Sally Rayl that, to my knowledge, was never mentioned in any other interview. Penniston said that he was standing next to the object and the next thing he knew, he was about twenty feet away, standing next to Burroughs—*apparently with no idea how he got there.*

This detail could be of significance, as we will see later. Unfortunately, the site containing this interview no longer exists; however, I did print out a copy for my files.

Penniston said the object then lifted off the ground and maneuvered through the trees before rising up, and in the blink of an eye, it was gone.[2] A few minutes later, he said they saw the same array of lights in the sky about a mile away but were unable to follow. They went back to the clearing, where Burroughs discovered three evenly spaced triangular depressions in the ground where the object had been sitting.[3]

In an appearance on *Unsolved Mysteries,* John Burroughs said they came to a clearing and saw an object on the ground, surrounded by a bank of blue lights, and that it appeared to be strobing. The object started to rise, and not knowing what to expect, the men dove to the ground. Burroughs described the peculiar sensation of distorted time: he said his perception of the sky, trees, air, and the ground all seemed different—like everything was happening in slow motion. After the object took off, he said his senses returned to normal.[4] In this interview, he said nothing about Penniston approaching the object and taking pictures of it. If he did mention it, it may have been edited out for time.

The details are sketchy as to whether it was the next night, December 27, or the following night, December 28, when security police went to the officers' club where Colonel Halt was attending a belated Christmas party with his family and advised him that lights were again being observed in the woods. Halt left the party and quickly put together a search team, heading into the woods with the intention of debunking the whole thing.

They brought large portable lighting units known as Light-alls into the woods; however, they failed to work. They'd worked fine when tested before leaving the base, but now they were useless. They brought in more Light-alls, which were also tested before leaving the base, but once in the woods, they, too, failed to work.[5] Whether this is relevant appears moot at this time because according to UFO investigator James Easton, the people he interviewed at the base claimed the lights were old and had seen a lot of use, and it was a well-known fact that they were not very reliable.

Halt brought a portable tape recorder to document everything. The first thing he and his team encountered was a red blinking light maneuvering through the trees; he said it looked almost like an eye. He said they followed it into a clearing, where it suddenly burst apart into five small white objects and disappeared.[6] Proceeding onward, they came to an open field and saw three bright objects circling in the sky to the north, emitting beams of light down at the ground. According to Sergeant Robert Ball, the pattern in which they maneuvered resembled a grid search.[7] Then another bright object was spotted rapidly approaching from the south. When it was overhead, it stopped, hovered, and projected a thin laser-like beam down to the ground directly in front of Halt and his men, almost at their feet. Halt said the beam remained for about ten seconds and then went out. The object shot back across the sky.[8] He said it headed toward Bentwaters and continued emitting beams of light. He also said that from the chatter on the radio, they knew it was near the weapons storage facility.[9]

About the same time, Sergeant Randy Smith claims that he and other security personnel were observing three hovering objects from the tower in the weapons storage area (WSA). Smith said he stayed for about an hour and then left, at which point he claims to have experienced a period of missing time. He said he doesn't remember anything after leaving the tower but has a vague memory of standing on the roof of one of the buildings. The next thing he knew, he was riding home on his bicycle.

The most bizarre account, however, came from Airman Larry Warren. He claims he was in the woods with another team, about a quarter of a mile from Colonel Halt's team. He said there was a bright glow coming from an open field ahead of them, illuminating the surrounding trees. As they approached, he said he saw military police and other security personnel scattered around the field, and a video camera and a motion picture camera had been set up at one end. In the center of the field, Warren said there was a strange patch of glowing fog, and he was trying to make sense out of this when his attention was drawn to a red ball of light moving across the sky. At first, he thought it was one of the fighters on a landing approach to Woodbridge, but then it suddenly turned and came directly toward the field. He said it descended into the glowing fog and there was an explosion of color. It transformed into a solid, structured object. He estimated it to be about thirty feet at the base, and it had a bank of blue lights around it. He said some of the men fled back into the woods, but that he and a few others just stood there, too stunned to move.[10] Later, in another documentary, he embellished his story by claiming alien beings were standing outside the craft and communicating with senior officers.[11]

Aside from these extraordinary claims, one civilian witness's testimony suggests that something was going on. Gerry Harris lived directly across the road from the runway at the Woodbridge base. He said he went outside to watch the spectacle from his front yard after he noticed lights bobbing up and down and zigzagging over the woods. Because the wind was blowing in his direction, he said he could hear excited voices shouting from within the base and vehicles starting up: he said it was evident that something was going on.[12]

James Easton believes the red light that Colonel Halt and his men saw maneuvering through the trees was the beam from the Orford Ness Lighthouse. When viewed through a starscope, which the men had with them, the beam would have created the impression of a red winking light. In one documentary, Halt was asked about the lighthouse, and he said they could see it, but that it was about thirty to thirty-five degrees to the north, and it was not the same light they were observing. In another documentary, he said that as the red light moved through the trees, it appeared to be dripping, like molten metal from a crucible.[13]

He also stated that it exploded into five small white objects and disappeared. Might it possibly have been some kind of remote-controlled probe or flare being used to detect, or maybe distract, anyone who came into the woods to investigate the lights? Exploding into five small white disappearing objects suggests it burned out, the white objects being like sparks that simply dissipated. But this is only speculation.

Easton also suggested that the lights Halt's team observed in the north, which were emitting beams down at the ground, were search helicopters because at the time, no one knew for certain if the lights in the woods were from a downed aircraft. However, that makes no sense. It was suspected that the lights might be from a downed aircraft on the first night, so logically, one would assume that a helicopter search would have been conducted at that time—why would they wait for over twenty-four hours? And if it was a downed aircraft, it probably would have been found since the search area was restricted to the woods and the area separating the two bases. However, Halt was quite certain that no helicopters were in the air. If it were a helicopter projecting the laser-like beam down in front of him and his men, surely they would have recognized it as such.

So was it a lighthouse beacon that caused security police to get all excited? It seems doubtful, for if it were, why was it not seen on previous nights? Was no one patrolling the east gate sector? That seems highly unlikely since this was a strategic nuclear weapons facility; security personnel would have been thorough in its patrol coverage.

However, a recent investigation by a team from the History Channel seemed to discount the idea that the lighthouse beacon could even be seen in the woods. They interviewed Keith Seaman, who has been keeper of the Orford Ness Lighthouse for many years. He showed them that a metal panel affixed to the back of the lighthouse would have prevented the beam from being seen in Rendlesham Forest, and he said the panel had always been there. He said that the only thing that might possibly be seen from the woods was the ray of the beam sweeping out across the water.[14]

Initially, fragmented accounts of the incident were presented on the TV programs *Sightings* and *Unsolved Mysteries* as well as in several documentaries, each having interviewed different witnesses who gave different accounts of the event. Only after consolidating the footage from the various sources did I gain a better perspective of what took place. Yet there were still many details in conflict, such as the affidavit Jim Penniston submitted to Colonel Halt. In it, he stated that he was never closer than fifty meters to the object, and he mentioned nothing about touching, walking around, or photographing it. And the sketch he submitted showed the object some distance away, behind trees.

Penniston still has his notebook with the original notes and sketches he made that night. One depicts a flat triangular-shaped object with a pyramid-shaped protuberance on the top.[15] Another is of the symbols that he said were engraved into the craft.[16] So why did he not submit these drawings to Colonel Halt with his affidavit? And if he did walk around the object as he reported in media interviews, why did he state in his affidavit that he was never closer than fifty meters to it?

There were also questions regarding Larry Warren's account. If there were cameras set up as he claims, then it would appear that someone was prepared to record the event, suggesting it may have been a prearranged demonstration of some kind. Either Warren has a vivid imagination, or he witnessed something extraordinary. Witnesses sometimes report details that seem too incredible to believe; however, we should not discount them just because they may not fit within the parameters of logical perception— at least where UFOs are concerned. We might better assess such claims based on the credibility of the witness.

What made me suspicious of Warren's story is what he said about military police and security personnel scattered around the field. If that were true, they were there to keep the area secure. Such a display (or demonstration) suggests a level of technology that would be highly classified and restricted only to those with the proper clearance. Therefore, their duty would have been to secure the area, making it inaccessible to anyone else. That means they would have also been in the woods, in which case Colonel Halt's team probably would have encountered them. So if Warren and the others were able to approach the area without being challenged, I can only conclude that the security people were completely derelict in their duties. I cannot believe that Warren's presence would have gone undetected and unchallenged.

Initially, I entertained the idea that Jim Penniston (and maybe others) had intentionally toned down the information in their affidavits in order to allay any concerns of their superiors that they were being distracted from their duties. Since the event became a major item in the UFO circuit, I even considered the possibility that it may have been advantageous from a disinformation standpoint to exaggerate details to the media and that they were coerced into doing so for this purpose. As we will see in a moment, I wasn't too far off the mark.

Halt and Penniston, now both retired, were brought back to Rendlesham Forest by the Sci Fi Channel to put together a special two-hour documentary on the incident. And something new was learned when they retraced their steps of the nights in question. While standing at the landing site that Halt said was shown to him the next day by security police, Penniston said that it was not the same place where he and Burroughs had their encounter, and he led them to the other site. For twenty years, Halt had assumed they were the same. Now it was learned that the same identical indentations existed at two different locations, suggesting that either two craft were present or else the same one landed twice.[17] And as I had theorized, Penniston said he did submit a sanitized version of the events in his affidavit. He was afraid that if he were too specific with the details, his mental stability might have been questioned, which could have jeopardized his career.[18]

As for the pictures he took, the film was completely blank—they never come out. Sergeant Monroe Nevels and Master Sergeant Ray Gulyas had also taken pictures of the landing site the next day and said their film came back all fogged.[19] Although it could have been caused by some form of radiation, Halt suspects that someone substituted their film with the fogged rolls.

And something else was revealed in the program—something that suggested a major cover-up.

Jim Penniston said that in 1994, he was seeing a psychiatrist because he was having terrible nightmares. The psychiatrist suggested it might be best to use hypnosis to get to the root of the problem, and Penniston said he finally consented, and what he revealed during the session was quite disturbing. Under hypnosis, he explained that Sodium Pentothal was injected into his arm by DS8 agents during an interrogation—and he had no conscious memory of it. He said he'd never heard of DS8 and had no idea what it was.[20]

According to Nick Pope, who for a few years handled UFO reports for the British Ministry of Defence, DS8 stands for "Defence Secretariat 8," a civilian division within the air force side of the MoD, which handled UFO investigations.

When Penniston was asked (under hypnosis) if he thought that what he saw might have been extraterrestrial, he said he thought it probably had something to do with the military. During the filming in Rendlesham Forest, he said that from a professional standpoint, he does not believe in extraterrestrials, although his personal views are quite different. However, he did state that after the hypnosis session, his nightmares stopped.

Halt suggests that Larry Warren may also have been mentally "meddled with" by OSI agents, so his memories would include a series of bizarre details as a form of disinformation intended to muddy the waters of those looking into the case. Warren's later claim of approaching the craft and seeing aliens did tend to diminish his credibility. Warren claims he was interrogated by what he believed were OSI agents. They told him that what he saw has been known about for a long time, and that there was a legitimate reason why it had to be kept secret. He also said that he was shown gun camera footage of UFOs taken from military aircraft.[21] But how much of his story may be true and how much may be programmed memories is anyone's guess.

Airman Ed Cabansag, who was in the woods on the first night, said that when he was interrogated, the investigators would not allow him to present his own account of what happened; he said he was coerced into signing a statement claiming that what he saw was the lighthouse beacon.[22]

Sergeant Adrian Bustinza said that intelligence agents interrogated him for hours and told him that what he really saw was the beam from the lighthouse. He persistently stated that was not true, until they casually mentioned that "bullets are cheap," at which point he relented and signed the statement saying it was the lighthouse beacon.[23] Larry Warren claims that the same statement ("bullets are cheap") was also made during his interrogation.

But Warren's account still lies under a cloud of suspicion because Colonel Halt stated in a later documentary that he interviewed everyone who was in the woods that night, and no one remembered seeing Larry Warren there.[24] Another reason to doubt his story is that although he stated that he was part of a second search, not one member of that team has come forward to confirm any part of what he claims to have seen. So Warren is either a liar or he was singled out as a patsy to create disinformation with the false memory of the events he described, thereby making him appear to be a publicity-seeking opportunist. The least credible parts of his story would seem to be his claim of seeing aliens, shown gun camera footage of UFOs, and being told that what he had seen has been known for a long time. If the government was trying to hush up the incident, why would they divulge such information, especially to someone with the lowest rank of airman? And if no one saw him in the woods on the night in question, as stated by Colonel Halt, it would appear that he was just using the event as an opportunity to get his own name in the newspapers. However, we cannot rule out the possibility that he was being used to create disinformation. He was the only one who claims to have seen cameras set up and a red ball of light descend into a glowing patch of fog and transform into a structured object. So perhaps this is the truth part of his "programmed memory" that actually happened. Of course, this is only speculation.

There are a couple of other details that warrant attention. First is Sergeant Penniston's claim that he was standing next to the craft and was suddenly twenty feet away, standing next to Airman Burroughs. He apparently does not remember moving to that position—or how he got there. Second is Airman Burroughs's statement that everything was like slow motion during the encounter. I refer to these aberrations as perceptual distortion. It is an element of the puzzle that has been described by many UFO witnesses, and in the preface, I described my own personal experience that occurred in 1955.

There are theories that UFO propulsion systems use a technology that distorts time and space; this could explain why they sometimes appear to morph and can make ninety-degree turns at phenomenal speeds. So perceptual distortion could be a side effect of being too close to the craft, at least where Sergeant Penniston and Airman Burroughs are concerned.

However, considering the other testimonies in this case regarding OSI and DS8 agents, it could also be the result of mental manipulation designed to suppress, alter, or distort details of people's memories as a form of disinformation.

Then there is Sergeant Smith's missing time and his vague memory of standing on the roof of a building. This is difficult to account for since, unlike the others, he was never in close proximity to any craft, at least that he remembers. If he was, then it happened after leaving the WSA tower, in which case his memory could also have been altered.

Another interesting detail is that Colonel Halt sent a memo to the British Ministry of Defence regarding the events, yet he never received a response. He expected that someone would pay him a visit and debrief him, but it never happened. Why? James Easton corresponded with the MoD regarding this matter and received a reply stating that Halt's memo was received—two weeks after the events occurred—and although the incident had been investigated, there was no indication that the security of the base had been compromised.

So the MoD claims they did investigate, yet they never talked to Colonel Halt. If they had conducted an investigation, they surely would have debriefed Halt, and after hearing his account, they may not have dismissed the incident so quickly. Even allowing for the fact that he sent the memo two weeks later (because he knew the liaison officer he was sending it to was away for that period), would they not at least owe him the courtesy of a reply? Even if there were nothing to the events, would it not have been to their advantage to brief Halt? He could have debunked the whole thing from the start.

I am not a conspiracy freak, but something smells here. The Sci Fi Channel's presentation revealed that witnesses were forced to sign false statements playing down the significance of the event, and that DS8 and OSI agents intimidated witnesses and mentally manipulated the memory of at least one with Sodium Pentothal. This implies that mind control tactics were used to control how and what a person would remember of the event. It has a very strong odor of disinformation.

Now, to make another point, I need to refer back to Roswell.

Assuming that a disc did crash on the Foster ranch in Corona, New Mexico, the remains of its crew lay out in the open for almost a week, exposed to the elements and in plain sight of any search team looking for them. Other evidence suggests these recoveries may have been made at one or two different locations. Regardless of where the crash, or crashes, occurred, it would appear that no attempt was made by the aliens to locate and recover them. Why?

We can assume that the crash victims were not alone—that they had a base, probably on a mother ship somewhere in the earth's orbit, and that they would have been missed when they failed to return. When we have missing aircraft, we launch an intensive search that can last for days. We recover aircraft wreckage and literally reassemble it in an effort to learn what happened, and we also retrieve bodies. We even plan for such situations by installing locater beacons in aircraft to aid in finding them should they go down. So are we to believe that beings capable of traversing light-years of space would not possess the means to locate one of their own missing craft?

One possibility is that they purposely left the wreckage and bodies for us to retrieve, and if so, we have to question why they would allow us such an opportunity. Surely they would have known we would take advantage of the situation in order to study their technology. However, if extraterrestrials are accelerating our evolution in order to survive a future cataclysmic event, it suggests that they are a benevolent species, which raises the question of why they would show no compassion for their dead. I draw no conclusions on this matter, but I do consider the possibility that there is more than one alien race visiting Earth. If one happened to be an adversary, there may be occasional confrontations. Could this be what happened in Roswell, the crashed ship and its crew being the losers?

The point is that regardless of where the crash (or crashes) occurred, it would appear they did not attempt to find it, nor was any attempt made to prevent us from recovering the wreckage and the bodies. Why? Was it a gesture on their part—a means of providing us with something as a prelude to actual contact? I suspect that if contact was established, it occurred sometime later, after the government became desensitized to their presence. They may have revealed who they were and why they were here, after which they reached an agreement whereby they would provide us with some limited technology, but only if we agreed not to use nuclear weapons in warfare and *not to interfere in their activities*, such as abducting people for whatever purpose they were abducting them for. But again, this is only speculation.

If an extraterrestrial spacecraft was retrieved from Roswell, it may have taken decades to unravel some of the technology because it probably would have involved a dimension of science that was incomprehensible at the time. It would be like transporting a new automobile back in time to the seventeenth century. The people might eventually figure out how to turn the ignition key and start it, and maybe even drive it around a little, but they would not understand the technology. They would not have the fuel to make it run, nor the tools and machinery, let alone the faintest idea of how to build one. With no electricity, satellites, or radio stations, they would have no idea what an AM/FM radio or a GPS system was for. So if a UFO did crash, it is unlikely that even by 1980 we would have learned enough to put on the show that Jim Penniston, John Burroughs, and Colonel Halt witnessed—and especially what Larry Warren allegedly observed.

Halt suggests that Warren's memory may have been altered for the purpose of creating disinformation. Disinformation is false information salted with some of the truth. The question is, what part of Warren's story is true and what part is false? If what he said about cameras being set up in the field is the truth part, I am left with the impression that the lights Colonel Halt and his men followed were decoys luring them away from the demonstration area. If we had perfected the technology to duplicate what any of these men described, the unfortunate events of the following night in Huffman, Texas, in all probability would never have occurred.

The Huffman Incident

It was about nine o'clock on the night of December 29, 1980, when Betty Cash, Vickie Landrum, and Landrum's seven-year-old grandson, Colby, were returning to Dayton from New Caney. They were driving south on Highway 1485, just outside of Huffman, Texas, when they noticed a bright light about three miles ahead. As they drew closer, the light approached the road and began to maneuver up and down. Whenever it got close to the ground, it would emit a burst of flame and then rise and hover above treetop level.

Betty stopped about 150 feet from the object; it was larger than her car and diamond shaped, with a bank of blue lights around the middle. It emitted a glow that hurt their eyes and illuminated the trees along both sides of the road. Betty got out, walked to the front of the car, and stared at the object. Vickie kept urging her to get back inside the car. Betty said that an intermittent beeping sound was coming from the craft, and that she could feel a heat burning her skin. When she went to open the car door, the handle had become so hot that she burned her hand and had to protect it with her coat to get it open.

The temperature was about forty degrees, and they had been using the car's heater to keep warm. Now the heat had become so intense that she had to turn on the air conditioner. Then, as the object started to move away, a swarm of large helicopters appeared overhead. Betty started the car and continued down the highway. She said the object was still visible in the distance and lighting up the surrounding area as well as the helicopters.

Upon reaching Dayton, she dropped off Vickie and Colby and went home. Within a few hours, her skin turned red, as though she had severe sunburn. Her neck swelled up, and her face broke out in blisters; she became nauseated and spent most of the night vomiting. Although not as severe, Vickie and Colby suffered the same symptoms. Within a few days, Betty became so weak that she had to be hospitalized. Her hair began falling out; her eyes became sore and were practically swollen shut for a week.[25] All three continued to suffer from these symptoms for the next two years. Betty, however, suffered the most: her health continued to decline, and she developed various types of cancer. She was hospitalized numerous times, had to give up her business, and suffered financial ruin. Ironically, on December 29, 1998, the eighteenth anniversary of her encounter, Betty Cash died.

I think the key element to this event is the helicopters. Colby and his grandmother counted twenty-three. The sketches they made suggest they were CH-47 Chinooks, huge helicopters with two overhead rotors, designed to transport troops and equipment. Air force investigators later interviewed everyone and showed them silhouettes of various types of helicopters, and they all identified the Chinook.

Detective Sergeant Lamar Walker of the Dayton Police Department was off duty that night and driving through the Huffman area with his wife when they encountered a number of large helicopters. They were flying low to the ground with searchlights turned on, and one of them sidled toward his car, blinding him with its light. At first, he thought they might be searching for a downed aircraft, but then he said they moved out of the area.[26] Could it be that one of the choppers intentionally blinded him to prevent him from seeing the same craft that Betty Cash and her companions encountered?

But why were twenty-three troop-carrying helicopters in the Huffman area that night, flying low to the ground with searchlights on, as witnessed by Detective Walker, and following the strange craft that Betty Cash and her companions encountered bobbing up and down over the highway? Could it be that they were escorting the craft? Chinooks are not pursuit aircraft; again, they are designed to transport troops and equipment. This implies that they were escorts, and that the craft was probably experimental. If something went wrong and it had to make an emergency landing, armed security personnel riding in the helicopters (which in this case is what one would expect to be aboard the large troop-carrying craft) would immediately be available to secure the area. What would be the point of having twenty-three empty troop-carrying helicopters escort the craft?

It would appear that Cash and her friends were victims of the military's experimenting with a new technology. The air force denied any knowledge of the incident and refused to accept responsibility. The victims were never compensated for the hospital and medical expenses they incurred, and since there was no possible way for them to substantiate their claims, the government simply ignored them; to honor them would be admitting they did know something.

So where did this craft come from—from what base? What was it doing near Huffman, and where was it going? What base were the Chinooks from? Investigators attempting to find answers to these questions have run into a brick wall. However, the big mystery would seem to be the diamond-shaped craft—with what kind of technology were they experimenting? Betty Cash said it was surrounded by a bank of blue lights. Larry Warren described something similar in Rendlesham Forest during his encounter, and so did Airman Burroughs. These similarities raise the question of whether the events might be related in some way.

Warren's account (if it is true) suggests a demonstration of technology that defies logic, and it was carried out with extreme precision by materializing a solid structured object out of a glowing patch of fog. By contrast, the object in the Huffman encounter demonstrated a lack of polished precision by bouncing up and down over the highway and exposing three civilians to a severe dose of radiation poisoning. If Warren's story is on the level and cameras were set up to record the event, then the aliens may be teaching us something about interdimensional technology or providing us with demonstrations of its applications, which could mean that somewhere along the way, we did establish contact.

Area 51

Over the last two decades, the Groom Lake area of Nellis Air Force Base in Nevada has attracted the attention of many UFO buffs. It has been called Dreamland and Paradise Ranch, but it is commonly known as Area 51. Each day, government passenger jets depart from a secured section of McCarran International Airport in Las Vegas, shuttling approximately fifteen-hundred workers to the site. In monitoring the aircraft frequencies, we find they are identified by the code name "Janet." A bus with blacked-out windows transports those who are afraid to fly. For years, the air force denied the existence of the Groom Lake base, and it no longer appears on maps. It is where the F-117 stealth fighter and the B-2 bomber were developed and kept secret for nearly a decade. Until several years ago, you could view the base from Freedom Ridge or Whitesides Mountain, about twelve miles to the east. Recent satellite images and the video footage taken from these locations reveal a huge complex of large hangars and the longest runway in the world.

Rumors of UFO crash retrievals being tested at this facility resulted in many people coming to these remote desert locations to see for themselves. But all the sudden attention prompted the air force to take over another four thousand acres of public land, which included these prime viewing sites. However, with a good telephoto lens, it can still be seen from Tikaboo Peak, twenty-six miles to the east.

The area around Freedom Ridge and Whitesides is now patrolled by heavily armed Wackenhut security personnel driving unmarked four-wheel-drive vehicles. Motion detectors and devices that can detect human odors further enhance security. Signs posted along the perimeter indicate that they are authorized to use deadly force against intruders, which means if you take one step over the line, they have the right to shoot you. Video footage taken from these sites before the military took them over suggests that the government is experimenting with new aerodynamic technologies: one clip shows an extremely fast object literally looping around a conventional aircraft.[27]

It appears that aliens may also be interested in the activities there. A video clip that was allegedly smuggled out of Area 51 several years ago shows an anomalous object that suddenly appeared out of nowhere. One of the radar-controlled cameras was tracking it on the range, and judging from the radio chatter in the background, it had everyone a little unnerved because it wasn't supposed to be there. When the clip was analyzed, it appeared by its actions that the object reacted to the fact that it was being tracked and seemed to show an interest in the radar camera tracking it. It also revealed that the object continuously morphed and manifested a black area from which no density reading could be obtained, even though the equipment being used was state of the art and could define detail in the blackest of images.[28]

From what researchers have learned about Area 51, security is extremely tight. All personnel plus anything they carry, such as briefcases, purses, and bags, are searched when they enter and leave the facility. So it would seem very unlikely that a video clip like the one described would have actually made it off the base. But if the clip is authentic, one must consider the probability that it was purposely intended to create disinformation. Since Area 51 is used primarily for the development and testing of new top secret aircraft, it seems rather unlikely that UFO crash retrievals would be kept there. It is more probable that any reverse engineering of alien technology or spacecraft would be conducted at a location that is even more secret than Area 51.

Allegedly, there is such a site, called S-4, and it is completely hidden from view behind a mountain fifteen miles southwest of Area 51. Those claiming to have worked there say it is where UFO crash retrievals are actually being back-engineered and tested. They are allegedly housed behind large hangars doors that are camouflaged to blend with the base of the mountain. There are no photographs or notarized testimonies to substantiate these claims; however, one cannot rule out the possibility.

The S-4 site was originally brought to the public's attention by Bob Lazar, a scientist who claims to have worked there, reverse engineering the propulsion system of a UFO. I tend to have mixed feelings about Lazar because on one hand, he comes across as completely legitimate, but on the other, his credentials lack credibility. He claims that he has a master's degree in physics from MIT and one in electronics from the California Institute of Technology, yet he cannot name any of his professors. Why? When Stanton Friedman investigated his background, he found no records of him having attending either institute. Lazar also claimed that he worked at Los Alamos National Laboratory. A phone directory from the time he worked there does list his name, but Friedman says that he was there as an employee of an outside contractor. So Friedman believes he is a phony.[29]

George Knapp, a newsman at KLAS-TV in Las Vegas, Nevada, interviewed Lazar extensively, and he believes he is credible. And so does John Lear, whose father founded the Learjet Corporation. Lear claims that Lazar took him out into the desert near Area 51 on the nights he knew they would be test flying the craft he was working on, and Lear claims that he witnessed these flights.[30] So if Lazar knew when these tests would be conducted, it would seem to give him some measure of credibility.

There are only three possibilities to consider regarding Bob Lazar and his claims: he is a well-educated crackpot who very cleverly put one over on a lot of people; his credentials and educational records were "erased" by the government in order to discredit him (which they have apparently done on other occasions), or he is part of a government disinformation campaign designed to gradually educate the public on the reality of the UFO issue. Disinformation will be covered in the next chapter.

Official Disinterest

Over the last thirty years, one detail that I believe is both important and revealing has become evident. It appears there has been a gradual decline of official interest regarding what is clearly hard evidence. Take the Mansfield, Ohio, incident, where a UFO lifted an army helicopter in a beam of green light. There were four men on that chopper, and the pilots filed an official report, yet there never was an investigation or a debriefing. Why? The Rendlesham Forest case occurred at a major nuclear weapons facility and involved the deputy base commander. Several witnesses were intimidated into signing false statements, and one was subjected to mind control using Sodium Pentothal. Aside from this, there was once again no official debriefing of any of the witnesses, including Colonel Halt. One can only conclude that the evidence was purposely ignored, and we have to ask why.

Today, people all over the world are videotaping UFOs, and there is a noticeable similarity in many of the images, suggesting they are not hoaxes. Different people in Gulf Breeze, Florida, have videotaped similar metallic objects hovering in the sky and suddenly zooming away at four thousand miles per hour. There is footage of a cylindrical object hovering over the coastline, appearing to have rotating parts, and it closely resembles an object videotaped near Las Vegas.[31] With state-of-the-art technology, the military can enhance and analyze these images, so why wasn't this done? Unless they are holograms or someone has found a way to videotape hallucinations, these objects are real.

In the past, many photographs and film footage of UFOs taken by civilians were confiscated or borrowed by alleged military or government investigators with the promise that they would be returned, but they never were. Fifty years ago in Roswell, the military cleaned up all evidence at the crash site and confiscated little souvenirs picked up by individuals, and if the accounts are true, they terrorized some witnesses into silence with death threats. All of a sudden, encounters by military personnel and the best civilian video evidence seem not to arouse even the slightest interest—why? Why is it being ignored? *How can the government not be interested?*

The only logical theory is that further pursuit and acquirement of evidence is unnecessary because contact has been established and the government knows exactly what these objects are and who is flying them. If there really was a movie and video camera set up in Rendlesham Forest, it means someone knew the event would take place at that location and at that particular time and was prepared to record it. And if it were a scheduled demonstration, it would preclude any need for an investigation. But you would think they at least would have gone through the motions; completely ignoring the incident should have aroused some suspicion and curiosity.

We know that several witnesses were intimidated into signing false statements, and that the memory of at least one witness was altered with chemicals. However, using coercion and mind control tactics is not an investigation; such actions are indicative of a cover-up. In an investigation, a witness is debriefed and information is collected—this did not happen in either the Mansfield, Ohio, or the Rendlesham Forest case. Except for Colonel Halt, the memories of some witnesses were altered to confuse details, and others were coerced into signing statements that were contradictory to the facts. This can only mean one thing—something was being covered up. A legitimate UFO investigation would include the debriefing of witnesses in an attempt to learn what they are, who is in control of them, why they are here, and possibly, to learn something about their technology. Since the government no longer seems to show any interest in good hard evidence, the implication is that they already have the answers.

◆◆◆◆◆

So far, the evidence seems to be building a strong case for UFOs. I suppose it is possible that the US and British governments were covering up some new top secret technology in the Rendlesham Forest case, but logistically, it seems that mind control tactics would be counterproductive to maintaining secrecy. Eventually, these stories were sure to be revealed, and once that happened, it would only draw more attention to the incident. A simple debriefing would have been more effective; the witnesses would have been questioned and their statements taken, and that would have been the end of it. Using underhanded tactics like intimidation and mind control would leave a bad taste that would linger for years and might never be forgotten. Could this have been done purposely as a form of disinformation meant to maintain the public's interest in UFOs?

Of course, this is only theoretical, but as we will see in the next chapter, it could be a real possibility.

Notes

1.   Penniston's description of craft
       UFO Invasion at Rendlesham. Documentary. Prod. John Gengl.
       THC.

2.   Object gone in the blink of an eye
       UFO Invasion at Rendlesham. Documentary. Prod. John Gengl.
       THC.

3.   Indentations at landing site
       UFO Invasion at Rendlesham. Documentary. Prod. John Gengl.
       THC.

4.   John Burroughs's Account
       Rendlesham Forest Incident. Documentary. Unsolved Mysteries.
       Lifetime.

5.   Malfunctioning Light-alls
       Rendlesham Forest Incident. Documentary. Unsolved Mysteries.
       Lifetime.

6   Object exploded into five small white objects and disappeared
       Rendlesham Forest Incident. Documentary. Unsolved Mysteries.
       Lifetime.

7.   Sergeant Robert Ball suggesting grid search pattern
       Rendlesham Forest Incident. Documentary. Unsolved Mysteries.
       Lifetime.

8.   Object emits beam in front of Colonel Halt's team
       UFO Invasion at Rendlesham. Documentary. Prod. John Gengl.
       THC.

9. Lights seen over WSA
    UFO Invasion at Rendlesham. Documentary. Prod. John Gengl. THC.

10. Larry Warren's account
    UFO Invasion at Rendlesham. Documentary. Prod. John Gengl. THC.

11. Larry Warren's claim of seeing aliens
    Britain's Roswell. Documentary. Prod. David Digangi. THC.

12. Civilian witness Gerry Harris
    "UFOs: Then and Now? Cause For Alarm." *UFO Files.* Prod. Joshua Alper. THC.

13. Red light dripping like molten metal from a crucible
    "UFOs: Then and Now? Cause For Alarm." *UFO Files.* Prod. Joshua Alper. THC.

14. Interview with lighthouse keeper
    "Military vs. UFOs." *UFO Hunters.* Prod. Chad Horning/Autumn Humphries. THC.

15. Rendlesham forest incident—Penniston drawing #1
    Link to image: www.ufocasebook.com/Rendlesham2.html

16. Rendlesham forest incident—Penniston drawing #2
    Link to image: www.ufocasebook.com/Rendlesham2.html

17. Two different landing sites
    UFO Invasion at Rendlesham. Documentary. Prod. John Gengl. THC.

18.   Penniston submitted sanitized version in affidavit
        UFO Invasion at Rendlesham. Documentary. Prod. John Gengl.
        THC.

19.   Fogged film
        UFO Invasion at Rendlesham. Documentary. Prod. John Gengl.
        THC.

20.   Penniston's hypnosis session
        UFO Invasion at Rendlesham. Documentary. Prod. John Gengl.
        THC.

21.   Warren's bizarre interrogation
        UFO Invasion at Rendlesham. Documentary. Prod. John Gengl.
        THC.

22.   Cabansag coerced to sign false statement
        UFO Invasion at Rendlesham. Documentary. Prod. John Gengl.
        THC.

23.   Bustinza coerced to sign false statement
        Britain's Roswell. Documentary. Prod. David Digangi. THC.

24.   Larry Warren not seen in woods
        Britain's Roswell. Documentary. Prod. David Digangi. THC.

25.   The Huffman incident
        "The Huffman Incident." *Unsolved Mysteries.* NBC. WPTV. West
        Palm Beach.

26.   Detective Walker saw helicopters
        "Alien Fallout." *UFO Hunters.* Prod. Jon Alon Walz. THC.

27. Video of object over Area 51
UFOs and Alien Encounters. Documentary. Prod, Michael Tetrick. TLC.

28. Video analysis of object over Area 51
"Intruders on the Range." *Sightings.* Dir. Ted Mesirow. Sci Fi (now Syfy).

29. Stanton Friedman on Bob Lazar's credibility
Web link:
www.stantonfriedman.com/index.php?ptp=articles&fdt=2011.01.07

30. John Lear on Bob Lazar's credibility
"Area 51 Revealed." *UFO Hunters.* John Walz. THC. 2009.

31. Similar cylindrical objects over Florida coastline and Las Vegas
UFOs Above and Beyond. Documentary. Prod. Chris Wyatt. TLC. 2003.

Chapter 9

DISINFORMATION

The government surely had to be concerned about what was going on during the First and Second World Wars when strange little balls of light began buzzing our planes. The pilots nicknamed them "foo fighters," and they outperformed our most advanced aircraft in both speed and maneuverability. Initially, military officials feared the enemy had developed a new secret weapon. However, after the war we learned pilots on all sides of the conflict had encountered them, thinking it was something the United States had developed. We know that the pilots photographed them on many occasions, so we can be sure the government made some attempt to learn what they were and to whom they belonged.

After the war, sightings increased dramatically. In December of 1947, six months after the Roswell incident, the government created Project Sign to investigate the phenomena. After studying less than 250 sightings in a little over a year, they concluded that UFOs posed no threat to national security. So Project Sign was discontinued—or so it seemed. Actually, it continued under a different name—Project Grudge. Like Sign, Grudge studied less than 250 cases and then announced that UFOs were nothing but hoaxes, hallucinations, conventional aircraft, weather balloons, ball lightning, or the planet Venus. But if, according to Project Sign, UFOs were no threat, then why was there a need to continue the investigation—and under a different name? What is wrong with this picture? What was the real purpose of Project Grudge?

When we read between the lines, we have to assume that "posed no threat" meant UFOs proved to be nothing more than weather balloons, hoaxes, conventional aircraft, or what have you—or that the government knew exactly what they were because they had acquired one or more that had crashed ... or possibly that contact had been established. Let's use a little common sense. Creating a second project to explain further their original conclusion makes no sense—unless they had learned something during Project Sign's investigation that they were not revealing. If they actually determined that UFOs were not a threat, they apparently presented some kind of a problem—one that they felt had to be kept from the public. So either Project Grudge was an attempt to discredit UFOs completely ... or it was the beginning of an organized disinformation campaign.

There are only two reasons I can think of that would logically explain the need for secrecy: communications and religion. Communications were not as sophisticated as they are today, and there was concern that a sudden and massive increase in reports could hinder strategic communication during a national defense emergency—something an enemy might take advantage of to launch an attack on the United States—and that would certainly justify the need for secrecy. On the other hand, if contact had been established during Sign's investigation, the knowledge that alien beings were visiting Earth would have upset the fabric of many religious beliefs. However, that alone would not have been world shattering; there had to be something more—something that would have had a devastating effect on the public and maybe the entire world if it were to become known, which, I suspect, points back to religion. This will be covered thoroughly later.

Project Grudge's "rational explanation" strategy stirred up controversy because it discredited reputable witnesses like air force and commercial airline pilots. To claim they did not, or could not, recognize Venus, weather balloons, or other aircraft, or to suggest that they were hallucinating, was to imply that they were unfit to pilot a plane. This was an insult to the intelligence of both military and civilian pilots, and it established a paradigm by which pilots who filed future UFO reports would be ostracized. If it was an attempt to tone down the UFO issue, it failed because it only drew more attention to it with the controversy it stirred up. Could this possibly have been the beginning of a campaign to desensitize the public to the facts?

If contact had been established, or was in the process of being established, the government would have needed a buffer—a pseudo organization to focus attention away from what was going on, and their next endeavor, Project Blue Book, fit that profile perfectly.

Project Blue Book was created in 1952 and headquartered in a small office at Wright Patterson Field in Dayton, Ohio. It was staffed by an air force major, a sergeant, and a secretary. Their facilities included a few desks, telephones, and filing cabinets. There were no computers back then, at least none comparable to what we have today, and there was no communications network. There were no scientists or engineers on staff to study and analyze data. Therefore, Blue Book was not equipped to carry out any scientific studies or evaluations. Its meager setting suggests that it was nothing but a low-budget facade used to control and shape public opinion. The project only investigated sightings that fell within the boundary of conventional explanation or hoaxes; many of the significant cases never appeared under the jurisdiction of Blue Book. Why?

The answer is that they were told what to investigate, or so it appeared. Those running the project had no idea what was going on because they were puppets with someone at a higher level pulling their strings. They did not run out the door to investigate a UFO sighting every time someone reported one—they did not have the workforce. And since their facilities precluded serious evaluation or scientific analysis, all they did was interview witnesses. Each case they were assigned could usually be explained as a weather balloon, hoax, or some natural phenomena; however, they were occasionally assigned a case that defied explanation, which of course left the door open to the possibility that at least some UFOs might be extraterrestrial. This could have been a strategy to ensure that public interest would not completely fade away. If there came a time for the public to be told the truth, they would have to be psychologically prepared to deal with it in order to avoid social and religious problems. And that is something that could not be done overnight. It would take time—fifty or sixty years, possibly even a century.

To enhance Blue Book's image as the air force's primary UFO investigative agency, they did have one consultant on their payroll: Dr. J. Allan Hynek, a former professor of astronomy at Ohio State University who, in 1960, became chairperson of the astronomy department at Northwestern University. He came into the program as a skeptic and attempted to explain each sighting using scientific methods of evaluation. However, he eventually realized that the air force was using him to whitewash the UFO issue by pressuring him into creating rational-sounding explanations for sightings in which there were none. It became evident to him that there was more to UFOs than the air force was admitting. In an interview filmed before he died, Hynek was diplomatic in suggesting that the air force was only doing its job, which was to prevent the public from becoming overly concerned by the fact that they had no control over the strange craft flying around in our skies.[1]

One case that impressed Hynek occurred in 1964 in Socorro, New Mexico. It began when Police Officer Lonnie Zamora was chasing a speeder on the outskirts of town and saw a bright glowing object shoot across the sky. He abandoned pursuit of the speeder and turned down a dirt road in an attempt to follow the object. Coming over a rise, he observed what he first thought was an overturned car. Then he saw that it was a white egg-shaped craft sitting on four legs; there were two rather small beings in white clothing standing on the ground beside it. When he tried to call his headquarters, he found that his radio had suddenly gone dead (a common occurrence in many UFO cases). Zamora exited his cruiser and started to approach the craft. Then he heard what sounded like a door slam and realized the two small beings had disappeared. Flames suddenly erupted from beneath the craft in a loud roar, and it began to rise from the ground.

Startled, Zamora ran behind his car and crouched down. As he watched, he said the noise and flames stopped and the object just hovered silently in the air for a while before drifting westward.[2]

After the object was gone, Zamora's radio crackled back to life, and he called for assistance. His friend Sam Chavez of the New Mexico State Police responded to the site and found Zamora quite shaken. They noted that the ground was scorched where the craft had been sitting, and branches on surrounding shrubs were scorched on the side facing the landing site. There were also indentations in the ground from the craft's landing gear, measuring eight inches long, nine inches wide, and nine inches deep.

Officials at White Sands Missile Range were notified, and within ninety minutes, a team led by Army Captain Richard T. Holder arrived at the site. In an interview on *Unsolved Mysteries*, Holder said he first thought that it might have been something classified that got away from the range, but he soon realized that that was not the case. He looked for clues that it might be a hoax, but everything seemed to back up Zamora's story.[3]

Dr. Hynek went to Socorro to examine the landing site and came away impressed by Zamora, convinced that he'd had a real encounter.[4] The air force, however, adopted the explanation that the object was probably an experimental craft. Hynek was disappointed by the air force's stand and that they would not let him present his own views on the incident.[5] Yet Hynek stayed with Blue Book until it ended in 1969. After the air force had stifled his attempts at being more objective in his investigations for so many years, he became convinced that there had to be something to the phenomena, and he founded CUFOS, the Center for UFO Studies.

But had the air force manipulated Hynek? Could this have been a strategy designed to put him in a position to where he would have a positive influence in the public sector regarding the UFO reality? Surely they knew he would eventually conclude that something was going on if they forced him to provide rational explanations for sightings that suggested extraterrestrial activity. Someone of his reputation would surely have a positive impact in the public arena if he suddenly reversed his stand as a skeptic and began his own uninhibited investigations into the phenomena. But again, this is only speculation.

Twenty-one years later, the air force came out with a new explanation for the Socorro incident. They stated that Zamora probably saw the lunar landing module that was being tested at White Sands. They produced logs from Whites Sands showing that the lander had been tested on the same day as Zamora's encounter.[6] But why? Why, twenty-one years later—after the incident had been forgotten—would they want to resurrect it with a new explanation? Surely, they knew there were some savvy UFO researchers who would launch their own investigation to see if it was true. And they did. And it wasn't!

They learned from the official records that although the lunar lander had been tested on the same day as the Socorro incident, the test ended hours before Zamora had his encounter. They also learned that at the time, the lunar lander could not fly because it was only a mock-up with no propulsion system and the test was an impact experiment in which it was dropped from a tower. Another fact was that the lander was trapezoidal in shape and in no way fit the description of the white egg-shaped craft described by Zamora. One might easily suspect this as another disinformation ploy. Why would the air force revive an old incident with a new explanation that they knew would be shot down unless it was meant to keep the UFO controversy alive?

Project Blue Book eventually outlived its usefulness, and in 1966, the air force initiated a two-year research project designed to justify its termination. And this made no sense at all. If Blue Book was of no further value, why spend thousands of taxpayer dollars on a two-year study to justify its termination? Why not just simply terminate it? Or was this another tactic to keep the controversy going?

In any case, the study was known as the Condon Committee and was headed by Dr. Edward Condon at Colorado University. It is interesting to note that a few members of the panel felt the investigation was biased from the beginning, and two committee members, David Saunders and Norman Levine, were later fired for questioning its lack of objectivity. In 1967, Condon was quoted in the New York *Star-Gazette* as saying that studying UFOs was nothing but a waste of time, and then he added, "But I'm not supposed to reach a conclusion for another year."[7]

That statement, it would appear, clearly defined the intended purpose of the committee and meant that Condon had already reached a conclusion. With a year to go and Condon's biased statement to reporters that the study was a waste of time certainly suggests it was never taken seriously from the beginning. Nevertheless, when the report was completed in 1968, the air force had the excuse it needed, and on December 17, 1969 Project Blue Book became history.

For some, the end of Blue Book was sufficient reason to believe that there never was anything to the UFO enigma. After all, if the air force was no longer interested, maybe it was all nonsense. However, an incident that occurred twelve years earlier, as recounted by the late Colonel Gordon Cooper, the astronaut who flew the longest space flight in the Mercury missions, confirmed that not only did UFOs exist, but that there was also a concerted effort by the government to cover up the evidence.

While supervising flight-testing at Edwards Air Force Base in 1957, Cooper said a saucer-shaped object flew over the heads of a film crew, lowered three landing gear, and set down a short distance away, on the dry lakebed. As the camera crew immediately headed toward the object, filming as they went, the craft suddenly lifted up, retracted the landing gear, and then tilted up and flew away at an enormous rate of speed. While the film was being developed, a courier waited in Cooper's office to pick it up. When the processing was finished, he took it straight to Washington and nothing more was ever heard about it.[8]

This is the testimony of a highly credible witness—a NASA astronaut—that a saucer-shaped craft landed on an air force base, was filmed by air force personnel, and the evidence was swiftly whisked off to the Twilight Zone.

MJ-12

Next we have the MJ-12 documents that appear to be a further dissemination of disinformation (figs. 4, 5, 6, 7, and 8). Allegedly, government agents provided film producer Jaime Shandera with a roll of undeveloped thirty-five-millimeter black-and-white film containing photos of top secret briefing documents given to then president-elect Dwight D. Eisenhower. They described a project called MJ-12 (also referred to as Majestic, Majestic-12, and MAJIC), set up by President Harry Truman. On page three was a brief outline of Kenneth Arnold's historic sighting as well as the Roswell crash, in which it says that several alien bodies had been recovered; they had been found about a week later, two miles east of the crash site, badly decomposed and partially eaten by predators. It alleges that they died after ejecting from the craft before it crashed.

On page two were the names of the twelve men running the project, one of which was the late Dr. Donald Menzel, director of Harvard College Observatory. This raised the eyebrows of many researchers because Menzel was a hard-nosed skeptic who had written three books debunking UFOs. It made no sense. Why would he be on this panel unless, as some speculate, the documents were phony and Menzel's name was included as a joke—or if it was part of an organized disinformation campaign.

Stanton Friedman was able to access Menzel's archives at Harvard University in Cambridge, Massachusetts, where he discovered that Menzel had been leading a double life. Aside from being an astronomer, he was a consultant to the CIA and the NSA and held a top secret Ultra clearance. He had worked on many classified projects and frequently visited Washington, DC, and New Mexico—all at government expense. Apparently, this part of his life had been a well-kept secret. In addition, three of Menzel's close associates were among the names listed on page two: Lloyd Berkner, executive secretary of the Joint Research and Development Board; Detlov Bronk, chairman of the National Research Council; and Vannever Bush, one of the nation's leading scientists. In spite of Menzel's public image as a devout UFO skeptic, Friedman felt that his role in MJ-12 might have been to spread disinformation, which he did by writing three books debunking them.

There has been much debate regarding the authenticity of the MJ-12 documents. Many believe they are disinformation, and if they are right, then they were created to enhance public interest in the UFO phenomena. Why would the government deny their existence and at the same time covertly spread information guaranteed to promote interest in them? There is no point to it unless it was purposely done to maintain attention through controversy.

One clue suggesting that the documents may be phony is that they were photographed on thirty-five-millimeter Tri-X black-and-white film. Now, common sense tells us that the level of security dealing with a situation as phenomenal as that described in the documents would surely negate any opportunity to photograph them. Microfilm, maybe. A microfilm camera could have been concealed in a fountain pen, a tie clip, a cigarette lighter, and so on; however, a thirty-five-millimeter camera would have been too conspicuous. It just seems too unlikely. Of course, it is possible that they were originally photographed on microfilm and later transferred to thirty-five-millimeter film for Shandera's convenience since he may not have had the facilities to work with microfilm.

If government agents really were the source of the film, then regardless of whether the documents are real or phony, it has to be disinformation. It would certainly spike the public's interest in UFOs and promote the belief in a cover-up, thus sparking more controversy. However, any subsequent publicity would provide the powers-that-be an excellent opportunity to evaluate public reaction. So unless it was someone's idea of a joke, I see no other logical explanation. Everything considered, Majestic or some other cleverly named operation probably does exist. But it would not exist unless there was a need for it. In this case, the need could only be based on the possibility that the government was somehow involved with UFOs or their occupants, thereby suggesting that contact was established with extraterrestrials, or that they recovered one or more of their ships that crashed—or both.

Being that MJ-12 is a clandestine organization, the last thing they need is publicity or some tenacious investigator nosing around and turning up clues as to what is going on behind the scenes. Sightings by air force pilots draw attention to the military and the government, as do those made by commercial airline pilots who fall under the jurisdiction of the FAA, which is a government agency. If too many investigators begin asking too many questions of too many government people, too much attention increases the risk of a leak. It seems there is always someone who knows someone who knows something.

Further evidence suggesting that the government is involved in a campaign of disinformation is the testimony of Edgar Mitchell, one of the Apollo 14 astronauts who walked on the moon on February 5, 1971. In a telephone interview from his home in Lake Worth, Florida, Mitchell was asked about Roswell. He said he has talked to many high-ranking government and military people from various countries who admitted their involvement with alien technology and hardware. He said the government is creating disinformation and the Roswell event was real, that an alien spacecraft did crash, and that material was retrieved from that crash site. When asked how the government kept the truth secret for so long, he said they were never able to maintain it, that it has been getting out into the public for fifty years or more.[9]

Until the Russians shot down Francis Gary Powers, how many people mistook a high-flying U-2 spy plane or the SR-71 Blackbird for a UFO? More recently, how many made the same mistake with an F-117 fighter or B-2 bomber? Would the air force have openly admitted that it was really a new top secret stealth aircraft they saw? Of course not. That would be announcing our secrets to the entire world, which would have included our adversaries. Therefore, it was convenient to let people believe they saw a UFO; it was the perfect diversion and another form of disinformation that kept UFOs in the news.

These stealth aircraft are now old news, and the government is developing newer, more technologically advanced aircraft that will probably generate a whole new wave of sightings. And we may already be witnessing this new era. Triangular-shaped craft, like the one photographed in Belgium,[10] and their *suspiciously frequent* appearances today suggest that many are of terrestrial origin.

The Phoenix Lights

One event involving a triangular or V-shaped craft that stirred up a cauldron of controversy (and reeks of disinformation) is the Phoenix Lights. It involved multiple witnesses and plenty of video footage. There is still some confusion in the public arena regarding the event because of the way it has been presented in various news clips and documentaries. There were two separate incidents, and many reports combined the details of both, often talking about one while showing video footage of the other. So here are the real facts as we know them.

It started around 8:15 p.m. on the evening of March 13, 1997. Police, radio, and television stations in the Phoenix area suddenly began receiving calls about a large V-shaped object with lights on the bottom, saying it was moving south. It had been observed from as far north as Henderson, Nevada, all the way to Tucson, Arizona, where it then reversed direction and headed back north.[11] Witnesses said it was extremely low, made no sound, and was as large as two or three football fields. A few witnesses said it was so low and so huge that it blocked out the entire sky above them as it passed over. Only Terry Proctor in Scottsdale is known to have videotaped this object, which is not too surprising considering that the flight path was mostly over desolate and uninhabited areas.

At 10:15 p.m., media and police switchboards again lit up with calls about a huge V-shaped craft over the Estrella mountain range behind Luke Air Force Base. This was a completely separate incident, and it created confusion in the media because people were still calling about the 8:15 sighting: it took a little while before they realized they were two separate events. This time, people all over the city were grabbing their video cameras and recording the lights. Nine different lights had appeared—one by one—forming a V-shaped pattern that many thought were lights around the edge of a large craft estimated to be at least a mile in length. Then, five minutes after the lights appeared, they began disappearing one by one, but in a different sequence than which they appeared.[12]

Originally, a spokesman at Luke Air Force Base suggested that they might be flares dropped from aircraft as part of a night exercise, which did not rate much media attention. However, in a later interview, Captain Drew Sullins of the visiting Maryland Air National Guard confirmed that on the night of March 13, a group of A-10 Thunderbolts (also called "Warthogs") conducted night illumination exercises over the Barry Goldwater test range on the south side of the Estrella mountains as part of "Operation Snowbird," in which they dropped a series of flares.[13] This was likewise confirmed by Lieutenant Colonel David Tanaka, also of the Maryland Air National Guard, in a separate and unrelated interview. Tanaka presented a map showing how they had taken off from Davis-Monthan Air Force Base in Tucson and flown northwest to the TAC range at Luke Air Force Base.[14] Logically, this would seem to explain the lights seen in Phoenix at 10:15. Most witnesses, however, were adamant that the lights were not flares and were on the north side, in front of the mountain.

A TV crew filming a documentary on the incident took the video shot by Mike Krzyston from his backyard to Leonid Rudin of Cognitech, Inc., an image-processing firm in California, along with their own daylight image of the same scene from the same location in the Krzyston's backyard. Technicians at Cognitech adjusted the images on a computer screen until the foreground details such as the ridge line of a small escarpment was perfectly matched up. This means they used a lens with basically the same focal length as that of Krzyston's video camera in order to get the closest match. Then they superimposed the daylight image over Krzyston's video footage so that both the mountains and the activity of the lights were visible. In this composite, the lights disappeared precisely where they descended behind the ridges of the mountain. Some ridges crested higher than others, revealing how, and why, they disappeared in a different sequence than which they appeared.[15] It is difficult to dispute this visual evidence: it clearly shows that the lights were not hovering in the air; they descended behind the mountain, so they probably were flares. Flares attached to parachutes slowly descending behind the mountain would only be visible for approximately five minutes, and the way they appeared fits the pattern of how they would have been dropped from aircraft.

There are basically two types of flares that are dispatched from aircraft: illumination flares and decoy flares, and they vary in color and intensity. Illumination flares are much brighter than decoy flares because their basic function is to illuminate ground targets. They can last for several minutes and are attached to parachutes. They descend slowly. Decoy flares are used mostly by fighter planes to misdirect heat-seeking missiles fired at them. They are usually dropped in clusters and normally last about ten seconds. In close-up footage, the smoky trails of illumination flares are clearly visible. However, in the footage shot by Krzyston on March 13, there is no evidence of smoky trails. But the Krzystons only had an average-style Sony video camera, and they were recording images about thirty-five miles away. Even at maximum zoom, it is doubtful that the smoke trails would be discernible at that distance. From thirty-five miles away and at night, without the mountains visible as a reference point, the slowly descending flares gave the impression of hanging in the air, like lights on a large hovering craft. This would seem to close the book on the 10:15 event. However, no one has yet been able to come up with an explanation for the 8:15 sighting.

Reports of the earlier sighting are fairly consistent regarding the size, shape, and direction of travel. Since these lights were observed across the entire state, obviously they were not flares. However, similarities evident in both sightings appear more suspicious than coincidental: (a) the flares formed a V-shaped pattern just like the lights on the craft observed earlier; (b) they gave the impression of being affixed to a solid object; and (c) the object appeared to be about a mile in length. Were the flares intended to create confusion or muddy the waters of those investigating whatever it was that flew over the state earlier? Since the object seen earlier came out of Nevada and headed back that way, many speculate that it probably came from Area 51.

Then there is Operation Snowbird, the name applied to the mission of the Maryland Air National Guard that night; allegedly, "snowbird" is a military code name for *diversion*.

So what is going on? Do we have a secret aircraft that is a mile long? Some rather large planes have been built in the last three decades, but something that large seems impractical, unless it was some new kind of lighter-than-air blimp-type craft. But why would anyone need something that big, especially if it was a new type of stealth aircraft? Unless it could become invisible, it would present one hell of a large target for an enemy to shoot at—unless it was a hologram. But who or what could project a mile-long hologram and move it across the entire state of Arizona? According to some sources, the military may have been testing a new type of holographic laser technology.

Chris and Janet Morris are experts in the field of nonlethal weapons technology who have written several books and are consultants to the Defense Department and various intelligence agencies. They said that we do have the means at our disposal to create such a hologram, but because of their work, they could not elaborate. However, they did mention Fort Huachuca, the Army's electronic proving ground located on the Arizona/Mexican border, the most likely place to develop such technology.[16] This presents the possibility that the object that flew across the entire state of Arizona may have been a hologram—possibly generated from a satellite in a geosynchronous orbit. It also brings into question the large low-flying UFO videotaped over Mexico City six months later, on August 6, 1997.

The Mexico City UFO Video

The Mexico City video was featured in the TV documentary *Danger in Our Skies: The New UFO Threat*, which aired on the UPN Network (now the CW Television Network). It showed a huge wobbling disc-shaped object slowly passing behind several tall buildings before vanishing behind one of them. The tape was originally sent to Jaime Mausson, a television personality who hosted Mexico's version of 60 Minutes, but because the videographer was anonymous, its validity was in question. And such a huge craft flying so low over the city should have been noticed by thousands of people, yet no one reported seeing it.

Mausson aired the tape making no claims to its authenticity, but he asked the viewers to contact him if they recognized the buildings or the area where the tape was shot. By the next day, he received numerous responses from people familiar with the location. The next step was to pinpoint the videographer's location, and it didn't take long for Mausson and his crew to narrow it down to one building. From the outside, it looked like any average multistory office building, except there were no signs or any indication as to who occupied the structure or what kind of business was being conducted inside. In attempting to gain entry, they found the doors locked. A security officer who refused to answer any questions soon confronted them and escorted them off the property. Apparently, someone inside the building shot the video. But who? And what was going on inside that was so secret? Was there a connection?[17]

The visible haze over the city when the tape was shot would have enhanced a holographic image, but from where was it projected? Logic suggests that it was from a different location simply because the craft moved in and out of sight as it passed behind buildings, something that would seem rather impossible to control from the videographer's location. And why a UFO? Why not something more conventional like a balloon, a kite, or a small plane? When you consider the technology and the cost of the equipment needed to create such an illusion, it is well beyond the means of most people, so the logical assumption is that the government or some large corporation was involved. And if they were only videotaping a holographic experiment, why leak it to the media with no explanation? Was it just another form of disinformation sponsored by the government? If not, then who could afford to perpetrate such a hoax—and why?

The footage was only thirty seconds long, at least what was shown on the air, which might explain why no one reported seeing it. However, Mausson found one witness, a little girl who described the object perfectly, including its wobbling motion. Her testimony seemed credible because she did not know Mausson and had never seen his program. And what about the videographer? He had to know when and where it would be projected in order to videotape it. Since the building from which it was taped seemed to be off limits to the public, for the videographer to be inside suggests that he was involved with whatever was going on there. And the fact that his tape was anonymously leaked to the media strongly suggests disinformation.

If the government is playing around with holography, it could explain the spectacular maneuvers executed by many UFOs, especially some of those videotaped in Gulf Breeze, Florida. On more than one occasion, a metallic-looking object was filmed hovering motionless in the sky before instantly zooming off at four thousand miles per hour.[18] Was it the result of suddenly swinging the projector away from the point of focus? It would be the same as shining the beam of a laser pointer on the ceiling and then swiftly turning it away. The higher the ceiling, the farther the image of the beam is from the source (projector) and the faster it moves when the source is turned away. And the fact that the exact same maneuver of the same type of object was recorded by different people at different times appears rather suspicious. When you consider that Pensacola Naval Air Station is situated directly across the bay from Gulf Breeze, it presents some interesting possibilities. Was someone generating the sightings from this base, and if so, why?

Of course, it is only theoretical, but holography could account for many recent sightings of huge triangular craft. This could be a strategic defense tool, so why risk its exposure by using it to create UFOs for people to get excited over—unless it is part of a disinformation campaign.

When it comes to holography, it appears that UFOs may also be applying this technology in some cases. There have been many recorded sightings in which a UFO suddenly seemed to split into two or more objects … and where one or more objects seem to merge into one. Was the UFO utilizing holographic technology to create the illusion of being more than one craft? Over two decades ago, Irene Granchi, one of South America's leading UFO researchers, investigated a sighting made by a little girl in southern Brazil. The girl said she saw a UFO hovering in the sky, adding that it was emitting a beam of light. She said the beam was aimed a short distance away, at the place where her mother and sisters were. According to Granchi, the girl's mother said they were just sitting there watching the clouds when suddenly images of Christ and the Blessed Virgin appeared before them. Granchi suggests it was a hologram projected from the UFO.[19] But why would a UFO be projecting images of a religious nature? If this event is true, it tends to suggest that UFOs and the deity may somehow be related.

One event that occurred in 1995 may have provided an opportunity to create even more disinformation. Transcripts and tape recordings of the incident were acquired through the Freedom of Information Act, so it is a highly credible case, and the evidence cannot be disputed. Although the size of the craft involved was immense, what truly makes it unique is that it involved communications between an airline pilot, an air traffic control center, an air force base, an F-117A fighter pilot, and NORAD.[20]

It began on the evening of May 25, 1995, when America West flight 564 took off from Tampa, Florida, headed to Las Vegas, Nevada. It was a Boeing 757 piloted by Captain Eugene Tollefson, and in the copilot's seat was his first officer, John J. Waller. At a certain point over Texas, they switched the radio frequency to the air traffic control center in Albuquerque, New Mexico.

AW-564:   *"Cactus 564 going direct Crow; Crow 6 arrival Las Vegas."*

ATC: *"Cactus 564 ... Albuquerque Center. Good evening."*

AW-564:   *"564 at 39,000."*

A short time later, they encountered something unusual over Texas.

AW-564:   *"Cactus 564 ... Off to our 3:00. We got some strobes out there. Could you tell us what it is?"*

169

ATC: *"Uh- uh ... I'll tell you what—that's some ... uh, right now I don't know what it is right now. That is a restricted area that is used by the military out there during the daytime."*

AW-564: *"Yeah ... it's pretty odd."*

ATC: *"Hold on. Let me see if anybody else knows around here."*

AW-564: *"Cactus 564 ... Can you paint that object at all on your radar?"*

ATC: *"Cactus 564 ... No, I don't, and in talkin' to three or four guys around here, no one knows what that is, never heard about that."*

AW-564: *"Cactus 564 ... Nobody's painting it at all?"*

ATC: *"Cactus 564, say again?"*

AW-564: *"I said there's nothing on their radars, on the other centers at all ... on that object that's up in the air?"*

Apparently, the fact that it was airborne took the controller by surprise.

ATC: *"Uh ... IT'S UP IN THE AIR?"*

AW-564: *"A-ffirmative!"*

ATC: *"No ... no one knows anything about it. What's the altitude about?"*

AW-564: *"I don't know—probably right around 30,000 or so. And it's ... uh ... there's a strobe that starts ... uh, going, uh, counterclockwise, and uh, the length is unbelievable."*

When the object moved in front of an active thundercloud and lightning flashed, the crew got a better look and estimated it to be three to four-hundred feet long.

Air traffic control called Cannon AFB in Clovis, New Mexico, to see if any military aircraft or weather balloons were in the area.

ATC:	*"Cannon 21."*
Cannon:	*"Cannon—go ahead."*
ATC:	*"Hey, do you guys know if there was anything like a tethered balloon released that should be above Taiban?"*
Cannon:	*"Uh, no, we haven't heard nothing about it."*
ATC:	*"A guy at 39,000 says he sees something at 30,000, and the length is unbelievable, and it has a strobe on it."*
Cannon:	*"Uh-huh."*
ATC:	*"This is not good."*
Cannon:	*"Uh, wha ... what does that mean?"*
ATC:	*(laughing) "I don't know. It's a UFO or something; it's that Roswell crap again!"*
Cannon:	*"Where's it at now?"*
ATC:	*"He says it's right in Taiban."*
Cannon:	*"It's right in Taiban?"*
ATC:	*"Yeah!"*

Cannon: *"No, we haven't seen nothing like that."*

ATC: *"Okay, keep your eyes open."*

Cannon: *"I'll talk to you. (mumbled)"*

An F-117A Nighthawk from the 49th Fighter Wing at Holloman AFB was in the air, and air traffic control alerted the pilot to look out for the object. His call sign was "Hawk 85."

ATC: *"Hawk 85, in the next two to three minutes, be looking off to your right side … If you see anything about 30,000 feet … One aircraft reported something … It wasn't a weather balloon or anything; it was a long white-looking thing with a strobe on it. Let me know if you see anything out there."*

Hawk 85:   *"You got any traffic off our left wing right now?"*

ATC: *"I've got something passing off your 9:00 in about 12 at 31 westbound …"*

Hawk 85:   *"It actually looks like something about a little lower than us just went off our left wing."*

Moments later the object flew by flight 564, and the pilot contacted Albuquerque again.

AW-564:   *"We're all huddled up here talking about it. With the lightning, you could see the dark object. It was like a cigar shape from the altitude we could see it, and the length is what got us sort of confused because it looked like it was three to four hundred feet long. So I don't know if it's a wire with a strobe on it, but the strobe starts going left, then goes right counterclockwise, and it was a pretty eerie sight."*

The object disappeared from 564's view, and ATC then contacted NORAD's Western Air Defense Sector headquarters at McCord Air Force Base in Tacoma, Washington.

ATC: *"I've got something unusual, and I was wanting to know if you all happened to know of anything going on out here. I had a couple of aircraft report something three hundred to four hundred feet long, cylindrical in shape with a strobe ..."*

NORAD: *"Oh?"*

ATC: *"At 30,000 feet."*

NORAD: *"We don't have anything going on up there that I know of."*

ATC: *"This guy definitely saw it run all the way down the side of the airplane. It's right out of the X-Files. It's a definite UFO or something like that."*

NORAD: *"And you all are serious about this?"*

ATC: *"Yeah, he's real serious about it too, and he looked at it, saw it."*

NORAD: *"Holy s#@*!"* (It appears the tape may have been edited, changing the expletive to "holy smokes.")

Thirteen minutes later, NORAD called Albuquerque back.

NORAD: *"We had someone call here earlier about a pilot spotting an unidentified flying object."*

ATC: *"Yep, that's us."*

NORAD: *"We're tracking, uh, a search only track where that might have happened … It's tracking about 390 knots. Uh, we, uh, we've been tracking it for about three, four minutes now. I mean, to be going that fast, it's gotta' be up kind of high."*

ATC: *"Yeah. And we got no code on it, huh?"*

NORAD: *"Nope. It's search only."*

"Search only" means that the object was not emitting a transponder code. All aircraft are required by law to have a working transponder that provides the data necessary to avoid midair collisions.

NORAD later denied the whole thing. But why? It seems rather pointless considering that documentation and recordings of the incident exist and have been made public. Yet denial appears to be standard procedure by the government and the military in such cases. If what the crew of America West 564 saw was a new top secret aircraft, then there would be justification for secrecy. But if that were the case, why did NORAD not block the information from being released through the FOIA? It makes no sense. Considering the fact that records exist proving the authenticity of the event, official denial only generates more controversy and is yet another reason to suspect disinformation.

Men in Black

Men in Black are one of the more bizarre facets of the phenomena. MIBs, as they are commonly called, are people who show up at the door of a UFO witness wearing black suits and driving shiny black cars, frequently older models. Their descriptions are fairly consistent: large heads; long, thin faces; and abnormally large eyes. Their walk is often described as awkward, as though they have trouble maintaining their balance, and some witnesses have commented that they appeared to be wearing lipstick. They also appear to be—fragile, would be the best description. An extrapolation of information from numerous accounts suggests that some of them might actually be extraterrestrials trying to disguise themselves as government agents.

The purpose of these visits is to silence a witness about a sighting that he or she had. Sometimes they are alone, and sometimes they arrive in groups of three or more and flash badges or government ID cards. They sometimes use threats to keep a witness from talking, but as far as is known, no harm has ever come to those who did report the incident.

After seeing a UFO near Toronto, Ontario, Pat De LaFranier was visited by a MIB. She described him as being about five feet six, extremely thin, and having a slightly enlarged head. His eyes were long and wrapped around his temple, and she said she felt like he was "mentally intruding" upon her. What is especially strange is that she said he was carrying a photo album under his left arm.[21]

Why would he be carrying a photo album? He never offered to show her any of his pictures, and it is unlikely that any witness trying to maintain credibility would include such a farcical detail in their story unless it was true. Yet absurd behavior seems to be common in many MIB encounters. Could it be that in his attempt to impersonate a government agent, he carried a photo album not knowing the difference between it and a briefcase?

Another rather bizarre MIB event happened to Ray Muniz from Austin, Texas. He operated an auto tinting business on the outskirts of the city and had also started a television show called *Project UFO* on the local public access channel. In June of 1996, a viewer sent in a home video of a UFO he filmed over Georgetown, Texas, which Muniz aired on the show. Several days later, a few men wearing black suits, black ties, and dark glasses showed up at his shop and handed him a summons from the IRS. He said he stepped into his shop and showed the paper to his employee, and they agreed it looked authentic. He then went back outside to talk to the men, only to find that they had disappeared. He said there wasn't enough time for them to have driven or walked away; in those few short seconds, they had simply vanished.

Muniz gathered his records and took them to the downtown address listed on the summons, where he encountered another man dressed in black. Muniz identified himself and put the box containing his tax records on the desk. He said the man just looked at him and said "Okay. Thank you. You can leave now." Rather taken aback, Muniz said, "Excuse me?" and the man said "Thank you. You can leave now." Muniz asked, "Aren't you going to look at my stuff?" The man said "No. Thank you. You can leave now." Somewhat perplexed, Muniz went home, only to find that his video collection had been ransacked. He believes the whole thing was a ruse to get him away from home so they could steal the UFO tape. However, he said they didn't find it.[22]

One characteristic commonly reported in MIB visits is that when they leave, they often seem to disappear into thin air. A witness who looks out the window after they leave the house will often find they are nowhere in sight—even though they did not have enough time to walk to their car. One witness who lived at the end of a long street ran outside to see which way they would turn when they reached the corner, and just as in the Muniz case, the car and the MIBs had vanished. He said there was no way they had enough time to drive the length of the street.[23] So where did they go? Were they beamed up to their ship? Since this disappearing act is frequently reported, teleportation would seem to be a plausible explanation. It could also be that the witnesses were "switched off" for a few minutes to prevent them from seeing where the MIBs went. A common occurrence in abduction cases, switching off will be explained in the next chapter.

It seems that the reason people are visited by MIBs is because they had a UFO sighting that the aliens would prefer not be known. Why? What is truly scary is how they knew they were seen by a particular individual, and how they knew where that person lived, since many of these sightings were made by people who were away from their homes at the time.

It seems that whenever someone tries to check on a MIB using the name on the ID he showed, or the license plate number of the car he was driving, the results are always the same: no one by that name works for that agency, and the license plates are of numbers that do not exist.

There is no doubt that some MIBs are government agents, and we cannot exclude the possibility that some of the more bizarre accounts were staged events designed to discredit witnesses. Reporting a UFO sighting is one thing, but when a witness claims he was visited by fragile-looking men in black suits wearing lipstick, who disappeared into thin air after walking out the door, he is more likely to be branded as a nutcase. However, the consistency of absurd details as reported by numerous witnesses only adds to their credibility and might easily be another form of disinformation.

TOP SECRET / MAJIC
~~EYES ONLY~~
NATIONAL SECURITY INFORMATION

• • • • • • • • • • • • • •
• TOP SECRET •
• • • • • • • • • • • • • •

001

EYES ONLY

COPY ONE OF ONE.

BRIEFING DOCUMENT: OPERATION MAJESTIC 12

PREPARED FOR PRESIDENT-ELECT DWIGHT D. EISENHOWER: (EYES ONLY)

18 NOVEMBER, 1952

WARNING: This is a TOP SECRET - EYES ONLY document containing
compartmentalized information essential to the national security
of the United States. EYES ONLY ACCESS to the material herein
is strictly limited to those possessing Majestic-12 clearance
level. Reproduction in any form or the taking of written or
mechanically transcribed notes is strictly forbidden.

• • • • • • • • • • • • • •
• TOP SECRET •
• • • • • • • • • • • • • •

TOP SECRET / MAJIC
EYES ONLY

T52-EXEMPT (E)

EYES ONLY

(1)

MJ-12 Document #1

TOP SECRET / MAJIC
EYES ONLY
* TOP SECRET *
* * * * * * * * * * * * * *

0 0 2

COPY ONE OF ONE.

SUBJECT: OPERATION MAJESTIC-12 PRELIMINARY BRIEFING FOR PRESIDENT-ELECT EISENHOWER.

DOCUMENT PREPARED 18 NOVEMBER, 1952.

BRIEFING OFFICER: ADM. ROSCOE H. HILLENKOETTER (MJ-1)

NOTE: This document has been prepared as a preliminary briefing only. It should be regarded as introductory to a full operations briefing intended to follow.

* * * * * *

OPERATION MAJESTIC-12 is a TOP SECRET Research and Development/ Intelligence operation responsible directly and only to the President of the United States. Operations of the project are carried out under control of the Majestic-12 (Majic-12) Group which was established by special classified executive order of President Truman on 24 September, 1947, upon recommendation by Dr. Vannevar Bush and Secretary James Forrestal. (See Attachment "A".) Members of the Majestic-12 Group were designated as follows:

Adm. Roscoe H. Hillenkoetter
Dr. Vannevar Bush
Secy. James V. Forrestal*
Gen. Nathan F. Twining
Gen. Hoyt S. Vandenberg
Dr. Detlev Bronk
Dr. Jerome Hunsaker
Mr. Sidney W. Souers
Mr. Gordon Gray
Dr. Donald Menzel
Gen. Robert M. Montague
Dr. Lloyd V. Berkner

The death of Secretary Forrestal on 22 May, 1949, created a vacancy which remained unfilled until 01 August, 1950, upon which date Gen. Walter B. Smith was designated as permanent replacement.

* * * * * * * * * * * * *
* TOP SECRET *

TOP SECRET / MAJIC
EYES ONLY

T52-EXEMPT (E)

0 0 1

MJ-12 Document #2

TOP SECRET / MAJIC
EYES ONLY
* TOP SECRET *
●●●●●●●●●●●●●

U 1 3

EYES ONLY   COPY ONE OF ONE.

On 24 June, 1947, a civilian pilot flying over the Cascade
Mountains in the State of Washington observed nine flying
disc-shaped aircraft traveling in formation at a high rate
of speed. Although this was not the first known sighting
of such objects, it was the first to gain widespread attention
in the public media. Hundreds of reports of sightings of
similar objects followed. Many of these came from highly
credible military and civilian sources. These reports resulted in independent efforts by several different elements
of the military to ascertain the nature and purpose of these
objects in the interests of national defense. A number of
witnesses were interviewed and there were several unsuccessful
attempts to utilize aircraft in efforts to pursue reported
discs in flight. Public reaction bordered on near hysteria
at times.

In spite of these efforts, little of substance was learned
about the objects until a local rancher reported that one
had crashed in a remote region of New Mexico located approximately seventy-five miles northwest of Roswell Army Air
Base (now Walker Field).

On 07 July, 1947, a secret operation was begun to assure
recovery of the wreckage of this object for scientific study.
During the course of this operation, aerial reconnaissance
discovered that four small human-like beings had apparently
ejected from the craft at some point before it exploded.
These had fallen to earth about two miles east of the wreckage
site. All four were dead and badly decomposed due to action
by predators and exposure to the elements during the approximately one week time period which had elapsed before their
discovery. A special scientific team took charge of removing
these bodies for study. (See Attachment "C".) The wreckage
of the craft was also removed to several different locations.
(See Attachment "B".) Civilian and military witnesses in
the area were debriefed, and news reporters were given the
effective cover story that the object had been a misguided
weather research balloon.

●●●●●●●●●●●●●
* TOP SECRET *
●●●●●●●●●●●●●

EYES ONLY TOP SECRET / MAJIC
EYES ONLY   T52-EXEMPT (E)

003

MJ-12 Document #3

TOP SECRET / MAJIC
EYES ONLY

****
* TOP SECRET *
****

EYES ONLY   COPY ONE OF ONE.

A covert analytical effort organized by Gen. Twining and
Dr. Bush acting on the direct orders of the President, resulted in a preliminary concensus (19 September, 1947) that
the disc was most likely a short range reconnaissance craft.
This conclusion was based for the most part on the craft's
size and the apparent lack of any identifiable provisioning.
(See Attachment "D".) A similar analysis of the four dead
occupants was arranged by Dr. Bronk. It was the tentative
conclusion of this group (30 November, 1947) that although
these creatures are human-like in appearance, the biological
and evolutionary processes responsible for their development
has apparently been quite different from those observed or
postulated in homo-sapiens. Dr. Bronk's team has suggested
the term "Extra-terrestrial Biological Entities", or "EBEs",
be adopted as the standard term of reference for these
creatures until such time as a more definitive designation
can be agreed upon.

Since it is virtually certain that these craft do not origin-
ate in any country on earth, considerable speculation has
centered around what their point of origin might be and how
they get here. Mars was and remains a possibility, although
some scientists, most notably Dr. Menzel, consider it more
likely that we are dealing with beings from another solar
system entirely.

Numerous examples of what appear to be a form of writing
were found in the wreckage. Efforts to decipher these have
remained largely unsuccessful. (See Attachment "E".)
Equally unsuccessful have been efforts to determine the
method of propulsion or the nature or method of transmission
of the power source involved. Research along these lines
has been complicated by the complete absence of identifiable
wings, propellers, jets, or other conventional methods of
propulsion and guidance, as well as a total lack of metallic
wiring, vacuum tubes, or similar recognizable electronic
components. (See Attachment "F".) It is assumed that the
propulsion unit was completely destroyed by the explosion
which caused the crash.

****
* TOP SECRET *
****

EYES ONLY TOP SECRET / MAJIC   T52-EXEMPT (E)
EYES ONLY   004

MJ-12 Document #4

TOP SECRET / MAJIC
EYES ONLY

00!

•••••••••••••
• TOP SECRET •
•••••••••••••••

EYES ONLY   COPY ONE OF ONE.

A need for as much additional information as possible about
these craft, their performance characteristics and their
purpose led to the undertaking known as U.S. Air Force Project
SIGN in December, 1947. In order to preserve security, liason
between SIGN and Majestic-12 was limited to two individuals
within the Intelligence Division of Air Materiel Command whose
role was to pass along certain types of information through
channels. SIGN evolved into Project GRUDGE in December, 1948.
The operation is currently being conducted under the code name
BLUE BOOK, with liason maintained through the Air Force officer
who is head of the project.

On 06 December, 1950, a second object, probably of similar
origin, impacted the earth at high speed in the El Indio -
Guerrero area of the Texas - Mexican boder after following
a long trajectory through the atmosphere. By the time a
search team arrived, what remained of the object had been almost
totally incinerated. Such material as could be recovered was
transported to the A.E.C. facility at Sandia, New Mexico, for
study.

Implications for the National Security are of continuing importance in that the motives and ultimate intentions of these
visitors remain completely unknown. In addition, a significant
upsurge in the surveillance activity of these craft beginning
in May and continuing through the autumn of this year has caused
considerable concern that new developments may be imminent.
It is for these reasons, as well as the obvious international
and technological considerations and the ultimate need to
avoid a public panic at all costs, that the Majestic-12 Group
remains of the unanimous opinion that imposition of the
strictest security precautions should continue without inter-
ruption into the new administration. At the same time, contingency plan MJ-1949-04P/78 (Top Secret - Eyes Only) should
be held in continued readiness should the need to make a
public announcement present itself. (See Attachment "G".)

•••••••••••••••
TOP SECRET.MAJIC
EYES ONLY   ## EYES ONLY   T52-EXEMPT (E)

005

MJ-12 Document #5

Notes

1.   Dr. J. Allen Hynek's experience with Project Blue Book
     UFOs: 50 Years of Denial. Documentary. Prod. James Fox. TLC.
     1997.

2.   Lonnie Zamora's description of Socorro incident
     "Contact at Socorro." *Sightings.* Dir. Eric Gardner. Sci Fi (now
     Syfy).

3.   Captain Richard T. Holder's investigation
     "Encounter at Socorro." *Unsolved Mysteries.* NBC. WFLX. West
     Palm Beach.

4.   Dr. J. Allen Hynek on Socorro incident
     "Encounter at Socorro." *Unsolved Mysteries.* NBC. WFLX. West
     Palm Beach.

5.   Hynek's ideas suppressed by Air Force
     "Contact at Socorro." *Sightings.* Dir. Eric Gardner. Sci Fi (now
     Syfy).

6.   New air force explanation
     "Contact at Socorro." *Sightings.* Dir. Eric Gardner. Sci Fi (now
     Syfy).

7.   The Condon committee
     "The Conspiracy in Shutting Down Project Blue Book." *This Week
     in History.* THC.

8.   Gordon Cooper's account of UFO landing
     Out of the Blue. Documentary. Dir. James Fox/Tim Coleman. Sci
     Fi (now Syfy).

9. Disinformation statement by Edgar Mitchell
    UFOs: 50 Years of Denial. Documentary. Prod. James Fox. TLC.
    1997.

10. The triangle photographed over Belgium
    Link to image:
    www.ufocasebook.com/Belgium.html

11. The Phoenix lights—8:15 p.m. incident
    "UFOs Over Phoenix: Anatomy of a Sighting." *Discovery Sunday.*
    Dir. Richard Ross. Discovery.

12. The Phoenix lights—10:15 p.m. incident
    "UFOs Over Phoenix: Anatomy of a Sighting." *Discovery Sunday.*
    Dir. Richard Ross. Discovery.

13. Capt. Sullin's testimony
    Danger in Our Skies: The New UFO Threat. Documentary. UPN
    (now CW).

14. Lt. Col. Tanaka's testimony
    "UFOs Over Phoenix: Anatomy of a Sighting." *Discovery Sunday.*
    Dir. Richard Ross. Discovery.

15. Cognitech's composite of day and night images
    "UFOs Over Phoenix: Anatomy of a Sighting." *Discovery Sunday.*
    Dir. Richard Ross. Discovery.

16. Mexico City video—possible laser hologram
    Danger in Our Skies: The New UFO Threat. Documentary. UPN
    (now CW).

17. What was going on in building?
    Danger in Our Skies: The New UFO Threat. UPN (now CW).

18. Gulf Breeze Videos
"Gulf Breeze Encounters." *Sightings* segment. FOX. WFLX. West Palm Beach.

19. Brazil UFO report with images of Christ and Mary
"Messengers of Destiny." *Sightings* segment. Sci Fi (now Syfy).

20. America West flight 654 encounter
"UFOs: Then and Now? Cause For Alarm." *UFO Files*. Prod. Joshua Alper. THC.

21. Pat De LaFranier's MIB encounter
"Men in Black." *Sightings* segment. Sci Fi (now Syfy).

22. Ray Muniz's MIB encounter
"Men in Black" *Unsolved Mysteries*. FOX. WFLX. West Palm Beach.

23. Disappearing MIBs
"Men in Black." *Sightings*. Sci Fi (now Syfy).

Chapter 10

ABDUCTIONS

The idea of people being whisked aboard a spaceship by little grey creatures and subjected to strange examinations seemed rather far-fetched, and I, too, found it hard to believe at first. For a long time, these stories were ignored because investigators associated them with the contactee cults of the 1950s and '60s. It wasn't until the mid-'70s, after the Barney and Betty Hill case became known, that researchers began to look at abductions in a more serious light. However, alien abductions attracted a bunch of wackos, whose stories were featured in tabloids, and the others were usually judged by this fringe element. But when you look beyond the tabloids and the fanatics and examine the core of the subject, several factors suggest it may be real.

- Abductees are from all over the world. They come from different races, different religions, and from all walks of life, and their financial or social status seems not to be a factor.

- With very few exceptions, none of these people know each other.

- Early on, many abductees were under the impression that their experience was unique, completely unaware that it was happening to others.

- Researchers eventually began recognizing similarities that were simply too numerous to be coincidental, especially in the seemingly unimportant and trivial details.

- Because most of the early cases had received little or no publicity, many details had not been publicized, so it would have been virtually impossible for someone in Tupelo, Mississippi, to know the details of what happened to someone in Boise, Idaho.

- Most abductees shun notoriety. They fear ridicule and are afraid any publicity will be detrimental to their job security. So they have everything to lose and nothing to gain.

Many psychologists and psychiatrists who have worked with an abductee have used hypnosis to unlock details of the event buried in his subconscious. However, many professionals, who claim it is an unreliable method of acquiring credible information, dispute hypnosis. Still, there are professionals on the other side of the fence who claim the exact opposite. In the beginning, many trivial details that were revealed through hypnosis were never publicized but were described by other abductees, people whom they had never met, and living in cities, states, and countries they had never visited. Since much of this information was accrued before abductions gained widespread public attention, hypnosis would appear to merit some credibility.

The first publicized case was that of Barney and Betty Hill. Their abduction occurred one night in 1961, on a remote stretch of highway in the mountains of New Hampshire, while driving home from Canada. It wasn't until a few years later, when memories began to surface, that their story was revealed. They had sought counseling from Dr. Benjamin Simon, a prominent Boston psychiatrist who used hypnosis to probe their memories, and he recorded their sessions on audiotape. Since then, hundreds of cases have come to light, paralleling many of the same details as well as those that Dr. Simon had not allowed to be made public, such as the sperm extraction from Barney. At the time he thought that aspect was a bit too controversial.

As other professionals became involved, they eventually recognized many similarities in the accounts and began to consider the possibility that these people were describing real experiences. However, obtaining credible information necessitated fine-tuning the method of how abductees were questioned under hypnosis, and new techniques were developed by Dr. Richard Haines and Budd Hopkins. Once they were able to recognize and filter out false memories, researchers gradually gained a better perspective of the phenomenon.

Memory Suppression

The most common factor in abductions is that the memory of the event is suppressed into the subconscious mind but can usually be brought out through hypnosis. Whether erasing the memory is something the aliens do to prevent a traumatic reaction or is an attempt to conceal from the world what they are doing is anyone's guess. However, there are rare cases where an abductee was able to recall a portion and even the entire experience without hypnosis. Whether it was intended or whether these individuals exhibited a stronger mental resistance to the alien's influence is unknown.

Telepathic Communication

Communication between an abductee and the aliens appears to be on a telepathic level, even though the abductee may not possess telepathic abilities. No words come from their mouths, yet abductees seem to be aware of communication. A few have described hearing words in their minds, while others claim they just knew what was being said to them. And this seems to be the case regardless of what language the person may speak.

Alien Descriptions

Abductees have described the aliens they allegedly encountered in a variety of shapes, sizes, and colors. Some have ears and noses, and some do not. Some are said to have three fingers, while others are said to have four, five, or even six. On rare occasions, some creatures have been described as insect-like in appearance, with claw or pincerlike appendages, and other descriptions suggest that some may even be robotic in nature. Such a variety could mean there are several alien races visiting Earth, or it could be that each person is describing the same creature according to his or her individual perceptions, based on his or her state of mind at the time.

Nevertheless, in the greater majority of cases, the creatures are described as about four feet tall, with huge heads and large dark liquid-like almond-shaped eyes, and there is a little bump with two tiny holes where the nose should be. They are commonly referred to as "the greys" because their skin is grey with a texture often described as reptilian. However, variations have occasionally been reported in skin color: white, light grey, grey, dark grey, and even brown.

One commonality is that the greys appear to have an overseer. He is taller, about five feet, and his mental powers appear stronger, as he is able to manipulate an abductee's thoughts and emotions.

The greys do not exhibit any of the obvious signs of gender distinction, such as female breasts or male genitalia. This raises the question of whether they are drones that were created to do the work.

There were times when an abductee referred to a grey as "she." But considering the mental control they demonstrate, it might be a false impression they exert in order to reduce fear and apprehension during an abduction; resistance may be minimized if a person believes he is dealing with a female. But this is only speculation.

One species referred to as the "Nordics" look very human. The men are described as tall and well built, often with blond hair, and the females are said to have excellent well-proportioned figures. They are seen on rare occasions—sometime with the greys—and judging from the cases I have read, I get the impression that they prefer to remain out of sight ... Why?

Mind Control

Although it is pure speculation, mind control, in some cases, may be related to the alien's eyes. When the greys first appear, they will sometimes stick their face right in front of the abductee's—just inches away. When this happens, abductees say they are unable to look away. This might suggest that mental control is easier to achieve at close range. Occasionally, these face-to-face incidents are reported to occur in the room where the examinations take place, usually by the taller grey. The subject is forced to experience visions and different emotions, and according to some abductees, human emotion is something these creatures do not seem to understand.

Removal of Clothing

In almost every case, abductees state that after being brought to the ship, the next thing they remember is being completely naked and lying on a table or else sitting on a chair or bench, often with other abductees, waiting their turn to be examined. So it appears that before an examination, the aliens remove their clothing or somehow persuade the abductee to do it. In some cases, it appears the aliens dress them prior to their being returned. Apparently, they are not familiar with our clothing because a few people reported waking up in their beds after being abducted, with shirts or pajamas that were put on inside out and, in some cases, wearing articles of clothing that did not belong to them.

Switching Off

'Switching off' is term that seems to have evolved in the study of abductions. Apparently, these beings are able to immobilize people who are either with or around an abductee. It has been described in numerous cases that when a person was taken from the bedroom, the spouse continued to remain asleep, unresponsive to any physical or verbal stimuli. If the spouse was awake, he or she was usually put to sleep or "switched off." It has even been reported with family pets. In one case, an abductee said that the family dog was just standing there as if frozen in place.[1] Another abductee said that during her experience, she saw her mother just standing motionless, looking out through the screen door of the kitchen.[2]

It is hard to picture man and beast being put to sleep while on their feet without falling over; it almost sounds as if they were frozen in a moment of time—that what may have seemed like hours to the abductee may have actually occurred in a nanosecond to those who were switched off. This probably sounds like another far-fetched idea; however, if the aliens come from thousands of light-years away, they probably have the ability to manipulate the space-time continuum. However, this is something that is rarely reported and may be a procedure they use in certain situations since most abductees experience a two- or three- hour period of missing time. But again, this is only speculation.

Automobile Abductions

In cases where a subject is taken from an automobile, it usually occurs when a person is driving on an isolated country road or on a long, deserted stretch of highway. The next thing he knows is that his vehicle is somehow being brought to a stop, usually out of sight on an isolated dirt road. At this point, he usually encounters small creatures that bring him into a craft that has landed in a clearing in the woods. However, there have been a few reports where vehicles were actually lifted off the highway and into a ship, most likely by some sort of tractor beam. The next thing the person remembers is driving down the road miles from where the encounter took place, sometimes traveling in the opposite direction from which he was originally headed.

Imaging and Envisioning

In compiling information from the numerous abductees with whom he has worked, Dr. David Jacobs of Temple University noticed a consistency in some of the procedures conducted by the aliens. Two of these procedures he calls the "imaging" and "envisioning" experience. According to his studies, envisioning generally occurs in the room where examinations and tests are conducted, and seem to be for the purpose of eliciting emotional responses. These visions are mentally induced into the abductee's mind, usually by the taller grey that seems to be in charge. The imaging experience usually takes place after an examination, wherein the abductee is shown scenes on some sort of projection screen. They may range from beautiful pastoral scenes to those depicting the person's daily routine. However, one common and very disturbing factor is that they frequently include apocalyptic scenes of destruction, and the abductee is told that these things are going to happen. This aspect could be a most important detail and will be discussed later.

Multiple Abductions

Another detail uncovered by Jacobs and other researchers is that under hypnosis, many abductees revealed more than one experience. Numerous cases seem to follow a pattern in which abductions begin at the age of six or seven and a tracking device is implanted in the person's body so he can be located again in the future. The pattern also revealed that the abductions continued into their teen years and then stopped for a while before they resumed.

Implants

Another aspect is implants. Many people have awakened after an abduction to find blood on their pillows or cuts and scoop marks on their bodies. Others have found strange lumps in earlobes, arms, and legs. Under hypnosis, many described that an instrument was inserted through a nostril, usually with a small metallic ball on the end. As it was pushed up inside their heads, they felt and heard a crunching sound, as if cartilage had been broken. When the instrument was removed, it was usually without the little ball.

One case investigated by the Canadian chapter of MUFON, the Mutual UFO Network, was that of Andrea Shale. After her abduction, one eye became extremely swollen. When an X-ray was taken, it revealed a foreign object behind the optic nerve. However, her doctor advised against trying to have it surgically removed because it would be extremely dangerous and would probably leave her blind.[3]

Another interesting case involved a woman from Salt Lake City who prefers to remain anonymous. She and her son experienced a period of missing time after encountering a bright light while driving down the highway one night. A year later, she was knocked unconscious when she tripped at home and hit her head on the fireplace. She was taken to the hospital for x-rays to determine if there were any fractures, and the doctor was completely taken aback by what he saw: there was an oval metallic object embedded in the right parasagittal area of her brain. Excited and concerned, he ran into her room and asked her what it was. She was dumbfounded because she had never undergone any surgery that could account for it.[4]

Unfortunately, the woman has chosen not to pursue the matter. Whatever the object is and how it became embedded in her brain remains a mystery. Was her and her son's encounter with a bright light and their missing time experience a year earlier an abduction? The details certainly fit the profile, but unless she decides to undergo regressive hypnosis, we can only wonder.

Implant Removal

In 1995, Dr. Roger Leir, a podiatrist, assembled a medical team to remove implants from abductees. On the afternoon of August 19, 1995, three identical triangular objects were removed from the toe and hand of two people—people who were complete strangers to each other. The objects were imbedded in something like a cocoon and glowed brilliant fluorescent green when exposed to ultraviolet light. When the surgeons tried to cut through them, they found that even their sharpest scalpels were ineffective. Leir stated that during the operation, one of the patients literally came off the table when they tugged at the object, indicating that it was connected to a nerve.

The objects were analyzed by different laboratories, and the preliminary findings were interesting. They were enveloped in a keratinous substance that appears to have come from each subject's own body. It seems that using the person's own biological material as a protective cocoon provided total immunity to infection. Leir stated that if we could duplicate this technology, it would virtually eliminate organ transplant rejection.[5]

Hybrids

The abduction of male subjects appears to be random. Although they are frequently subjected to rigorous physical examinations and anal probes, it appears that the primary interest in men is the extraction of sperm. This detail has remained consistent from the beginning. With women, however, a most disturbing pattern was revealed: their abductions usually coincide with their fertility cycle—when they are ovulating—and it appears the aliens are extracting their eggs for fertilization purposes.

Another pattern that became apparent is that women are often impregnated by insemination. This is followed by a subsequent abduction before the end of the first trimester, and the fetus is extracted from the womb. It is then placed in a transparent container where gestation apparently continues. These fetuses are sometimes described as having both human and alien features, so it would appear that in some cases, the aliens may be fusing their own DNA material with the DNA in sperm collected from male abductees. In subsequent abductions, each woman is often given one of these infants to hold, presumably the same one she carried in her womb. They are frequently encouraged to breast-feed the infant, even though they may not be lactiferous. According to some women, the aliens seem extremely emphatic about this contact being important to the child. However, the purpose of these hybrids still mystifies researchers.

I have a question. If the aliens can fertilize an egg in vitro and artificially gestate the fetus in some type of incubation chamber, then why do they use a female womb for the first three months? This could be a significant factor that is being overlooked. I am not an authority on genetic engineering; however, the only logical purpose I can see for this temporary womb gestation might be to enable the fetus to assimilate into its own biological system the mother's natural immunities to earthly germs and disease. If this is the case, it opens the door to many possible scenarios. Considering this, I would think researchers would focus on this temporary womb gestation period and try to learn more about its real purpose.

Teleportation
In the Hill abduction, Barney noticed scuff marks on the tops of his shoes when he returned home, and he was confused as to how they got there. It wasn't until Dr. Simon let him hear the tapes of his hypnosis sessions a few years later that he learned how it happened. It appears he was putting up a strong resistance and the creatures had to physically drag him to their ship. However, in recent cases, abductees say they walked or were led to the ship and were somehow unable to resist. Could it be that the Hill abduction was the first, or one of the first, of recent times, and that

the ETs now exert a stronger mental influence against resistance? Some cases suggest the use of a tractor beam or even teleportation as a more convenient method of transport. I know it sounds crazy, but according to how people describe being taken from their bedrooms, it may be more of a reality than we think.

The common bedroom abduction usually consists of one or more beings suddenly appearing out of a brilliant light and acting as an escort. In one case, a woman said that one of these creatures took her by the arm and maneuvered her toward the window. Suddenly, she was outside and rising into the sky. When asked if she could tell where she was going, she described approaching the bottom of a dark grey object that appeared to be oval shaped. She said she felt as if they (her and her alien escort) were in some kind of a light, rising toward the center of the bottom of the craft, and suddenly they were inside.

In another case, a fifty-year-old businessman described how he passed right through the Venetian blinds and a closed window when he was taken.

A patient of the late Dr. John Mack said that she felt that all the air was suddenly pushed out of her, and she was sucked out the window as if in a vacuum.[6]

Jim Weiner described the sensation of his body being ripped apart on a molecular level—as if he were being "torn apart atom by atom." This occurred when he and his twin brother Jack, along with two friends, were abducted during a fishing trip in the Allagash wilderness of Maine.[7]

Another man explained that he suddenly felt compelled to go outside and stand on his lawn. He said he saw small creatures silhouetted against bright lights and was forced to enter a large dark cloud from which a bright light was emanating. He also described stepping out of a cloud and back onto his lawn when he was returned. And there are other accounts of abductees describing how they passed through the wall or the roof of a building and even through the windshield of a car.

From these descriptions, the implications are obvious: the sensation of disembodiment, being molecularly disassembled, passing through closed windows, and then turning up inside a strange craft with little grey creatures suggests teleportation. However, it seems that when an abductee is taken into a cloud, it usually occurs outside. I have yet to hear of such a cloud appearing in an indoor abduction.

I realize the skeptics laugh at such ideas (and I have to admit to it myself) because it sounds like something you would see on *Star Trek*. Although these descriptions bear an uncanny similarity to *Trek*'s transporter beam, I doubt it is the influence behind what abductees are describing, for many such incidents occurred long before *Star Trek* was ever thought of. And most people are completely unaware of the fact that similar descriptions were recorded thousands of years ago in ancient manuscripts—the same manuscripts that were later compiled and assimilated into what we call the Holy Bible. For example (and I am paraphrasing):

Soon after the Hebrews were liberated from Egypt, the Lord frequently came down in a "cloud" to speak with Moses in front of the temporary meeting tent that had been set up outside the camp. (Ex 19:9)

There is the angel who visited Samson's mother to tell her she would have a son. Upon his departure, it says that he ascended in what was described as "fire." (Jdg 13:20)

The story of the Transfiguration describes how Christ became enveloped in a "bright white light" at the exact instant Moses and Elijah materialized at his side. Would it not suggest that he was engulfed in the same light from which the two men appeared? When Moses and Elijah departed, it says they were enveloped by a "cloud" into which they disappeared. (Mt 17:2, Mk 9:2, and Lk 9:29)

When the angel appeared at Christ's tomb, it was in a bright flash of light. It says he appeared "like lightning," and that his clothes were "as white as snow" and "gleamed like lightning." (Mt 28:2, 3 and Lk 24:4)

At his ascension, it says the disciples watched as a "cloud" enveloped Christ and then rose slowly into the sky. (Ac 1:10)

When the angel rescued the apostle Peter from the prison cell where he was being held, his appearance was accompanied by a "bright light." (Ac 12:7–10)

I find it difficult to ignore these similarities between the abductions and the biblical texts of what appears to be teleportation. If it walks like a duck and quacks like a duck, then the odds are that it probably is a duck. David Jacobs notes that in the numerous cases where people have passed through closed windows, there is rarely an outside witness. He theorizes that whatever it is that allows abductees to pass through solid objects may also render them invisible. The idea makes sense because in order to pass through a solid object, the molecular composition of the body must be thinned out, so to speak. Every atom would have to be spread far apart to reduce molecular density. Assuming that such a thing is possible, it should easily allow a person's individual molecules to pass between those of solid obstacles like windows and walls, and it would most likely render the person invisible. To anyone witnessing the process, it would seem that the person simply dissipated into thin air. It would be the same as how evaporating water becomes invisible until it condenses and forms into clouds.

Many researchers now feel that abductions may be more prevalent than was first believed. Literally thousands of cases have been uncovered through the hypnosis of people who were merely seeking help for inexplicable feelings of anxiety, stress, and other related symptoms such as missing time. They estimate there may be millions of abductees who are completely unaware of their experience and have not sought counseling because they cannot afford the expense of professional help, or they simply may not have experienced any of these symptoms.

The Skeptic's Corner

There are always going to be skeptics. Professionals in the psychiatric field who are too rational in their thinking often approach the subject with their minds already made up and not open to other possibilities because, according to their mind-sets, what the patients described could not possibly have happened. And so they ignore the testimony of witnesses and the evidence compiled by researchers in the field and substitute it with their own opinions and conclusions, which are usually based on little, if any, background research. However, they have made a few valid points.

One of their theories involves the hypnagogic and hypnopompic states, often referred to as sleep paralysis. It is what occurs between the last moments of consciousness and falling asleep, or between sleep and awakening. During these periods, one may experience temporary paralysis and dreams that seem real. Since most abductees claim they were unable to move or physically react during the onset of an abduction, some psychiatrists feel this transition period between consciousness and sleep is a catalyst for many abduction claims. And it is true that a large percentage of abductions seem to occur after the person has gone to bed. They also suggest that a person's own belief in the reality of the experience can trigger psychosomatic symptoms, causing scoop marks, bruises, and scars to appear on the body.

Another theory is that the brain's temporal lobe is stimulated by energy released during seismic activity, such as earthquakes or volcanic eruptions. This energy generates electrically charged particles into the atmosphere, which often appear as glowing balls of light. A common occurrence over fault lines and regions of volcanic activity, they have often been mistaken for UFOs. Doctor Michael Persinger, a Canadian neurologist, believes it may also explain many abduction cases. He has conducted experiments in his laboratory by duplicating the hypnagogic state to demonstrate his point.

A subject is isolated in a room and blindfolded—completely deprived of any sensory perception. He is wired with sensors through which patterns of electromagnetic waves are transmitted, stimulating the temporal lobe area of the brain. The result is a series of false perceptions somewhat similar to those reported in abductions. The person may feel a presence in the room. He may experience paralysis, moving through a dark tunnel, or approaching a bright light. Persinger suggests that people who are sensitive to this energy might easily experience what they believe to be a real abduction.[8]

These are all valid points, and they probably do explain some cases, but not all. First, abductees are not blindfolded or deprived of sensory perception. Second, it does not explain the bruises and scoop marks that appear on people's bodies. How could one person's subconscious create (in some cases identical) psychosomatic manifestations exhibited by someone he or she has never met, someone who lives in a different city, state, or country? Third, sleep paralysis does not explain abductions that occur while people are wide-awake or driving down the road in their cars. And fourth, just because it can be done in a laboratory does not constitute proof that seismic activity is responsible for abduction experiences, nor does it explain those that occur in places where seismic activity is rare and relatively nonexistent. But skeptics continue to be skeptics, and when their ideas are applied to individual cases, they rarely hold much water.

An Extraterrestrial Alliance

If alien abductions are as real as the evidence seems to suggest, the idea of an extraterrestrial alliance is reinforced by the variety of alien species that have been described, especially the Nordics, who are occasionally seen working with the greys. In her book *Encounters,* Edith Fiore reports that one woman in regressive hypnosis described two average-looking men with blond hair who looked as if they could have been football players. They performed tests on her, and another man with light brown hair assisted during another examination. She also claims that there were several different alien species present on the ship. It is rare that more than one alien species is reported during an abduction, but if what she said is true, it does suggest that different races may actually be working together, suggesting that some sort of a planetary alliance may actually exist.

Take the case of Travis Walton, which occurred in 1975. He was struck by a blue-green beam of light from a UFO that he and his companions encountered in the Arizona wilderness. While on their way home from doing contract work in the Apache-Sitgreaves National Forest, Walton and his companions encountered a large glowing circular craft hovering off the side of the Road. Walton jumped out of the truck and approached the object, ignoring the pleas of his companions to come back. He walked up to the craft and was standing almost underneath it when it suddenly started to wobble and emit a rumbling sound, so he ducked behind a log and crouched down. Deciding he had better get out of there, he stood up, and that is when a beam of blue-green light shot out of the craft, striking him in the head and chest. The beam hit with such force that it actually lifted him into the air, throwing him back about ten feet, where he landed on the hard ground. His companions sped away in panic, thinking Walton had been killed. A few minutes later, they calmed down and returned, thinking that Walton might still be alive and seriously injured, only to find that the craft was gone and so was Walton.

The occupants of the craft had apparently brought him aboard, I suspect to give him medical attention for his injuries. While on the ship, he encountered both human and nonhuman beings. But I seriously doubt he was abducted, for he was on board for five days, whereas abductees usually experience a two or three-hour period of missing time. Walton had full recall of the event while abductees have no memory until they undergo regressive hypnosis. And he'd apparently been healed of his injuries caused by the blue-green beam. There are many other reasons why I believe Walton was not an abduction victim, which I will not go into because it would be like writing another book.

In any case, we again have greys and Nordics on the same ship. But who are these human-looking aliens? Are they aboard all the ships where abductees are taken, and if so, why do they stay out of sight? Are they subservient to the greys, or are they the ones who are actually in charge? If they are extraterrestrials, the fact that they look exactly like us is an intriguing characteristic that should arouse some curiosity. But could it be that it is really *we* who look like them as a result of hybridization conducted millennia or even eons ago? Could they possibly be the angels described in the Bible? These are issues we will begin examining in the next chapter.

◆◆◆◆◆

If alien abductions are as real as the evidence suggests, then we cannot ignore the fact that people are being transported to alien craft by some process of teleportation. This technology is presently beyond our understanding; therefore, it seems more suited to the realm of science fiction. It is hard to believe that alien creatures are snatching people out of their bedrooms and performing strange experiments on them, and it is even more difficult to believe they are inseminating women and later removing the fetuses from their wombs. And expecting us to believe that they were molecularly disassembled and passed through closed windows or even solid walls and rose into the sky in a beam of light only to have their molecules reassembled on board an alien spacecraft is pushing believability to the max. Yet it seems to be a common factor in most cases, and it is a detail that should not be ignored. There is not enough of a deviation in these accounts, or the details thereof, to warrant classifying these people as crackpots or victims of sleep paralysis. And I feel this teleporting process parallels biblical accounts of people appearing and disappearing in clouds and bright lights too closely to be a coincidence. It certainly suggests that there may be a link between the UFO phenomena and many biblical events. And as we will see in the next chapter, this connection seems to be further strengthened by evidence that hybrids were also created in biblical times.

Notes

1. Switching off of dog
    Abduction Diaries. Documentary. Prod./Dir. Tina DiFeliciantonio/
    Jane C. Wagner. Sci Fi (now Syfy).

2. Switching off of person
    "Abducted." *Sightings* segment. FOX. WFLX. West Palm Beach.

3. Implant behind optic nerve
    "Canadian MUFON Investigations." *Encounters* segment. FOX.
    WFLX. West Palm Beach.

4. Brain implant
    "Strange Beings and UFO." *Mysteries of the Unexplained.* Prod./
    Dir. Steve Eder. TLC.

5. Implant removal
    "Removal of Alien Implants." *The Paranormal Borderline.* UPN
    (now CW).
    Link to image:
    www.ufodigest.com/surgeon.html

6. Sucked out window as if in vacuum
    "Secrets of Alien Abduction." *Sightings.* Prod. Susan Michaels. Sci
    Fi (now Syfy).

7. Feeling of being molecularly torn apart
    UFOs II: Have We Been Visited? Documentary. Prod./Dir. Lisa
    Bourgoujian. A&E. 1997.

8. Dr. Michael Persinger's experiment
    UFOs: Then and Now? Nightmare. Documentary. Dir. Joshua
    Alper. THC. 2004.

Preface to Part 2

I believe I have presented sufficient evidence suggesting that UFOs are real, and that one or more extraterrestrial races are visiting our planet. There is evidence suggesting the government knows what is going on and is withholding it from the public. Yet they have consistently kept the subject alive through the dissemination of disinformation—why? The only reason that seems to make any sense is that it has to do with religious doctrine and the chaos that would result if they were to make the truth known. Eventually, the truth will have to come out, but first we must be prepared psychologically to deal with it.

In the public arena, theories abound about what the aliens are up to, one being that they are simply studying and/or monitoring our evolutionary progress. Another is that they created the human race as an experiment or as a slave race to suit their own agenda. Others believe their intention is to wipe us out with plagues so they can colonize our world. They have cited numerous plagues that wiped out millions of people over the ages, yet despite this, the earth's population has increased to billions of people today. If they really wanted to wipe us out, I would assume they possess the technology to have done so long ago—and very quickly.

As I have hinted at throughout part 1, a situation could arise in the next millennium or two and threaten our very existence. If this is true, our only chance for survival is to migrate to another planet that will sustain human life, and to do so, we need to develop the technology to travel far beyond the speed of light. On our own, we might never accomplish this in time, but there is evidence suggesting that extraterrestrials may have initiated a plan to accelerate our advancement not only on a technological level but socially and morally as well. This will become evident as we explore the biblical scenario.

The Bible is a compilation of stories that were passed along in oral tradition for thousands of years. There is evidence that some of the stories in the Torah (the five books of Moses) may have been borrowed from earlier Mesopotamian writings, while others were created simply to make a moral statement. Although some stories may possibly have a basis in fact, it is almost certain that over the centuries, people added their own spin according to how they perceived them. Stories about Sodom and Gomorrah, the crumbling walls of Jericho, and the ten plagues of Egypt may possibly be the result of natural disasters that were portrayed by later writers as God's punishment of man for his corrupt and evil ways, or they could be fictional writings by someone who only wanted to make a moral point.

So anyone who is familiar with how the Bible actually evolved knows that it is not a record of historical fact. Therefore, some scholars suggest that the scriptures are only allegorical and should not be viewed in a literal sense.

When studying the Bible as presented in its current form, there appears to be a consistent series of events sanctioning a moral and ethical evolution of the human race. Many other stories that appear inconsequential and even inappropriate to the overall scenario were included in the Bible for reasons known only to those who included them.

You may wonder what all this has to do with UFOs. Maybe nothing or maybe a great deal; it all depends on how you choose to interpret the Bible from the stories printed between its covers. For example, the first chapter in the book of Ezekiel describes his encounter with five beings that came down from the sky in what certainly sounds like a mechanical flying craft. You can interpret this as a spiritual or prophetic vision that Ezekiel experienced, or you can interpret it as an encounter he had with extraterrestrial beings. In view of the fact that there are numerous technological references throughout the Bible, which most people are completely unaware of, I have chosen the latter.

I am not saying my choice is the correct one, but when we apply this concept to the sequence of biblical events starting with Adam all the way through to the resurrection of Christ, it presents a most interesting scenario. Whether or not it has any merit is something that only you, the reader, can decide. Nevertheless, I guarantee it will be an interesting read.

All scriptural quotes are from:
The Holy Bible, New International Version (1984). International Bible Society

Part 2

THE BIBLICAL CONNECTION

Chapter 11

HYBRIDS

One element seems to stand out in both the Old and New Testaments: technology. Many of the miraculous events described in the Bible can be reproduced with technologies that exist today. So if the biblical miracles really were technological demonstrations, then whose technology was it? After years of studying the chronological sequence of events as they appear in the Bible, I began to recognize that a specific series of events was interrelated. A scenario began to take shape, suggesting that extraterrestrials were actually accelerating the evolution of the human race on a social, moral, and technological level. After examining some of the amazing architectural achievements produced by men of ancient times, plus the laws given to Moses by the Lord, it made a lot of sense. Yet there was always the question of *why*. There had to be a reason for it, and that reason did not become apparent until later.

There are suggestions in the book of Revelation that the earth will suffer a major cataclysmic event that will either destroy it or cause the extinction of the human race. It also says that a millennium after Christ's return, he will take people off the earth to a place called the New Jerusalem or Holy City. In 1 Thessalonians 4:17 and 1 Corinthians 15:51, it tells how this will be done, and from the description, it sounds exactly like teleportation. Yet it seems unlikely that Christ will be able to take everybody. So does that mean the only survivors of this disaster will be those chosen by Christ? Not necessarily. If the evolution of man's technology proceeds on schedule, he will then be able to save himself by migrating to another habitable planet that he discovers in his exploration of the galaxy.

The only logical reason for accelerating the evolutionary process seemed to be time—time was a critical factor. In order for humanity to survive, there was a deadline to meet, and it created a problem: man's wisdom would never be able to keep pace with accelerated technological development, something that is evident today. And this may possibly be the reason behind the current alien abduction cases. They may be trying to bring man's wisdom into balance through a process of genetic engineering.

This, of course, may sound like an off-the-wall theory, and it very well may be. However, as we examine the evidence pertaining to each issue, you will see how they logically fit together. So as we delve into the biblical aspects of UFOs, I again wish to emphasize that the evidence presented is in theory only. Although some of my ideas may be compelling, I am not claiming them to be fact—only a possibility based on a logical evaluation of situations and events as described in the Bible and, of course, the possibility that they even occurred.

However, the biblical scenario will make more sense once you become familiar with the technological aspects involved. First, we will examine clues that hybrids were created to fulfill the various phases of the project, and in the next chapter, we will examine the technologies that were applied. Then, in chapters 13–19, we will see how these details logically relate to the biblical events as they unfold chronologically—events suggesting aliens are involved in a project to expedite the moral, social, and technological evolution of the human race. But as I stated, it is only a theory based on a logical evaluation of the stories. It is up to you, the reader, to decide if it has any merit.

No one knows for certain in what language Moses spoke or wrote his texts, or if he even wrote them down at all. Bible scholars tell us that until the first written accounts were transcribed, the stories had been passed down orally in Aramaic. So Moses probably spoke a very ancient version of Hebrew or Aramaic that became obsolete long before the first written accounts. However, we know that many words had more than one meaning, forcing scribes to make decisions according to what *they* felt the correct interpretation should be, and the mysticism of their own beliefs is reflected in many of the words they chose. Every Bible has footnotes denoting optional meanings for many of these words, but people often ignore the footnotes and accept what is written in the verse as fact, which can lead to misconceptions as to the reality of the event being described.

One example is in how the name "Adam" was applied to an individual whom the writers had been conditioned to believe was the very first human being. However, the word from which Adam was derived also means *all of mankind*. So when we factor in the alternate definitions attributed to many of these words, the stories often change in context to a more logical scenario. In this case, it could very well mean that Adam referred to an entire civilization.

According to the Bible, Adam arrived on the scene about six thousand years ago. Now archaeologists have confirmed that many civilizations and cities existed long before then, such as Jericho and Tiahuanaco, which have been around for at least ten thousand and twelve thousand years, respectively. So there is plenty of evidence that man was around long before the alleged creation of Adam. Therefore, it is possible that the timeline of biblical events is wrong and the creation story was invented by early fundamentalists or may even have been derived from earlier Mesopotamian writings. In any case, organized religion has conditioned our minds with the belief that Adam was the only human being on the earth at the time of his creation.

Everyone is familiar with the Genesis story of how God created Adam and then later used one of his ribs to create Eve. Yet some scholars believe the first chapter in Genesis proposes man and woman were created simultaneously, thus suggesting there may have been another woman before Eve.

So God created man in his own image, in the image of God he created him; male and female he created them. (Ge 1:27)

213

Since the second chapter specifies that Eve was created after Adam, it led to speculation that there was another woman before Eve. Supposedly, she was a demoness called Lilith, who was the epitome of untamed female sexual power. As the story goes, she left or divorced herself from Adam because of sexual incompatibility: he wanted her to lie beneath him for sexual intercourse, and she wanted to be on top.[1] But since no names are mentioned in this first account, it's an issue open for debate.

In this chapter, I will present what could be evidence that Adam, along with many of the primary biblical characters, were genetically engineered hybrids. Thirty-five years ago, I would have considered the idea ridiculous, but after examining the basic details of each story logically, without the supernatural embellishments created by religion, the idea seemed to make sense. However, that is something you will have to decide for yourself; I am only presenting the evidence that suggests it. Although the details in this chapter may seem a bit bizarre, I am not claiming them to be fact. They will begin to make a lot of sense once we begin examining the complete biblical scenario in chapter 13.

One fact clearly stands out in the Old Testament: the intent to create a new race. According to Genesis 1:28, after creating man and woman, God told them to be fruitful, to multiply, and replenish the earth. However, in Genesis 2:7 and 2:22, it says it was the *Lord God* who created two particular individuals called Adam and Eve, which may or may not be an extension of the first reference. Either way, it presents the possibility that Adam and Eve were hybrids. Why would there be a need to create two particular individuals when man already existed, unless their purpose was to incorporate upgraded genetic qualities into the existing population. It may sound far-fetched, but when we examine the details surrounding the miracle births described in the Bible—miracles in the sense that they occurred to elderly women who were sterile to begin with and also to a young virgin—we realize that if these stories are true, they can only be describing either miracles or insemination.

Another detail worth noting is that these miracle births were announced in advance by a personal visit to either the women or their husbands. The first visit was from the Lord himself, and the others were by those who represented him, such as angels or prophets, so they all had a connection to the Lord. So unless you choose to believe in miracles, the only way an elderly woman could become pregnant, especially one who was sterile, was if she had been impregnated by artificial means.

There are no accounts of miraculous conceptions taking place in modern times; however, there are many women whose memories of their abductions had been buried deep into their subconscious, and they suddenly found themselves pregnant with no idea of how they got that way, because they were not sexually active at the time of conception. Then, within a few months, they suddenly turned up not pregnant, without having aborted or miscarried. Just like the sterile old women in the Bible, they, too, appeared to have "miraculously conceived", their pregnancies defying any rational explanation. Each one who later underwent regressive hypnotherapy then learned of her abduction, insemination, and a subsequent abduction in which the fetus had been removed from her womb.

Were those old and barren women abducted and inseminated in the same manner described by abductees, and were the events blocked from their conscious memories? If these stories are true, there can only be two possible explanations—miracles or insemination—and if we remain logical, we have to go with insemination.

In all probability, the first hybrids were Adam and Eve. The others (in chronological order) were Isaac, Samson, the son of a Shunammite woman who is not named, John the Baptist, and Jesus Christ. Except for Christ, whose mother was said to be a young virgin, these sons were born to old and sterile women. However, there are subtle clues that other fertile women may also have given birth to hybrids, the most famous being Enoch, Noah, Solomon, and Elijah. And the details surrounding some of them suggest they were used to test a particular series of characteristics and abilities that had been enhanced on a genetic level—the same characteristics that were later evident in Christ.

Adam and Eve

Being created from the dust of the earth, as the Bible claims, does not necessarily mean that Adam popped up out of the ground with a fully developed brain preprogrammed with all the knowledge that an adult male of six thousand years ago would normally have acquired. It may simply be a metaphor indicating that the human body is composed of the same elements as the soil. The roots of any life-form can be traced back to life that evolved from the soil or, as the Bible describes it, "the dust of the earth." Now, wouldn't you think that God could have merely *willed* Adam into existence—why would he mess around with dust? So logic suggests there was a physical being involved. And if Adam really was "created," then he had to be a hybrid, probably infused with certain elements of his creator's DNA. In order to create Eve, the Bible tells us that the Lord God had to put Adam to sleep and take something out of his body, after which he closed up the place with flesh. This means that the creation of Eve required a material substance that, according to Genesis 2:21, was one of Adam's ribs. Therefore, he was dealing with physical matter and the mechanics of physical activity, certainly outside the realm conducive to miracles. Again, let's be logical; God could have simply willed her into existence.

The description of this event parallels surgical procedures performed today in any hospital. The fact that Adam had to be put to sleep suggests that he was anesthetized so an operation could be performed. Closing up the place with flesh describes the closing of an incision—what every surgeon does after an operation. Also, the footnote referring to Genesis 2:21 explains that the words interpreted to mean *the Lord God took a rib out of Adam* can also mean *he took part of the man's side,* which could have been anything. Since we already suspect genetic engineering, might it have been a sample of Adam's hybrid DNA? What other logical reason could there have been to remove something from his body?

All indications are that Eve was a hybrid, but not of the same caliber as Adam. Of all the miracle births mentioned in the Bible, none were female. Therefore, if they did not create female hybrids, one might question how Eve fits into the picture.

If Adam's intended purpose was to produce a genetically improved race, he would need a mate, and since he allegedly lived for 930 years, his mate would require a comparable life span. We don't know what the average life span of the general population was at that time, but it seems doubtful that it was 800 or 900 years, as the Bible attributes to Adam and many of his direct descendants. Therefore, we might consider the possibility that the operation performed on Adam was to remove DNA samples so they could incorporate into Eve certain elements of his genetic structure that related to longevity. I might consider Eve a sub hybrid—one created from human seed but genetically enhanced with certain elements of Adam's hybrid DNA.

Genesis 1:26 quotes God as saying, "Let *us* make man in *our* image, in *our* likeness," not "Let *me* make man in *my* image, in *my* likeness." Does this not suggest that the creation of Adam involved more than one individual, and that he resembled his creators in appearance? The words "us" and "our" suggest that the one identified as God was talking to someone else, which certainly implies that more than one individual was involved. From what is known about the earliest texts, the translation relating to the word God could have been singular or plural in meaning.

This is a rather confusing point when considering the origins from which the word God was derived. The name for God used by the Hebrews who allegedly settled in Judah was Yahweh, and it is thought to have originally been associated with a pagan deity. Elohim, used by those in Jerusalem under Solomon's rule, was derived from El Shaddai, indicating plurality, and is also thought to have pagan origins.[2] Since the scribes who originally translated the words of Moses lived closer to his time period, we might assume they were more familiar with whatever language he spoke, even though it had most likely become obsolete. So there is a higher probability that their interpretations were correct in this case, but not probable enough to justify a conclusion.

Now we see that basically the same phrase is used to describe the birth of Adam's third son, Seth:

When Adam was 130 years old he *had a son in* his *own likeness, in* his *own image.* (Ge 5:3)

So if Moses wrote the book of Genesis as dictated to him by the Lord, then the Lord used basically the same words to describe the birth of Seth as he did the creation of Adam. In Seth's case, the words indicate that he shared the same physical features as his father, meaning there was a physical resemblance. Therefore, would not the same interpretation apply to the same words in the creation of Adam? And would it not suggest that Adam and those who created him were likewise identical in appearance?

Another clue that Adam was part of a genetic engineering project is the fact that he was put to a test. If we look at the story logically, we must assume there was a reason for it. Why would there be a need to test him unless it was an evaluation—to see if he measured up to their expectations—to find out if there was anything wrong. If it really was God who created Adam, it seems only logical that he would have made him flawless, and there would have been no need to test him. Why would God make him imperfect? And why would God, who is described as an all-perfect and all-powerful Supreme Being, even have a need to create a physical life-form? To create one such as man who is imperfect and then spend thousands of years trying to change him makes no sense. What would be the point? And if, according to beliefs promoted by organized religion, God is all-knowing, meaning he knows the past, the present, and the future, then he would have known that Adam would be imperfect before he even created him, and he would have known all the problems that would follow, so bothering to create him at all is illogical. What *is* logical is that Adam was a genetically engineered hybrid created by physical beings for a specific purpose, and it was necessary to test him in order to make sure he met the qualifications for the job.

When he ate the forbidden fruit, Adam broke the only law he was required to obey. I always wondered why such a big deal was made over something as mundane as a piece of fruit. However, common sense suggests that it was not the fruit but Adam's actions that confirmed there was a problem. He was not the perfect law-abiding specimen that was intended, and this imperfection would multiply through his descendants to the point where they would never be masters of their baser instincts, nor would they develop the wisdom to be a positive, productive, and peaceful race; they were destined for immoral, unethical, and violent behavior. So it would appear that because of this imperfection, Adam was disqualified from the game. He and Eve were forced to leave Eden, and as they assimilated into the local population, the children they produced were contaminated with his negative genes, which, for lack of a better definition, I will henceforth refer to as "Adam's virus."

Not to get ahead of myself, but as the scenario unfolds, it suggests that Christ was not part of the original plan. After Adam's failure, it appears a contingency plan was implemented, requiring someone like Christ to ensure its success, and it would be necessary that he possess certain superior abilities. This required the use of other hybrids to be sure certain characteristics and abilities could be enhanced genetically. It seems that although Isaac was selected to replace Adam as the progenitor of a new race, he was also used to conduct the first experiment.

It may appear that I am trying to stretch the facts to fit my own beliefs and interpretations. However, if my ideas on Adam and Eve were the only basis for my theory, you would not be reading this book. Most of my interpretations were derived from specific information and evidence that appear later on in the sequence of events; it necessitated a lot of backtracking to see how and why certain events came about. You might compare it to reverse engineering a UFO in order to learn how it works. When I first began studying the Bible stories, I was curious to see if my thoughts concerning teleportation had any merit. It was only after ten years of examining the information that a project of genetic engineering designed to accelerate mankind up the ladder of evolution, plus the reason behind it, gradually fell into place. It was the only scenario that seemed to make any sense.

Isaac

If Adam was a hybrid created to improve the genetic quality of the existing human race, he was a failure. Thus the story of Isaac, born to Sarah, the wife of Abraham, suggests that he, too, was a hybrid created to continue the project.

The Lord first contacted Abraham (then called Abram) when he was seventy-five years old, and it would seem that the decision to use his wife,

Sarah (then called Sarai), had already been made. However, twenty-four years elapsed before it actually happened, and it would appear that this interim was used to prepare for the event. Judging from what transpired, the Lord wanted to make sure Isaac would not be exposed to the perversion that prevailed in the nearby cities of Sodom, Gomorrah, Admah, Zeboiim, and Zoar. And in order for him to receive the proper upbringing from his parents, it was necessary to provide them with a lifestyle free of the hardships that prevailed in those times. Having fewer problems to contend with would allow them to devote more time to teaching the child to adhere to proper moral and ethical standards. This would have been very important if he was to complete the job originally intended for Adam.

It appears a plan was initiated that enabled Abraham to acquire wealth, and twenty-three years later (a year before Isaac was born), the nearby corrupt cities of Sodom, and Gomorrah, and possibly Admah and Zeboiim, were destroyed. Zoar, however, was spared as a safe haven for Abraham's nephew, Lot, and his family who lived in Sodom.

According to Genesis chapter 12, the Lord instructed Abraham to take Sarah on a journey that would ultimately lead them to Egypt. Apparently, Sarah was an extremely beautiful woman, and Abraham was afraid that if anyone knew she was his wife, someone might kill him in order to claim her for himself, so he had her pretend to be his sister. When they finally arrived in Egypt, the pharaoh became overwhelmed by Sarah's beauty, and believing she was Abraham's sister, chose her to become one of his wives. In turn, he rewarded Abraham with much wealth; he gave him sheep, cattle, donkeys, camels, and many servants as well. But before the pharaoh had a chance to wed Sarah and become intimate with her, the Lord brought down a sickness on his household. Then he threatened the pharaoh in a dream and told him that Sarah was really Abraham's wife. Even though he was innocent of ill intentions, the pharaoh was intimidated into returning her to Abraham and letting him keep all the wealth he had bestowed on him.

Many scholars admit to their confusion about this incident because it suggests that Abraham prostituted his wife for monetary gain. How could such a righteous man—the patriarch of the Israelites—do such a thing?

It seems that the scholars are too absorbed in their mystical beliefs to recognize that it was the Lord's idea, not Abraham's. More evidence of this is revealed in chapter 20 of Genesis, when they did the same thing a second time. Abraham and Sarah pulled the same brother and sister act on Abimelech, the king of Gerar, and like the pharaoh, he, too, became enamored with Sarah and chose her to become one of his wives. It was only after the Lord threatened him in a dream (and laid a heavy guilt trip on him) that he returned her to Abraham and lavished him with even more riches as a means of atonement.

Prior to this, the Lord had visited Abraham and told him that Sarah would bear a son, and as we follow the sequence of events, it will become obvious that Sarah's pregnancy had been planned from the beginning. With this in mind, we can assume that he was concerned for her well-being and Abraham's as well. And since the Lord had been in contact with Abraham, and Abraham was following his instructions by going to Egypt, why would he need to fear for his life if anyone knew Sarah was his wife? Surely the Lord would have protected him. Another thing: when the pharaoh took Sarah into the palace to prepare her to become his bride, why didn't Abraham tell him then that she was really his wife, not his sister? Had the Lord not intervened, would Abraham have actually let Sarah marry the pharaoh? And what was the purpose of having them go to Egypt in the first place? Please consider the following points:

- If it was really Abraham's idea to have Sarah pose as his sister, why did the Lord not admonish him for putting her in such a precarious situation with the pharaoh? And why did he let him keep all his ill-gotten wealth?

- They pulled the same stunt on the king of Gerar, and like the pharaoh, the Lord threatened the king, who ended up giving Abraham more wealth, which he was allowed to keep. And again, Abraham was never chastised, suggesting it had been the Lord's plan all along.

- There was much wealth in Egypt, and Abraham and Sarah would be virtually unknown there. It was the ideal place for him to acquire his riches.

Since the Lord apparently assisted Abraham in pulling the same ruse on two separate occasions, are we to believe that it was really God Almighty who stooped to such levels of deceit in order to extort wealth from these rulers? And does it not suggest that it was a preconceived plan to make Abraham a wealthy man?

Prior to the incident with the King of Gerar, the Lord had never revealed to Abraham who he was. However, during his next visit, he told him he was "El Shaddai," which through later interpretations was redefined to mean God Almighty. During this visit, he told Abraham that Sarah would bear a son and he was to be called Isaac. He also made a covenant with him in which he would give Isaac's descendants their own land. Then when Abraham was ninety-nine years old (a year before Isaac was to be born), he paid him another visit.

The story as related in Genesis chapter 18 says that Abraham was sitting inside the entrance to his tent when he suddenly saw three men standing nearby. It does not say he saw them approaching from the distance or that they were even walking, only that they were suddenly standing where no one was standing a moment ago. Is this a clue that they had teleported down to that location?

Genesis 18:2 describes the Lord and his two companions as *three men* and says they ate and drank with Abraham, so we can assume that they were normal-looking individuals. They were actually en route to Sodom, presumably to arrange its destruction. During this visit, the Lord reminded Abraham that by this time next year, Sarah would bear a son (this suggests that she may already have been in the first stages of pregnancy during her later encounter with the king in Gerar). In any case, the Bible says that Sarah overheard this conversation from inside the tent and laughed at the idea.

In light of what we know about alien abductions, we might speculate that she was abducted and inseminated in the same manner. If the event were blocked from her conscious memory, wouldn't she have believed her pregnancy was a miracle?

While Isaac was still young, Genesis 22:2 describes a rather strange turn of events when the Lord ordered Abraham to sacrifice him as a burnt offering. But why? Abraham followed the Lord's instructions: he brought Isaac to the designated place and prepared an altar. Yet nothing is said about how he prepared Isaac or what Isaac's reaction was when he learned that he was to be the sacrifice. Did he simply lay across the altar, ready and willing to give up his life, or did Abraham have to overpower him and tie him up? This detail seems to have been conveniently omitted from the story. Nevertheless, it states that just as Abraham was about to plunge his knife into him, an angel intervened and saved his life.

None of this makes any sense. What kind of god would order a man to kill his son? And why? This was the same god who predicted Isaac's miraculous birth and promised Abraham that he would give his descendants their own land. Unless the Lord was considering reneging on his promise, I think we can be reasonably certain that he was not about to let anything happen to Isaac. It is also hard to believe that a man such as Abraham would even consider killing him. Could it be that Abraham knew this was only a situation created to test Isaac, and that he was not really expected to kill him?

The Bible, however, relates this story as a test of Abraham. Considering his age and all their previous contact, what reason would the Lord have for testing him at this stage of the game? And what would he be testing him for? No. The logistics suggest that this was a test of Isaac. Isaac was being groomed by his parents to abide by proper moral and ethical values and thus was not subjected to a test of temptation like Adam. However, he was now the star of the show because it would be from his seed that the new race would emerge. It would appear that in this particular case, they needed to know if he would be willing to surrender his life—a quality that was later evident in Christ. It would seem that the new plan required that Christ be willing to accept his fate when the time came, so I would assume this was a priority issue and the most important of all the tests that followed. Had they been unable to genetically enhance this particular characteristic in Isaac, they may not have created Christ and proceeded in a different direction. Since the scriptures fail to describe Isaac's reaction, we really don't know if he was willing to die or not. It is possible that he was, but other factors lead me to believe he may not have been too thrilled with the idea. One is the fact that this same test appears to have been repeated on their next hybrid, Samson.

Samson

Like Isaac's mother, Samson's mother was also old and infertile, and she worked out in the fields, which would have provided many opportunities for abduction. And just as the Lord had informed Abraham in person that Sarah would give birth, an angel personally visited Samson's mother and told her that she would have a son. He advised her not to drink wine or any other fermented drink and not to eat any food that was unclean. He also told her that her son would set in motion the process of freeing his people from Philistine domination, which might suggest that it was a another reason for his creation.

She believed her visitor was an angel of God because his appearance was so awesome. He returned again one day when she was working in the fields, and this time she went to get her husband, Manoah. Manoah came and prepared a burnt sacrifice for the visitor, and as the fire blazed from the altar, the Bible says that the angel ascended in the flames (Jdg 13:20).

That makes no sense. However, when we consider that the only light source familiar to the scribe translating the story would have been from fire, would he not logically interpret the description of the bright light associated with the teleporting process as fire?

Most everyone knows the story of Samson. He allegedly possessed the strength of one hundred men and killed one thousand Philistines with the jawbone of an ass. He became enamored with Delilah, who coaxed him into revealing that the secret of his strength was his hair. While he was asleep, she shaved his head, thereby rendering him helpless and setting him up for the Philistines, who then gouged out his eyes and put him in prison.

When the Philistines gathered in their temple for a celebration, they had Samson brought in for amusement. He amused them by pushing apart the pillars supporting the temple, thereby causing it to collapse, killing all who were present, including the Philistine rulers and himself.

While it's an interesting story, I find it unlikely that Samson's hair had anything to do with his strength; it is more believable that it was the result of genetic enhancement. It appears that Samson's genes may also have been programmed with the same attribute they had previously tested on Isaac—a willingness to sacrifice his life. Whether or not it worked on Isaac is uncertain; however, since it appears to be the first of a series of experiments that were performed, we might assume that it was the most important and may have required a backup test. If, however, it had not been successful with Isaac, they may have found a way to make it work on Samson. Either way, it suggests that the test was done twice.

Everything the Bible says about Samson is written in Judges, chapters 13–16. He was not a righteous person, as were Abraham, Isaac, Noah, and Moses; he patronized prostitutes and murdered many Philistines. So why is he portrayed as a biblical hero? And why would the Lord create a hybrid with such iniquitous qualities? Could it be that in Samson's case, character may not have been an essential factor? Could it be that emphasis was on the enhanced genetic qualities being tested ... and that it was planned for him to be expendable? Almost everything he did was designed to incite the rage of the Philistines, so it is not surprising that they took advantage of his interest in Delilah in order to capture him. She had been constantly pressing him to learn the secret of his strength, and each time she questioned him about it, he made up a different story, so he probably knew they were using her to set him up.

The only way to end the Philistine's domination was to eliminate their rulers, and in order for it to work, he had to get them all at one time, leaving the people with no leadership. He knew they would soon be celebrating a feast to their god, Dagon, and that they would gather in their temple for the occasion, thereby providing the perfect opportunity. However, it meant letting himself be captured. If he were their prisoner, would they not use such an opportunity to get revenge by making him a public spectacle? But he knew his strength was an intimidating factor, so he had to create a situation in which he would appear vulnerable. He knew they would take advantage of his affair with Delilah, and he willingly played right into their hands. If they believed the story that his hair was the source of his strength, he knew he had it made.

After finally telling Delilah his "secret," he let her get him drunk, probably thinking he would wake up shackled by the soldiers. Moreover, I think he only expected to be put in prison; I don't believe he expected them to gouge out his eyes. We will never know for sure, but gouging out his eyes may be an embellishment that was later added over centuries of oral tradition. Once he started to go along with the plan, he had to see it through. Sure, he could have broken free and escaped, but then he would never have another opportunity like this, and the Philistines would never believe any other story he might concoct about what made him so strong. So if they were to believe he was truly powerless, he had to let them do whatever they wanted to him.

At this point, I think he actually accepted the fact that to accomplish his goal would probably mean his own death. The angel had told his mother that he would begin the deliverance of his people from the Philistines, so I believe it was known all along how things would turn out. And regardless of Samson's lack of moral qualities, the fact that, like Christ, he placed his mission above his life meant the test was a success.

The Shunammite Boy

I can understand if you think this is all off-the-wall speculation. However, consider the account described in 2 Kings 4:8–37 regarding the Shunammite boy. When we carefully examine all of the details in this story, it fits the pattern of what could be the creation of another hybrid.

The woman, a Shunammite who is not named, offered the prophet Elisha the use of one of the rooms in her house whenever he visited the region. Elisha wished to repay her kindness but had no idea of how to do it; however, it may have provided the Lord with the perfect opportunity to conduct another test. From what the Bible tells us of Elisha, he was in frequent communication with the Lord, so to solve his problem, the Lord instructed him to tell the woman that she would have a son. Like the mother of Isaac and the mother of Samson, she, too, was elderly and sterile, but this time there was a problem because the child *allegedly* died.

Certain details of this story suggest that he may have been used to test another quality that was evident in Christ—genetically enhanced telepathic abilities, which Christ apparently used to communicate with the Lord. While he was still very young, it appears the child's mental awareness may have "switched on" suddenly. He was probably somewhere between three and five years old when it happened and he went out to where his father was working, complaining, "My head! My head!" His father, who was very old, had a servant take him to his mother. As she sat trying to give him comfort him in her lap, the boy allegedly died. Since the child was complaining about his head, we get the impression that he may have suffered a brain hemorrhage or even an aneurysm, either of which is unlikely to occur in a young child. However, according to how he was revived by Elisha, it sounds as if he was being brought out of suspended animation.

The child may have suddenly become aware of other people's thoughts collectively, without being able to sort them out. It would have been a frightening experience hearing the thoughts of many people all at the same time. Think of how a deaf person might react if his hearing was suddenly restored while standing in the middle of Times Square on New Year's Eve. The child would not know or understand what was happening and would desperately try to block out all the "noise" happening in his head.

Lying in his mother's lap probably helped. He may have reacted instinctively, taking deep breaths and relaxing his muscles, and assuming he was a hybrid, he was able to concentrate on these relaxing techniques to a greater degree. He most likely induced himself into a state of suspended animation; it acted as a safety valve. His metabolism slowed down to where his pulse was undetectable. His skin then became cold, and his mother would naturally have assumed he was dead.

You may think I am pushing the envelope on this one, but it is a fact that infants, when severely traumatized, can fall into a state of suspended animation. I remember watching a program several years ago that featured a story on the 7.4 earthquake that struck Kobe, Japan, in 1995. It showed infants being pulled from the rubble of a collapsed hospital—two weeks later—who had managed to survive in this state. This, of course, is all speculation, as there is no way to know what really happened to the Shunammite boy. Considering the miraculous aspect of his birth and the fact that he was complaining about his head, the idea seems plausible. But wait, there's more.

His mother put him on the bed in Elisha's room and ran out to find Elisha. When Elisha saw her approaching, he realized she was in great distress and asked what was wrong. After she explained, he handed his staff to his servant and ordered him to run on ahead and "lay my staff upon the face of the child" (2Ki 4:29). The woman stayed with Elisha, who, because of his advanced age, could not walk too fast.

The servant soon returned and met them on the road. He said he had lain the staff on the boy's face, but there was no sound or response. When they reached the house, Elisha went directly to his room and closed the door. Then it says he climbed up on the bed and lay on top of the boy. Elisha may have been using his own body heat to stimulate the boy's metabolism because it says his body began to warm up, so apparently it was working. Elisha then paced the floor for a while, waiting for him to come around. After a few minutes passed and nothing happened, he stretched out over him again, and this time the child began to stir. It says he sneezed several times, probably a reaction to his changing body temperature, and he woke up.

This story raises some intriguing questions. How did Elisha know that lying on top of the boy would revive him? And having his servant place his staff on the boy's face was a rather curious act—what was that supposed to have accomplished?

Since Elisha was in frequent communication with the Lord, is it possible that his staff contained some sort of communicating device, one that could be used to detect the slow-motion breathing of suspended animation when laid on the boy's body? Once the problem was diagnosed and Elisha was alone in his room behind the closed door, instructions on how to revive the child were communicated to him.

Nothing more is said about the boy. If this was a test to enhance telepathic abilities, he should have developed an awareness of other people's thoughts and feelings from infancy and adapted to it as he grew. Turning on so suddenly was a very traumatic experience. The child was totally unprepared for, and unaware of, what was happening to him.

Because the author of 2 Kings is unknown, one might doubt the veracity of this story by questioning how he knew the details of what occurred between Elisha and the boy in the bedroom since there was no one there to bear witness. Therefore, it could be a work of fiction. However, since the story was passed along, it is possible that Elisha recounted the details to someone who later wrote them down.

Solomon

If the Lord truly was creating hybrids, I might suspect Solomon was next. His mother, Bathsheba, was a young fertile woman, which seemed a deviation from using old and sterile women. However, the fact that he allegedly exhibited a phenomenal wisdom presents the possibility that he possessed hybrid genes. One clue is that when he broke the Lord's covenant by taking wives from other nations and even worshipping their gods, the Lord did not dispose of him as he did other unfaithful kings—why? When King Ahaziah broke the rules, he did not think twice about eliminating him. Allegedly, the Lord was not happy with Solomon's activities, so why would he be partial to him—unless he was a hybrid playing a crucial role in his plan?

Being that Solomon was the son of King David and destined to become a high-profile public figure, he was an ideal subject, providing the maximum test of wisdom to deal with the many important decisions he would be required to make during his own reign as king. And if the Lord was testing enhanced attributes to be incorporated into Christ, the wisdom of Solomon would certainly seem like a logical step in the testing sequence since it would be important that Christ also possess superior wisdom.

John the Baptist

Another old and sterile woman who seems to have miraculously conceived was Elizabeth, the cousin of Christ's mother, Mary, and the wife of a priest named Zechariah. One night while Zechariah was performing his duties in the temple, he was visited by an angel who told him that Elizabeth would bear a son and that he was to be called John. Because of their advanced age and the fact that Elizabeth was sterile, Zechariah naturally questioned the angel's words. The angel then identified himself as Gabriel and said the Lord had sent him to deliver this news. But because he questioned the word of the Lord, Zechariah was struck mute as a punishment, and supposedly his voice did not return until the day the child was circumcised.

So did the angel really do something that caused Zechariah to become mute, or was it an embellishment that was added later? That is something we may never know, but we do know that the ETs involved with the abductions seem to be great at mind control.

John the Baptist appears to be the last hybrid they created before Christ. Since his mother was old and sterile, it makes sense that she, too, may have been inseminated during an abduction in which her conscious mind was programmed to block out any memory of the event. Up to this point, the creation of hybrids had been separated by centuries. However, John and Christ were born only six months apart, which suggests that John was created to set the stage for Christ—he did baptize him, and they were also related.

John became a hermit who lived in the wilderness and survived on locusts and wild honey. He began his preaching before Christ and told his followers that someone more powerful than himself was coming—someone whose sandals he was not worthy of carrying. So it appears highly probable that John was used to set the stage for Christ's debut.

Christ

According to the Bible, six months later the Lord sent Gabriel to Nazareth to visit a young virgin named Mary and tell her that she was about to become the mother of a very special child. He also informed her about the "miraculous pregnancy" of her cousin, Elizabeth. Unlike the others, Christ was to be the perfect hybrid created from the alien's own gene pool, and it may well have been from the Lord himself; he always referred to Christ as *his Son*, and Christ likewise referred to him as *his Father*. And it appears that Christ possessed the same genetically enhanced qualities previously tested on the other hybrids, except of course for Samson's superhuman strength. That would have been impractical.

If we allow logic and common sense to prevail, we can only conclude that if Mary was a virgin at the time of conception, it could only have occurred through artificial insemination. So why, after using sterile older women, did they use a fertile young virgin to bring Christ into the world? Since the prophecy was given to Isaiah seven hundred years earlier, it had apparently been decided from the beginning, so we must assume that it was part of the plan. However, it seems unlikely that prophesying the Messiah's mother would be a virgin was meant as a means of identifying the event when it actually occurred. How would anyone know, or even have reason to suspect, that Mary was still a virgin, and under what circumstances would she have found it necessary to tell anybody? Could it be that using a virgin was a precautionary measure to assure there would be no anomalies in Christ—genetically or otherwise? Most doctors will tell you that if you have a one-night stand with a member of the opposite sex, you are not only having sex with that person but everyone that person ever had sex with, plus all his or her partners … and so on and so on. I am not implying that Mary and Joseph led promiscuous lives, only that during intercourse there is an exchange of bodily fluids and hormones. Was this a factor that could possibly affect Christ later—and the reason that intercourse had to be avoided until after his birth?

Hybrid Factors

I would like to highlight particular details regarding these biblical characters so you will better understand why I have labeled them as possible hybrids. I suggested that Isaac was tested to see if he would willingly sacrifice his life, and I suggested that the same, or a follow-up test, was conducted with Samson. I proposed that Solomon was created to test an enhanced capacity for wisdom, and that the Shunammite boy was an experiment of enhanced telepathic abilities. It is apparent in the New Testament that Christ possessed each of these traits, suggesting that after Adam's failure, a contingency plan was instituted. It also suggests that Christ was not part of the original plan, for had it been successful, there would have been no need to bring a Messiah onto the scene.

Except for Solomon, whose mother was young and fertile, and Christ, whose mother was a young virgin, these sons were born to old and sterile women. There are subtle clues that other fertile women besides Bathsheba and Mary may also have given birth to hybrids; however, there is not enough information provided to substantiate it further. Nevertheless, the details surrounding those that I have mentioned tend to suggest that a sequential series of tests was conducted.

One clue to Adam's hybrid status is the fact that he had been isolated. Initially, it was necessary to create a secure environment where the first hybrids could be tested and groomed. The Garden of Eden might be compared to a highly restricted test facility—like Area 51—a place completely isolated from the rest of the world. Bringing a woman into this environment to give birth to Adam and raise him may have defeated their purpose because she would have brought with her the influence of the outside world. I would think the eventual purpose was for the outside world to be influenced by the hybrids, not the other way around. Therefore, if Adam had been born in the normal fashion, it probably would have occurred on the outside. Then, in order to isolate him in Eden, he would have to be taken from his birth mother, which would have been a rather cruel thing to do. But if she only carried him in her womb for three months, and if she had no memory of her abduction or pregnancy, it would have been the kindest way to proceed. The balance of Adam's gestation in an incubation chamber makes sense, and we might also consider this to be the case in their creation of Eve.

There are two factors suggesting that the birth of sons to old and sterile women were preplanned events. First, the women, or their spouses, received a personal visit from the Lord or one of his agents announcing the birth in advance. Second, it was announced that all births would be sons. However, the fact that the mothers of Isaac, Samson, the Shunammite boy, and John the Baptist were old and sterile and the mothers of Solomon and Christ were not raises an important question: *What was the purpose of using old and sterile women in the first place?*

Since this practice began with Isaac, perhaps it had something to do with what happened to Adam. The Bible mentions nothing of Adam's birth and childhood, nor is there any mention of parents; therefore, we have been led to believe that he simply "popped" into existence as a full-grown adult. But common sense tells us that was unlikely. The Bible does tell us that Adam was *"placed in"* or brought to, the Garden of Eden *"in the east"* by the Lord God. This suggests that his womb gestation may have occurred somewhere in the West, which could have been in Egypt or even on another continent, such as North or South America.

We know that somewhere around the third month, the little greys remove the fetuses from the women they inseminate, so fetus extraction and incubation may be standard procedure in the creation of certain hybrids. Since there is no mention of Adam having been born, it is possible that his birth, as well as Eve's, originated in an incubation chamber after a short gestation period in the womb of a human female.

However, since he broke the rules, he was not the perfect specimen that was intended: there was a flaw in his enhanced attributes. And if they did create him for the purpose of spawning a new and genetically improved race, this would have been a major problem.

It is possible that Adam's defect occurred during the period of womb gestation. He was the first hybrid infused with elements of alien (or genetically modified) DNA, and they had probably selected the most perfect young and healthy woman they could find as his gestation host. However, the fact that they began using old and sterile women right after this suggests that there possibly may have been a problem with young, fertile women because a fertile woman's body undergoes chemical and hormonal changes that would not occur in a sterile older woman. Might this have been the factor responsible for the problem? Since they used a sterile older woman to create Isaac, it could be a sign that this was the case.

Isaac was strong in character; he obeyed all the rules and adhered to proper moral and ethical values. And since his descendants did not fall into the abyss of decadence as did Adam's, it would appear that they had solved the problem. However, if I am correct in assuming that he was not too enthused about becoming a burnt sacrifice for no particular reason, there was still a problem enhancing certain characteristics. So although an older sterile woman may have proved more effective regarding moral and ethical aspects, there were still some problems that needed to be ironed out.

From what we know about the hybrids created after Isaac, the Lord may have found a way to prevent further contamination, and it would seem that Samson's genes may have been protected by such an immunity. Perhaps his strength was used as a gauge to measure its effectiveness. Since he allegedly had the strength to push apart the pillars of a stone temple and he willingly sacrificed his life, it would appear that the system was effective. But would it work on a young fertile woman?

Before they took that risk, it seems that they conducted one more test with the sterile old Shunammite woman, and it may have been an experiment to enhance telepathic abilities. The child should have been able to sense the thoughts and emotions of others from infancy and, as he grew, adapted naturally to this ability. Instead, it appears to have remained dormant for a few years before suddenly kicking in at full power. Does that mean they still had a problem, or was it the result of overcompensating for the system's effectiveness in protecting the child's *enhanced* ability?

If, as I suspect, Solomon was the next hybrid, I am inclined to think they may have overcompensated—and the immunity somehow prevented the child's enhanced attribute from manifesting until he was a few years old. Since Solomon's mother, Bathsheba, was a fertile young woman, it would seem that if they were still not sure, they would have used another old and sterile woman. And since they were planning to use a young, fertile virgin with Christ, it is only logical that if young fertile women were the source of the problem, they would have to use another one to make sure they had the problem solved. Bathsheba may simply have been that test.

Now, if success with Bathsheba meant the problem was solved, then why did they not use a fertile young woman for John the Baptist? If they were simply picking women at random to be surrogate mothers for hybrids, and if it really didn't matter if they were young, old, fertile, or sterile, then my whole theory goes down the tubes. Everything I have proposed so far makes sense except old and barren Elizabeth. However, from a logistical perspective, if John's role was to set the stage for Christ, he would have to be born around the same time as Christ, and they would have to grow up together. What better choice could they have made than Mary's cousin, Elizabeth?

Moses allegedly recorded the stories of Adam and Isaac as the Lord dictated them to him. Those of Samson and the Shunammite boy were written by a person or persons unknown, as were those of John the Baptist and Christ in the New Testament. The question is, are they describing a supernatural god performing miracles, or are they part of the record describing how the Lord was manipulating the advancement of the human race through genetic engineering? Let's examine a few more details.

The Incredibly Long Life Spans

Some people think it is all a myth, but if you take the time to study biblical chronology, you can actually determine that the creation of Adam occurred about 6,000 years ago, circa 4004–4000 BC. Chapter 5 in the book of Genesis, and a few other scriptures, provide sufficient information by which it is possible to backtrack through the early years of Genesis. If the information is accurate, then Adam and many of his descendants did live to the ages described in the Bible. So what happened? Why don't we live that long today?

The evidence suggests that the tree of life, or whatever it really was (it may only be a symbolic reference to something else), was responsible for their longevity. I also have a suspicion that it was a certain element in Adam and Eve's genetic makeup that made it work. It was also an element their children would inherit and pass on to their children, and they to their children, ad infinitum—something we may still possess today. Because Adam and Eve had eaten from this tree for many years, they had accumulated enough of its benefits to provide them and their offspring with extremely long lives before the effects would eventually wear off and they would grow old and die.

Although some of Adam's descendants also lived for 900 years, life spans for most gradually decreased. It all ended with Noah; although he allegedly lived for 950 years, his sons only lived 400 to 600 years, after which life spans dwindled to about 120 years. So the Bible is telling us that Adam's descendants did experience a gradual decrease of life cycles, and the only thing it can logically be attributed to is the tree of life. And the scenario described in Genesis suggests that the only reason for Adam and Eve's expulsion from Eden was to prevent them further access to it.

There is one aspect of their longevity that has never been explained: the length of time it took for them to procreate. Because Adam and Eve produced no children while living in Eden, it is possible that they were evicted before reaching puberty and had not yet experienced intercourse, which seems unlikely. It also seems unlikely that Adam would have been tested before he reached an age of mature reasoning, so it is doubtful that they left Eden before becoming sexually active.

Their first son, Cain, was born sometime after they left Eden. Exactly how many years elapsed before Abel was born is unknown, but the Bible says their third son, Seth, was born when Adam was 130 years old. You would think that once they began having intercourse, they would have had children almost immediately. Producing only three children in the span of 130 years gives the impression that they did not have sex very often—unless due to the genetics supporting their extended life cycles, puberty was not realized until they were over 60 or 80 years of age, in which case it still took 50 to 70 years for them to produce three children. The Bible says that Adam lived for 930 years ... but nothing about how long Eve lived. It does state that she lived a long life and had many children, so logically the question would seem to focus on the frequency of her fertility cycle.

A woman can only conceive during her fertile period. Based on the average life cycle today, this period occurs about once a month (every 28 days). If her life span were several hundred years, would it be natural for her fertility period to be on a monthly cycle? If that were the case, she could literally have hundreds of children in her lifetime. And the strain her body would undergo giving birth to a multitude of children would likely have a negative effect on her life span. With Eve, it would make sense that her menstrual cycle was synchronized with her longevity—she may only have become fertile every ten or twenty years.

The chronicles of Adam's descendants reveal that many of the men did not become fathers until they were at least 65 years old—and in many cases, not until they were over 180. Therefore, it is possible that they did not reach puberty until the age of 50 or 60. Also, the deterioration rate of the tree of life factor may have varied as Adam's descendants melded into the local population. Men who did not produce children until they were 180 suggests that they married women of Eve's descent with fertility cycles that were probably separated by decades. Those who took wives from the local population with normal life spans and fertility cycles would naturally have produced children at a much younger age. We must also consider that the Bible predominantly mentions the birth of first sons and little or nothing of daughters. So it is possible that many men produced one or more daughters before a son, in which case they, too, may actually have become fathers at an earlier age. Sons were the progenitors of the bloodline, and much importance was placed on this factor; they were the ones who would carry on the family name. Daughters, however, would marry into other families, and their children would bear their new family's name. Therefore, a number of variables could explain the wide range of ages in which the Bible states that men became fathers. Everything supposedly changed after the flood, when the average life span of Adam and Eve's descendants began to stabilize at around 120 years and women's fertility periods decreased proportionately into a monthly cycle. So it would appear that the potency of the tree of life inherited from Adam and Eve decreased in each succeeding generation.

There are two questions about this extended life span that I feel are important and, to my knowledge, they have never been addressed: At what age did a woman reach menopause, and at what age did men and women actually begin to show their age?

The Bible tells us that Abraham lived to be 175, and Sarah lived to be 127. Abraham was 100 and Sarah about 90 when she became pregnant with Isaac, and both are described as being elderly at this time. That means Sarah was approximately 65 years old when she and Abraham were in Egypt and the pharaoh was so taken with her beauty that he wanted her as one of his wives. Logically, this made me wonder how old Sarah looked at 65. This was long after the flood, when life spans supposedly had decreased to approximately 120 years. Sarah's life span would have fallen within the norm, however, considering how long Abraham lived, it would appear that the effects of the tree of life had not yet completely worn off and were still manifesting in some people.

Today, most people maintain youthful appearances as adults until at least the age of 35 or 40, at which time they begin to exhibit signs of aging. Wrinkles become more prominent, and many men begin to experience hair loss; eventually, both men and women's hair turn grey. Without any major medical complications, most will live to be 70 or 80, and in some cases, over 90 and 100. So there is approximately a 35- to 40-year span between when a person starts to lose his youthful appearance and when he dies. We might expect that with Abraham and Sarah, the average might have been 60 or even 70 due to their life spans of 127 and 175 years. At 65, she may have appeared to be 35 or a youthful-looking 40.

Every now and then, a genetic factor from the past will show up unexpectedly for no apparent reason. A child with blond hair and blue eyes may be suddenly born to a family who for generations has had predominantly dark hair and brown eyes. Usually you will find that the child inherited the genes of some long-forgotten ancestor with blond hair and blue eyes who married into the family. Such genetic flukes are rare, but they do occur periodically, and it may explain the circumstances surrounding Jacob's wife, Rachel.

Rachel was a healthy young woman when she became Jacob's wife, but it was possibly ten or even twenty years before she conceived and gave birth to their son, Joseph. It was not for lack of trying, because she was Jacob's true love, and he wanted desperately for her to produce his first son. Meanwhile, he fathered eleven children with her sister, Leah, and two maidservants.

I had considered the possibility that Rachel may have been sterile and that Joseph was a hybrid because, as you will see later, he did play a key role in the biblical scenario. However, the fact that Rachel had a second child seemed to discredit that idea. It was years later, in her old age, when she conceived Benjamin; however, because she was elderly, she suffered a difficult labor and died while giving birth.

Since Joseph, at the time of his birth, was the youngest of ten brothers and one sister, we can assume that at least ten or more years had elapsed before he was conceived by Rachel. It is believed that Joseph was about seventeen years old when his brothers sold him into Egyptian slavery, and since Benjamin had not yet been born, we can assume that more than seventeen years had elapsed before Rachel became pregnant with him. Did she inherit Eve's genetic code for fertility as a fluke? Actually, the scenario suggests another possibility: her fertility cycle may have been altered.

To fit the project's schedule, Rachel's fertility cycle may have been reprogrammed with the same cycle possessed by Eve. In order to move Jacob's family to Egypt and away from Adam's virus, the Lord manipulated the events that brought Joseph into power in Egypt. It would not have happened had he been born first. He had to be the youngest and the son of Rachel in order for him to become Jacob's favorite and thus generate the resentment that would lead to his older brothers selling him into Egypt, where he eventually became governor. Her conception of Benjamin in her old age was a by-product of this reprogramming. She may have been programmed with Eve's fertility cycle, but not her genetic code for longevity, thus her body was too weak to survive the stress of Benjamin's birth. There will be more about this later.

The Iceman

In 1992, two Germans hiking in the Austrian Alps near the Italian border discovered the frozen body of a Stone Age man who died over 5,000 years ago. Commonly referred to as "the Iceman," scientists named him Ötzi for the locale of his discovery. However, he is forcing them to reevaluate their beliefs about the era in which he lived, which was about 700 years after the alleged creation of Adam and Eve, so Adam would still have been alive. Since his body had been frozen in ice for 5,000 years and was fairly well preserved, it provided an opportunity for extensive study.

It was confirmed through radiocarbon dating of bone and skin samples that he died between 5,200–5,300 years ago. But his clothes, tools, and hunting gear were much more sophisticated than what scientists thought possible for that time. His hat, jacket, and leggings were made from leather and fur, and his shoes were stuffed with grass for insulation. His ax was almost pure copper. High levels of copper and arsenic were found in his hair, suggesting that he may have smelted the copper himself.

Further tests revealed that he suffered from osteoarthritis, and it was speculated that he might have been treated for it with acupuncture. There were tattoos on his body that corresponded to acupuncture points associated with treating back and leg pain. Now, this was 1,000 years before the first known tattoos were used in Egypt and about 2,000 years before acupuncture was thought to have originated in China.

X-Rays and CAT scans revealed that the Iceman's carotid artery was partially closed and that he suffered from arterial sclerosis, suggesting that he may have been 60 to 70 years old at the time of death; however, chemical analysis conducted on his bones suggested that he was in his late forties. But the scientists were in for yet another surprise: X-rays of the jaw revealed that the Iceman's wisdom teeth had not broken through—something that typically occurs during adolescence today.[3]

Naturally, this presented many questions regarding the Iceman's real age at the time of death. Was he an older man, around 60 or 70, with arterial sclerosis? Was he in his late forties, as indicated by his bones, or was he an adolescent, as suggested by his wisdom teeth? None of this fits the pattern of human maturation today, so it would appear that people matured differently 5,000 years ago. That seems to be the logical hypothesis, but his wisdom teeth suggest that he may have matured at a much slower rate and may have had a life span far beyond what is common today. Naturally, this contradicted many mainstream beliefs about the history of the human race; however, it could add credibility to the Genesis account of people living for hundreds of years. It wasn't until they took a closer look at the X-rays that they discovered there was an arrowhead embedded in Ötzi's back, which might explain his seemingly premature death. Perhaps one day science will advance to a level that will allow us to determine what Ötzi's expected life span really was.

Is it possible that the Iceman was one of Adam and Eve's direct descendants? If so, he was in the snow-covered mountains of Austria, far removed from the region where his ancestors were believed to have lived. There are, however, many ancient Roman, Chinese, and Egyptian writings that tell of people who lived to be 900 or 1,000 years old, suggesting there may have been more than one Adam, more than one mitochondrial Eve, and more than one Garden of Eden—and that ETs were manipulating the evolution of mankind all over the world.

Notes

1. Lilith
    "Adam & Eve: Lost Innocence." *Biography*. Prod. Bill Harris.
    A&E. 1996.

2. The names of God
    Web link:
    www.bidstrup.com/Bible.htm

3. The Iceman
    "How Old Are Humans?" *Encounters with the Unexplained*. Dir.
    David Priest. PAX (now ION).

Chapter 12

TECHNOLOGY

W hen I first began exploring the Bible, I was merely looking for information on the great Egyptian pyramids, hoping it might provide a clue as to when they were actually built. Then I became intrigued by the accounts of how the Lord often came down in a cloud to speak with Moses, and how angels would appear and disappear in a flash of light. Having become familiar with the alien abduction enigma, I could not help but notice how remarkably similar these descriptions were to abductee accounts of the little greys appearing in a bright light. It sounded just like the transporter beam on *Star Trek*, and I began to wonder if they might actually be describing some sort of teleportation process. So I decided to take a closer look at these biblical accounts to see if there was any real substance to the idea. However, once I got into it, I was amazed at the number of references there were to other technologies. It was difficult initially, having been indoctrinated with religious beliefs from childhood to avoid being absorbed into the mysticism surrounding some of the stories. However, once I began to focus on the basic elements of each event logically, not from a supernatural or religious perspective, the technical implications seemed quite evident. Beginning with flying craft, this chapter will focus on what I perceive to be references to the various technologies.

Flying Craft

The most famous incident occurred around 575 BC and is described in the first chapter of Ezekiel. It appears to be a unique account of the contact he had with a being who called himself the Sovereign Lord and came down out of the sky in a large metallic craft. But then I had to ask *why*. Why this personal contact? Ezekiel's book is a compilation of prophecies he received in the form of visions from the Lord or his angels, so why does this first contact describe so vividly the landing of a ship? Only after reading it through several times did I begin to recognize clues that the landing may actually have been an unplanned event.

It began when Ezekiel saw a windstorm (whirlwind) approaching from the north. It was a "large cloud with flashing lightning and surrounded by brilliant light" (Eze 1:4).

We must understand that if it really was some type of flying machine or spacecraft, then Ezekiel was exposed to something far beyond his understanding: he could only describe it in relation to that with which he was familiar. Here is a logical analysis of his encounter:

The center of the fire looked like glowing metal. And in the fire was what looked like four living creatures. In appearance their form was that of a man. (Eze 1:4–5)

Obviously, the glowing metal would be the craft itself, and the fire would be the brilliant glow or aura surrounding it. Inside, apparently through a large window, he could see four men.

But each of them had four faces and four wings. Their legs were straight; their feet were like those of a calf and gleamed like burnished bronze. (Eze 1:6–7)

To believe these beings actually had wings is to suggest they could fly, and if that were the case, then why would they have need of a flying craft? Therefore, what Ezekiel described as wings may have been some kind of mechanical structure or apparatus behind each man that was connected to the craft's landing gear, as this seems to be suggested later on.

Their legs being straight indicates that they were standing and probably operating controls on a panel in front of them. Describing their feet as those of a calf suggests they were wearing something like shiny brown boots. The only footwear known to Ezekiel would have been sandals, so the hoof of a calf was probably the only thing he could compare to the likeness of smooth, shiny boots. Moreover, the fact that he could see their feet suggests that the window he looked into was large.

> *Under their wings on their four sides, they had the hands of a man. All four of them had faces and wings, and their wings touched one another.* (Eze 1:8–9)

The hands of the four men were at their sides—where any normal person's hands would be. He then repeats the fact that they all had faces and wings. And as I suggested, that which Ezekiel took to be wings may have been the design of a structure, or structures, behind the men.

> *Each one went straight ahead and they did not turn as they moved.* (Eze 1:9)

At this point, the craft was moving straight ahead, the same way the men were facing, and it did not make any turns. This may be describing the craft as it was coming in for a landing.

> *Their faces looked like this: Each of the four had the face of a man, and on the right side each had the face of a lion and on the left the face of an ox; each also had the face of an eagle.* (Eze 1:10)

A being with four faces seems highly improbable, especially when one is human, one feline, one bovine, and one a bird of prey. But if we apply a little common sense, there is a logical interpretation.

These faces may have been patches or emblems, similar to what a military pilot might wear on his flight suit. On the right side of each chest was an emblem with a lion's face, and on the left was one with the face of an ox. Since Ezekiel specified that these faces were on the right and left sides, it is only logical to conclude that the other two were in the front or center. He already said they each had the face of a man, so the third face would be that of the men themselves, and the last one, depicting an eagle's face, could represent an emblem on the fronts of their uniforms, centered between the others. Some Bibles describe the eagle's face as being on the men's backs; however, Ezekiel mentions nothing of the men turning around so he could see their backs. This may have been an assumption made by later writers.

But what did these images represent? They probably signified something. We can only speculate, but they may have represented different missions or projects they were involved with on our planet.

The appearance of the living creatures was like burning coals of fire or like torches. (Eze 1:13)

I think this statement was misunderstood by the scribes during translation. Their interpretation suggests the men were glowing, which seems rather unlikely. A logical interpretation is that the craft's interior lighting, or possibly lights from control panels in front of them, were reflecting off their faces and clothing. Any kind of manufactured light would have been unfamiliar to Ezekiel, as the only light he knew was produced by fire.

Fire moved back and forth among the creatures; it was bright and lightning flashed out of it. (Eze 1:13)

If there were control panels in front of the men, they may have had banks of flashing and blinking lights that gave the impression of lights ("fire") moving back and forth. Ezekiel would naturally compare these flashing and blinking lights to fire. However, the "lightning" flashing out of the panels suggests that it may have been a bright strobe light—possibly a visual alarm. They may have been experiencing some sort of problem.

The creatures sped back and forth like flashes of lightning. (Eze 1:14)

This gives the impression that they were running amok. Ezekiel already stated that their legs were straight, suggesting they were standing. They could have been leaning over control panels and moving from side to side as they manipulated different controls, especially if they were dealing with some kind of problem. It may have been an optical illusion created by all the flashing and blinking lights, or it could even mean that the craft made rapid side-to-side movements as it came down—a maneuver frequently described in UFO sightings.

As I looked at the living creatures, I saw a wheel on the ground beside each creature with its four faces. (Eze 1:15)

Logically, wheels on the ground suggest that it was the ship's landing gear. They came out of the craft's underside, and since it is unlikely that the men were riding on the outside of the vehicle, it may have appeared from Ezekiel's position that each wheel was located in close proximity to each man inside.

This was the appearance and structure of the wheels: They sparkled like chrysolite and all four looked alike. Each appeared to be made like a wheel intersecting with a wheel. (Eze 1:16)

The wheels sparkled in a yellow or greenish gemlike quality, suggesting they were probably metallic. Since airports were nonexistent in 575 BC, the craft could not have landed like an airplane; it would have to come down vertically, and a vehicle that can land vertically would have minimum use for wheels, so we might speculate that they probably were pods. And if they sparkled like gems, they were probably solid, and solid wheels would be impractical, making for an awful bumpy ride. The description of wheels intersecting with wheels may simply have been the design of the pods.

> *As they moved, they would go in any one of the four directions the creatures faced …* (Eze 1:17)

This gives the impression that the craft moved in four different directions on the ground: right, left, forward, and backward. However, if the craft had landing pods, such a maneuver seems improbable unless it occurred just before the craft actually touched down. It may also be that this was when the craft started bouncing into the air, as he begins to describe in verse 1:19.

> *The wheels did not turn about as the creatures went.* (Eze 1:17)

"As the creatures went" could pertain to when they were leaving—or bouncing into the air. The wheels not turning could also mean they did not rotate, suggesting they were pods, not wheels.

> *Their rims were high and awesome, and all four rims were full of eyes all around.* (Eze 1:18)

I am not certain what this is referring to, because it makes no sense that the rims were up high and the wheels were on the ground. In some Bibles, these "rims" are referred to as "rings." Could it be that the scribes doing the translating misinterpreted this? Could it be that there were four separate rims, or rings (which were higher up and awesome looking), rotating around the outer edge of the craft and having nothing to do with the landing gear? This seems like a more logical interpretation and in line with many current UFO descriptions, and the "eyes all around" is probably indicative of their design. But this is only speculation.

When the living creatures moved, the wheels beside them moved. (Eze 1:19)

We have what appears to be synchronous movement between the men in the craft and the wheels. Could it be that they were operating separate mechanisms to lower the landing gear? It seems rather primitive, as one would expect the landing gear of a flying craft to be powered by some kind of motor. But if they were dealing with a problem, it is possible that they may have had to lower the gear manually.

And when the living creatures rose from the ground, the wheels also rose. (Eze 1:19)

This tells us the craft bounced a few times, another indication that they may have been experiencing a problem and were making an unscheduled and awkward landing.

Wherever the spirit would go, they would go, and the wheels would rise along with them, because the spirit of the living creatures was in the wheels. (Eze 1:20)

When the craft rose into the air, so did the men and the landing gear. Again, this suggests that the craft bounced up and down several times, a maneuver that seems inconsistent with a higher technology—unless, of course, they were having problems.

One possibility is that they were having a problem with the landing gear. It should have locked into place when the gear made contact with the ground. And if they had to lower it manually, it may have taken several attempts before the locking mechanism engaged.

Spread out above the heads of the living creatures was what looked like an expanse, sparkling like ice and awesome. (Eze 1:22)

This seems to refer to the top outer hull of the craft. He perceived its smooth, shiny metallic surface as sparkling, or icy, in appearance.

When the creatures moved, I heard the sound of their wings, like the sound of rushing waters, like the tumult of an army. (Eze 1:24)

Ezekiel is saying that there was a loud noise, which was probably the propulsion system. He would naturally assume that to fly, one would need wings, and he was merely associating the revving sound of the engine each time the craft rose into the air with wings. "Rushing waters" is probably a good description of what it sounded like as the craft bounced about in its attempt to land.

When they stood still, they lowered their wings. (Eze 1:24)

The interior structure, which he described as wings, may have been mechanisms that were linked to the landing gear and descended behind the men, locking the gear in place after the craft finally touched down. In the first few attempts, perhaps the gear did not engage, forcing them to rev the engine, rise back into the air, and try again. When it finally did engage, the structures behind the men lowered, locking the gear in place.

Then there came a voice from above the expanse over their heads as they stood with lowered wings. (Eze 1:25)

Ezekiel heard a voice coming from the top of the craft.

Above the expanse over their heads was what looked like a throne of sapphire, and high above on the throne was a figure like that of a man. (Eze 1:26)

This throne of sapphire may have been a bluish hatch door that flipped open, with a man emerging from the open hatch.

I saw that what appeared to be from his waist up he looked like glowing metal, as if full of fire, and that from there down he looked like fire. (Eze 1:27)

As with the four men inside the craft, whom he described as glowing "like torches," he is describing the man standing above the open hatch on the upper section in like fashion. This further supports the idea that the glow was produced by interior lighting. It reflected off the upper part of the man's uniform (from his waist up), which may have been comprised of a shiny metallic fabric, thus giving him a "glowing metal" or "full of fire" appearance. From the waist down, he was closer to the light emanating from the open hatch, where the reflection was much brighter (from there down, he looked like fire).

Since the man was high above him and he could see below his waist suggests that he was standing above an open hatch. Had he been sitting, like a pilot in the cockpit of a plane, his lower torso probably would not have been visible.

We should also note that Ezekiel mentions no wings associated with this person as he did with those inside the craft, an indication that they probably were part of the interior structure.

And brilliant light surrounded him. Like the appearance of a rainbow in the clouds on a rainy day, so was the radiance around him. (Eze 1:27–28)

This most likely refers to the light reflecting off the open hatch door, providing a radiant background behind the man.

This was the appearance of the likeness of the glory of the Lord. When I saw it, I fell facedown, and I heard the voice of one speaking. (Eze 1:28)

Note that Ezekiel was comparing the bright glow of light emanating from within the craft to the "glory of the Lord." It is a common term in the Old Testament, usually associated with flying craft, which we will be coming across frequently.

Is it any wonder that Ezekiel believed he was face-to-face with God? After all, a huge metallic craft bathed in an aura of bright light appeared out of the sky and descended in front of him. There were four men inside, standing behind control panels with flashing and blinking lights—lights that bathed them in a fiery glow. Landing gear appeared from the underside of the craft, which bounced several times before finally settling on the ground. Then, from above, he heard a voice and looked up to see a fifth man in a shiny uniform standing above an open hatch, also bathed in the glow of light from within the ship. It was like nothing he had ever seen before. Surely this had to be God. Who else could display such awesome wonder?

Except for when Moses received the Ten Commandments, which I will cover shortly, landing a ship right in front of someone was an unprecedented event. So why now?

Again, it appears there may have been a problem. It would explain Ezekiel's description of the men as they "sped back and forth like flashes of lightning" while they were trying to deal with the situation—or lock the landing gear in place. It would also account for the bouncing he described as the ship was landing. This first contact was probably meant to be in the form of a vision since he had many after this, but for some unknown reason (possibly a mechanical problem), they may have been forced to land, thus making this first contact face-to-face.

Some of you may have read *The Spaceships of Ezekiel* by the late Joseph F. Blumrich, a former NASA space engineer. Although he was not the first to recognize the technological implications in biblical scripture, he was one of the first to publish his ideas. He perceived the craft shaped somewhat like a child's toy top, with four long legs, or poles, extending vertically from its underside down to the ground. He suggests that there were four helicopter-like blades in the center of each pole, and all the blades folded down after they stopped rotating, which he perceived as being the four wings. He perceived a jet or rocket-like engine located in the underside of the craft as being its propulsion source, and he provided a valid scientific evaluation of the wheels intersecting with wheels. He even presents a detailed schematic of how they could rotate in all directions.

When I first began researching information for this manuscript years ago, my original ideas concerning Ezekiel were much more primitive in their concept and were actually laughed at by a couple of my friends who were familiar with his book. Since he was a space scientist and I was not, they heartily ridiculed some of my ideas. As my research evolved, so did my perception of Ezekiel's encounter. I wish to point out that Blumrich's ideas are valid. However, they were based on the technology he was familiar with over three decades ago, when his book was published.

Readers who are old enough may remember the ENIAC and the UNIVAC, the forerunners of modern-day calculators and computers. The ENIAC (Electronic Numerical Integrator And Computer) was created in the late 1940s by the army to compute ballistic firing tables during World War II. Costing $486,804.22, it contained 1,500 relays, 17,468 vacuum tubes (or 19,000, depending on whom you reference), weighed over 30 tons, and took up about 1,000 square feet of floor space.[1] The UNIVAC (UNIVersal Automatic Computer) was built in the early 1950s at a cost of about $1 million. It only contained 300 relays and 5,600 vacuum tubes and was the size of a one-car garage.[2] At the time, it was state of the art, even though it performed fewer functions than a pocket calculator costing $17.95 today. Could the engineers who built UNIVAC have perceived their million-dollar monstrosity becoming small enough to fit in the palm of your hand, performing a multitude of other functions at speeds millions of times faster and selling for less than twenty dollars? Probably not.

Another example of our ever-changing perception of the future is exemplified in the technology depicted on *Star Trek*. From the original series with Captain Kirk to *The Next Generation* with Captain Picard, there was a radical design change in the bridge and computer panels of the *Enterprise*. Comparing the old *Enterprise* to the new is almost like comparing the UNIVAC to a new laptop. The updated *Enterprise* was a reflection of our own technological advancement. As we evolved on a technical level, so did our perceptions of future technology. Likewise, the spaceship described by

Blumrich represented his ideas of futuristic or alien technology as it was perceived over thirty years ago, which by today's standards seems primitive.

Please do not misinterpret this as a put-down of Blumrich or his ideas. I thoroughly enjoyed his book and was greatly inspired by his commonsense approach. However, as time passes, we acquire new knowledge, we develop new technologies, and our views change accordingly. Today, our ideas of the future are viewed from a perspective based on the tools and technologies currently at our disposal. If Blumrich were still alive and wrote his book today, I am sure it would likewise reflect an evolution in his perceptions.

Getting back to the biblical account, Ezekiel could see the metallic surface of the craft and the four men who were inside. This means there was no aura or glow around the craft after it landed. The only mention he made of such a glow was when he first sighted it in the sky. His description of the craft just prior to and after touchdown suggests that the field creating the glow had been turned off. This could be a clue that they switched to an alternate propulsion system. To see the detail he described, Ezekiel had to be close to the craft, and if current UFO events are any indication, had this field been operating, the glow probably would have hurt his eyes, and he would have been in danger of suffering from radiation exposure—like Betty Cash and her companions experienced in Huffman, Texas, with the craft that bounced up and down over the highway.

If there was a problem that necessitated landing, I speculate they could have done so without the bouncing; I suspect they switched to an alternate non-radiation-producing (or backup) propulsion system for Ezekiel's safety. If they were on a mission to enlighten him with visions, as seems to be the subject of his book, the information he received in this first contact was probably also intended to be through a vision. If it was a problem that forced them to land, it happened right in front of him. To prevent him from being exposed to dangerous radiation, they had to make the switch in mid-flight, which may also account for the awkward bouncing as the ship landed. Again, this is only conjecture.

Another important detail is the "glowing metal" or "full of fire" appearance of the man standing above the open hatch on the upper section of the craft, not to mention the "burning coals of fire" appearance of the men inside. Logically, it sounds as if Ezekiel was describing interior lighting reflecting off a silvery or metallic fabric of the men's uniforms. The only mention of clothing worn by anyone associated with the deity is in the New Testament. Starting with Christ's resurrection, all the angels were suddenly wearing white, and I think that the reason for this, when we come to it, will be rather obvious. Except for this, no other accounts of appearances by the angels, or the Lord himself, mention how they were dressed. This suggests that nothing about their attire was unusual or worthy of mention: they wore clothing that allowed them to blend in with the general populace. And the fact that Ezekiel's description suggests a reflective quality in their attire is another indication that this may have been an unscheduled landing. Had it been planned, it seems only logical that they would have remained consistent with established procedures and dressed inconspicuously, and it is unlikely that they would have landed their ship right in front of the person they were contacting.

So we have a biblical eyewitness to the landing of a metallic flying craft and personal contact with one of its occupants. We also have reason to believe that their technology was not infallible—it was susceptible to mechanical problems.

Ezekiel's encounter also presents a strong case that aliens were manipulating history. The man standing above the open hatch called himself the Sovereign Lord and revealed future events that were to take place regarding the Israelites; how could he know of such things unless he was involved in creating them? Most important, however, is the link connecting the deity to technology. This has been established by virtue of the fact that the Sovereign Lord landed in a flying craft.

We can adhere to the miraculous and mystical concepts of organized religion and believe that God manifested himself to Ezekiel in this physical and *mechanically oriented form*, or we can be logical and accept the fact that Ezekiel described the landing of a metallic craft with five men aboard. To remain logical is to accept the idea that flying machines, or spacecraft, were around in biblical times and their occupants were perceived as gods.

And by virtue of their imparting knowledge of future events regarding the Israelites, they were manipulating the course of history.

The Glory of the Lord

Those subscribing to religious mysticism believe that when the Lord met with Moses, he manifested a human appearance because it would have been fatal for him to see the Lord in his true form. This probably refers to Exodus 33:20, in which he told Moses that no man may see his face and live. Other verses, however, contradict this idea by describing how he frequently met with him face-to-face.

> *The Lord would speak to Moses face to face as a man speaks with his friend.* (Ex 33:11)

> *When a prophet of the Lord is among you, I reveal myself to him in visions, I speak to him in dreams, but this is not true of my servant, Moses, he is faithful in all my house. I speak to him face to face, clearly and not in riddles; he sees the form of the Lord.* (Nu 12:6–8)

So if Moses spoke to the Lord face-to-face, and saw him as he really appeared, he had to be a physical being.

In a meeting that took place about three months after the Hebrews left Egypt, Moses was seeking reassurance that the Lord would not abandon him at this time. He was afraid that once the Hebrews were free, the Lord would leave and someone else would take charge, so he said to the Lord:

> *If you are pleased with me, teach me your ways so that I may know you and continue to find favor with you. Remember that this nation is your people.* (Ex 33:13)

If taken in the context that Moses knew the Lord was not really God, these words suggest that he was expressing his eagerness to learn more. Being a curious person, he was probably fascinated by the Lord's ship—how it could fly and hover for days and weeks and by the technology it displayed ("teach me your ways so that I may know [more about] you …")—and he was looking for something tangible to justify his own participation ("and continue to find favor with you."). And by reminding the Lord that the Hebrews were his (the Lord's) people, he was emphasizing the fact that *he* was the one giving up forty years of his life to assist him. Yet for some reason, he had the idea that once the Hebrews made it out of Egypt, the Lord would leave and someone else would take over—someone with whom he had not established a relationship. The Lord, however, assured Moses that would not happen:

> *I will do the very thing you have asked, because I am pleased with you and I know you by name.* (Ex 33:17)

Knowing Moses by name merely exemplifies their close personal relationship. Their meeting concluded, Moses then said to the Lord, "Now, show me your glory," as if he were urging him to fulfill a promise that he had made. The Lord responded:

> *"You cannot see my face, for no one may see my face and live." Then the Lord told Moses that he would cause his goodness to pass in front of him and there was a place near him where he could stand on a rock and he said; "When my glory passes by, I will put you in a cleft in the rock and cover you with my hand until I have passed by. Then I will remove my hand and you will see my back; but my face must not be seen."* (Ex 33:20–23)

This makes absolutely no sense. Taken literally, it suggests that the Lord was going to stick Moses in the crack of some rock and then reach out his hand and cover his eyes so he would not see his face as he walked by. This has to be a misinterpretation. I think the key to understanding this statement is this part: "When my glory passes by …"

Since the Lord's own words confirm that he met and spoke with Moses face-to-face, we must assume they were face-to-face during this meeting.

Moses's request to have the Lord show him his *glory* and the Lord's response that no one could see his *face* suggest that *glory* and *face* mean the same thing: *the Lord's ship*. An analogy would be referring to a Cadillac as a *car* or *automobile*. However, I suspect what the Lord was really referring to was the exterior—the face or facade of his ship and the dangerous radiation he would be exposed to if the energy field surrounding it were turned off while in flight. Moses knew about the ship, but all he ever saw was the glow that surrounded it whenever the Lord moved it out of the cloud. He was a curious fellow and wanted to see what it really looked like.

Like many researchers, I suspect the glow associated with UFOs is created by an electromagnetic field. For Moses to see the ship without the glow, the field would have to be turned off, which, while in operation, may have allowed radiation to extend beyond normal safe limits. So the Lord had to put Moses in some kind of protective shield as the ship passed by. So Moses went to where the Lord told him to stand. The Lord then brought his ship out of the cloud and made a close pass in front of him. As he drew near, he projected a protective shield around Moses ("I will put you in a cleft in the rock"), which apparently blocked his vision as the ship passed in front of him. After reaching a safe distance, the Lord deactivated the shield, and Moses probably got a good look at the back of it.

I find it illogical that the Lord would tell Moses that he would die if he looked upon his face when he was standing right in front of him. Since they were already together, the words "when my glory passes by" only make sense if the glory referred to his ship. It was impossible for the scribes who translated the story over a thousand years later to understand its technological implications; it was something to which they had never been exposed. Trying to adapt a spiritual significance to the many technological references would have been confusing; they could only equate such things with the supernatural.

The Ship on the Mountain
Another incident alluding to the Lord's ship is described in Exodus 19:11. In preparation for receiving the Ten Commandments, the Lord informed Moses that he would come down on Mount Sinai in sight of everyone.

When the ship came out of the cloud, it descended on the mountain, engulfed in a bright glow. It says there were sounds like trumpet blasts and thunder, and there were flashes of lightning. Then it says smoke covered the top of the mountain in a thick cloud. It does not say how long this cloud remained, but if it were more than a day or two, it would have presented a problem. Moses and Joshua would have had to enter it when they went up to receive the Ten Commandments, and prior to that, Moses had taken his brother Aaron and seventy elders there. So if it really was a thick cloud of smoke, how were they able to breathe? Perhaps it was removed before anyone actually went up the mountain. It is also possible that the cloud was holographic image being projected around the perimeter of the mountaintop and clear within. Whatever it was, we will probably never know.

Landing the ship on top of the mountain suggests that the plan was for Moses to come aboard to receive the Ten Commandments; what other logical reason could there have been for a landing? Therefore, it would have been necessary to create a landing site. Disintegrating rocks and boulders with lasers may have sounded like thunder, and the trumpet sound could have been the whine of high-powered machines. Debris was probably blown off the mountain, which would have necessitated creating a safety perimeter. The people were warned that they faced death if they approached the mountain, so to keep them away, Moses declared the mountain and the area around it as holy ground.

Sometime after the ship landed, Moses made his first trip up the mountain with Aaron and his two sons, Nadab and Abihu, and seventy of the elders. This visit may have been a special privilege allowed the elders, possibly as an attempt to create a more positive influence regarding the new teachings with which they were about to be indoctrinated.

Moses and Aaron, Nadab and Abihu, and seventy of the elders of Israel went up and saw the God of Israel. Underneath his feet was something like a pavement made of sapphire, as clear as the sky itself.

God did not raise his hand against these leaders of the Israelites; they saw God and they ate and drank. (Ex 24:9–10)

Logic suggests that the feet were the ship's landing gear, and that the ship was concealed in a smoke screen. It says there was a pavement of sapphire underneath his feet, which may have been a specially constructed landing pad of polished metal, or sand and stone could have been melted to create a reflective glass-like surface. Since the feet were mentioned but there was no description as to whom or what they were attached to, common sense dictates that they had to be attached to someone—or something. The most logical "thing" would be a ship enveloped in a smoke screen, except for the landing gear protruding from the bottom. Though they did not know what God looked like, they would naturally have assumed he was inside the cloud.

Note: Here we have one of the many examples of biblical misdirection in which the word *God* is being substituted for *the Lord*. It was the Lord who told Moses that *he* would come down on the mountain (Ex 19:11). Then it says, "God did not raise his hand against them" and "they saw God and they ate and drank." However, it was not God that landed on the mountain—it was the Lord. The God of Israel was a physical being they would never see but knew only by the title of the Lord.

For sixteen hundred years, Jebel Musa in the southern Sinai Peninsula has been accepted as the original Mount Sinai, even though there is no archaeological evidence to justify that belief.[3] If the Lord did land a ship on top of the mountain, it seems unlikely that it was Jebel Musa because of its incompatible terrain. The top would have to be relatively flat or else landscaped to accommodate a landing, and judging from the Bible's description, there would probably be evidence of burning and scorched rocks. There should also be a cave somewhere on the mountain where Elijah was said to have stayed after fleeing the wrath of Jezebel, who was out to kill him. There is a mountain in the Negev Desert with such a cave. It's called Har Karkom and has a flat mesa-like top, and one of the many glyphs found at the base of the mountain was a tablet depicting the Ten Commandments.[4] However, there is another possibility: Jebel el Lawz, a mountain in northwest Saudi Arabia. It is relatively flat, and it, too, has a small cave that one might associate with Elijah.[5] Authors Larry Williams and Robert Cornuke explored this site in 1988 and found the rocks and the whole top of the mountain blackened as if scorched. Could this be where the landing took place? Unfortunately, soon after this discovery, the Saudi government sealed off the site for military use, thereby preventing further access.

Most scholars believe that Horeb, Sinai, and the mountain of God all refer to the same mountain. If so, this was the same mountain where the Lord first made contact with Moses through the burning bush, where he met with his brother Aaron on his return to Egypt, where he produced water from the rock, and where he also received the Ten Commandments. Could it have been a temporary land base?

Elijah's Encounters

According to the Bible, the prophet Elijah had two encounters with the Lord's ship. The first occurred at Mount Horeb (Sinai), where he fled to escape the wrath of King Ahab's wife, Jezebel. After exposing the king's prophets as fakes, they were executed. When Jezebel found out, she became enraged and sought vengeance on Elijah, so he fled across the desert to Mount Horeb. It would seem that the angels were keeping close tabs on Elijah because in chapter 19 of 1 Kings, it reveals that one of them brought him bread and water a few times to sustain him during the long trek.

Upon reaching Horeb, he spent the night in a cave. In 1 Kings 19:9–11, it says the Lord spoke with Elijah, asking why he had come there. After explaining, the Lord told him to step outside because he was about to pass by. What Elijah saw is described only as a fierce wind, then an earthquake, and then fire. A logical interpretation suggests it was a ship taking off from the top of the mountain. It apparently kicked up a lot of wind; as the propulsion system kicked in, it made a loud rumbling sound that shook the ground and then flew away enveloped in a bright glow. Inviting Elijah to watch him take off suggests that a working relationship existed between them, much as it did with Moses. And he probably knew as much about what was going on as Moses did. I believe this is verified by the fact that the Lord later took Elijah with him.

But why did Elijah go there in the first place? He was fleeing from Jezebel, who wanted to kill him, so it is only logical that he would seek the Lord's protection, *But how did he know where to find him?* And how did the Lord communicate with him in the cave? According to Exodus 4:17 and 4:20, the Lord gave Moses a staff with special powers just before he returned to Egypt. So I speculate that Elijah, Elisha, and Moses were all provided with staffs that contained a device for communication, as they all appear to have had frequent non-face-to-face contact with the Lord.

Elijah's second encounter is found in the second chapter of 2 Kings. In his dramatic departure from the earth, a chariot of fire and horses of fire appeared out of the sky and took him up to heaven in a *whirlwind.* This suggests that they actually beamed up Elijah but not his cloak, because it says that right after that, Elisha picked up the cloak that had fallen from Elijah.

If the craft had landed, the pilot would have had to shut down the propulsion system so Elijah could go aboard safely. Elisha would then have seen the ship clearly, without the glow around it, and he would have provided a more detailed description other than just a chariot of fire. But since he did not, we might assume that the ship hovered above the men, kicking up a vast amount of wind, and amid this whirlwind, Elijah was beamed aboard.

Because it picked up Elijah, it is only logical that it would have been perceived as a chariot. As for it being a chariot of fire, the bright glow surrounding it would have been perceived as fire, as the only source of light known at the time was provided by fire. As for the horses of fire, it could have been a second craft or an embellishment created during all the years the story was passed down orally by those who took it too literally and assumed that horses were needed to pull the chariot.

Jonah

Comprised of four short chapters, the book of Jonah describes what is probably the last event in the Old Testament suggesting technology.

The Lord wanted Jonah to go to Nineveh and warn the people that unless they reformed their ways, they were about to face his wrath. Not wanting to do the Lord's bidding, he attempted to flee on a boat bound for Tarshish. The winds soon became strong and the seas rough, threatening to break the boat apart. Jonah had told the crew earlier that he was running from the Lord, so they believed they were being punished because of him.

As the storm gained force, they pleaded with him, asking him to pray to his god to calm the seas and the wind. Jonah said it would do no good; the only way it would stop was if they threw him overboard. Being decent men, this was not an option they favored, so they attempted to row back to shore. However, this proved futile, as the winds and waves became even stronger. Finally, in desperate fear for their lives, they relented and threw Jonah into the sea. Then it says that the Lord sent a large fish to swallow Jonah and he spent three days in its belly before it spit him out onto dry land. He then went to Nineveh and delivered the Lord's warning. Apparently, he was extremely persuasive with words; the people reformed their ways, and the city was spared.

The question is—was this a real event or a fictional writing by someone who wanted to make a moral statement? Personally, I am not totally convinced it is authentic. I also challenge the idea that Jonah was ever swallowed by a fish. If it were true, it would have to be the size of a large whale, which raises other questions: How could he have survived inside the belly of a whale? What prevented him from being digested into its system? Where did he get the air to breathe for three days and the light to see everything he described?

So I don't buy the fish story. If Jonah really was thrown into the sea during a violent storm and survived to tell about it, I can accept the possibility that he spent three days in something—but not a fish. Jonah 2:6 says he was taken to the depths—to the bottoms of the mountains and the earth—and he said there were bars all around him. What were these bars, and how did he know he was at the base of the mountains?

If Jonah was describing a real experience, then he had to be inside an underwater craft. Since he was able to breathe for three days, common sense tells us he was in a room with an air supply, a ventilation system, and surely some kind of toilet facility. And if he knew he was at the base of the mountains, it means he could see the mountains underwater and his descent to the bottom, and that means there was a window. Since fish and whales are not equipped with windows, it had to be some kind of underwater craft. I have no idea what the bars were that he says were all around him, unless perhaps he was in something similar to a holding cell. It may be that he was pulled into some sort of underwater vehicle, but this was over two thousand years ago. There have been many reports of UFOs appearing out of oceans as well as diving into them, so we know that at least some, if not all, UFOs are both aerodynamic and hydrodynamic, and Jonah being picked up by one of these craft would seem to be the only logical explanation.

At first, I thought the book of Jonah was a work of fiction written by someone who simply wanted to make a moral statement. The idea that Jonah walked into Nineveh and converted its inhabitants so easily just seemed too incredible to believe. And how could the author picture him surviving inside a fish for three days? There isn't a fish large enough to swallow a full-grown man. Even the largest whale, which is actually a mammal, would not have been able to do it. The idea that he could see the cliffs underwater and his descent to the bottom, and that he was surrounded by bars, suggests that he was inside of some sort of submersible vehicle with a window. Surely the author knew that fish do not have windows. So there is the suggestion of a technology that the writer could not possibly have known about two thousand years ago. As to whether there is an element of truth to the story is something we may never know.

The Stars of the Magi

Two thousand years ago, there was no way an event could be known by people hundreds of miles away until someone brought word of it in person. So the only way to attract attention to the birth of Christ was to promote it in advance. It had been prophesied by Isaiah (7:14) and Micah (5:2) that a Messiah would be born, but no time was given, because when the word was given to the prophets, it is possible the Lord didn't know himself. The only clue given was that his star would shine in the east.

It is believed the Magi probably came from what is now northern Iran. Herod, who was king of Jerusalem at the time, felt threatened by the prophecy of a new king being born, and when he learned the Magi had arrived in town, he had them brought in for a meeting. He wanted to know where the child was, and they told him that according to Micah's prophecy, he would be in Bethlehem. Herod asked that they stop in on their way home and tell him the exact location so that he might go and worship him. Then it says an angel warned the Magi in a dream of Herod's intention to kill the child, so they took another route home in order to avoid him.

Whatever it was the Magi saw has generated a great deal of controversy. It has been explained as a comet, a planetary conjunction, and a supernova (an exploding star). Since the prophecy indicated the sign would be a star, I think it eliminates the comet theory. The Magi were said to be astrologers and well educated, so they would have known the difference between a comet and a star. And they would have been familiar with the planets and recognized a conjunction if one had occurred. A supernova would have been much brighter, but we must consider the fact that no one reported seeing it in Jerusalem, Bethlehem, or anywhere else, for that matter. The real problem with the nova theory is that to coincide the birth of Christ with an exploding star, the Lord would have had to know in advance about the star going nova.

If a star one thousand light-years distant exploded today, we wouldn't know about it for a thousand years—until the light of the explosion reached Earth. Now, someone with interstellar travel capabilities might have knowledge of a star that had gone nova millennia before its light would reach Earth. So it is possible that the birth of Christ could have been planned to coincide with the arrival of its light. Even if that was the case, there are other factors that would have to coincide exactly. They would have to know that the star was in the precise location where it would be visible from Earth, and in the eastern sky of a particular country.

However, stars rise in the east, and they do not stay there. As the earth rotates, they move across the sky and set in the west. No. There are too many elements of uncertainty making the nova theory unlikely. In order to predict that a bright star would appear in the east, it seems only logical that the Lord would have to make sure one would be there at the appropriate time, and I am inclined to believe that what the Magi probably saw was one of his ships. Like many UFOs reported today, it would have appeared as a distinct bright light, one that they would interpret as Isaiah's predicted sign. This would explain the appearance of a star in the east and why it would not have been seen in Jerusalem, Bethlehem, or anywhere else.

Since the Magi were the only known observers of this star, we might wonder if Isaiah's prophecy was meant for them or for people living in that region of the country. And if it was an alien craft, they had no way of knowing this, or that people in the cities west of them did not, or could not, see it. It would be from their arrival in Jerusalem and Bethlehem that the sighting of this star would become known. It wasn't until after their meeting with Herod that they saw the same or another bright light in the sky, which led them the few short miles to Bethlehem (Mt 2:9). To reach Bethlehem from Jerusalem, it would have traveled due south, and the Bible says it stopped directly over the child's location. If true, it had to be a craft under intelligent control—stars do not move from north to south, nor do they stop in the sky. If the event occurred today, it would undoubtedly go on record as a UFO sighting.

The scriptures also say that an angel (or bright glowing craft) appeared to some shepherds out in a field that night as they stood watch over their sheep. Was it the same craft that the Magi followed to Bethlehem? Possibly. It scared them half to death when it suddenly illuminated them with a bright light and a voice announced the birth of Christ. The Bible says the angel (or craft) was then joined by a host of others (Lk 2:8–13).

The Pentecost Visit
Another event suggesting flying craft (and other technology) is the Pentecost. In one of his last visits to the disciples after his Resurrection,

Christ told them to remain in the city until his Father delivered the gift that had been promised them. When the time came, they were gathered in the temple, and according to Acts 2:1–4, there was a sound like a violent wind, and tongues of fire appeared and touched upon each one of them. Suddenly, they were able to speak in different languages, and they had also acquired the power to heal.

Today, we would describe these tongues of fire as beams of light, and if they touched upon each individual, then they were under intelligent control. And since the disciples suddenly acquired their new powers at this time, we might assume these beams had something to do with it. I think their healing power probably emanated from a natural energy within their own bodies, and perhaps the beams somehow stimulated the particular brain cells that gave them the ability to utilize this power. However, their sudden ability to speak in different languages would seem to be a knowledge that can only be acquired through a learning process. I could be wrong, however. I know nothing about the intricacies of the brain, so it could be a collective but dormant knowledge that is genetically inherent in everyone and these beams of light somehow activated the specific brain cells containing this knowledge. Another possibility is that the disciples had been taught these languages and their memory was suppressed. They could have been "programmed" to respond to the beams of light so they would suddenly remember what they had been taught, but not the method of how it was accomplished. And a familiar detail by now is the sound of thunder, a whirlwind, rushing waters, etc., sounds associated with aircraft. Should we not suspect that the sound of a *violent wind* was probably a ship hovering above the temple?

Lasers and Beam Weapons

To suggest that someone possessed lasers in biblical times may sound a bit off the wall. However, when I first opened the Bible and began reading Genesis, I was immediately struck by what seemed like a reference to this technology. It is found at the very beginning, in Genesis 3:24. It says that after Adam and Eve were expelled from the Garden of Eden, cherubim and *a flaming sword flashing back and forth* were placed on the east side of the garden to protect the tree of life. According to the footnotes, the word translated from the ancient texts meaning *east side* also means *front of.* So I think we can logically assume that this flaming sword was placed at the entrance to the garden.

Webster's Third New International Dictionary, unabridged, defines "cherubim" as "a "biblical figure frequently represented as a composite being, with large wings, a human head, and an animal body and regarded as a guardian of a sacred place and as a servant of God." Common sense tells us this was not a real-life creature—rather, it was something designed to discourage intruders. The flaming sword flashing back and forth suggests that it was a mechanical device with moving parts—a scanning beam of light, just like a security device today that uses a sweeping laser beam. Since this allegedly occurred six thousand years ago, where could such technology have possibly come from if not extraterrestrials?

The Bible says it was put there to protect the tree of life, the source of Adam and Eve's longevity. Due to a genetic imperfection, their life spans had to be cut short. If I am wrong about this, then I can find no other reason, either logical or supernatural, that would explain why a security device had to be installed to prevent them further access to it.

So what happened to the tree of life? Since a device was installed to protect it, it suggests that it remained for some years. Perhaps if the Lord solved the problem of Adam's imperfection soon enough, he might have resumed operations in the garden. But I would suspect that after Cain killed his brother, he decided against it. The garden was probably abandoned and the tree of life either removed or destroyed.

Further use of laser technology is suggested in three separate incidents in which the Bible claims people were struck blind. The first is noted in Genesis 19:11, when the angels struck blind the mob that wanted to rape them at Lot's house in Sodom. The second is described in 2 Kings 6:8–23, when the Lord struck blind the Aramean army sent to capture the prophet Elisha. However, the story of Saul in the New Testament seems to be the most enlightening.

An avid persecutor of Christ's disciples and their followers, Saul pursued them throughout the land. Acts 9:1–18 says he was struck blind on the outskirts of Damascus by a flash of light that came from the sky. He then heard a voice say, "Saul, Saul, why do you persecute me?" The men traveling with Saul were dumbfounded because they saw no one there. The voice identified itself as Jesus and told Saul to go on into the city. Saul remained blind for three days, until an apostle named Ananias came and healed him. During the process of cleansing, it says that something like *scales fell from his eyes*, suggesting it was dead cells or scab tissue, which means his eyes had been burned in some way.

So now we have two clues: the flash of light and the scales. It was probably a device that emitted a high-intensity laser burst, causing flash burn on the outer protective layer of the cornea—the ectodermic conjunctival epithelium. The dead cells of this membrane would eventually dry up like a scab and flake off—like dead skin from sunburn. I checked with my eye doctor to verify the feasibility of this idea, and he agreed that it could happen just as I have described it. So it seems Ananias didn't cure Saul's blindness; he merely washed away the scab tissue. Whatever the device was that caused the blindness, it demonstrated amazing flexibility. In Elisha's case, it was used to incapacitate an entire army. With Saul, precision and accuracy was demonstrated in how it could pinpoint one individual out of a crowd. I might assume the intensity could be adjusted to cause permanent blindness, something the angels may have done to the mob in Sodom.

Soon after Moses led the Israelites out of Egypt, the Lord began eliminating the gripers and others who exhibited negative behavior, and some of the stories describe how he literally killed thousands at a time. He gave them a warning at first. When they began complaining about their hardships, fire came out from the Lord and consumed some of the outskirts of the camp (Nu 11:1). If anyone was killed in this instance, it is not mentioned.

Chapter 16 in the book of Numbers describes how the Lord turned his wrath on 250 council members who were in league with Korah, Dathan, and Abiram, a trio of dissenters. They had instigated a rebellion against Moses, and according to Numbers 16:35, the council members were consumed by a fire that came out from the presence of the Lord. However, according to what allegedly occurred the next day, I have serious doubts that 250 were killed. I suspect it was only a handful, if any at all. You would think the deaths of 250 people would have struck fear into the hearts of everyone and put an end to the problem, but apparently, it did not make a big impression, because it says thousands gathered the next day to protest these killings. Then it says that the *glory of the Lord* came out of the cloud and 14,700 more were killed. Exactly how they were killed is not mentioned, but I would suspect that if it really happened, it was by the same method.

These high numbers could very well be an exaggeration attributed to later writers who simply embellished the count as a means of stimulating a greater fear of God's wrath into the hearts of men. Though only speculation, it is something to consider when examining similar accounts.

What appears to be another demonstration of laser weaponry is described in Leviticus 9:24. Eight days after the new tent of meeting was erected, the first offering was made on the sacrificial altar in front of it. Then it says the *glory of the Lord* came out of the cloud, and *fire came out from the presence of the Lord* and consumed the offering.

When Moses led the people to the border of their Promised Land, the Lord had them camp near Moab where it appears he made one final sweep to eliminate the rest of the troublemakers. They now had the opportunity to make contact with others and those prone to negative influences revealed themselves by giving in to temptation and corrupt behavior. According to chapter 25 in the book of Numbers, many let themselves be seduced by the local women and even bowed down to worship their gods. The Lord then unleashed a plague in which another 24,000 were killed. Again, keep in mind that this number could be highly exaggerated.

After entering the Promised Land, one of the first things Joshua did was agree to a treaty with the Gibeonites. When the Gibeonites came under siege by their enemies, they sent word to Joshua, requesting help. Joshua responded with the Lord, and the Lord blasted them from the sky with large hailstones that killed more of them than did Joshua's men. Joshua, however, wanted more time to pursue the remnants of the fleeing army, and he asked the Lord to stop the sun and moon in the sky—in other words, stop time, and according to Joshua 10:13, the sun and moon stood still for about a full day.

Now, unless the Lord had the technology to manipulate the space-time continuum and actually freeze time around the area of battle, I don't believe the sun and moon held their place in the sky for a whole day. This is probably another exaggeration that grew from years of oral tradition by those absorbed in supernatural beliefs.

Another incident of *fire from the Lord* occurred on Mount Carmel, when Elijah challenged the king's false prophets. He had them prepare a sacrifice but not set fire to it, and he did the same. All day long, they danced around their altar, calling on their god, Baal, to ignite their sacrifices, but nothing happened. When evening came, Elijah dug a trench around his altar and had the people saturate his offering with four large jugs of water, which drained down and filled the trench. According to 1 Kings 18:38, as Elijah prayed, fire came from the sky and incinerated not only his sacrifice but also burned the altar and evaporated the water in the trench.

Another event suggesting the use of weapons is described in 2 Kings 19:32–37. It was when the Assyrians were on their devastating campaign annihilating much of the Israelite population throughout the land and destroying their cities. It alleges that the night before they were to attack Jerusalem, an angel went out to their camp and killed 185,000 of them as they slept. Again, this seems like a gross exaggeration. Who dug the graves to bury that many dead bodies? Some scholars suggest that the Assyrian king may have found it necessary to withdraw his army to ward off an impending invasion by armies moving up from the south, and it certainly sounds like a more logical explanation.

These accounts describe how the Lord allegedly eliminated hundreds and even thousands of people at a time with a fire that issued forth from his presence. When this happened, it was generally preceded by his presence, which was described as the "glory of the Lord" (a bright light or glowing craft) emerging from the cloud that constantly hovered above their camp.

Nuclear Weapons

What may seem like another ridiculous idea is the use of nuclear weapons. However, the destruction of Sodom and Gomorrah as described in Genesis chapter 19 suggests such a possibility, although probably on a much smaller scale than what occurred in Hiroshima. And remember the account described in the Mahabharata, of what appeared to be the use of nuclear weapons thousands of years ago, plus the vitrified sand and the stones in the buildings of Mohenjo-Daro. Could it be that nuclear weapons were known to someone back then?

The Bible tells us that the angels Lot had welcomed into his home told him he had to leave because the city was about to be destroyed. Lot was reluctant to go, so they physically led him and his family out of the city and told them to head for the mountains. Lot didn't think they could make it there in time but thought they could make it to Zoar. The angel agreed. He said he would not destroy that town and told him to get moving.

Other ancient manuscripts state that five cities were slated for destruction: Sodom, Gomorrah, Admah, Zeboiim, and Zoar, a detail not mentioned in the Genesis account. However, it coincides with the angel's statement that he would spare the town (Zoar) where Lot wanted to go. Then the Bible says they reached Zoar at just about sunrise, at which time the Lord rained down burning sulfur that consumed Sodom and Gomorrah and all the vegetation in the area. It does not reveal what happened to Admah and Zeboiim, but if they were as corrupt as Sodom and Gomorrah allegedly were, it is likely they would have been destroyed as well. However, it does tell us that Zoar was spared. Since it was slated for annihilation, it, too, was probably contaminated with perversion, and since it was not destroyed, it is only logical to assume that its inhabitants survived.

One theory proposed in *The Wycliffe Bible Commentary* is that the destruction was caused by an earthquake that created fissures in the rocks, releasing stored-up gasses that exploded and threw vast amounts of flaming petroleum into the air. In other texts, it describes burning sulfur falling from the sky, which could have been debris thrown into the air from the force of the blast, and there are sulfur deposits in the area, which would explain the odor of sulfur in the aftermath. But who saw what happened? The only alleged witness was Lot's wife, whom the Bible claims was turned into a pillar of salt when she looked back. However, this is another clue suggesting nuclear weapons.

According to Genesis 19:17, the angels advised Lot and his family not to look back. But why? What difference would it make if they witnessed the destruction of Sodom? Since nothing was mentioned about any consequences they might suffer if they did look, one might interpret these words as a metaphor to not look back on the sinful ways of the city—or simply as a figure of speech meant to denote the importance of getting as far away as possible and as fast as possible for their own safety. But if it were meant as a warning, the only real justification for it would be if a nuclear device were used; the flash of a nuclear detonation would cause blindness to anyone looking at it without protective goggles.

If Lot's wife witnessed a nuclear explosion, it would have been a tremendous shock to her senses. The device used on Gomorrah, which was farther away, may have been detonated first. Unable to overcome her curiosity, she turned around and looked. Then, as she was looking back in that direction, a second device detonated over Sodom. If this is what happened, the last thing she would have seen was a mushroom cloud forming over Gomorrah and the flash that struck her blind when the device detonated over Sodom. Then she would have been hit by the shock wave and high winds. To her, it would have been a horrifying experience and could have generated enough fear to trigger a heart attack. Nevertheless, the description of her death might simply be an embellishment that developed over the centuries in which the story had been passed along orally.

The Bible says that in the morning, Abraham stood near his camp, looking down toward the plain, in the direction of Sodom and Gomorrah, and saw dense smoke rising into the air as if from a huge furnace. Since these cities allegedly were located around the Dead Sea, which at 1,299 feet below sea level is the lowest elevation in the world, it had to be along its south end because the northern part of the Dead Sea is bordered by high cliffs. Some old biblical maps (if they are correct) show Zoar located at its southern tip. Hebron, where Abraham lived, was said to be about eighteen miles away, and it is approximately eighteen miles west of the Dead Sea.

After Lot and his daughters arrived in Zoar, the Bible says they were afraid to stay there and went to live in a cave in the mountains. Then it says that Lot's daughters got him drunk and had sex with him for the purpose of getting pregnant because "Our father is old, and there is no other man around here to lie with us, as is the custom all over the earth" (Ge 19:30–31). Surely they didn't believe they were the only ones left—Zoar was spared, so its inhabitants obviously survived. However, if the people of Zoar were as perverted as those in Sodom, perhaps they felt it was the same throughout the whole world, that there were no prospects for ever finding a husband to bear them children. This is something we will probably never know.

Sonic Weapons

We know that sound generated at the proper frequency can cause matter to break down and disintegrate. Today, machines emitting sound pulses are being used in many hospitals to disintegrate kidney stones, and although some people think it was just an advertising trick, from what I have been told, Ella Fitzgerald really did shatter a glass with her voice in the old TV commercial for Memorex.

The story of Joshua bringing down the walls of Jericho, if true, is an event that can also be associated with sound. According to the biblical account described in Joshua 6:1–20, everyone was to march around the city once each day for six days with the priests blowing on trumpets. Then, on the seventh day, they were to march seven times around the city with the priests blowing on trumpets. On a given signal, they were then to begin shouting. That was when the walls allegedly crumbled.

Although the story implies that this shouting brought down the walls, it seems unlikely. For that to work, everyone would have to shout at the proper frequency and pitch long enough to effect the molecular structure of the stones in the walls. So if it really was sound that collapsed the walls, it had to be produced by a device designed to generate it at the proper frequency. The noise probably would have been deafening unless it was accomplished by the harmonic of a frequency that was inaudible to the human ear. Either way, the vibrations may have caused serious damage to the ear drum unless proper precautions were taken. Logic suggests that the shouting may have been a precautionary measure to prevent injury by equalizing pressure in the ears while the device was in use. Let's use a little common sense; to have people just stand there shouting their lungs out seems like a pointless act—unless it was done as a safety precaution.

Force Fields
Another example of technology in which one can find numerous references scattered throughout the Bible is force fields.

Just before the chariot of fire took Elijah up to heaven, he and Elisha arrived at the Jordan River accompanied by fifty prophets. Elijah rolled up his cloak and struck the water with it; it soon stopped flowing. He and Elisha then crossed over (2Ki 2:8). After Elijah was picked up by the chariot of fire, Elisha carried Elijah's cloak back to the Jordan and slapped the waters with it; again, the river stopped flowing so he could go back across (2Ki 2:13–14). What could possibly halt the waters of a flowing river—twice in one day—if not some kind of force field?

The most notable event involving a force field would seem to be the parting of the waters as described in Exodus chapter 14. When the Egyptian army pursuing Moses and the Israelites caught up to them, the Lord blocked their path with a smoke screen that the Bible describes as a pillar of cloud. There is no reason the Egyptians could not have circumvented this cloud unless it completely surrounded them. Or perhaps the terrain was such that access to the area where the Hebrews were camped was restricted by a narrow passage leading down from a higher elevation such as the top of a mesa. Yet it would seem that something more than a cloud was involved. Since there is no description of the terrain, and unless they were surrounded by this cloud, we can assume that there was a narrow gap that the Egyptians had to pass through with their horses and chariots. If the cloud did contain a force field, we might assume that contact with it would have been unpleasant and possibly fatal. The horses could probably sense this field and would not go near it, leaving the Egyptians no choice except to sit there and wait.

In the movie *The Ten Commandments*, when Charlton Heston, who played the part of Moses, raised his hands, the waters separated into two giant walls, and everyone immediately went through to the other side. Had it actually happened that way, I might consider it a miracle. However, according to Exodus 14:21, it took all night, which reinforces the idea of technology; God could have done it in an instant or materialized a bridge for them to cross.

The Bible would have us believe that Moses parted the Red Sea, but we know today that this was not the case. Even at its narrow points, the Red Sea spans about one hundred miles, and it would have taken weeks for the people to make it through. It is also too far south from where they left Goshen, south of the pharaoh's city, making it unlikely they covered that distance within several days, especially with the erratic back-and-forth direction of travel in which the Lord had been leading them (see Ex 13:18–14:2).

The northern part of the Red Sea forks around the Sinai Peninsula, and the west fork—the side where Moses and his people probably would have been—is the Gulf of Suez, which connects to what is now the Suez Canal. During Moses's time, there were many areas in this region where the water was shallow and less than a mile wide. This area is also dotted with many small lakes, so it is likely that the event (if it occurred at all) took place somewhere in this region. In Hebrew, the sea is called Yam Suph, which means Reed Sea, a name that because of its similarity is often misinterpreted as the Red Sea.

The Bible says the Lord used an east wind to part the waters and dry the seabed. However, because an east wind blows from the east, logistically— whether it was on the banks of a small lake or the Gulf of Suez—the people would have been on the west side. To be on the east bank would mean they were heading back toward Egypt, which would seem unlikely. So logic tells us that if an east wind pushed back the waters, it would have pushed them up on the west bank, where the people were camped. Therefore, it seems unlikely that an east wind was responsible. Of course, it is possible that they were on the north end of a small lake, where they would not have been affected. But for a wind to part the sea, it would almost have to be of hurricane force, making it very difficult for anyone to pass through.

Separating the waters with a force field probably took a short time—that was the easy part. Drying the seabed was what took all night. To facilitate the crossing of several hundred thousand or more people with their animals, carts, and wagons, it had to be dried to a hardened surface. This may have been accomplished by microwave energy that dried the seabed from the inside out.

Once the people were safely on the other side, the smoke screen was lifted, and the pharaoh, determined to get back his free labor force, ordered his army to proceed through the parted waters after them. Then, according to Exodus 14:25, the Lord blew the wheels off the lead chariots, thereby disabling them and creating obstacles for those behind. He then turned off the force field, and the walls of water came crashing down over the entire Egyptian army, allegedly leaving no survivors.

One clue that this was a small body of water is the Lord disabling the lead chariots. It caused a backup—a traffic jam—grouping them close together. This would have been unnecessary in the Red Sea because of its vast expanse. Only in a small body of water would it have been necessary to bunch them up in the middle in order to get them all when the force field was released.

Another event is described in Joshua 3:16, when the waters of the Jordan River ceased to flow, allowing Joshua and the people to cross over. It says the water piled up in a heap about twelve to fifteen miles away, near a town called Adam, in the vicinity of Zarethan. The priests carrying the Ark of the Covenant then stood in the center of the riverbed as everyone crossed on dry ground.

Here again is a clue that this was no miracle. If it were, why not halt the river at the point of crossing so the people could see it—where it would have made a big impression. But it was not logistically feasible. Unlike the Sea of Reeds, the Jordan was a flowing river; the water would have piled up against the force field and spilled around its edges, onto the riverbanks and onto the land. So it had to be far enough away to prevent the spillover from posing a hazard. The Jordan, for the most part, is a narrow river, which would have facilitated a speedy crossing, even though this supposedly occurred during its annual flood stage, when it was higher than normal. The force field probably spread well beyond the boundary of the riverbanks in an isolated area, where the spillover drained off without posing a threat to anyone. After everyone had crossed, stones were gathered from the center of the riverbed to construct an altar. The priests carrying the ark then came ashore, the force field was turned off, and the river resumed its flow.

But who actually saw the water pile up twelve to fifteen miles away? The author of this scripture did not reveal how he came by this information, so its validity is questionable. Except for the first five books attributed to Moses, the authors of Joshua and all the other scriptures are unknown.

The following account in the book of Daniel is one of the most difficult stories to believe. It has to be a work of fiction or a story that has been exaggerated to extreme proportions. Daniel 3:21–30 describes what happened when Shadrach, Meshach, and Abednego were allegedly thrown into a fiery furnace for refusing to bow down and worship a golden idol that King Nebuchadnezzar had erected on the plain of Dura in Babylon. It says they were bound fully clothed and thrown into a furnace that was heated to a temperature seven times hotter than normal. Then it says the king saw four men walking around in the fire. He called to the three men to come out, and they walked out of the furnace completely unscathed, with no scorch marks on their clothing or any odor of fire about them.

If this is a true story, the real mystery is how the three men survived. The only logical answer is that a powerful force field shielded them from the heat and the flames just as they were thrown into the furnace. The fourth person would have been an angel that teleported into the force field with the men and untied them. Since nothing further was mentioned about the angel, we can assume he beamed out as soon as the three men were safely outside.

The story certainly sounds like a work of fiction, but if there is any truth to it, it is an amazing demonstration of the versatility that can be applied to the use of force fields. Nevertheless, we must continue to keep in mind that most of these stories were passed down orally for many centuries before they were actually written down, leaving them subject to misperception and exaggeration. In this case, I am inclined to think it may have been a fictitious story that was created by someone who simply wanted to make a moral point.

Replication

Another item of technology suggested in scripture is replication—the method of creating something out of nothing. Well, not exactly nothing. Everything has molecular structure, and molecules are made up of atoms, so technically, it would be juggling atoms and molecules into the specific pattern of whatever it is you want to create. It is alluded to several times in the scriptures and sounds like something out of *Star Trek*, as do all of the other technologies, which seriously makes me wonder if Gene Roddenberry and his writers didn't get their ideas from the Bible.

According to Exodus chapter 16, when the people started to complain about the lack of food, the glory of the Lord appeared out of the cloud. This was usually a sign that someone was going to die. He instructed Moses to tell the people that they would get meat that night, and starting the next morning, they would get bread every day except on the Sabbath. It appears that under the cover of darkness, quail were gathered some distance away and made to stampede straight into the Israelite's camp.

In Numbers 11:31–34, we find that this was one of the first events in which the Lord actually eliminated troublemakers. Before they had a chance to eat the meat, it says the Lord struck them down as a punishment for their complaining, and many died. Although it was labeled a plague, we find that in most cases, these plagues are described as a *fire* that was dispatched from the Lord. Even though it is not spelled out, we must wonder if something similar did not occur in this instance.

In the morning, when the dew evaporated, thin flakes like frost appeared in its place. Moses told them it was bread from the Lord, and they called it manna (Ex 16:15). It was white like coriander seed and tasted like wafers made from honey, and it was to be their staple for the next forty years. Whatever the manna was, it had to contain the nutritional value necessary to sustain them for the duration.

So what was this manna and where did it come from? The Bible says that when the dew evaporated, it appeared in its place, so we might suspect that it was teleported there. However, that makes no sense, for it means the Lord would have had to store enough on board his ship to feed several hundred thousand people each day for forty years. No. The only thing that makes sense is that it was replicated.

Now, before you dismiss this idea, consider the information compiled on alien abductions. If the aliens possess the technology to break down the molecular structure of the people they abduct, transport them through solid walls and windows, and reassemble them aboard their ship, they are manipulating matter on a molecular level. So it may also be possible for them to manipulate the molecules of any substance and rearrange them into the pattern of whatever they want to reproduce.

In 2 Kings 4:1–7, a widow approached the prophet Elisha, telling him her creditors were about to take her two sons as slaves because of unpaid debts. He asked if she had anything of value in her house, and she said she only had a jar of oil. Elisha told her to gather all the empty jars she could from her neighbors, and then, behind closed doors in the privacy of her house, pour the oil from her jar into the empty ones. She did as Elisha instructed ... until she ran out of empty jars. Elisha then told her to sell the oil and pay off her debts; she and her sons could then live on what was left over.

If this really happened, the only way she could have poured out more oil than was in her jar was if some process of replication was replenishing it.

I know it sounds crazy, and as a logical thinker, I am skeptical of miracles; however, I do believe in technology, and replication is the only explanation that seems to make sense. But because it is a technology beyond our present capability, we can only equate it with science fiction, just as we did with the idea of going to the moon a century ago. Just as we did with Dick Tracy's two-way wrist radio fifty years ago … But there is more . . .

In 2 Kings 4:42–44, it says that the Lord aided Elisha by allowing him to feed one hundred people with only twenty loaves of bread. In Matthew 14:17–19, Mk 6:34–42, and Lk 9:13–17, it says Christ fed five thousand people with only two fish and five loaves of bread. Again, on a mountain near the Sea of Galilee, Matthew 15:29–38, Mark 8:1–9, and John 6:7–13 tell us that he fed another four thousand people with only two fish and seven loaves of bread. In each case, when policing the area after the people had left, it says the disciples filled baskets with the leftover pieces of bread that amounted to more than the number of loaves they started with.

What is probably the most significant demonstration is the first miracle that Christ performed; it was at a wedding in Cana, when he turned water into wine. From what the Bible says, his mother coerced him into doing it. She told him that the host had run out of wine, and he told her that it was not his problem, nor was it his time, that he was not ready to perform such acts in public. But it appears she may have put him on the spot in front of all the guests, so he had to do something.

According to chapter 2 in the book of John, Christ requested that the six stone jars sitting on the floor be filled with water—but why? If he could perform miracles, why couldn't he just materialize the wine into the empty jars? Therefore, we must assume that there was a reason for needing water in the jars first. The logical assumption is so the water's molecular structure could be reformatted into that of wine. Christ probably had to prevail on his Father (the Lord) to rescue him from this predicament with his technology—a replicating system.

In each incident, it seems there was an agent involved. With the manna and wine, it was water; dew on the ground and water in the jars. So we can speculate that the molecular structure of the water was reformatted into the manna and wine. Just like *copy* and *paste* on your computer, the oil and the bread were probably the easiest to reproduce since samples were already on hand for quick analysis. However, replicating life-forms such as fish seems rather doubtful, although they were probably able to reproduce a reasonable facsimile. These stories may sound like miracles, but collectively, they suggest that there was much more going on. And we are now beginning to realize that such things may not be impossible.

Tractor Beam

One incident alluding to the use of a tractor beam is when Christ allegedly walked on water, as described in Matthew 14:22–31, Mark 6:45–51, and John 6:16–21. He had sent the disciples out in the boat while he stayed behind to pray and meditate. Later, after dark, it says they were straining with the oars against a strong wind when suddenly Christ appeared, approaching them on the water. At first, they thought he was a ghost, but he told them not to be afraid and climbed into the boat. And since this was the only time he allegedly did this, it seems unlikely that he actually had the power to levitate.

Of the three books describing the event, Matthew is the only one that claims Peter also attempted to walk on the sea. After Jesus identified himself, Peter said, "Lord, if it is really you, bid me to come to you on the water." And Jesus said, "Come." Peter climbed out of the boat and began to walk toward Jesus, but he became frightened by the high winds and rough seas and began to sink. Jesus caught him and said, "You of little faith, why did you doubt?"

Now, whether Peter actually took a few steps on the water is debatable. It is not mentioned in the other gospel books, so it may be an embellishment of later translators. If the seas were rough and choppy, as the Bible says, and if Christ was actually walking *on* the water, then he would have been bobbing up and down on the rough surface, and he would have had a very difficult time maintaining his balance. Yet nothing like this is described. The impression we get is that he was gliding across the water—as if he were being *floated* by a tractor beam.

The energy of this beam, as it is being concentrated or focused on a subject, must create a glow or aura around it—just like the teleporting beam. Unless he was illuminated, how else would the disciples have been able see Christ in the dark?

Teleportation

One of the major technical issues suggested in the Bible is teleportation. Initially, it was one of the reasons I began studying the scriptures—because of what appeared to be similarities between alien abductions and certain biblical events. Let us now examine in detail the stories suggesting this technology.

In the first months after the Hebrews left Egypt, the tent of meeting had not yet been created, so a temporary tent was set up a short distance outside the camp, where Moses could meet with the Lord. The Lord recognized the need to reinforce the people's trust in Moses, so he decided to begin making some appearances by coming down in a cloud in front of the tent, where everyone could see (Ex 19:9). When Moses went out for these meetings, the people saw the cloud descend and watched as Moses stood there and conversed with a voice from within. This set the precedent for all future visits by the Lord, up to and including the time of Christ, in which he concealed himself within a cloud. Previously, his association with Enoch, Abraham, Isaac, and Jacob had all been in the flesh, but from this point on, it appears he felt it necessary to conceal the fact that he looked like a normal human being. Except for his private meetings with Moses inside the tent, the cloud cover allowed him to maintain the supernatural mystique of a deity figure during the time in the desert.

One rather unorthodox use of teleportation is suggested in chapter 16, in the book of Numbers. It was when three dissenters, Korah, Dathan, and Abiram, attempted to usurp Moses by instigating a rebellion. They were the ones in league with the 250 council members that the Lord allegedly incinerated, as described earlier. It says the Lord got rid of these three by causing the ground to open and swallow them, along with all their tents and family members.

This can be perceived as a miraculous act, but I prefer to examine the technological possibilities, one being that a vast amount of subsurface sand could have been beamed out, creating a large and deep cavity into which everyone fell. They were then buried under the subsurface sand as it rematerialized over them.

Another event suggesting teleportation is found in Judges 13:20, when the angel who visited Samson's mother to announce that she would give birth to a son departed by rising into the sky in a bright light described as fire.

However, I think the most misunderstood event is the Transfiguration. As noted in Matthew 17:2, Mark 9:2, and Luke 9:29, Jesus brought Peter, John, and James up on top of a mountain to pray with him. While they were there, it says he was suddenly engulfed in a bright white light. I can't think of anything that would explain why Christ would suddenly start glowing. The clue to what happened is that it occurred at the exact same moment Moses and Elijah appeared standing beside him. So how did they get there? The fact that they did not come walking out from behind a tree or from up the mountain path—they just suddenly materialized next to Christ—is sufficient reason to suspect they were beamed down. In this case, the writer had his attention focused on Christ, who was apparently engulfed by the light of the teleporting beam that delivered the two men at his side.

After talking for a while, a cloud suddenly appeared and covered them, and a voice from within the cloud said, "This is my son, whom I have chosen; listen to him" (Mt 17:5, Mk 9:7, Lk 9:35). The next thing that Peter, John, and James knew, there was nobody there except Christ.

I have already pointed out that from the time of Moses, all subsequent appearances by the Lord were in a cloud, so logically, we might assume that the voice the disciples heard coming from within this cloud was none other than the Lord himself. He may have come down to accompany Moses and Elijah back to his ship and at the same time take advantage of the opportunity to say hello to his son. The purpose of this visit by Moses and Elijah is an important issue that will be covered later.

More clues to teleportation are found in Matthew 28:2–3 and Lk 24:4, in which it describes a bright light associated with the appearance of angels at Christ's tomb. It says they appeared like "lightning" or in a "flash of light"—just like the little grey creatures in an abduction experience.

According to Acts 1:10, when Christ left the earth, a cloud suddenly materialized around him and began rising slowly into the sky. His disciples stood there intently watching as the cloud rose higher and higher. Then it says two men dressed in white appeared standing beside them and said that Christ would return to Earth the same way they were watching him leave it. The fact that a cloud materialized around Christ suggests that the Lord may have personally come down to escort him up to his ship. The two angels appearing beside the disciples might suggest they were teleported there; however, no bright light was mentioned with their appearance. But if the disciples were intently watching the cloud that had enveloped Christ as it was rising into the sky, the odds are that they never noticed it. However, as we will see later on, there is good reason to believe that these men had been standing in the background all the time.

Another event suggesting teleportation is described in Acts 12:7–10, where it says that an angel appeared out of bright light in the prison cell where the apostle Peter was being held. Two guards had been stationed in the cell with Peter for extra security and were apparently switched off (put to sleep)—something that frequently happens to people around abductees when they are taken. The angel then released the shackles from Peter and led him out of the prison past other guards that also appeared to have been immobilized. And let's not forget the angel that *allegedly* appeared in the fiery furnace and saved Shadrach, Meshach, and Abednego. No one saw him walk into the furnace; he just appeared there. Unless it was by teleportation, how did he manage that?

Other stories in the Bible could also be describing teleportation, but I have not mentioned them because they are ambiguous. However, those that I have mentioned, assuming of course that they really occurred, present the most compelling arguments in support of this technology.

The Ark of the Covenant

Probably the most highly profiled symbol of technology in the Bible, the Ark of the Covenant—is a mystery that has never been completely understood. Its intent and purpose, although clearly defined in the Bible, has become shrouded in the mysticism created by religion. There are questions as to what happened to it and whether it even existed, but since it seems to be an object shrouded in many technological issues, we will assume that it did.

The ark was housed behind a curtain in the sanctuary (tabernacle), which was a separate enclosure centered inside the tent of meeting. According to the Bible's description, the tent was located in the center of a courtyard that was 300 feet long, 150 feet wide, and surrounded by a wall of curtains about 7½ feet high. The ark was 3¼ feet long, 2¼ feet high and wide, and made of acacia wood and plated with gold inside and out. Four gold rings were fastened to its legs, through which poles also made of acacia wood and plated with gold were placed. They were used to carry the ark when moving camp, and the instructions were that they were never to be removed. A separate cover of gold called the atonement cover was placed over the ark, with two cherubim carved into its sides facing each other and looking down toward the lid at an angle. When the Lord gave Moses the instructions on how to build the ark, he clearly specified that it was a system through which they would communicate:

> *There, above the cover between the two cherubim that are over the ark of the Testimony, I will meet with you and give you all my commands for the Israelites.* (Ex 25:22)

The Lord told Moses that he would communicate with him through the ark's gold cover and dictate all the laws the Hebrews would be required to follow. Further evidence is also noted:

> *Moses entered the tent to speak with the Lord and the Lord's voice was speaking to him from between the two cherubim over the atonement cover.* (Nu 7:89)

The same message is reiterated in Leviticus 16:2, so it seems obvious that the ark's primary purpose was for private communication between Moses and the Lord.

On the day it was completed, the ark was taken into the tent and placed behind a curtain in the sanctuary. According to Exodus 40:34–35, a cloud descended and hovered over the tent, and a bright light described as the glory of the Lord filled the tabernacle.

Since the scriptures clearly state that the Lord conversed with Moses through the atonement cover of the ark, the logical assumption is that a communication system had been installed in it. So the only reason I can see for a bright light appearing in the tent at this particular time is that someone beamed down to install the system. And it appears that something else had also been installed—something deadly.

According to Leviticus 10:1–3, Aaron's two sons, Nadab and Abihu, entered the tent of meeting one night and made an unauthorized entry into the sanctuary. In the morning, their bodies were discovered virtually incinerated, apparently by a blast of fiery energy that presumably came from the ark. After this incident, the Lord said to Moses:

Tell your brother Aaron not to come whenever he chooses into the Most Holy Place behind the curtain in front of the atonement cover of the ark, or else he will die, because I appear in a cloud over the atonement cover. (Lev 16:1–2)

The Lord was emphasizing the fact that the sanctuary was reserved for private communication between himself and Moses—and that he appears in a cloud over the atonement cover (communicates with him through it). If Aaron enters at any other time than when he is supposed to, the system will recognize him as an intruder and the same thing will happen to him that happened to his sons.

Warnings had been given about the privacy of the sanctuary and the danger of touching the ark. Orders were that when the ark was moved, only the Levites were allowed to do it:

Anyone else who goes near it shall be put to death. (Nu 1:51)

This is what the Lord first told Moses when he said to appoint Aaron and his two sons to serve as priests:

Anyone else who approaches the sanctuary must be put to death. (Nu 3:10)

It is again mentioned in Numbers 3:38

So apparently, the ark was more than a storage place for the Ten Commandments. It was kept in seclusion behind a curtain in the sanctuary, where only Moses and certain priests were allowed access. The priests were allowed entrance in the performance of their duties, which was only at a designated time. The sanctuary was a private conference room for Moses and the Lord to discuss the business at hand. To maintain security, the ark was armed, and anyone attempting unauthorized entry would be eliminated on the spot. Due to the nature of the discussions taking place, security was important Whatever it was that allowed the Lord to speak with Moses, and maybe even project a visual image, it would have aroused unwanted curiosity if anyone were to see it.

When the ark was moved, only the Levites were allowed to do it. The poles used to carry it were set into rings that had been cast into its legs, with instructions that they were never to be removed. So it appears that the legs, or the rings, were insulated to prevent its bearers from being harmed. It is also logical to assume that whenever they moved camp, the system would have to be reset for transport when the ark was out in the open, in full view of everyone. But the Bible does mention two incidents when people who made physical contact with it were struck dead.

The first incident is described in chapter 4, in the book of 1 Samuel. When the Israelites went to battle the Philistines, they thought that if they brought the ark with them, they would automatically be victorious. Mystical beliefs were now beginning to cloud their concept of the Lord.

They had no idea that in the past he'd been physically present and had used powerful weapons against their enemies; they were just stories that had been passed down for generations. However, they believed that the Lord's presence was in the ark, and that his divine powers would somehow ensure their victory. This, of course, was not the case; they lost the battle, and the ark was captured by the Philistines.

In chapter 5 in the book of 1 Samuel, it says the Philistines placed the ark in their own temple, next to a statue of their god, Baal. Allegedly, the statue was mysteriously knocked over twice, the second time with the head and hands broken off, and the implied message is that the ark had something to do with it.

At some point, the people became plagued with boils and sores erupting on their bodies. This may have been caused by natural circumstances, or perhaps it was a tactic the Lord used to intimidate the Philistines into returning the ark to the Israelites, but instead, they moved it to the city of Gath. It wasn't until an outbreak of boils began plaguing that city that they decided it was probably a good idea to return it. They put it on a cart along with a chest of treasures as a gesture of atonement, and two cows pulled it back across the border, into the Israelite's land. The people were overjoyed by its return, so they set it up on a rock and sacrificed the cows.

According to 1 Samuel 6:19, 70 people were killed when they looked inside the ark. Again, this seems like an exaggerated number. Some Hebrew manuscripts say it was 50,070 people, but that's absurd; I am more inclined to believe that it may have been less than ten. In any case, the Israelites forgot the dangers associated with the ark or did not take the stories seriously. Supposedly, the Philistines had it for two years, and surely they would have opened it … or at least tried to. But even if they did, there is nothing on record about it.

It is doubtful that the Israelites ever managed to open the ark, let alone look inside, since it was rigged to kill anyone who physically touched it. The Bible doesn't say whether the people died at the same time or in separate incidents, but it makes sense that if one person was struck down, it would have served as a warning to others, so it was probably a small group that had gathered, becoming too curious for their own good. If they were crowding around the ark, they would have been in physical contact with each other, and the system was triggered by the first hand that touched it. It could be that they were electrocuted. A high-voltage discharge would have been fatal to whoever touched the ark— and anyone in a chain of physical contact with him. With its plating of pure gold, it was a perfect conductor of electricity.

The second incident is described in 2 Samuel 6:1–8 and occurred many years later, when David was having the ark brought to Jerusalem. The ark was being transported on a cart pulled by oxen. When the oxen stumbled, a man named Uzzah, who was walking beside it, reached out to steady it, but the moment his hand touched the side of the ark, he fell dead. The fact that no one around him was harmed would also suggest electrocution.

Whoever wrote (or translated) the book of 2 Samuel interpreted Uzzah's death as God's punishment for his act of irreverence. This is either an obvious misperception or an intentional distortion of the facts to portray an image of a vengeful God. If the incident occurred as described, common sense suggests that Uzzah's act was not one of irreverence but rather a reflex action—he acted instinctively. Nevertheless, it suggests that the systems in the ark were still activated.

As the time of Christ drew near, the Lord began to back out of the limelight. In the process, it was necessary to remove any evidence of technology, and the Ark of the Covenant would have been of particular concern. The communication and security systems had to be removed, which was difficult because the ark was a symbol of inspiration to the people, and it was always well guarded. The deaths of those who allegedly tried to open it and a man who tried to steady it on an oxcart is evidence that it remained "hot" long after the time of Moses. Since its primary purpose was to facilitate communication with Moses, there was really no use for it after he was gone. No longer was the tent of meeting being used, so there was no sanctuary to provide seclusion to remove the system without being seen; they had to wait until it was placed in another sanctuary.

Their opportunity came during Solomon's fourth year as king, when he built a new temple in Jerusalem and had the ark brought in and placed in its inner sanctuary. Unlike the light that was observed when the ark was placed in the original tent of meeting, this time 1 Kings 8:10–13 says that immediately after the ark was placed inside, a cloud filled the temple. Since the cloud was mentioned, it stands to reason that any light from a teleporting beam would also have been mentioned had it been seen. But because this new sanctuary was now in a large stone temple instead of a tent, any light emanating from within the inner sanctuary probably would not have been visible outside. In this case, I think the cloud was simply a means of keeping people away while the angels did their work. Since it occurred immediately after the ark was placed inside, it probably gave the event a supernatural flavor. However, since there were no further incidents mentioned about the ark being responsible for anyone's death, a reasonable assumption is that the communication and security systems had been removed.

The ark has long since disappeared, and until it is found, assuming it has not already been dismantled for its gold, we may never know for certain that it ever really existed. Many theories have been tossed around as to what became of it, one being that the Knights Templar spirited it away and have it buried in a secret vault.[6]

Author Graham Hancock has conducted extensive research on the ark and believes it was moved from Jerusalem to the island of Elephantine, where it remained for about 240 years. It was then taken to Tana Kirkos, a small island in the middle of Lake Tana, in Ethiopia. About eight centuries later, it was moved to the town of Aksum, where it now rests concealed from view in the Zion of Mary Chapel. Unfortunately, no one other than the man appointed as guardian of the chapel is allowed to see it, and he steadfastly maintains that it is there. According to the monks at Debre Damo, an isolated Ethiopian repository of Holy Scriptures, they also claim that the ark was taken to Tana Kirkos, where it remained for several centuries before being moved to Aksum.[7]

Until the time comes when it can be viewed by the public, there is no way to corroborate the story. If the ark is there, it could provide the evidence that will either prove or disprove that it once contained a device of alien technology.

♦♦♦♦♦

Now, as we begin examining the major biblical stories, you will see how these various technologies logically fit into the scenario. The major events of the Old Testament describe the trials and tribulations that went into the creation of a new race. Genesis describes how the first attempt was a failure, and how their majority had to be destroyed. It describes the implementation of a contingency plan in which another race was created, and in order to preserve their (hybrid) genetic purity as they grew into a nation, you will see how they had to be isolated from the remnants of the first race until they had grown into a small nation. You will also see how these events were orchestrated by a physical being that the people knew by the title of the Lord, and you will see how the technologies described in this chapter were applied—and why I suspect certain major characters were genetically engineered hybrids created to fulfill the various stages of the plan.

Before we begin our journey from the Garden of Eden to the Resurrection, I want to emphasize the fact that The Old Testament is simply a collection of books expressing the views of the people who wrote them down many centuries after the fact. There are numerous manuscripts that were not included in the Bible, presenting the same stories from different points of view, so no one really knows if there is any truth to them, or to those that were included, or how much they may have been altered or embellished over the centuries. And the same applies to the New Testament. It took many years to shape the contents of the Bible into what it is today, and I sometimes wonder if it was due to extraterrestrial influence in order to awaken us to the fact that they are helping us prepare for what is to come in the next millennium or two. Nevertheless, my ideas are simply a logical evaluation, and I do not claim them to be fact, only a possibility based on the sequence of events described in the Bible as presented in it its current form.

Notes

1.   ENIAC
      Web link:
      www.pbs.org/wgbh/aso/databank/entries/dt45en.html

2.   UNIVAC
      Web link:
      en.wikipedia.org/wiki/UNIVAC_I

3.   Jebel Musa
      Web link:
      www.ldolphin.org/franz-sinai.html

4.   Har Karkom
      Web link:
      ancientneareast.tripod.com/Mount_Har_Karkom.html

5.   Jebel el Lawz
      Web link:
      www.arkdiscovery.com/MtSinaiPAX.htm

6.   Theory that Knights Templar has the ark in secret vault
      "The Ark of the Covenant." *History's Mysteries*. Prod. Roel Oostra.
      TLC. 1994.

7.   Theory that the ark is in Aksum, Ethiopia
      "The Ark of the Covenant." *History's Mysteries*. Prod. Roel Oostra.
      TLC. 1994.

Chapter 13

THE FIRST RACE

The evidence alluding to ancient extraterrestrial visitors could probably fill a book the size of *Webster's Complete and Unabridged Dictionary*. What I have presented so far regarding hybrids and technology in the Bible may cause some of you to reevaluate your beliefs, but I have barely scratched the surface. As we explore the major biblical events, you will see how these various technologies (or at least what I perceive as such) logically fit into the scenario of an alien agenda. If my ideas are correct, the plan is revealed in the scriptures, but its meaning has been obscured by the supernatural embellishments of organized religion. Nevertheless, it reveals what appears to be a series of controlled events designed to accelerate and upgrade the technological evolution of man.

Now I am not claiming this to be a fact of life, I am only presenting the evidence that suggests it. Some of my ideas are original, and some are not. I will be covering areas that others have only skimmed over in the past and raising questions that no one has ever thought to ask; however, I am going one step further by connecting all the dots to show the relationship between everything. But as I stated, it is only theory based on logical interpretations—you must draw your own conclusions.

I cannot count the number of times I have heard preachers and evangelists claim that the Bible is the word of God. The truth is that there was no such thing as a Bible until approximately three hundred years before Christ, when religious leaders began to incorporate the five books of Moses (known as the Torah, or Pentateuch) into the Hebrew doctrine. Other books were eventually added and it became known in Christianity as the Old Testament. After the time of Christ, Christianity gradually evolved into a major religion, and twenty-seven new books were canonized, making up The New Testament. So except for the Torah, which was allegedly dictated to Moses by the Lord, the other books are simply a collection of stories written by unknown authors who were expressing their personal views of events that occurred long before their own time, and no one really knows if they are based on fact, derived from earlier Mesopotamian writings, or were simply written to make a moral statement. And when you consider that these books were chosen from literally hundreds of others, many telling the same stories from a different point of view, it is difficult to look upon the Bible as a record of historical fact. Many scholars believe some of these stories were created simply to inspire man with the moral and ethical values they promote—and that they should not be viewed in a literal sense. As for the extraterrestrial connection, it is based solely on the possibility that there is an element of truth to at least some of the stories as currently presented in the Bible.

From childhood, our minds have been conditioned to accept a variety of mystical and supernatural beliefs as fact. Through the teachings of organized religion, we have been coerced into believing it is wrong not to believe what the Bible says because that would be questioning the word of God, and questioning God could result in spending eternity swimming in the fires of hell. This is religion's brainwashing at its best. Growing up intimidated by this belief makes it difficult, even as adults, to perceive the biblical stories in any other fashion except through interpretations deeply rooted in the supernatural and mystical. Exploring alternative ideas may strengthen or diminish our belief in their reality, depending on how we choose to perceive them, but the existence of a supernatural god can neither be proved nor disproved—and probably never will be. For all we know, God may simply be the personification of that which we call Nature. The basic definition of Nature is "a natural creative and controlling force in the universe." Would not the same definition also apply to God?

Adam's Test

The Genesis account of Adam mentions no parents or even a birth mother, thereby allowing religion to perpetuate the idea of a miraculous creation. After examining the details of the creation story from a logical perspective, I could not help but suspect that Adam was a genetically engineered hybrid. When compared to the other Bible stories, it fit comfortably into the overall pattern of events. If we use the alien abduction pattern as a guide, in vitro fertilization may have been followed by a three-month gestation period in the womb of a human female. I would assume it was for the purpose of assimilating her biological immunities to earthly germs and diseases into the fetus. The fetus was then removed and gestation completed by artificial means. Like many of today's abductees, Adam's female host may never have been aware of her abduction or the fact that she was ever pregnant.

The Bible tells us the Lord God placed Adam in a special environment located in the east, called the Garden of Eden, after which he created his mate, Eve. In all probability, this would have occurred while Adam was still very young. It would have been necessary to introduce them into the garden before they were old enough to imprint on any technological aspects of the environment of their creation. Had they become acclimated to such an atmosphere, relocating them to an outdoor setting could have been a traumatic experience. So the logical assumption is that they were moved to the garden at an early enough age to where they would easily adapt. Yet our perception of Adam and Eve living in the wild could be wrong. We know that many civilizations lived in cities earlier than six thousand years ago, before Adam supposedly was created, so it is possible that they lived in a comfortable dwelling both in and outside of Eden.

Nevertheless, someone had to take care of them until they were old enough to survive on their own, and in order to create a positive influence during their formative years, that person (or persons) would have had to play a parental role. It is likely that as they grew older, anyone tending to them gradually faded out of the picture. The only person with whom it appears they had occasional contact was the Lord God, who would have represented the ultimate authority figure.

The only rule they were given was not to eat the fruit from a tree referred to as *the tree of knowledge of good and evil.* They were told that if they disobeyed this rule, they would die (be denied the opportunity of an unlimited life span). Breaking this rule would mean there was a flaw in their genetic programming. They would then be considered imperfect and susceptible to negative influences—unacceptable role models for any future hybrids or the inhabitants of the outside world. It also meant that this imperfection would be passed on through their children. (As suggested earlier, this could have resulted from something that occurred during the period of womb gestation.)

While growing up, it is only natural that they would have been curious about the forbidden fruit, but apparently, they never touched it. It wasn't until they were older that their wisdom and willpower were put to the test. Hebrew scripture indicates that the tree of knowledge may have been a banana tree, but what it really was will probably never be known, assuming it even was a tree; it may only be a symbolic reference for whatever the real test was that they faced. But because it is usually depicted as an apple tree, many people have come to accept it as fact.

If everything had gone as planned, Adam should have developed the wisdom to avoid temptation and the willpower to resist even the strongest efforts of intimidation. However, the Bible clearly states that it was not Adam who was tempted; it was Eve. It appears they used her to expose his weakness. She was Adam's mate, his friend, his companion, and his lover, and she knew everything there was to know about him. If anyone had the power to influence him to act irresponsibly, it was she. Nevertheless, Adam was the star player in the production—his actions would determine how things would proceed from that point on.

The Bible portrays Eve's tempter as a talking snake. That might possibly be attributed to later translators acclimated to beliefs more oriented in mysticism. Let's be realistic—how many people believe that a snake can talk? We know it is a ridiculous idea today, and why would it be any less ridiculous 6,000 years ago. Ancient Hebrew legends describe Eve's tempter as a being who stood upright, and it is a much more logical idea to conceive. What is printed in the Bible is the scribe's choice of what he thought the interpretation should be, and it is very misleading. Eve's tempter was probably a humanoid being, although not necessarily human. As speculated earlier, it may be that he was of the same grey species currently involved with the abductions.

He tried to persuade Eve to eat from the tree of knowledge, but she said that doing so would mean her death. He told her that she would not die, that instead she would become like God, knowing good and evil. This implies that she lacked the knowledge, or the ability, to differentiate between right and wrong. Both she and Adam knew it was against the rules to eat this fruit; therefore, they did know the difference between right and wrong (good and evil). The fruit looked and tasted good. Eve then gave some to Adam, and as we all know, neither of them died, at least then. In fact, the Bible says Adam lived for 930 years, and that Eve also lived a very long life. So why were they told they would die if they ate the fruit?

The logical interpretation is that it was *the act* of eating the fruit—disobeying the rule—that was their death sentence. Their longevity depended on the tree of life. It was the fruit of this tree, combined with their enhanced genetics, that sustained them, and it was their eviction from Eden, with no further access to it, that condemned them to eventual death. The plan was for them to have virtually unlimited life spans, providing, of course, they proved to be perfect specimens whose positive qualities would be passed on to each new generation. Unfortunately, they turned out not so perfect, a factor that would also be passed on to their children. So it appears this imperfection was the factor that disqualified them from the game—and the reason why they were put out of Eden and denied immortality.

As a child growing up in the Catholic religion, I learned from the nuns that we are all born with original sin on our souls—that we are automatically guilty of the sin committed by Adam. But I always thought that was ridiculous. How can we be guilty of a sin before we are born—it is illogical. The logical interpretation of original sin is Adam's imperfection. It is a genetic factor we have all inherited (are guilty of) to some degree.

After eating the fruit, they suddenly realized the seriousness of their actions and were genuinely afraid of what the consequences would be if the Lord God found out. The Bible says they suddenly realized they were naked and sewed fig leaves together to cover themselves, and when they heard the Lord God coming, they went into the woods and hid among the trees.

The fact that they knew how to sew fig leaves together and conversed with the Lord God implies that they were intelligent, so suddenly realizing they were naked makes no sense. To know they were naked means they knew about clothes. Surely they remembered that those who tended them in their younger years wore clothing, and whenever the Lord God paid them a visit, it is difficult to picture him arriving in the nude, so it was obviously just an excuse they made up for why they were hiding. They were afraid the Lord God would find out they had broken the rule, so they hid in the woods, hoping he would not see them and leave. Obviously, the Lord God monitored the test and knew. After confronting them, he proceeded to chastise the tempter. But if this was really a test, why admonish the one who conducted it? Restrictions were placed on the couple to see if they possessed the positive qualities to be the progenitors of the new race who would obey all the rules, in which case it would have been the tempter's job to do everything in his power to make them break the rules. So would he not have been working in concert with the Lord God?

In his diatribe, the Lord God said that he would create enmity between the seed of the tempter and the woman, which makes no sense since they would probably never see each other again. He also said that the woman (meaning women) would now suffer pain in childbearing. Since they would now be deprived of its fruit, the only thing that can logically be associated with this discomfort is the tree of life. It probably would not have affected Eve for many years, if at all, but as the beneficial effect of the fruit wore off and life spans became shorter, childbirth would gradually become painful for women of later generations.

Since no trees on Earth provide immortality, the tree of life (if it was a tree) had to be something that the aliens either created or brought with them from their own or another world. It is also mentioned in the book of Revelation, which says it will provide immortality to those living with Christ in a new city after his return and one-thousand-year reign. The implication is that this fruit somehow retards the aging process and those who regularly eat of it will be blessed with unlimited life spans. However, if suddenly cut off from this fruit, its effects would wear off, and they would eventually grow old and die. The number of years they had consumed the fruit was a factor that would determine how long they (and their immediate descendants) would actually live. To ensure their mortality, a security device in the form of a flaming sword flashing back and forth was installed at the entrance to Eden to prevent further access to it.

Adam allowed Eve to seduce him into breaking the law; the positive genetic qualities that he should have manifested did not take hold for some reason. Something, perhaps in the biological makeup of the woman they used to initiate his gestation, inhibited (or contaminated) certain enhanced elements of his genetic programming. So the plan to create more hybrids was put on hold. Depending on how things went, Adam's descendants could present a major problem, so each succeeding generation would have to be closely monitored.

The book of Enoch suggests that the decision to destroy them had been made early on, so why did they wait for over a thousand years? A reasonable assumption is that they needed to make a complete evaluation and see how long Adam and Eve and their immediate descendants would actually live. They had to get some idea of how long it would take for life cycles to return to normal. If they digressed rapidly, there would be no problem. However, if it were going to take a few thousand years, the race would have to be eliminated so they could start over in time to meet the project's deadline.

After the couple left Eden, it was necessary to create an authority figure—someone they would have to answer to for their indiscretions. This is when deity worship and sacrifices to the deity suddenly came into play.

The Deity Image

If Adam's purpose was to spawn a new race by infusing improved genetic qualities into the existing population, it is logical to assume that if he passed his test, more hybrids would have been created to speed up the process. However, due to his imperfection, it appears that this phase was put on hold. If things had worked out, the ETs may have maintained an open relationship with man. Eventually, we would have benefited from the association and may have moved out among the stars a long time ago. But now we would have to do it alone, without the knowledge that we were under the influence of an alien power; they could no longer let themselves be known for who they really were. Consistent interaction with them would have eventually yielded technological secrets that man would never be mature enough to handle, or he could grow dependent on them and not develop his own skills for survival. So direct involvement had to be avoided, which meant control could only be maintained through an image that man would fear and respect—thus we came to perceive them as gods.

During the time in Eden, the Bible mentions no rituals of sacrifices being performed, *nor was there any worshipping of a god*. It was only after they were evicted that deity worship and making sacrifices to the Lord began. Nothing in the Bible explains how or why this practice originated, but in the time of Moses, the Lord dictated specific instructions on the preparation and offering of animal sacrifices; only the best animals with no imperfections were to be used. It was considered an act of atonement for sins committed, and since it appears this same ritual was practiced by Cain and Abel, it is reasonable to assume that it was instituted by the Lord in order to perpetuate the belief in a higher authority.

The Changing of the Gods

Once Adam and Eve were out of Eden, the Lord God seemed to disappear. The responsibility of Adam and his descendants suddenly shifted to a different individual known simply as the Lord. The titles of *Lord* and *Lord God* have the same connotation as *manager* and *assistant manager* or *general* and *major general*. So it is possible that these titles were actually designations of authority or rank. Evidently, the Lord's rank was higher because it seems that he made all the important decisions after he took over. So if, as the Bible claims, the Lord dictated to Moses all the information contained in the Torah, it would appear that in Genesis, he made a clear distinction between himself and the Lord God.

Adam and Eve now had to fend for themselves in the outside world, and after the birth of their third child, Seth, nothing more is said about them. I would assume they had always been aware of the people on the outside and had even been brought up speaking their language. If it were intended for them and future hybrids to blend with these people, being able to speak their language would have been a great advantage.

Nevertheless, an indication of what was to come was evident in their first offspring, Cain. Cain did not have the power to control his emotions, nor did he apply his talents to their fullest potential. In their offerings to the Lord, Abel, who raised animals, sacrificed only the best of his flock, but Cain, who worked the fields, provided a meager offering. While complimenting Abel on his sacrifice, the Lord admonished Cain, telling him he could have done a lot better. Adam's defect manifested strongly in Cain, and he let his emotions get the better of him: he became jealous of his brother and murdered him.

Actually, I suspect that there was more involved than belittling Cain for an unacceptable sacrifice. I suspect the Lord had been riding him all along by purposely showing favoritism toward Abel. He pushed Cain to the breaking point. He needed to know how far he would actually go—it would be an indication of what to expect in future generations. When the Lord learned that he had killed his brother, he went to Cain and asked him where Abel was. Cain responded, "Am I my brother's keeper?" Because of his arrogant and violent nature, it was necessary to relocate him for fear that he may commit more acts of violence, possibly on his parents. It was important that they be monitored to learn how long they would actually live. So the Lord banished Cain from the land. He went (or was transported) to a place far to the east, called Nod, where the Bible says he took a wife, had a son, and even built a city.

Who Was Cain's Wife?

Bible buffs argue that Cain's wife had to be one of his sisters, one of the many subsequent children produced by Adam and Eve. Others, in a feeble attempt to rationalize, believe that Cain's son resulted from a sexual union with his mother, Eve. They all believe the same myth—that Adam and Eve were the only people on the earth at that time. However, if Cain was banished to a land far away from his parents, then he couldn't have mated with his mother. As for marrying one of his sisters, it is possible, but the statistics, according to the Bible, make it a very unlikely theory. Up until the flood, most men did not become fathers until they were at least 65 years of age—and in many cases, over 180. Starting with Seth, if we average it out, the first son born to each of his descendants occurred about every one-hundred-plus years for the next 900 years. Each time a first son was born, grew up, took a wife, and had his first son, an average span of about 100 years had elapsed. And this is how it went for 900 years. How long did it take them to produce a second child? It's likely that daughters were born first in some cases, but there is no mention of them, and even if there were, it might have been decades before Cain encountered any of his sisters or other female relatives such as nieces and cousins.

This chronology accounts for the descendants of Seth, not the later children of Adam and Eve, who assimilated into the native population. Those men produced children at an earlier age, with women whose fertility cycles were normal; it was well over a thousand years before the fertility cycles of Adam's female descendants began a gradual return to normalcy. In any case, it is more probable that Cain married a woman native to the region in which he had been relocated, and the most convincing evidence of this is Genesis 4:14. It states that when Cain was being banished, he expressed to the Lord his fear that "whoever finds me will kill me." To whom was he referring? This was before Seth was born, and since he killed Abel, there were no other siblings. So to whom was he referring if not the native population?

According to Genesis 4:15, the Lord put a mark on Cain that was supposed to protect him from any potential slayer. Whatever the mark was, it had to be something the general population would recognize as a symbol that he was under the protection of a higher authority, and it could have been in the form of a tattoo or a brand, such as is put on cattle. So what kind of mark or symbol would be recognized, respected, or even feared by the general population? That is something we may never know.

It soon became evident that things were deteriorating. Although not all of Adam's descendants were affected, it was apparent in many. As they began mating with the local population, Adam's virus was passed on through their children. A great number exhibited weakness of character. Many developed abnormal and perverted sexual habits, and deviant sexual behavior gradually became a major factor. However, not all were affected. One such person was Enoch, Adam's great-great-great-great-great grandson, who, according to the Bible, had developed a close association with the Lord. After the birth of his son Methuselah when he was sixty-five years old, he and the Lord became close for the next three hundred years. Then it says the Lord took him from the earth (Ge 5:24).

As we will see later on, going with the Lord appeared to be the ultimate reward for those with whom he had established a personal relationship and worked with him on the project. Enoch may have provided valuable assistance in its early phase, and it is possible that he, too, was a hybrid. However, the Bible passes over the first thousand years in just three pages; many people are mentioned, but little or nothing is said about them.

According to Erich von Däniken, the book of Enoch had been accepted into the canon of the early Abyssinian (Ethiopian) Church. Part of the scripture tells how the guardians of heaven transported Enoch up to their leader (the Lord), who, from the description, sounds like he was in a large ship in orbit around the earth. Among the things he described of this visit was receiving astronomical information, particularly on the orbits of the planets, and even advance knowledge of Noah's flood (which did not occur until several hundred years later). It also says that these "guardians" were in trouble; they had become sexually involved with the women of Earth and fathered many children. It resulted in a mixing of genes that produced children of extremely tall stature. Hoping to lessen the degree of trouble they had gotten themselves into, they asked Enoch to speak to the Lord on their behalf.[1] This implies that Enoch had influence with the Lord, which also suggests that, like Moses, he knew who he really was.

Since these Guardians fathered children with Earth women, it would appear they were stationed on Earth for many years during the Lord's absence; had the Lord been around, they probably would not have gotten away with it. So it seems there were times when he returned to his own world or went elsewhere and left the Guardians as monitors to take care of any problems that might arise until he returned. In Aramaic texts, they are called *watchers*.

It would appear that in the course of their duties, they began mingling with the local population; this socializing led to intimate relationships with many young women and, inevitably, the birth of many children. But we have no way of knowing if the women they were involved with were only the direct descendants of Adam and Eve or if they included the local women. I think the most logical assumption would be both because after leaving Eden, Adam and Eve and their later children would have melded into the local population. Therefore, Adam's virus was being spread all over the place, and I think we can assume that many of the alien's offspring eventually became affected.

Their sexual involvement is clearly described in the Bible, as is the Lord's intention to eliminate the hybrid race he had created.

> *When men began to increase in numbers on the earth and daughters were born to them, the sons of God saw that the daughters of men were beautiful, and they married any of them they chose. Then the Lord said, "My Spirit will not contend with man forever, for he is mortal; his days will be a hundred and twenty years. (Ge 6:1–3)*

> *The Nephilim were on the earth in those days—and also afterward—when the sons of God went to the daughters of men and had children by them. They were heroes of old, men of renown. (Ge 6:4)*

"Nephilim" is defined in *Webster's Dictionary* as a "biblical race of giants or demigods," and "demigod" as "the offspring of a deity and a mortal." This suggests that they were the offspring of angels—normal human-looking beings whom the people considered to be the sons of God because they had come down from the heavens. It says, "They were heroes of old, men of renown," but it is unclear if "they" pertains to the sons of God or their children—you can take it either way. If they really were heroes and men of renown, then who were they? The Bible mentions nothing about them except that their offspring were men of extremely tall stature. Goliath, the giant killed by David, supposedly was one of their descendants and was said to be over nine feet tall.

In Hebrew, Nephilim is defined as "the fallen ones" and does not mean they were giants in the literal sense. Referring to them as giants may simply indicate that they greatly excelled (were giants) in their particular fields of endeavor. Unfortunately, religion has exacerbated the literal translation, leading people to believe that giant men were actually walking on the earth at the time. Nevertheless, the book of Enoch mentions many of them by name and says they numbered about two hundred. In chapter 8, it says they taught men a great deal about astronomy, how to work with metals and dyes, and introduced them to weapons of war. They also taught them many other things that would eventually lead to technical advancement. They provided Adam's descendants with knowledge they were not meant to have, thereby compounding an already serious situation.

The Nephilim are later referred to in Exodus as Anakites or Anakim, the descendants of Anak, and were wiped out when the Israelites first entered the Promised Land. It says they "were on the earth in those days—and also afterward ..." This adds emphasis to the fact that the Nephilim were around before as well as after the flood. We know that "those days" means before the flood and "and also afterward" refers to after the flood. So why does organized religion teach us that Noah and his family were the only survivors? Allowing for the possibility (or in this case, the probability) that religion has completely distorted the context of the story, Noah and his family were not the only survivors. The Bible clearly states that the descendants of the Nephilim were still around and were one of the first to be defeated by the Israelites in the Promised Land. If this is true, it means the flood could not have been as devastating as the Bible makes it out to be.

Now let me bring your attention to this:

Then the Lord said, "My Spirit will not contend with man forever, for he is mortal; his days will be a hundred and twenty years." (Ge 6:3)

The footnote relating to this verse states that the word translated from the ancient texts meaning *contend* also means *remain*. So depending on which word is correct, the sentence could have two different meanings. Although some Bibles may use different words in this passage, the general interpretation is the same. Apparently, the scribes who did the original translation favored the *contend* definition because they assumed the Lord was expressing his anger for the evils that men were doing. They say that the Lord's spirit will not contend (struggle, strive, or put up) with man forever, because he is mortal and he will only live for about 120 years. But that is because the Lord cut them off from the tree of life. And man never really was immortal; he was always susceptible to death by accident, murder, or even suicide.

If we use the word *remain* instead of *contend*, it appears to be a distinct reference to the hybrid genes that failed to manifest in Adam's bloodline. The Lord is saying that his own genetic qualities (My Spirit) were deteriorating in man's body (will not *remain* with man forever) because he no longer has access to the tree of life, and for this reason, his life span will diminish and he will die (for he is mortal; his days will [now] be a hundred and twenty years).

The benefits acquired from the tree of life were ebbing away; fewer people were living for 900 years. They began dying at 800 and 700 years of age and younger. At this rate, it would have taken a few thousand years before life cycles stabilized at around 120 years, and by then the problem would have multiplied to uncontrollable proportions. To meet the project's deadline, they had to start over much sooner. The Lord said:

> *"I will wipe mankind, whom I have created, from the face of the earth ..."* (Ge 6:7)

This seems to be a double entendre suggesting that the Lord was going to wipe out the entire human race ... or just those of Adam's lineage. Since man existed long before the time of Adam, the words "mankind, whom I have created" would seem to refer to the direct descendants of Adam (the hybrid race), whom he created—the ones who were the problem. Their numbers were now great, and they were scattered throughout the entire land, so the only logical solution was to wipe them out with a flood; it was the only sure way of eliminating the majority of them. There were sure to be survivors, but they would be an insignificant number, at least for a while.

Like Enoch, there were those unaffected by Adam's virus. Noah was one of these exceptional ones; he was not influenced or intimidated by the evil and perversion that prevailed throughout the land. His genes represented the positive qualities infused into the first race. He and his family were considered righteous people, and so it was decided to use them to salvage the project.

◆◆◆◆◆

When we look at the creation story from a logical perspective, it suggests that the intention was to upgrade the technical evolution and moral behavior of the human race on a genetic level. The fact that Adam and Eve were told not to eat from the tree of knowledge suggests it was meant to be a test—a test to determine if their programmed genetics would enhance positive qualities and eliminate, or at least minimize, any negative characteristics. It was important that they possessed the wisdom to make the right decision when the time came. What other possible reason could there have been to subject them to a test of temptation? Since they failed the test, it appears there was a problem. The next step: what to do about it.

We should also note that the Bible makes no mention of events that occurred prior to Adam's creation, so whatever transpired previously may be considered irrelevant. Nevertheless, the Lord allegedly had Moses document everything that occurred from that point on—up to and including what took place during his own lifetime.

Notes

1.   The book of Enoch
       Web link:
       www.altheim.com/lit/enoch.html

Chapter 14

THE FLOOD

We now move ahead to the period circa 2344 BC, in which the Bible describes how the decadence spawned by Adam's descendants had grown to intolerable levels. Adam's race was a failure, and the time had come when something had to be done about it if the project was to continue. Another race was needed, which meant the first one had to be eliminated (or at least the greater majority of them) or their perversions could become a dominant influence that would have an adverse effect on their replacement. The Bible says this was accomplished by a flood.

If the flood was a real event, the biblical account is an exaggeration because there is not enough water on the planet to create an inundation of the magnitude it describes. If the northern polar ice cap were melted, scientists estimate it would only raise ocean levels by approximately 350 feet, and if we include the southern polar ice cap, it would still fall far short of what the Bible claims. And if the water level was raised on a global scale to the height described in the Bible, we would all be underwater right now because there would have been no place for it to go, and that much water would have had to come from somewhere else.

It is possible that the Lord had the means to control the weather. He may have created a storm system that generated several weeks of heavy rain over the land, which would have produced devastating flood conditions, causing widespread death and destruction. However, according to Genesis 7:11, much of this water was unleashed from deep underground reservoirs. But there is another possibility to consider.

We know that as the Ice Age came to an end, melting glaciers caused a gradual rise in ocean levels. Marine geologists William Ryan and Walter Pitman theorize that as the level of the Mediterranean Sea rose, it penetrated an earthen dam in what is now the Bosporus, spilling saltwater hundreds of feet down into the Black Sea. They estimate that the spill rate would have been two hundred times greater than that of Niagara Falls, and the entire basin region would have been inundated with water rising at approximately six inches per day. They estimate that this inundation would have occurred between 5,500–7,500 years ago.[1] Adding credibility to this idea are fossilized shells of freshwater sea life that were recovered from the Black Sea, indicating that it was originally a freshwater lake. Then, in 1999, an ancient shoreline and a flat beach area were discovered at a depth of 550 feet. Robert Ballard, the man who found the *Titanic*, also came up with more evidence. In September of 2000, his team discovered what appears to have been human habitation at a depth of over 300 feet. They took underwater photographs and video footage of what looks like stone tools and the remnants of a structure.[2]

Ryan and Pitman said the location is right, and they claim that the 5,500-year estimate is close to the timeline in the biblical account. However, the biblical account places it circa 2344 BC, and Ryan and Pitman's estimate would place it around 3500 BC, when Adam was only 500 years old. There is archaeological evidence suggesting that many of the biblical events took place at a much earlier time than what the Bible claims. Some of the data is hard to dispute, which suggests that timelines associated with many of the biblical stories could be totally inaccurate.

According to Erich von Däniken, one of the Qumron texts discovered near the Dead Sea is the scroll of Lamech, Noah's father. Although it is in fragments, it suggests that Noah may not have been Lamech's biological son. Lamech had apparently been away for a long time (how long is not specified), and when he returned, he did not recognize Noah as being one of his sons, because he bore no resemblance to his other children.

Lamech accused his wife, Bat-Enosh, of being unfaithful, possibly with one of the "sons of heaven" (the Nephilim). Yet she swore by everything that was holy that he was the father. Lamech went to his father, Methuselah, and told him of the child and his suspicions, and Methuselah in turn sought counseling from his father, Enoch. Enoch told Methuselah that the Lord was going to wipe out the evil of the earth and that Noah had been chosen to preserve the seed of mankind—and that Lamech should accept him.

However, biblical chronology places the birth of Noah some sixty-nine to seventy years after the Lord took Enoch from the earth. So if he was gone, how could Methuselah have talked to him? Where he was taken or what he was doing is unknown, but the fact that he was still alive presents the possibility that he returned periodically. Unfortunately, this is something we will probably never know. Considering the scroll is very fragmented—much of it missing—fitting together the existing pieces leaves much to speculation. However, it does present the possibility that Noah's father may have been one of the sons of heaven.

The fact that the sons of heaven are even mentioned is interesting. If their children were extremely tall men, as the Bible suggests, and if Noah was one of their offspring, it makes sense that he, too, would have been a giant of a man. Since nothing is said about his height, it is probably not true. And remember, the Hebrew word for Nephilim means "the fallen ones," not giants. On the other hand, it could mean that Noah was a hybrid. That would make sense since he was used for the specific purpose of continuing the project. And it never was affirmed, or denied, that Lamech was his biological father. As much as I would like to consider this a good piece of evidence, due to the condition of the scroll, it can only be considered unreliable information.

It appears that the Lord chose Noah to keep the positive genes of the first race alive until he created another hybrid to breed a second race, so he gave him specific instructions on how to build an ark. It was to be three hundred cubits in length, fifty cubits in width, and thirty cubits in height. No one has ever been able to agree on the exact length of the cubit; it was based on the length of the forearm from the elbow to the tip of the middle finger, and most estimates vary from eighteen to twenty-one inches. Scholars, however, suggest that it was probably about 450 feet long, 75 feet wide, and 45 feet high. In any case, it had to be large enough to hold Noah and his family plus all the animals and enough food to feed them for at least a year since that is how long they were said to have been on board.

There is nothing mentioned in the Bible as to how Noah collected the animals, so it remains a mystery. Left to the imaginations of those absorbed in religious beliefs, most films and literature depict the event as a miraculous display of God's power over all creatures. They show Noah calmly leading wild beasts from their habitats and into the ark, while others show a parade of animals magically arriving on their own, two by two. Obviously, no one knows how it was accomplished, although they continue to propagate their mystical beliefs in how they portray the event. It is nice to believe that things occurred in such an orderly fashion, but (assuming the story is even true) I think Noah and his sons would have had to set many traps, and the animals were probably not as docile as they have been portrayed.

Since it is illogical that the flood was worldwide, we might assume that it was confined to the local region, and that many of the local inhabitants were wiped out along with Adam's descendants. The Bible says it took forty days for the rains to flood the land and ten to eleven months for the water to recede. But the number forty is a misnomer in the context of how it is used. Anyone familiar with biblical history knows that *forty* and *seven* denote unspecified amounts. Forty was used in the same context that we use expressions like tons, heaps, and oodles to indicate large amounts or a lot of something. The term "forty days," as applied to the length of time the rains fell, simply means that it rained for a very long time. Exactly how long is something we will probably never know.

It is still the belief of many that when the waters began to recede, the ark came to rest on top of Mount Ararat. This is a perfect example of people accepting ideas for which there is no basis in fact. The Bible says that the ark came to rest on the *mountains* of Ararat, not *mountain*, which means it could have set down anywhere. And another piece of misinform1ation is that the flood was global, an erroneous assumption based on illogical beliefs. According to Genesis 7:20, the water rose to twenty feet above the mountain peaks. The *Rand McNally World Atlas* lists Mount Everest, located on the border of Nepal and Tibet, as the highest mountain in the world at 29,028 feet, and Mount Ararat in Turkey at 17,011 feet. Even if the water only covered Ararat, it is unlikely that the ark came to rest on the top of the mountain. Can you imagine large bulky-framed animals like short-legged hippos and rhinos, not to mention huge and cumbersome elephants, scaling their way down 17,000 feet from the top of a mountain—a mountain that is even a challenge for man? And if the flood did cover Mount Everest to twenty feet above the peak, and if it was worldwide, then the entire planet would have been under 29,048 feet of water. That means sea level would have been raised to that altitude! Even if it only covered Ararat, sea level would have been over 17,000 feet. Where did all that water go? Equally puzzling is where it came from.

Another point to consider is the altitude—the air becomes thinner above 10,000 feet. Granted, the body can adjust over a period to functioning at much higher altitudes, even above Ararat's 17,000-foot elevation. Noah and his family were acclimated to conditions existing at or near sea level; the daily routine of feeding and cleaning up after all the animals would have become a monumental task. Carrying sacks of feed up and down ladders or ramps to the different levels, shoveling hay, and wielding heavy implements would have been strenuous under any condition, but if the water level rose gradually, I suppose it is possible they could have adjusted.

We also have to consider that at such an altitude, there would have been a considerable drop in temperature. Whether they were able to build fires inside the ark is unknown, but because of the vast amount of hay that had to be stored and because the ark was made of wood, it would have been very risky, especially on a windy day if the ark was bouncing around in choppy water. One might theorize that a comfortable temperature was maintained from the body heat produced by all the animals.

Today, snow and a deep glacier of ice cover Ararat's peak all year long, making it a difficult trek for anyone. We don't know for sure what the climate was like five thousand years ago, but we do know that most regional climatic changes would have occurred approximately ten thousand years ago, at the end of the Ice Age. So the odds are that the climate on Ararat during Noah's time was not much different from what it is today. We know this to be the case in the Austrian Alps, where the Iceman lay frozen in a layer of ice for over five thousand years. But even if Ararat had been free of snow and ice, it still would have been impossible for large animals like elephants to scale their way down from the top.

Except for the creatures in the sea, the biblical account would have us believe that Noah collected every species of life that existed: animal, bird, reptile, insect, and so forth. Logic, however, tells us that he could only take those indigenous to the region in which he lived. I rather doubt that koala bears, kangaroos, penguins, and polar bears, plus a variety of other species, were native to the area, which means that Noah would have had to travel to the four corners of the earth to collect them, and if that were the case, he would have needed ten more arks to accommodate them. And if, as the Bible claims, it took him one hundred years to build just one, how would he have found the time? So a logical conclusion is that the flood (if it really occurred) was localized to a particular region and not quite as devastating as organized religion would like us to believe.

Of course, it is possible that the flood was a natural disaster, and Ryan and Pitman's theory currently presents a strong possibility. And the fact that Noah was instructed to build the ark one hundred years in advance suggests that the Lord knew it was going to happen. With the technology at his disposal, he surely would have been aware of the rising ocean levels and what was happening in the Mediterranean, and it would have provided a convenient solution to the problem.

As for the flood being a global event, anyone who has studied world history knows that Egypt's Fifth Dynasty was in existence before and after the flood (2465–2323 BC), as were the Sumerians who flourished from 4000 BC until almost 2000 BC. So logic, as well as historical fact, tells us that if biblical chronology is accurate, the flood could not have been the devastating event that the Bible makes it out to be.

Another notable point is that even if Noah was a hybrid or unaffected by Adam's virus, it was still possible for it to manifest in his descendants through his wife's bloodline, and according to Genesis 9:22–27, it did. Without being specific, it suggests that either his youngest son, Ham, or Ham's son, Canaan, sodomized Noah while he lay asleep in his tent, naked and drunk after consuming too much wine. According to Genesis 9:24, Noah cursed his grandson, Canaan, so it would appear that he was the one.

It is interesting to note that in chapter 10 of Genesis, it lists the clans that descended from Noah's sons and says that many of Canaan's descendants migrated toward Sodom, Gomorrah, Admah, and Zeboiim—the cities slated for destruction a year before Isaac was to be born, presumably for their perverted ways.

After the flood, long life spans decreased dramatically. Noah was the last to live an extended life and died at the age of 950, outliving his great-great-great-great-grandson Reu by twelve years. And his sons only lived for 400 to 600 years, after which life spans dwindled to about 120 years. However, many of Adam's negative genetic factors were carried forward through Noah's family and others who survived the flood. As these survivors repopulated over the centuries, they were eventually spread throughout the entire world to the point where today we are all affected to some degree.

The Tower of Babel
The majority of Adam's descendants demonstrated moral and ethical instability. Their wisdom could not keep pace with their technical potential, so it was necessary to stifle progress until after a new race was created and things could be brought into better balance.

After the flood, the Lord disappeared, while Noah's descendants grew in population. When he returned, it was evident that their creative abilities were beginning to flourish. Instead of wandering throughout the land, they wanted to settle in one place and establish themselves by building a city and a tower that reached to the heavens. Some moved onto a plain in Shinar (Babylonia), where they began to develop their construction skills. They started erecting buildings made from baked bricks and used tar for mortar. Although not as impressive as the monolithic structures in Egypt, the city of Babel was a manifestation of their desire and ability to progress.

The Bible states that when the Lord saw what they were doing, he immediately put a stop to it. But why? They were doing nothing wrong. They simply wanted to build a city with a very tall tower that would gain them status and recognition in the land. They were tired of being wanderers; they just wanted to settle down and grow roots. So why did the Lord interfere?

The answer is that they had to be stopped; they were in the beginning stages of technological progress. The Lord was speaking to a companion when he said the following:

"If as one people speaking the same language they have begun to do this, then nothing will be impossible for them. Come, let us go down and confuse their language ... " (Ge 11:6–7)

According to Genesis 11:1, the entire world spoke only one language after the flood. And organized religion relies on this passage to fortify the false belief that the flood encompassed the entire world and wiped out everybody except Noah and his family. Since we have proof that civilizations around the world were thriving at the time, it is an erroneous claim. As for the people of Babel, it seems that *speaking the same language* is simply a metaphor indicating unity—unity of people working together as a team to achieve greater accomplishments. Confusing their language suggests a creating of dissension to disrupt that unity and teamwork.

The people were exhibiting both desire and ability to progress. Had they completed their city, they would have gained more knowledge, increasing their confidence to advance even further *(then nothing will be impossible for them).* So they were manipulated into abandoning their project. Progress was being reserved for the next new race, which was still in the offing. Any advancement made by these people would have put them in a dominant position with a strong influence over the new race, and it had to be prevented. Although most were decent and righteous people, they had not developed the wisdom necessary to cope with major progress. It would only have been a matter of time before things got out of control, so they had to be stopped.

The Lord's words suggest that he and a companion actually came down and mingled with the people. They possessed strong powers of persuasion, so it would not have been difficult for them to plant a variety of conflicting ideas in the people's minds to create a disruption—a breakdown of their unity and teamwork. If everyone suddenly developed conflicting ideas, it would create arguments and dissension, and it would soon become impossible for them to agree on anything. Instead of working together as a team, they would allegorically be *speaking in different languages*. Eventually, they would become frustrated with the whole idea and go their own separate ways.

◆◆◆◆◆

Practically every civilization on the planet tells of a great flood that occurred at some time in their past. Ancient Sumerian writings describe a flood similar to the biblical account, and it would have occurred around eight thousand years ago. Some Bible scholars believe Noah's flood was just one of several stories that may have been derived from these earlier writings. Even if there is an element of truth to the biblical account, there is no geological evidence that a global flood ever occurred. So it was not the worldwide event that religion would have us believe.

Since the first race ended up in an abyss of decadence, it had to be removed so it would not have an adverse effect on its replacement. Logistically, it had to go before a backup plan could be initiated. Whether a planned or natural event, a devastating flood would have provided a convenient solution to the problem.

Notes

1.　The Black Sea evidence
　　Web link:
　　www.nationalgeographic.com/blacksea/ax/frame.html

2.　Robert Ballard's Black Sea discoveries
　　The Quest for Noah's Flood. Documentary. Prod. Marijo Dows/
　　Foster Wiley. PBS. 2001.

Chapter 15

STARTING OVER

The next events describe what appears to have been a contingency plan designed to keep the project going. A new race was created by a new hybrid, and Abraham's wife, Sarah, was selected to be his mother. Abraham was approximately seventy-five years old when the Lord first contacted him, and it was twenty-four years later (when Sarah was about ninety) that she gave birth to Isaac. In the meantime, Abraham became a rich man when the Lord assisted him in extorting wealth from an Egyptian pharaoh and the king of Gerar. This enabled them to devote all their time raising the child with proper moral and ethical values.

During that period, the Lord visited Abraham again. Although Abraham may have perceived him as some sort of god who came down from the heavens, the Lord had never told him who he was. It wasn't until a year before Isaac was born that he told him he was El Shaddai, the title that was later reinterpreted to mean God Almighty, the God above all other gods and the origin of the one-god concept in Judeo/Christian history.

It was during this visit that he first told Abraham that Sarah would bear a son and he was to be named Isaac. He made a pact with him, stating that he would give Isaac's descendants their own land, which he did about five centuries later. He also told him they would become enslaved in another land for four centuries, and that he would bring punishment upon those who enslaved them; ultimately, they would be delivered to their new land.

So the Lord was actually revealing his plan to Abraham—describing what he was going to do—and some of the events were to be five hundred years in the future. This suggests that the Israelite's move to Egypt, their enslavement, their release, and their subsequent deliverance into their Promised Land was a series of events that had been planned before Isaac was even born.

Meanwhile, the remnants of the first race that survived the flood still posed a threat. Many had moved to cities along the Dead Sea, such as Sodom, Gomorrah, Admah, Zeboiim, and Zoar, not far from Hebron, where Abraham had set up his camp. Sodom and Gomorrah were said to be rife with decadence, so to prevent Isaac from being exposed to their perversions, these cities had to go, and according to the Bible, they did—a year before he was born.

In the Lord's next visit to Abraham, two angels accompanied him, and according to Genesis 18:2, they were described as three men. He reminded Abraham of what he said about Sarah bearing a son and told him it would occur within a year. After sharing a meal, the Lord stayed to talk with Abraham, and his two companions went down into Sodom. While visiting Lot's house, a band of men gathered outside and demanded that Lot send them out so that *they may know them,* a biblical term meaning to have sex with them. The angels retaliated by striking the mob blind, and then they physically forced Lot and his family to leave the city, after which it was destroyed.

Other ancient manuscripts state that five cities were slated for destruction: Sodom, Gomorrah, Admah, Zeboiim, and Zoar. We really don't know for sure about Admah and Zeboiim, but if they were as corrupt as Sodom and Gomorrah allegedly were, it seems likely that they would have been taken out as well. And as we already know, Zoar was spared as a safe haven for Lot and his family, so we can assume that its inhabitants survived.

The tale of Sodom and Gomorrah is so fantastic that we are forced to question whether it was a fictional story that was intended to make a moral statement, and whether the cities even existed. Credibility will only be realized if and when archaeologists discover their ruins.

In 1924, noted archaeologist William F. Albright discovered the ruins of an ancient city on the Jordanian side of the Dead Sea. Due to political unrest in the country, he was unable to accomplish much in excavation. Years later, after things had settled down, research was resumed, and by 1965, archaeologists had uncovered enough evidence to know that the city had flourished some three thousand years before Christ.

The site, known as Bab edh-Dhra, met with some sort of disaster around 2350 BC. Archaeologists can't say for certain, but they are now considering the possibility that it may be the ruins of Sodom. Human bones were found under the debris of a huge tower that had fallen, and there was evidence that the city's walls had collapsed. A layer of ash was found, suggesting that the city may possibly have suffered a major fire. Their hopes grew high when they uncovered a huge cemetery containing a large number of skeletons that they thought might be the bodies of those who perished when the Lord allegedly destroyed the city. However, carbon dating of the bones revealed that the site had been used as a cemetery for at least a thousand years.[1] They figure that if it is Sodom, then the ruins of Gomorrah must also be in the vicinity.

In 1973, Dr. Thomas Schaub of Indiana University in Pennsylvania and Dr. Walter Rast of Valparaiso University in Indiana discovered a site called Numeira, seven miles to the south, with pottery identical to that in Bab edh-Dhra. The city appeared to have suffered the same fate as Bab edh-Dhra, as its walls and buildings had collapsed. The site also revealed evidence of massive burning, and carbon dating set the time of its demise at the exact same time as Bab edh-Dhra. Hopes were high that they had found Gomorrah.[2]

Speculating on what happened, they said that the destruction was similar to that caused by an earthquake, and the area is prone to earthquakes. Another possibility they proposed was military siege; it was not uncommon for armies of that era to burn the cities of their enemies.

One observation I would like to make is that they could have it backward. Bab edh-Dhra might be Gomorrah, and Numeira might be Sodom. Many old biblical maps show Sodom located south of Gomorrah, and Zoar, the city where Lot and his family sought refuge, at the south end of the Dead Sea. The Bible says that Lot and his family fled from Sodom to Zoar, which means they would have traveled south, and nothing is said about them passing through Gomorrah. So it is possible that Gomorrah was located somewhere north of Sodom. Of course, it is also possible that one or both of these ruins are Admah and Zeboiim, the two other cities slated for destruction. This can only be confirmed if they find Zoar.

Some believe that the city of Safir, located just south of the Dead Sea, sits on the site where Zoar was located. It is also near the cave of Saint Lot, which many believe is the cave where Lot and his daughters stayed after Sodom's destruction.

However, if Bab edh-Dhra and Numeira are Sodom and Gomorrah, or even Admah and Zeboiim, then a shadow of doubt is cast over what the scriptures say about them. The archaeologists claim that there is no evidence that they were ever as decadent as the Bible claims; they appear to have been well-structured societies that enjoyed a healthy commerce.

◆◆◆◆◆

The first race was wiped out in a flood. Whether it was the result of a severe weather system created by the Lord or a natural disaster, as proposed by William Ryan and Walter Pitman, may never be known. There were survivors, some of which migrated to cities located around the Dead Sea. It would appear that as these survivors repopulated, decadence again became a dominant factor. Since this was when a contingency plan was about to be initiated, it was necessary to get rid of these cities in order to minimize any negative effect they might have on the new race. And so the Bible tells us that the Lord destroyed at least two of them and left one as a refuge for Abraham's nephew, Lot, and his family.

The next step was to create another hybrid, and from his descendants, the Lord would select one family to breed a new nation. To accomplish this, they would have to be isolated in another land, far from any survivors of the first race, in order to prevent genetic contamination. After they had grown into a small nation, they would be sequestered in the desert for a generation, away from contact with all other nations, and indoctrinated with a new set of laws and moral values. Upon completion of this phase, they would be returned to the land of their ancestors, where the Lord would assist them in reclaiming it as their own.

Notes

1.   Bab edh-Dhra
      "The Real Sin Cities of Sodom and Gomorrah." *Digging for the Truth.* Prod. William Morgan/Jason Williams. THC. 2006.

2.   Numeira
      "The Real Sin Cities of Sodom and Gomorrah." *Digging for the Truth.* Prod. William Morgan/Jason Williams. THC. 2006.

Chapter 16

ESTABLISHING THE NEW RACE

For the project to succeed, it would seem logistically necessary that the new race maintain its hybrid genetic integrity for as long as possible. The survivors of the first race, though now fewer in number, were still around, and exposure to Adam's virus was inevitable. Therefore, in order to fulfill the plan that the Lord had revealed to Abraham, he had to isolate them away from their homeland for an extended period, and he accomplished this through Jacob's son Joseph.

Isaac grew up, married, and had twin sons, Jacob and Esau. Esau was born first, which meant he would be the one to inherit his father's estate. However, chapter 27 of Genesis notes that when the time came, Isaac's wife, Rebekah, conspired with Jacob to beat his brother out of the inheritance. Esau was described as a very hairy individual, and while he was out hunting venison for his father, Rebekah disguised Jacob to appear as Esau. Isaac was old, and supposedly his eyesight had failed, so when Jacob went to him, Isaac, allegedly thinking it was Esau, blessed him, thus making him the benefactor. When Esau found out, he was not happy, but there was nothing he could do; Jacob had fled the area.

Many years later, Jacob did return and make peace with his brother. In preparation for meeting with him, Jacob sent his servants ahead with hundreds of various animals as gifts. Then, according to Genesis 32:24, Jacob spent the night physically engaged in a wrestling match with the Lord. For some strange reason, it appears the Lord had to leave at daybreak, and since he was unable to overpower Jacob, he did something to dislocate his hip. It may be that this part of the story was created to make a moral point, and several ideas have been suggested, but I will not go into them because they are irrelevant to the events being discussed.

Some scholars theorize that Isaac knew all along that he had blessed Jacob and not Esau, which may be true. We know that the Lord told Abraham of his plan for Isaac's descendants long before Isaac was born, so I think we can assume that the events involving Jacob were part of the plan. Since Isaac had twins, the Lord may have had to decide which one was best suited to carry out the plan. And since he had had previous contact with Isaac, he may have made him aware of his decision to use Jacob. It may be that he felt Jacob was better qualified. In any case, it was from Jacob that the new race received its name. The Lord changed his name to Israel, and the tribes that grew from his twelve sons became the Israelites.

Jacob set out to marry his true love, Rachel, but was tricked by her father, Laban, into marrying her older sister Leah. On the wedding night, Leah entered the darkened tent where Jacob lay waiting, and he consummated the marriage with her. Supposedly, it wasn't until morning that he realized what had happened. But how could Jacob not have known that Rachel wasn't the one he was making love to? One would think that he had to be drunk out of his mind or completely stupid not to know. In any case, Jacob confronted Laban and demanded to know why he had done this. Laban said it was their custom for the oldest daughter to marry first but told him that if he agreed to finish the bridal week with Leah, then he would also give Rachel to him. However, there was a catch: he would have to work another seven years for Laban. Jacob agreed, and he took Rachel as his second bride a week later.

It was Jacob's desire that Rachel give birth to his first son, but it appears she was unable to conceive. Leah, however, produced four sons: Reuben, Simeon, Levi, and Judah. By this time, Rachel had become desperate for a child, so she gave her maidservant, Bilhah, to Jacob to produce children for her, and she had two sons: Dan and Naphtali. Then, when Leah had not conceived for a few years, she gave her maidservant, Zilpah, to Jacob to produce more children for her, and she had two sons: Gad and Asher. Then it appears Leah became fertile again and produced two more sons and a daughter: Issacher, Zebulun, and Dinah. It wasn't until after the other children were born (and possibly ten or twenty years later) that Rachel finally conceived and gave birth to Joseph, and because he was Rachel's son, Jacob favored him over the others. Of course, this fueled his brothers' hatred of him, but as I suggested in chapter 11, it appears to have been part of the plan. It was at least seventeen years later when Rachel conceived again and gave birth to Benjamin, but because she was an old woman by then, her body could not stand the stress, and she died while giving birth.

In his youth, Joseph had two prophetic dreams. He dreamt that he and his brothers were binding sheaves of grain out in the fields. His sheaf rose and stood upright, and their sheaves all bowed down to his. Then he had a second dream in which the sun, the moon, and eleven stars were bowing down to him. This truly riled his brothers because he was telling them that he would eventually hold great power over them.

One day while they were out tending their flocks, Jacob sent Joseph out to see how they were doing. When they saw him approaching in the distance, they conspired to kill him. However, they apparently did not have the heart. Instead, they only stripped him of the multicolored robe that Jacob had given him and threw him down an empty well.

When a caravan of merchants passed by on their way to Egypt, they decided that the best way to get rid of Joseph was to sell him. So they pulled him from the well and sold him to the merchants for twenty shekels of silver. To cover their deed, they took his robe, smeared it with goat's blood, and took it back to Jacob, saying that a predatory animal had attacked and killed Joseph. Jacob, of course, was devastated.

The merchants brought Joseph to Egypt and sold him to Potiphar, one of the pharaoh's officials, and he became a servant in his house. It is estimated that he was about seventeen years old at this time, and as he reached manhood, Potiphar's wife was taken with Joseph's handsome appearance and tried to seduce him. But he fought her off and escaped, leaving her standing there holding his cloak in her hand. Angered because he had scorned her advances, she charged that Joseph had tried to rape her, so he was arrested and put in prison.

It was during this time that the pharaoh's personal servant and baker were also put in prison. They'd both had a dream that troubled them, so Joseph asked them to describe their dreams, that he may interpret them. The servant said he dreamt of a vine with three branches that budded and produced grapes. The pharaoh's cup was in his hand, so he pressed the grapes into the cup and gave it to the pharaoh. Joseph told him that the three branches represented three days, at which time the pharaoh would reinstate him to his former position. And since Joseph had been falsely accused, he asked the servant to put in a good word to the pharaoh for him.

The baker then recounted his dream in which there were three white baskets on his head, the uppermost filled with bakemeats for the pharaoh. Then birds came along and ate all the bakemeats in the basket. Joseph told the baker that the three baskets represented the three days in which he would be hanged, and that the birds would come and eat the flesh off his body. Just as Joseph predicted, in three days, the pharaoh's servant was reinstated to his former position and the baker was hanged. The rest of the story is described in Genesis chapters 41–45.

Two years passed before the servant brought Joseph to the pharaoh's attention. It was only when the pharaoh had two dreams that troubled him, and no one seemed to know what they meant, that his servant told him of Joseph. So the pharaoh had Joseph brought to him, and he described his two dreams to him. In one, he said that seven healthy cows came up from the Nile and began grazing on the reeds. Then seven sickly cows came along and devoured the seven healthy cows. In his other dream, the pharaoh said there were seven heads of healthy grain growing on a single stalk. Then seven heads of scorched grain sprouted and devoured the seven heads of healthy grain.

Joseph told the pharaoh that both dreams represented the same thing: seven years of prosperity followed by seven years of famine. He then suggested that the pharaoh select a wise and discerning man to oversee the land of Egypt and appoint commissioners to gather one fifth of all the grain produced each year for the next seven years and preserve it in preparation for the seven years of famine. The pharaoh was genuinely impressed with Joseph's interpretation and his wisdom. After giving it some thought, he decided that Joseph should be the one to oversee the project, so he took off his signet ring and put it on Joseph's finger. He then dressed him in robes of fine linen, put a gold chain around his neck, and appointed him governor over all of Egypt. The pharaoh gave him the name Zaphenath-Paneah, and he gave him Asenath, the daughter of Potiphera, the priest of On (Heliopolis) to be his wife, and during the seven years of prosperity, she bore him two sons, Manasseh and Ephraim. But remember, like *forty*, *seven* also represented an ambiguous amount. The seven years of prosperity and famine may have only been three or four.

Since Joseph acquired the ability to interpret dreams—at least those that helped him achieve a position of power in Egypt—it would appear he was being manipulated, and the dreams he had as a child that so angered his brothers were also about to come true. Just as Joseph predicted, there was famine throughout the land, extending all the way to Canaan, his homeland. Now, it could be that this was a natural event that the Lord knew would occur, but we cannot rule out the possibility that he manipulated weather patterns to bring it about. Nevertheless, it was during this time that Joseph became reunited with his brothers.

Jacob had sent them to Egypt to buy grain, but he kept Benjamin, the second son of Rachel, at home. After losing Joseph, he didn't want to take the risk of something happening to him. Upon arriving in Egypt, the brothers approached Joseph to buy their grain, and because he was now an adult, they did not recognize him—but he recognized them. He began to harass them, accusing them of being spies who came to learn where the land of Egypt was unprotected. They all bowed down to him, proclaiming they were all brothers that had only come to buy grain so that they may provide for their families. Joseph questioned them at length. That is when he learned that his mother, Rachel, had died while giving birth, and that he had a true brother, Benjamin.

Nevertheless, he continued to taunt them. He said he would hold Simeon as ransom while they returned to Canaan and brought Benjamin back as proof of their story. Then, in secret, he ordered his servants to fill their sacks with grain, along with the silver each had used to pay for it. When they discovered the silver during their trip home, they became upset, thinking they would surely be accused of stealing it.

When they got back to Canaan, they explained to Jacob everything that had happened and said they would have to take Benjamin back to Egypt. Of course, Jacob was not too thrilled with this idea and was not about to let Benjamin out of his sight. However, he soon realized that there was no other choice if they were to get Simeon back, so he reluctantly let Benjamin return to Egypt with them.

Unsure of what consequences they might face because of the silver they had found in their grain sacks, they brought double the amount plus enough to buy more grain. When they arrived back in Egypt, they presented themselves to Joseph and introduced Benjamin to him. Joseph acted pleased and said he now believed them. Then he sent for Simeon. He invited them to dinner and ordered his steward to bring them to his house. On the way, they explained to the steward about the silver they found in their grain sacks. The steward told them that he had received the payment for their grain, so it must have come from their god.

But it appears that Joseph was not through giving them a hard time. Before they set out for home, he had his own silver chalice planted in Benjamin's grain sack to make it appear he was a thief. He then sent his men after them to search their sacks. When the chalice was found, they were brought back to Joseph, and they all bowed down in front of him, proclaiming their innocence. All this bowing down, of course, fulfilled the dreams Joseph had had as a child. Joseph then told them they could all go home—except Benjamin. Since it appeared that he was a thief, he would remain as Joseph's personal slave. They explained that this would have a terrible impact on their father because of his health and because he had already lost the only other son of Rachel. Losing Benjamin would surely devastate him, so Reuben offered to remain in his place. At this point Joseph could no longer hold back; he broke down and revealed himself to them. He explained that it was not really their doing, that a higher power had orchestrated the events that led to him becoming governor of Egypt and putting him in a position to aid them during the long famine. He had his brothers return to Canaan and bring his father, Jacob, and the entire family back to Egypt. By order of the pharaoh, they were given the land of Goshen to the south, where they could live comfortably, graze their animals, and grow their crops.

Initially, they were treated well, and they prospered. However, in the years following the death of Joseph and the pharaoh, the situation changed. As the Hebrew population grew in number, later Egyptian rulers began using them for forced labor. This continued for about four centuries, during which time they grew to the size of a small nation.[1]

Had it not been for Jacob's favoritism toward Joseph, his brothers never would have borne resentment toward him and sold him to the merchants. He never would have become governor of Egypt, and the family would have remained in Canaan. Of course, you can also say that if these events hadn't occurred, the Hebrews wouldn't have had to endure four hundred years of slavery, nor would they have had to spend an additional forty years wandering around in the desert. But neither would they have been isolated from Adam's virus while growing into the nation of Israel, a nation that may never have existed if not for these events.

The point is that they had to be kept together as they grew in population, and their migration to Egypt was part of the plan. It was important that they be isolated from Adam's virus in order to maintain their (hybrid) genetic purity, which could not have been accomplished any other way. They also had to be indoctrinated with a new code of ethics and morality. This was to be accomplished during forty years of isolation, and only then would they be permitted to enter their Promised Land. So a series of events was methodically executed to achieve this goal; it was a plan that had been mapped out and revealed to Abraham five hundred years earlier.

It was through dreams and visions that the Lord imparted information to the Old Testament prophets, and it is probable that the dreams of the pharaoh and the pharaoh's servant and baker were dispatched in this same manner, as was Joseph's knowledge of their meaning. Interpreting dreams is what brought him to the pharaoh's attention, so I think it is a fair assumption that the Lord manipulated these events. It was the only way to get Isaac's descendants away from their homeland and Adam's virus in order to fulfill the rest of the plan. And as mentioned in chapter 11, it also suggests that Rachel's fertility cycle may have been altered to ensure that Joseph would be the last, or one of the last, sons born. Had he been first, there would have been no reason for his brothers to resent their father's favoritism toward him, and he never would have ended up in Egypt as governor.

The next phase was to get them out of Egypt and indoctrinate them into a lifestyle of proper moral and ethical values. This would require a full generation—about forty years.

Notes

1.   The story of Joseph
      The Holy Bible, New International Version (1984). International
      Bible Society. Genesis chapters 27–47.

Chapter 17

INDOCTRINATION

One of the most significant participants in the project was Moses, for without him, liberating the Hebrews from Egypt and isolating them in the desert for forty years of indoctrination would never have been possible. Without his cooperation, the Lord had no way to relay his teachings to the people unless he came down and did it himself. Therefore, it was necessary to establish a relationship with someone who could do it for him.

During four centuries of enslavement, the Hebrews had grown into a small nation, which some have estimated to number about two million, but according to chapters 1 and 2 in the book of Numbers, a census was taken, totaling 603,550 people. The Levites, however, were exempted because the Lord made them responsible for setting up and breaking down the tabernacle, and for transporting the Ark of the Covenant when moving camp. The number of each tribe ranged from 35,400 (the tribe of Benjamin) to 74,000 (the tribe of Judah), and when you allow for the uncounted Levites, the total number of Israelites probably exceeded 650,000. Many Israelites brought Egyptian servants with them, and others brought Egyptian spouses, but none of them were counted in the census, so the total number of people in the camp may well have exceeded 700,000. Some scholars contend that the census counted only Hebrew men and not women, and if true, the total could conceivably have numbered between one and two million. However, I think a more realistic estimate would be somewhere around 700,000.

Moses

When Moses was born, the pharaoh was concerned about the growing population of Hebrews, so he decided to limit their numbers by killing off all their infants. In order to save his life, Moses's mother put him in a basket and set him adrift in the Nile, hoping someone would find him and provide him with a good home. As it turned out, the pharaoh's daughter discovered him some distance downriver. She took him into the palace and raised him as her own child right under the pharaoh's nose. She also managed to locate his mother and hired her as a nanny, therefore enabling her to nurse him. Moses was never told that his nanny was his real mother, so he grew up believing he was Egyptian: it wasn't until adulthood that he learned of his true heritage and who his real mother was.

Common sense tells us that the Lord needed an organized intelligence operation to keep him informed of the pharaoh's intentions regarding the Hebrews, and he probably had one or more spies who were relatively close to him planted in the palace. They would have known Moses and everything about him, which I believe might have been a factor in his being selected for the job of freeing his people. Moses, however, fled Egypt after he unintentionally killed an Egyptian taskmaster who was beating on one of the Hebrews. He fled across the desert to Midian, where he met and married a woman named Zipporah and had a son.

When the Lord first contacted Moses about going back to Egypt, he tried to convince him to do his bidding by waving his magic wand and performing a few tricks. Moses saw a bush that appeared to be on fire, yet it did not burn. With a curious and analytical mind unfettered of superstitious beliefs, he did not run away in fear—instead, he went to investigate. Then he heard the voice of the Lord telling him he was the God of his father, the God of Abraham, the God of Isaac, and the God of Jacob. From all that is written about Moses, I tend to doubt he was impressed. He comes across as being a practical person who was never impressed by the Egyptians gods or anyone else's, and I think that as the conversation progressed, he became less convinced. So when the Lord said he wanted him to go back to Egypt and free his people, Moses declined. In a further effort to persuade him, the Lord turned his staff into a serpent and even made his hand appear leprous, but Moses still refused. And the Lord actually became peeved at his reluctance (Ex 4:14). However, it proved Moses was a logical thinker, an indication that he would be able to deal with the facts when the Lord felt it was time to reveal them to him.

Growing up in the palace provided him many opportunities to see the pharaoh's magicians at work, so I think Moses knew these were only tricks of illusion. However, since the Lord eventually succeeded in convincing Moses to work with him, I can only surmise that he leveled with him regarding the importance of what he was doing and why. Moses would not have understood any of the technology, although it probably fascinated him. According to Exodus 4:17, before he left for Egypt, the Lord gave him a staff with which to perform miracles. However, all indications are that the Lord actually orchestrated all the miracles, and that the staff contained a device used for communication between them. When Moses set out for Egypt, "he took the staff of God with him," per Exodus 4:20.

It was arranged that Moses would first meet with his brother, Aaron, at Mount Horeb, and there it was decided that they would approach the pharaoh together. On their first visit, they simply asked him to let the people make a three-day journey into the desert to make sacrifices to God. This angered the pharaoh, and he put extra burden on the workers. He held back their supply of straw, which they needed to make bricks, but he still required them to meet their regular daily quota. Without straw, such demands were impossible to meet, and the workers were beaten when they failed to comply—and this really angered Moses. He met with the Lord a few days later and made it clear that he did not like what was happening and wanted to know why he was letting the pharaoh get away with it. The Lord assured Moses that he was about to do things that would break his spirit.

It seems that whenever someone angered or challenged the Lord, the person was always punished. When Zechariah questioned the angel's message that Elizabeth would give birth, he was allegedly struck mute. When the dissidents rose up in the desert, the Lord allegedly eliminated them by the thousands. Here is Moses boldly confronting the Lord and questioning his actions, or in this case, inaction, and the Lord does nothing except assure him that things will get better. This seems to indicate that Moses did not perceive the Lord as any kind of god, nor did he fear him as such. To have gained his cooperation thus far, I believe that the Lord had made him aware of what he was doing and why. Why else would he give up the remaining years of his life to wander around the desert playing guru to several hundred thousand people unless he knew what was going on? And the fact that Moses bared his anger may have caused the Lord to worry about losing his cooperation. If Moses abandoned him at that point, it would create a major problem; there was no one to take his place. That's when he revealed to Moses who he really was. Now, the Lord never told Moses that he was God. However, he said this when he first contacted him at the burning bush:

> *"I am the God of thy father, the God of Abraham, the God of Isaac, and the God of Jacob."* (Ex 3:6)

Again, I don't believe Moses was impressed. It appears that he set the parameters of their relationship right from the beginning when he made the Lord angry by refusing his request to return to Egypt. And although Moses may not have believed he was any kind of god, he never knew who he really was ... until the Lord admitted to Moses that he had purposely misled Abraham, Isaac, and Jacob into believing that he was God:

> *"I am the Lord. I appeared to Abraham, to Isaac and to Jacob as God Almighty, but by my name the Lord, I did not make myself known to them."* (Ex 6:2–3)

So he is telling Moses that he presented himself to these men as God but did not reveal who he really was, a physical being (from another world) who was known by the title of the Lord.

Then he instructed Moses to tell the people:

"I will take you as my own people, and I will be your God. Then you will know that I am the Lord your God, who brought you out from under the yoke of the Egyptians." (Ex 6:7)

The Lord is not claiming to be anyone's god. He is simply saying that he will take these people as his own and *will be* their leader (god figure) who freed them from Egypt. And the fact that Moses even recorded this information suggests that the Lord was having him keep a record of what was really going on.

It was now time to fulfill the plan the Lord had revealed to Abraham five hundred years earlier and liberate the Israelites from Egypt. But first Moses had to convince them to follow him. He couldn't just walk in and expect all the people to pack up and leave by telling them the Lord was now ready to take them to their Promised Land; they would never have believed him. And even if the pharaoh did release them right away, it would still have taken time to convince them. So it appears the Lord arranged for a series of plagues to hit the pharaoh's city. As each one was unleashed, the pharaoh promised to release the people, but when the plague was removed, he would always renege on his word. And it appears this had been planned because the Lord had told Moses earlier that he was going to "harden the heart of the Pharaoh" to prevent him from releasing the people prematurely (Ex 7:3). So it appears the pharaoh was being manipulated. It also suggests that the ten plagues were designed to allow Moses sufficient time to break down their resistance and persuade the people to follow him. Although they were being used as slave labor, they were not locked up in prison cells like criminals. They lived on their own land. Some had taken Egyptian spouses, and many even had Egyptian servants. They raised animals, grew crops, and had an ample supply of food. Although they were unhappy with the conditions of hard labor that had been forced upon them, there was a feeling of uncertainty as to what would happen if they went with Moses; the pharaoh would surely come after them with his army and force them to return. And the prospect of having unbearable hardships placed on them for having left hung like a dark cloud over them. If they thought they had it bad then, they could expect a lot worse if they were forced to return.

However, the stories of Moses calling forth godly plagues against the pharaoh and his people filtered back to them and gradually weakened their resistance. Then the death of all the firstborns, now called the Passover, gave them their first opportunity to see what he was truly capable of doing. It was the first event that directly affected them, and it helped reduce their apprehension about leaving.

A number of ideas have been proposed as to what caused the ten plagues. One is that they resulted from the volcanic eruption that devastated the Greek island of Thera (Santorini) when clouds of volcanic ash swept across the Mediterranean into Egypt. However, historians and Bible scholars are unable to coordinate the two events to a compatible time frame. Another possibility suggested by Dr. John Marr and Curtis Malloy is that a strain of algae called Pfiesteria may have appeared in the Nile River, causing a red discoloration and killing many fish. Without enough fish to feed off the eggs laid by frogs and toads, their population mushroomed out of proportion. After fleeing the toxic waters, they died in massive quantities on land. This in turn caused a vast increase in the insect population feeding off the dead amphibians as well as the crops. Thus a domino effect was in progress, contributing to the rest of the plagues.[1]

Although the idea seems to stretch the odds of probability in some areas, it is a logical theory. Therefore, we must consider the possibility that the plagues were a sequence of natural events that were portrayed by later writers as miraculous acts of God. However, when considering the technical aspects already discussed, there is also reason to suspect that these events were controlled by someone who had the technology to bring them about.

Turning the Nile to Blood
As an infant, Moses is alleged to have burned his mouth on a hot coal. This may have resulted in a speech impediment and been the reason he

was reluctant to return to Egypt and confront the pharaoh. He told the Lord he lacked eloquence and was slow in speech and tongue (Ex 4:10), so it was decided that his brother, Aaron, would carry the staff and do the talking for him. Therefore, according to Exodus 7:19–24, Aaron carried Moses's staff and dipped it into the Nile River, and the water turned to blood (turned red). It also says they caused the water to turn red in lakes, streams, and ponds throughout the entire region. Fish died, creating a terrible stench, the water became undrinkable, and the people had to dig along the riverbanks to get drinking water. Since Exodus 7:22 claims that the pharaoh's magicians performed the same trick, we can assume that the water returned to its normal color at some point.

Apparently, each year near the end of June, the waters of the Nile begin to rise, and prior to the construction of the Aswan Dam in the twentieth century, the silt carried down from the headwaters created a dark red discoloration. This was said to last for about three months. The silt fertilized the soil but made the water undrinkable, and it probably resulted in many dead fish. It has been suggested that Aaron performed his act just before the Nile's annual rising and discoloration, thereby exacerbating this period of inconvenience. If this is true, then the Bible may be crediting the pharaoh's magicians for what was actually a normal annual occurrence. It does not say where or when the magicians performed their trick, so there is a high probability that the story has been exaggerated.

If Moses and Aaron really walked throughout the land turning the water red in lakes, streams, and ponds, it probably would have taken days, maybe even weeks. It is possible that whatever Aaron did was a simple trick and the effect only lasted a short time. However, the idea was to impress the pharaoh and his people with the power of the Hebrew's God, so it probably lasted much longer. Devices could have been planted in the water, releasing something like red dye that lasted for several days, much like the sanitary agent we use in toilet tanks, which turns the water blue and lasts for weeks. In scripture, this event sounds much more dramatic than it probably was.

The Bible then describes nine more plagues that were released on the pharaoh's city: frogs, gnats, flies, the death of livestock, boils, a severe hailstorm, locusts, three days of darkness, and the death of all firstborns. Except for the deaths of the firstborns, none of these plagues affected the Hebrews who lived in Goshen, south of the pharaoh's city. And Moses set the stage for each event by announcing to the pharaoh in advance each plague he was about to unleash, thereby perpetuating the belief in a powerful Hebrew God.

Frogs
The invasion of frogs could have been accomplished by beaming ultrasonic waves down along the riverbanks. It could have driven the frogs into a frenzy, forcing them to flee onto the land. But according to Exodus 8:7, the magicians also duplicated this trick.

Scientific research allegedly has revealed that frogs are attracted to white or shiny reflective objects. This may explain how the magicians accomplished their trick: by placing white or reflective materials near the water. But whatever the Lord had done was apparently fatal (maybe causing nerve damage) because they reportedly died all over the place: in houses, courtyards, and fields.

Gnats, Flies, and Locusts
The three separate invasions of insects—gnats, flies, and locusts—could have been accomplished with sound. Sound waves generated at the proper frequencies could have produced vibrations that attracted the insects by stimulation or by reproducing mating sounds. They may have simply been lured into the city at the appropriate time, until the impact of their presence had been felt, then lured back out of the city in the same manner.

Death of Livestock
Any number of things could have killed the livestock, including weapons such as the ones used to destroy those who caused problems during the forty years in the desert or even crop dusting the grazing areas with poison. Unfortunately, not enough information is provided to suggest a particular cause.

Boils

The incident regarding the boils could have been caused by releasing a chemical agent over the pharaoh's city. When it encountered the body, it caused a reaction that resulted in boils or sores erupting on the skin. I suppose it is possible that the Lord gave Moses and Aaron a protective repellent to rub over their bodies so they would not be affected, but in reality, they had probably left the city before the event even took place.

Severe Hailstorm

We know that rain can be produced by saturating clouds with dry ice, so it is possible that the Lord manipulated the weather to create a severe electrical storm and used an agent that would produce large hailstones. They could control the hail by how they seeded the clouds to ensure it would not fall on the land where the Hebrews lived. It is alleged that these large ice balls killed many slaves and animals that were left out in the fields, and it is probable that many were killed by lightning striking the wet ground they were standing on. In some Bibles, the lightning is referred to as fire, which is very misleading.

Three Days of Darkness

It was then reported that darkness fell over the land for three days, and one could not see another standing right in front of him. However, it says the Hebrews had light in their land, which means that the sun was shining in Goshen. But this could be another exaggeration, as some scholars suggest the darkness was simply a bad sandstorm. If true, omitting this fact would seem that later writers made an intentional effort to portray the event as something more than what it was. However, if it was created by technology, then it is totally out of our league. As a logical thinker, I am inclined to go with the sandstorm.

Exactly how much time elapsed between these events is unknown, but two or three months would seem a reasonable amount of time. Up to this point, most Hebrews had not seen much of what occurred, because these things happened in the pharaoh's city, not in Goshen, where they lived. Only those who were working in or around the pharaoh's city as slave labor witnessed these events and reported what they had seen to the others. And the Lord did tell Moses that the Hebrews were a "stiff-necked" (stubborn) people, so they were probably not impressed since they had not been affected. That, however, was about to change.

The Death of All Firstborns

The pharaoh's consistent refusal to release the people provided the Lord with the excuse to execute his next move—one that would demonstrate how powerful he was and at the same time build the people's trust of Moses. He was about to cause the death of the firstborns of all the families in the land, except for those who followed certain instructions. According to Genesis 12:21–20, he told Moses to instruct the people that on the tenth day of the month, they were to select a lamb or goat that was one year old and free from any defect. They were to take care of this animal until the fourteenth, then slaughter it at twilight and roast it over a fire. They were to smear some of its blood on the sides and tops of their doorframes as a sign for the destroyer to pass by their homes and spare their firstborns. They were to eat the meat in haste—with their cloaks tucked into their belts, sandals on their feet, their staffs in their hands—and they were not to go outside until morning. On this day, they were also to get rid of any yeast in their homes, and for the next week, until the twenty-first, they were to eat only unleavened bread made without yeast. Now, I would think there had to be a reason behind all of this—it had to serve some purpose.

One hypothesis is that death was caused by a lethal agent they beamed directly into the person's body from their ship as they cruised over the city. The Bible claims that the firstborns of all the livestock and other animals were killed as well, but that may simply be an embellishment that grew over centuries of oral tradition. Nevertheless, these beams may have left a residual contamination floating in the air, which could seep into other homes and possibly be absorbed through the skin and cause serious illness and possibly death. It may have required several ships to complete the job in one night, thereby increasing the amount of airborne contamination and the need to take precautions.

Keeping their cloaks wrapped tightly around them and tucked into their belts would have protected their skin. If any settled on the floors, sandals would protect their feet. Keeping their staffs in their hands instead of leaning them against the wall would prevent them from contact with any contamination that might settle there. Eating the meat in haste meant that they were to eat it immediately after cooking it—before the killing started and the contamination began to build up. Yeast may possibly have been a product that would absorb the contamination and retain it, and if eaten, it might cause serious illness and maybe even death, so they were told to get rid of it on that day. Eating unleavened bread for the next seven days may have been an added precaution just in case any yeast they might have procured after the fourteenth was contaminated. It may be that the contamination would have dissipated within three or four days, so a safety margin of seven days was given. And the instruction to stay inside until morning may have been intended to reduce the danger of exposure.

It was important that when they left Egypt, they immediately put a lot of distance between themselves and the pharaoh in case he set out after them too soon. In fact, during the first several days, the Lord provided light so they could travel during the night hours (Ex 13:21). If anyone had become sick or died from the contamination, it would have seriously hindered travel during this time, so it had to be prevented. Therefore, the Lord provided a clear-cut list of instructions that were meant to be followed. If we accept the fact that technology may have been involved, then these instructions can logically be explained as precautionary measures. *What other purpose could they have served?*

In Exodus 12:12, the Lord told Moses that he would pass over the land of Egypt that night and smite all the firstborns. However, Exodus 12:23 identifies the destroyer as the one who would carry out the mission. This may actually have been a reference to the type of ship, or ships, that were to be used. And the fact that the people were given instructions to smear the blood of goats or lambs on their door frames to avoid having their firstborns killed tells us that this event occurred in their own land of Goshen as well as in the pharaoh's city.

My curiosity was aroused as to how they could tell which person in a household was a firstborn. If this event really occurred, it would appear that they had the technology to make that determination. It's not so incredible when you think about it. How can a doctor determine the age and the sex of a fetus in the womb of a pregnant woman without cutting her open? Fifty years ago, it was impossible, but ultrasound is a technology we take for granted today.

According to the Bible, this night of death also claimed the pharaoh's firstborn, which caused him great sorrow. Allegedly, in his moment of grief, he finally relented and let the Hebrews leave with Moses.

This is all speculation based on the kind of technology we might expect an alien race to possess, assuming that aliens truly were involved. The only other choices are to believe these events were miracles or a series of natural events, such as those proposed by Dr. John Marr and Curtis Malloy. However, if the covenant that the Lord made with Abraham is based on fact, then all the events leading up to this point were part of a plan that had been mapped out five hundred years earlier—before Isaac was born—suggesting they were methodically orchestrated and required the necessary technology to effect the outcome.

It appears that the next step was to put on an awesome power display to minimize the threat of desertion or rebellion when the people learned they would have to remain in the desert for the next forty years. The plan was to annihilate the Egyptian army in front of them—the ultimate sign of their freedom. But first the Lord had to make sure the Egyptians would pursue them. Once the people were far enough away, he had to prevent them from gaining too much headway, so he led them in an erratic back-and-forth pattern until he knew the Egyptians were coming. Exodus 13:18 through 14:2 says the Lord led them on a route toward the Red Sea. Then it says they went to Succoth and then to Etham, where they camped at the edge of the desert. Then (probably because they had gained too much headway) the Lord had them turn and head back to Pi Hahiroth, between Migdol and the sea. He had the people camp by the sea (or some small body of water), which would seem to place them in a vulnerable position.

When the pharaoh's army finally caught up to them, the Lord blocked their path with a smoke screen, which they could not penetrate. Then, using a powerful force field, the waters were parted, providing the Hebrews with a route of escape. When the smoke screen was lifted, the Egyptians attempted to pursue them through the parted waters, but when they were about midway through, the Lord blew the wheels off the lead chariots, creating obstacles to slow them down, forcing them to bunch up in the middle. He then turned off the force field, and the waters came crashing down over them, allegedly leaving no survivors.

I must point out that the parting of the waters seems to be an event of astounding proportion, even if accomplished by ET technology. To witness such an extraordinary event would surely enhance the people's belief, secure their loyalty, and convince them how powerful the Lord really was. Yet within a few months, while Moses was on Mount Sinai receiving the Ten Commandments, it seems many of them reverted to inappropriate conduct. This raises the question of just how impressive the parting of the water really was.

If any of us today were active participants in such a spectacular event, would we be apt to forget it so quickly? Would we not continue to hold in awe the powers that be for many years, even the rest of our lives? Yet according to the Bible, about three thousand people soon began worshipping the idol of a golden calf. It could be that there is some truth to the story, but we must keep our minds open to the possibility that the event has been grossly exaggerated.

The next phase was important: the people had to be groomed into a nation disciplined in proper moral and ethical behavior. This required a period of indoctrination, so it was necessary to keep them isolated for this purpose. They were never told they would be sequestered in the desert for so long, for had they known, they never would have followed Moses.

For those who think their forty-year isolation was a punishment for their complaining, as suggested in scripture, consider everything that was done during this period: the new knowledge and all the laws they were given. There were Sabbath laws; laws pertaining to Hebrew servants; laws pertaining to personal injuries through accident or assault; laws pertaining to death by murder, accident, or self-defense; laws pertaining to property; laws pertaining to social responsibility; laws pertaining to justice and mercy; a volume of medical knowledge; and a whole new routine of hygienic practices. They had to adapt to these changes and actually live them. This could not be accomplished in a few weeks or a few months—it required a full generation (about forty years). There was too much involved to believe this was a punishment. No. It was planned from the beginning; it was something that had to be done *while they were all still together*—before they entered their new land and began spreading out.

During their enslavement, they had acquired many customs and traditions and the laws by which they lived. However, these old ways had to be put aside. They had to conform to new philosophies and adopt new standards of ethics and morality. Had they proceeded directly into their Promised Land, it would have been tantamount to graduating school without ever having attended classes. So the indoctrination was necessary. A situation was created, forcing them to complain rather violently about the lack of water, and they came close to attacking Moses. This provided the Lord with an excuse (in the guise of a punishment) to sequester them for this purpose.

Many were killed by the Lord during this time, but it was only the gripers and dissenters—those who threatened the stability of the plan. In order to meet the deadline, this phase had to be completed within one generation, so it was imperative that the schedule be maintained. Whenever the dissenters banded together in a show of force, they were purportedly eliminated by the hundreds and even thousands by a "fire" that issued from the presence of the Lord. It ensured the indoctrination would proceed on schedule and with minimum interference.

The bond between family members was extremely strong, and the elders were a powerful influence on the younger generation. This presented a problem because they were too set in the old ways, which they would have to abandon. It is not difficult to understand how they must have felt, having to give up the lifelong traditions to which they were accustomed in favor of adopting a whole new set of values. It was an adjustment that many would find difficult to make. Although there were probably some exceptions, it would be impossible for the majority to conform. When you realize that the elders had the most to lose—that they would never live to see their Promised Land ... that they had been liberated from Egypt only to spend their final years wondering in the desert—we can only conclude that it was part of the plan. The younger generation—the children and those who were producing children—was the focal point of these changes. But the elders had done nothing wrong, so there was no reason to eliminate them. The only solution was to let them live out their lives; by the end of the indoctrination, most would be gone.

After a generation of adapting to the new standards, the people were led to the border of their Promised Land, and one final sweep was made to expose the last of the problem people. At that point, Moses appointed Joshua to take command. Moses then went to the top of Mount Nebo to die ... Or did he?

What Really Happened to Moses?

According to Deuteronomy 31:14 and 32:50, the Lord told Moses that he would die, and Deuteronomy 34:5 claims that he did. There is, however, evidence suggesting otherwise: his appearance over one thousand years later with Elijah at Christ's Transfiguration. If it really was Moses, how could he be standing there talking to Christ if he were dead? Logic told me it had to be one way or the other, so I began looking for clues that might shed light on the mystery. I carefully reread everything from Exodus on, focusing on everything that had to do with Moses, until I finally recognized the clue: the story of him producing water from the rock.

While camped at Rephidim, the people began complaining about the lack of water. The situation became so bad that they were ready to attack Moses, which caused him to complain bitterly to the Lord, saying the people were ready to stone him. Moses was told to take some of the elders and walk ahead of the people to the rock at Horeb, and the Lord said he would "stand there before him by the rock." According to Exodus 17:6, Moses was to take his staff and strike the rock, and then water would pour out from it. But here we find a discrepancy; according to Numbers 20:7–8, he was supposed to *speak* to the rock. Nevertheless, when Moses arrived at the site, nothing was said about the Lord standing there before him, so we can assume that the word "before" meant *prior to*, in that the Lord would go there before Moses arrived. But why?

One possibility is that he had installed a line into a rock from an underground stream and drilled microscopic-size holes to provide an outlet for the water. Then again, the rock could have been the side of a cliff that contained a well of collected rainwater. Either way, a valve designed to open from the sound of tapping had probably been installed ahead of time, and the Lord had to get there first to activate it. We have the same technology today; with The Clapper, you can turn your lights on and off by clapping your hands.

So why would the Lord need to get there first to turn on this device? Would it not have been more practical to have done it ahead of time?

The whole idea was to enhance the people's faith in Moses, so it had to appear as another miracle. Had it been preset, any number of things may have caused it to turn on prematurely, such as a distant clap of thunder or a loose stone falling from a cliff. Had the water been flowing when everyone arrived, it would not have made much of an impression. So the Lord waited until the last possible moment to activate it.

However, this story poses another question that to my knowledge no one has ever thought to ask: *How did Moses know which rock to go to?* It seems unlikely that he would trek across the desert and walk up to just any rock and expect water to flow from it by tapping on it—or speaking to it. Common sense suggests that he had to know in advance which rock to go to. Since this event supposedly took place at Mount Horeb, which is where the Lord first made contact with Moses through the burning bush, and where he met with his brother Aaron on his return to Egypt as well, we know that he had been there before. It also means he would have been familiar with the area, and the rock had to be one that he would be sure to recognize. And the Lord did tell him to go to *the* rock at Horeb, not *a* rock. So the Lord had probably identified this rock to Moses during his meeting with Aaron on his return to Egypt. It also suggests that the events at this location had been preplanned.

There is more to the story, though. It appears to have been a plan specifically designed to set the stage for when Moses would leave the people.

There is some confusion here because of the conflict between Exodus 17:6 and Numbers 20:7–8. One says Moses was to strike the rock with his staff, and the other says he was to speak to it. Which one is right? Probably both. Moses did *strike* the rock according to the Lord's orders, and he did *speak* to the rock in a rebellious manner, supposedly because he was upset with the Lord. According to Numbers 20:12, because of his irreverent behavior, the Lord became angry and told him that he would never live to lead the people into their Promised Land.

The fact that Moses complained and acted in a rebellious manner branded him a griper, automatically putting him in disfavor with the Lord. So the people believed that he, like most of the elders, would never live to see the Promised Land. But this made no sense. Since the Lord came down so hard on everyone else, why would Moses, of all people, complain so blatantly and rebel against the Lord in front of everyone when he knew what the consequences would be? It would seem that if anyone knew better, he did.

But remember how he bared his anger to the Lord back in Egypt, when the taskmasters were beating on the people for failing to produce their quota of bricks after the pharaoh withheld their straw? If the Lord did not come down on him then, it seems unlikely that he would he do it now.

Moses was saddled with the responsibility of keeping several hundred thousand people under control while indoctrinating them to new ways. The Lord had to dictate all these new laws so Moses could make a record of them before he passed them on to the people, and it was a time-consuming part of the project. There were no typewriters or word processors in his day, and if you look at the number of words in the Torah, you will see that it probably took a very long time to record. Moses had to write down each individual letter of every word (assuming, of course, that he did write them down), and with all his other responsibilities, probably a tiny portion of each day was set aside to do this. If he thought the Lord was going to effect his death simply because he voiced one complaint, it is unlikely that he would have remained so committed to him and his project, and it is unlikely that the Lord would have continued to put any trust in him. Why would he spend forty years of his life, considering that was about all he had left anyway, running around the desert trying to keep several hundred thousand people happy, as well as the Lord, only to be rewarded by climbing up on top of a mountain to die? It makes no sense.

Moses's job would be finished when they reached the Promised Land. It would then be necessary for a younger leader to take over, one with military expertise who was capable of leading the army in battle. Many people do not realize that Moses was 80 years old when he and Aaron were confronting the pharaoh back in Egypt, and that he was 120 and near the end of his lifetime when they reached their new land, certainly too old to be effective in a military capacity. His mission was to indoctrinate the people and keep them under control during the forty years. It necessitated dealing with the Lord on a personal level and knowing what was really going on. Isn't it more likely that he was rewarded for his forty years of faithful service by going with the Lord instead of dying on top of a mountain? If this was the case, which it certainly appears to be, then it would have been necessary to create a situation to validate his departure.

When the time came, Moses could not just stand up and say, "Well, folks, my job is finished, and now the Lord is coming to pick me up ... Y'all take care now." No. It would seem that this situation was purposely created so it would appear that the stress of the moment—the threat of being attacked by the people—caused him to complain to the Lord and act rebelliously in front of them. As far as they knew, he had angered the Lord, and his departure would then be an event they expected. According to the laws of justice with which they were about to be indoctrinated, they would never have believed the Lord was partial to Moses just because he was their leader. They would believe the same justice that applied to them applied to him, and that his departure meant his death, thereby providing him with the excuse he needed for leaving when the time came. There would be no witnesses. He would go to the top of Mount Nebo all alone, where he would be picked up; everyone would assume he had gone up there to die. Since he was seen over one thousand years later at Christ's Transfiguration with Elijah, whom the Lord took up to heaven in a "chariot of fire," does it not suggest Moses was still alive?

It is the consensus of most biblical scholars that Joshua or someone else later added the description of Moses's death. The Bible says he died at the ripe old age of 120, yet his eyes were not weak, nor his strength gone. Logically, I had to question how such a healthy individual could simply lie down and die. And why would he have to do it on top of a mountain, away from the people—why were they not allowed to witness his death, and why were they not allowed the privilege of burying him? Deuteronomy 34:6 says he was buried in Moab, in the valley opposite Beth Peor. However, no one really knew where his grave was or if he had been buried. Logic, as well as the evidence, suggests that he did not die but instead went with the Lord, as did Enoch and Elijah. It was reward for their many years of faithful service in assisting him in the project.

Notes

1.   The ten plagues
       The Ten Plagues of Egypt. Documentary. Dir. Bill Eagles. TLC.
       The Holy Bible. New International Version (1984). International
       Bible Society
       Exodus Chapters 1–39

Chapter 18

OTHER PLAYERS AND THE INTERIM YEARS

With the help of Moses, the indoctrination was completed on schedule. As the new ideas were being introduced, the older generation gradually died off, along with their traditional views of a justice based on vengeance. The younger generation was the focal point of these changes since they would inherit the new land. Adopting new laws of morality and justice made it easier for later generations to accept newer ideas instituted by Christ; they were better prepared to understand the higher wisdom of his teachings. Christ completely abandoned the *eye-for-an-eye* style of justice and stressed the importance of *turning the other cheek*. Once these values were established, future generations should acquire a higher level of tolerance and wisdom.

Obtaining their new land meant taking it away from the current inhabitants. Although it was the land of their heritage, none had ever seen it; their ancestors had left five hundred years earlier, only to become enslaved in Egypt. The current inhabitants were sure to defend their territory, and they had large armies to rely on, but they knew not of the arsenal of alien firepower they would be up against. The Israelites only had about forty thousand men who were battle trained—no match for the armies they were about to challenge. However, the Lord was going to give them the advantage. He told Moses:

I will be an enemy to your enemies and oppose those who oppose you. (Ex 23:22)

"I will send my terror ahead of you and throw into confusion every nation you encounter ..." (Ex 23:27)

I will send the hornet ahead of you to drive the Hivites, Canaanites and Hittites out of your way. (Ex 23:28)

Would this not suggest that "the hornet" was one of his warships? In reminding Moses of what he had done to the pharaoh back in Egypt, he said:

The Lord your God will do the same to all the peoples you now fear. Moreover, the Lord your God will send the hornet among them until even the survivors who hide from you have perished. (Dt 7:19–20)

In one of the final speeches Moses delivered to the people, he talked about the Anakites (descendants of the Nephilim). He emphasized the fact that the Lord would go in first and destroy their majority, and then the Israelites could come in and take care of whatever was left.

The people are strong and tall—Anakites! You know about them and have heard it said: "Who can stand up against the Anakites?" But be assured today that the Lord your God is the one who goes across ahead of you like a devouring fire. He will destroy them; he will subdue them before you. And you will drive them out and annihilate them quickly as the Lord has promised you. (Dt 9:2–3)

This confirms that the Lord was going to take out most of the enemy first: "*He* will destroy them; *he* will subdue them before [in front of or ahead of] you." All the Hebrews had to do was come in and wipe out whatever was left: "And you will drive them out and annihilate them quickly as the Lord has promised you."

More evidence of the Lord's participation is noted in what Joshua told the people in Shechem just before he died. He was delivering a message from the Lord, part of which described how he had gone ahead of them and destroyed the majority of their enemies.

I sent the hornet ahead of you, which drove them out before you—also the two Amorite kings. You did not do it with your own sword and bow. (Jos 24:12)

So the Bible clearly shows that the Lord guaranteed the survival of his new race by wiping out most of the opposition before they even got involved in the battles.

Aaron

The logistics suggest that Moses's brother, Aaron, was one of the key players because there were times when the Lord dealt with him directly. Arranging for him to meet Moses at Mount Horeb on his journey back to Egypt necessitated personal contact, and there were other occasions during the forty years of desert isolation when he talked to him directly. Aaron served as Moses's right-hand man in Egypt and did all the talking for him when confronting the pharaoh. And he continued to serve Moses after the people left Egypt. But when Moses went up on Mount Sinai to receive the Ten Commandments, he took Joshua with him, not Aaron. Why?

Moses was on the mountain for a long time—so long that many thought he had abandoned them, and they became restless. Their loyalty began to fade, and they wanted a god they could see, one that they could put in front of them to worship. Aaron was skilled in the art of working with gold, and they persuaded him to fashion a golden calf for them to worship. So it would appear that Aaron's loyalty also faded; he gave in and made them the idol they asked for.

It had been approximately three months since the people had left Egypt. and they had already witnessed the Lord do some amazing things. They saw how he provided light that enabled them to travel by night during the first several days; they saw him block the approach of the pharaoh's army with a pillar of cloud; they saw him part the waters for their escape; and they saw him destroy the pharaoh's army by closing up the waters over them. The Lord was monitoring the activities in the camp and could not believe that so many reverted to worshiping an idol after everything he had just done. According to Exodus 32:9–14, the Lord became disgusted and decided to put an end to it and wipe them all out. Moses, however, was able to convince him that such an action would be construed by their enemies that he was too weak of a god to maintain control over his own people. So Moses told him he would handle it himself. When he and Joshua returned to the camp and saw what was going on, Moses smashed the Commandments tablets on the ground in a fit of rage and then destroyed the idol. The Levites had remained faithful, so Moses ordered them to go through the camp and wipe out the idol worshippers, and the Bible says they killed about three thousand.

Yet Aaron, whom it appears abetted the disloyal activity by making the golden calf, was not harmed, and neither was he ever admonished by Moses. And since neither the Lord nor Moses ever held him accountable for his actions, it would appear that he was innocent of any wrongdoing. In fact, the Lord later had Moses appoint him to serve as a priest in the new tent of meeting. So it would seem that the reason for Moses's long stay on the mountain was to give Aaron sufficient time to weed out and identify those who would eventually be a problem.

When Moses went back up the mountain to get the second set of tablets, he was again gone for quite a while, probably to see if there would be a recurrence, but it would appear that this time there were no problems. However, upon his return, Exodus 34:29 states that his face was glowing and that the people were afraid to go near him. It says he became self-conscious of his appearance and wore a veil over his face for some time after. Now, I find it difficult to believe his face was actually glowing. I suspect this was either a mistranslation or another embellishment. Let's be logical—if you were to describe your wife or girlfriend as looking radiant, you would not be implying that she is glowing in a literal sense. Perhaps the atmosphere in the Lord's ship had a rejuvenating effect on his appearance after being exposed to it for so long during his two visits.

Joshua

After Moses left, an emissary from the Lord personally visited Joshua, the reason for which was not made clear. When Joshua saw him standing there, he asked him if he was for them or their enemies, and the man replied:

"Neither, but as commander of the Lord's army, I have now come."
(Jos 5:14)

That was a rather strange response. Why would he not be for one side or the other? If he was working with the Lord, wouldn't he have been for the Israelites?

Depending on how they were spoken, the meaning of his words can be taken two ways. Did he speak in a lighthearted tone with a smile on his face or did he project a serious no-nonsense military attitude? Considering the situation at the time, I would be inclined to think it was serious. To him, mankind was probably just a primitive race for which he had no particular like or dislike. It probably made no difference to him if they were the Israelites or their enemies; his job was to assure victory for the Israelites. When he said he was for neither side, he was probably just being honest. Nevertheless, the reason for his visit remains a mystery. He must have come to tell Joshua something other than that he was the commander of the Lord's army. Since he was operating in a military capacity, we might speculate that he came to discuss strategies pertaining to the upcoming battle of Jericho.

Not much is known about Joshua, yet it appears from the beginning that he was being groomed to take over for Moses. He accompanied him to Mount Sinai when he received the Ten Commandments, and the information suggests that Moses was inside the Lord's ship for maybe five or six weeks. Where was Joshua during this time? Did he just hang around outside eating the berries off bushes, or was he inside the ship too? Let's look at the logistics.

Joshua was being groomed to succeed Moses when the time came, and it would necessitate his own personal dealings with the Lord. According to Exodus 33:11, when the Lord met with Moses in the cloud in front of the temporary meeting tent set up outside the camp, *Joshua was usually with him.* Even after Moses returned to the camp, it says *Joshua remained in the tent*, probably to further discuss his personal role in the project.

Since the Lord dictated this information for Moses to record, why would he make it a point to mention that Joshua was in the tent, and that he remained there after Moses left, with no explanation as to why? This is one of those obscure details that can easily be overlooked because it seems an insignificant and irrelevant piece of information. However, the fact that it was mentioned tells us that Joshua was an active player. His presence at these meetings suggests that he, too, was well aware of what was going on. His expertise as a military leader would be crucial in bringing the people into their new land, and it would have involved much communication with the Lord.

The time was fast approaching when man would need to begin his technological development and begin to recognize the mechanics of technology associated with the Lord. If the Lord's ships continued to maintain a visible presence, it could lead to a premature discovery of alien involvement, so it was necessary to remove their physical presence from the picture. Man would soon begin to realize that the Lord was not a supernatural being, and that his *glory* appearing out of a cloud was really a ship. He would also come to realize that the *fire* that issued forth from this ship was a weapon. So before Christ's arrival, he began a gradual fade into the background, leaving the angels to make periodic contact.

After Joshua died, memory of the events in which the Lord had displayed his awesome technology gradually faded. The people eventually had trouble accepting an invisible god, and many turned to the gods of the locals. At one point, an angel was sent to inform them that because of their actions, the Lord was withdrawing his support; on their own, they didn't stand a chance. Yet whenever they fell to their enemies, another leader was appointed who would lead them to freedom, but once free, they would revert to idol worship and again succumb to oppression. The Lord was trying to impress on them the fact that worshipping idols was meaningless and a waste of time. To reestablish their loyalty, he would periodically make his presence known by briefly getting involved—but without an awesome display of firepower.

Chapters 6 and 7 in the book of Judges tell how he arranged the people's victory over the Midianite army, in which he did not become personally involved. He sent an angel to visit Gideon with a plan of attack. According to Judges 6:2, Gideon prepared an offering for him, but before he could set it on fire, the angel reached out and touched it with the tip of his staff, and it burst into flames. So apparently, it was more than just a staff.

Gideon had already recruited thousands of men, but the angel told him that the Lord said it was too many, so they narrowed it down to three hundred.

There is a clue that the Lord mentally manipulated the Midianite army. Just as he provided the prophets with information of future events through visions and dreams, he did the same with the Midianite soldiers by planting visions in their minds of being cut down by Gideon's sword (Jdg 7:7–21). This resulted in much unrest in their camp, and they turned on each other and began fighting among themselves. While this was going on, the Lord had Gideon position his men around the perimeter of their camp, blowing on trumpets and waving lanterns in the air. This caused the Midianites to panic; they jumped on their horses and fled. The Lord had Gideon leave an opening to provide them with an escape route but had him position another army hidden along the route that he knew they would have to take. When the Midianites passed by, Gideon's forces took them by surprise and wiped them out. So the Lord's strategy arranged Gideon's victory, thereby eliminating any need for his personal involvement and use of superior weaponry.

The only deviation the Lord seems to have made from appointing new leaders to rescue the Hebrews when they fell victim to oppression was Samson, whom I believe was a hybrid with genetically enhanced strength. The fact that he was not of the same moral fiber as the other major players were suggests that his expendability was intended. His willingness to sacrifice his life to free his people may also have been a characteristic that had been enhanced on a genetic level, a characteristic that had also been tested on Isaac. Because it was one of the qualities to be incorporated into Christ's genetic makeup, it was a priority issue and the first and most important test performed.

According to Judges 11:28–38, when the Israelites were at war with the Ammonites, a man named Jephthah was appointed as their leader. He vowed that if he was victorious, whatever came out of the door of his house to greet him when he returned home would be sacrificed as a burnt offering. Jephthah was victorious, and upon returning home, first out the door to greet him was not a chicken or a goat but his virgin daughter, his only child. He felt terrible because of his vow, which he felt he could not break. According to the rest of the story, Jephthah kept his vow and sacrificed his daughter.

Today, Jephthah would be labeled a religious fanatic. Can you imagine your next-door neighbor taking his daughter out to the backyard barbecue and using her for a burnt sacrifice because of his religious convictions? Of course, the validity of this story is open to question and may only have been intended as an example of fanaticism by showing how strongly some people can be influenced and controlled by their religious beliefs.

Over time, the Lord had become an invisible entity, and the people could not relate to a god they could not see. The physical presence of his ships and his use of powerful weapons against their enemies in the past was not understood by later generations because they were just stories that had been passed down through the ages. It was during this period that the Israelites lost the Ark of the Covenant while battling the Philistines. Two years later, it was returned, and allegedly a group of people were killed when they tried to open it.

About twenty years later, the Philistines were preparing to attack the Israelites, who were assembled at a place called Mizpeh. The Lord used loud, thunderous sound effects to uproot the Philistines and create confusion in their camp, thereby allowing the Israelites to overpower them (1Sa 7:10).

When the king of Aram sent his army to raid Samaria, the Lord blasted them with sound effects. The noise was so frightening that the

Arameans thought ten thousand armies were charging. It claims they fled on foot and in such haste that they left their horses, tents, and all their personal possessions behind (2Ki 7:5–7).

The Lord could have easily wiped them out, but instead he just scared them away with frightening and thunderous sounds. He still used weapons periodically, but in situations where there were no witnesses. One such instance occurred the night before the Assyrians were planning to attack Jerusalem. An angel went out to their camp and *allegedly* killed 185,000 of them as they slept (2Ki 19:32–37). But as suggested earlier, it may be that the army left to confront a more immediate threat of enemy forces advancing from the south.

Another lesson illustrated in the Bible is how power can corrupt. The luxurious lifestyles and the perks of high office led to the corruption of some Israelite leaders, and David, who is credited with killing Goliath, was one of them. Chapter 11 in the book of 2 Samuel describes the adulterous affair he had with Bathsheba, the wife of Uriah, one of his soldiers. When she became pregnant, David sent word to the captain of his army to send Uriah to him. When he arrived, David spent some time chatting with him about the war. Then he told him to go on home, with the idea that he would sleep with his wife and thereby provide an explanation for Bathsheba's pregnancy. Uriah, however, felt guilty about leaving his comrades in battle and chose to sleep on a mat in the palace with the servants.

Realizing that his plan would not work, David sent a sealed message back to the captain of his army, carried by Uriah, telling him to put Uriah on the front lines, where the fighting was heaviest and then withdraw all the other men from around him so that he would be killed. When this was done, David was free to take Bathsheba for his own wife. The Bible says this displeased the Lord, so he caused the death of their child. Now, in translating the story, the scribes may have incorporated into it their own "righteous" interpretation of the child's death—they may have *assumed* the Lord was punishing David, when the infant may simply have died from natural causes.

The fact that the Lord took no other action against David as he did with other kings who broke the rules is suspicious. In fact, it appears that the illicit affair between David and Bathsheba was condoned or at least tolerated by the Lord—why? They went on to have another child, Solomon, who possessed phenomenal wisdom and with whom the Lord found special favor. Does it not suggest there is something more to this story? I have already labeled Solomon as a possible hybrid, and perhaps now you can better understand why.

There was, however, one incident during David's reign when the Lord is alleged to have used his weapons, and it reflects yet another biblical discrepancy. In 2 Samuel 24:1, it says that the Lord ordered David to take a census of all the fighting men in Israel and Judah, and then he became angry with him for doing it. It makes no sense. In describing the same event, 1 Chronicles 21:1 says it was not the Lord but Satan who influenced David to take the census.

Nevertheless, it says the Lord gave David a choice of three punishments: three years of famine, three years of great loss under the siege of his enemies, or three days of an angel ravaging the land of Israel. David chose the latter, believing the Lord would surely have mercy on his own people. The Bible says that for three days, an angel traveled throughout the land and killed about seventy thousand people. According to 2 Samuel 24:17, David witnessed the angel approaching Jerusalem. In 1 Chronicles 21:16, it seems to be a little more specific in describing that "David looked up and saw the angel of the Lord standing between heaven and Earth with a sword in his hand extended over Jerusalem." Might this not be interpreted as a ship in the sky emitting some kind of beam weapon?

However, it seems the Lord was not immune to feelings of remorse, for it also says that when the angel reached out his hand to strike Jerusalem, he became grieved and told him to stop. It would appear that he suddenly came to his senses and realized what he was doing; he was taking his revenge out on David by killing thousands of innocent people.

Killing innocent people paints a picture of a rather vengeful god. What would people think if you became angry with your neighbor over something he did and took revenge by killing all the people on your street? I seriously think this story may have lost something in translation.

In his fourth year as king, Solomon built a new temple in Jerusalem and had the Ark of the Covenant brought in and placed in its inner sanctuary. Since it was now away from public view, it appears the Lord took this opportunity to remove the system he had used to communicate with Moses and the security system that had been responsible for the deaths of those who had the misfortune of coming into physical contact with it.

The next significant events are the Lord's dealings with Elijah, whom he took up to heaven in a chariot of fire, and with Elisha, his successor. It was during this time that the Lord created another hybrid, the Shunammite boy, which I suspect may have been to test enhanced telepathic abilities. Then, in 575 BC, Ezekiel had an encounter with the Sovereign Lord, who landed in a metallic flying craft, which (as described in chapter 12) I suspect was an unplanned event.

As the time for Christ's arrival drew near, the technological demonstrations ceased, and although a small percentage of the people lapsed in their loyalties, it was consistent with their behavior during the forty years in the desert—a statistical probability that was expected. However, idol worship and marrying outside of their race were considered serious offenses. Idols were nothing more than carved images, and they possessed no supernatural powers, nor did the imaginary gods they stood for. Worshipping them was a waste of time because they represented false beliefs. The Lord was emphasizing the fact that he was real, and only he possessed real powers.

Preserving their genetic purity was extremely important, and marrying outside of their race risked genetic contamination from Adam's bloodline. Although their numbers were fewer, descendants of the original race were still around. Mixed marriages were inevitable, however, and would be accepted in time, after Isaac's genes gained more dominance. And if Solomon was a hybrid, as I suspect, he seeded a large percentage of the population with his genes through the children he produced with his seven hundred wives. By the time Christ entered the picture, the genes of the new race were widespread, and intermarriages were then tolerated. Christ's teachings included all people—regardless of their ethnic or genetic heritage.

Chapter 19

THE SUPER HYBRID

W
e now enter the final stage of the biblical scenario. As we explore the significant events in which Christ was involved, the implied use of sophisticated technologies and genetic engineering is still evident. The interpretations are my own and based on a logical evaluation of the events described. The evidence suggests that Christ was not part of the original plan, for had it been successful, there would have been no need for the Messiah. Adam's descendants would have progressed peacefully to a technological level far beyond that which we have achieved today, and we probably would have already moved out among the stars. Although Adam's failure was a setback, the contingency plan still made it possible to achieve this goal before it was too late.

Due to Adam's imperfection, his children would never acquire the wisdom necessary to keep pace with their technical potential, so the new plan necessitated tighter control over advancement. After the new race (Isaac's descendants) had grown to sufficient numbers while isolated from Adam's virus in Egypt, they had to be indoctrinated with proper moral and ethical values. They had to rise above the primitive levels of justice they had known for centuries and adopt higher moral and ethical standards. Christ discouraged the style of justice that emphasized *an eye for an eye, a tooth for a tooth*. His teachings focused on tolerance and compassion—*turn the other cheek* and *love your enemy*—and he conveyed this wisdom to humankind with the hope that it would be absorbed by future generations.

Meanwhile, the Lord remained behind the mask of the deity so man would not discover prematurely that there was extraterrestrial involvement. However, in due time, he should come to realize it on his own—when he was better prepared to accept it—when the issue would no longer be problematic.

Conceivably, Christ could have carried out his mission without ever being known for who he really was. His recognition as a major player was accomplished through prophecy, as noted in Isaiah 7:14, that his star would shine in the east, and Micah 5:2, stating that he would be born in Bethlehem. When it occurred, however, these prophecies only served to identify the events to the few who were familiar with them. However, the story of the Magi focused attention on Christ from the time of his birth. Without this story, there would have been nothing to associate him with the Messiah prophecies when he emerged as an adult twenty-six years later, although he probably would have stood out in history as one of the Hebrews' greatest teachers and as a martyr who strongly believed in the principles that he preached.

Nothing in the Bible describes Christ's childhood, other than a brief mention in Lk 2:41–50. When he was twelve, the entire family went to Jerusalem to celebrate the Passover. But when they set out for home, Jesus stayed behind, and because the group was so large, a whole day passed before anyone realized he was missing. Mary and Joseph returned to the city and searched for three days before they found him in the temple courts with the rabbis, who were rather impressed by him.

Mary asked him why he had done this and said that she and his father (Joseph) had spent three days looking for him. He in turn asked why they had done so, saying that they should have known he would be in "his Father's house." Does this mean he already knew that his biological father was not Joseph but the Lord? Apparently, they did not realize the meaning of his words: "But they did not understand what he was saying to them" (Lk 2:50).

The next mention of Christ is his baptism by John, when he was approximately twenty-six years old. The Bible says that the sky opened up and the Holy Spirit descended on Christ like a dove. We might surmise that this was some sort of holographic projection from a craft hovering in the clouds, an event designed to elevate Christ's image to those who were present, making for a more impressive debut.

According to the books of Matthew, Mark, and Luke, Christ went directly from his baptism into the desert, where he was subjected to forty days of temptation by the devil. However, in the book of John, there is a discrepancy. According to John 1:29 and 1:35, Jesus was seen the next day and again the day following, and nothing is mentioned about the temptation. So which one do we believe?

The books of Matthew, Mark, Luke, and John were written decades after the fact by unknown authors. Their information was most likely gathered from oral tradition or from other ancient texts that no longer exist, so some discrepancies might be expected.

In spite of all the preliminary testing, it was still possible that something could go wrong. Unleashing a super hybrid into the world with a defect in any of his genetically enhanced attributes could prove disastrous. This phase was critical, so it is only logical that Christ would have to prove himself. And as it was in the Garden of Eden, someone had to put him to the test—someone had to tempt Christ with unimaginable things that only he would be susceptible to. Matthew and Luke identify the tempter as the devil, and Mark calls him Satan. Apparently, he was selected because he possessed powers of persuasion (or technology) comparable to those of the Lord. He was probably the only one capable of influencing him, if it could be done at all. But apparently, his efforts were in vain.

The Bible tells us that Christ exhibited many extraordinary abilities during his lifetime. It seems he possessed strong telepathic abilities, which he used to communicate with his Father, the Lord. He also displayed phenomenal wisdom and had the power to heal the sick. But contrary to popular belief, I suspect there were certain things he could not do, which I will discuss in a moment.

In all probability, Christ's healing power was an energy emitted from his own body, which had been genetically enhanced, and it required intense mental concentration. If he did too much at one time, he could be drained both mentally and physically. Rest and meditation seemed to replenish his energy like recharging a battery, which was probably the reason he spent many hours in solitude.

There are people today who possess similar powers, but they are probably not as powerful as what Christ was capable of. Those who have this ability are generally referred to as psychic healers or faith healers, and they are distinguished from the crackpots by remaining inconspicuous and seeking no monetary rewards for what they do.

It appears that whenever Christ intensely focused on his energy, it became so powerful that at times it would actually emanate through his clothing and a cure might be effected just by touching him or his robe. It is also evident that he was extremely sensitive to it, and could feel it drain from him when he healed, as suggested in the story of the bleeding woman. The Bible does not state whether the bleeding was nasal, oral, rectal, vaginal, or aural (from the ears), only that she had had the problem for twelve years, and when she came up behind Christ and touched his robe, she was allegedly cured. And apparently, it caught Christ by surprise and caused a startled reaction. He said:

"Someone has touched me; I know that power has gone out from me."
(Lk 8:46)

This suggests that he felt the sudden drain of power from his body— and this is a very important detail. As we will see later, it is relevant to an event that occurred after his resurrection.

Christ healed the crippled, the blind, people with skin disorders, and people with many other types of diseases and afflictions. Some of the stories seem exaggerated, but I suspect that he did have the power and did do the healing. However, it is doubtful that they were miracles; it was likely one of his natural physical abilities that had been genetically enhanced.

With all the technology currently at our disposal, I am amazed at how many people still let superstitious beliefs control and influence them. One such superstition is triskaidekaphobia, a fear of the number thirteen. This is especially evident in large cities, where you will not find a thirteenth floor in most tall buildings. By designating it as the fourteenth floor, people think they are less likely to be plagued with bad luck. However, the reality check is that regardless of what you choose to call it, the floor above the twelfth is still the thirteenth elevation of the structure. Other superstitious myths apply to black cats, walking under ladders, and breaking mirrors, etc., and organized religion relies on such gullibility to control the minds of the masses. For example, one myth promoted by religion is demons.

Many of the stories in which Christ allegedly expelled demons describe the classic symptoms of mental illness, epileptic seizures, and even Tourette's syndrome. It seems that Christ knew the difference, as noted in Matthew 17:14 and Mark 9:14, and he tried to explain it to his disciples after healing a boy who, judging from the description, had probably suffered an epileptic seizure. Christ had apparently taught the disciples psychological techniques to deal with people who supposedly were possessed, and since these were mostly mental aberrations based on superstitious beliefs, they were often successful in effecting a cure. In this case, however, their efforts were futile. Jesus is said to have cured the boy, but later, when they were alone, the disciples asked him why they had failed. Jesus told them:

"This kind [of demon] *can come out only by prayer."* (Mk 9:29)

He was explaining that this situation was different—it was not a mental problem but a physical disease that required "prayer" (a special healing power), something they did not acquire until the Pentecost.

Exactly why Christ went along with this demonic belief might be explained by the fact that to do otherwise would have also questioned the existence of God. The people were not ready for the truth, nor would they have understood it. Only when man outgrew these superstitious beliefs on his own would it be a sign that he was mentally maturing, that his wisdom was progressing and logic and common sense were taking precedence.

It wasn't so long ago that many people still believed in such myths. However, advances in medicine and a bit of common sense have now dispelled many of these archaic ideas. People who believe in demons today were taught to do so through religious indoctrination or by those dabbling in occult practices, or they have simply convinced themselves to do so. The only real demons exist in the power of their own minds—their own thoughts.

I could be wrong, but I believe the so-called ghostly activities such as those of poltergeists are nothing but the uncontrolled manifestations of someone's subconscious brain activity, most likely those of an adolescent or a young child. At least that is what the evidence suggests, so I am not going to waste time by presenting my thoughts on this subject, as it is irrelevant here. We know next to nothing about what the human brain is capable of, and we are only now beginning to recognize its psychic potential. A few centuries ago, such powers were perceived as demonic, and many who exhibited them were executed as witches or devil worshippers. So when it comes to demons, logic tells me that there are numerous other possibilities to consider.

There are stories suggesting that Christ had the power to raise the dead, and if they are true, they truly are miracles. However, there is nothing said of his bringing back to life a person who had been pierced through the heart by a sword or where vital organs were destroyed, giving evidence that a person was really dead. No. The people he allegedly raised from the dead were only said to have died; the causes of their deaths are not mentioned in the scriptures.

Christ was able to do many wondrous things, but bringing the dead back to life was likely beyond his capability. But if people thought his powers were limited, it would have seriously affected his Messiah image, so it appears that at least one and possibly two incidents were created to convince people that he did have this power. One involved a man named Lazarus, from the town of Bethany, who became sick and allegedly died.

When his sister, Mary, and other mourners came to Christ, he had them take him to Lazarus's tomb, which was a cave with a stone laid across the entrance (Jn 11:38), and he said:

"Take away the stone." Lazarus' other sister Martha said, "But, Lord, by this time there is a bad odor, for he has been there four days." Jesus said, "Did I not tell you that if you believed, you would see the glory of God?" (Jn 11:39–40)

The stone was removed, and Jesus called out:

"Lazarus, come out!" Lazarus came walking out, still wrapped in his burial linen. Jesus said, "Take off the grave clothes and let him go." (Jn 11:43–44)

Martha was correct in assuming there would be a bad odor, if indeed Lazarus had been dead. Since no mention was made of such an odor when the stone was rolled back, it suggests there was none. If he were dead, the stench of his decomposing flesh would have been mentioned because it would further substantiate the event as being a miracle.

Of course, this is an assumption on my part and proves nothing. However, when you put all the pieces of this story together, it appears to have been a setup designed to enhance Christ's image in Judea, and Lazarus was being used as a prop. We can only surmise that he was visited by an angel who put him into a state of suspended animation. And Christ's own words to his disciples tend to suggest that Lazarus's death was arranged to enhance his credibility as the Messiah. When he first received word that Lazarus was sick, he told them:

"This sickness will not end in death. No, it is for God's glory so that God's son may be glorified through it." (Jn 11:4)

Christ was telling his disciples that it was a setup. It was designed to fortify the Lord's deity image ("It is for God's [the Lord's] glory ...") and at the same time enhance his Messiah image ("… so that God's [the Lord's] son may be glorified through it"). Christ then waited two more days before going to Bethany because he knew Lazarus was not dead. When he did arrive, Lazarus had allegedly been dead for four days. When the stone was rolled away from the tomb, Jesus said to Martha, "Did I not tell you that if you believed, you would see the glory of God?" But then he said:

> *"Father, I thank you that you have heard me. I knew you always heard me, but I said this* [the quote to Martha] *for the benefit of the people standing here so they will believe you sent me."* (Jn 11:41–42)

Jesus was thanking his Father (the Lord) for helping him out ("Father, I thank you that you have heard me") and promoting his Messiah image ("so they will believe you sent me.")

The other person that Jesus allegedly raised from the dead is described in Luke 7:11–17. A woman said to be a widow was preparing to bury her dead son when Jesus came strolling by. Nothing is stated as to what the boy died of, and we don't know if he was truly dead. And since Christ just happened to appear at the appropriate time, it presents a strong possibility of being another setup.

Aside from Christ's alleged miracles, there were other situations created to inspire faith in his disciples, such as when he is said to have calmed the waters of a rough sea. He and the disciples were out in a boat, and Jesus was said to be sleeping. The disciples became frightened when a bad storm arose and waves began sweeping over the boat, so they woke him. Christ then said to them, "Oh ye of little faith, why are you so afraid?" (Mt 8:26). He then got up and is said to have calmed the winds and the waves.

I find it hard to believe that anyone could sleep on a boat bouncing about in rough waters with waves splashing over it. It would appear that this was an event created for teaching his disciples to have faith in themselves when confronted with a troubling situation. The storm may have been natural, and we can only guess that the angels were instrumental in creating the high waves from their ship. And it seems doubtful that Jesus was really sleeping; he may have been feigning sleep in order to elicit a reaction from them.

At some point before his execution, the angels would have begun guarding Christ around the clock. There were people who wanted to kill him, but his death appears to have been planned down to the last detail, and it is highly unlikely that the Lord would let anything happen to disrupt this plan. In fact, Christ told his disciples in advance that he was going to be executed in Jerusalem:

"We are going up to Jerusalem, and the Son of Man will be betrayed to the chief priests and teachers of the law. They will condemn him to death and will hand him over to the Gentiles, who will mock him and spit on him, flog him and kill him. Three days later he will rise." (Mk 10:32–34)

How could he possibly have known all of this in advance … unless it was something that had been planned? It is also mentioned in Matthew 16:21, Mark 8:31, Luke 9:21, Luke 18:31–33, and John 12:20. Christ was actually describing to them the plan for his execution, but it appears that the disciples did not realize at the time that he was talking about himself.

Back in chapter 12, I said I would discuss the reason that Moses and Elijah visited Christ at the Transfiguration, mentioning that it was a most important issue. This was the event in which Christ was engulfed in the light of the teleporting beam that delivered Moses and Elijah to his side. I think we can discount the idea that they were just cruising over the neighborhood and decided to drop in for a visit; we must assume they came for a reason. According to Luke 9:30, the conversation had to do with Christ's departure (execution), which he was about to bring to fulfillment in Jerusalem.

Christ may have been apprehensive about the pain and suffering that he was about to experience. Just before he was arrested, he allegedly took his disciples to a garden called Gethsemane, at the foot of the Mount of

Olives. There is no evidence that the place ever existed; nevertheless, it says he was sweating profusely. This suggests that he was extremely nervous; the thought of what he was about to experience would have been weighing heavily on his mind. It says an angel visited him at this time, probably for a last-minute counseling session and to help him get mentally prepared. So perhaps this visit by Moses and Elijah was intended to give him added moral support. Perhaps their appearance was meant to reassure him that when it was all over, he, too, would be like them—still alive.

We have to ask if it really was Moses and Elijah. They had been gone for centuries, so how would the disciples have known who they were? The only way they could have recognized them was from pictures, but there were no cameras, television, or newspapers back then to provide a visual image of these men, so I think the most probable explanation is that they heard Christ greet them by name.

According to Luke 9:29–36 Peter, John, and James became extremely sleepy at the moment Moses and Elijah appeared. It would seem that they, like those who are near abductees when they are taken, were switched off so they would not hear what was being discussed. According to Matthew 17:9 and Mark 9:9, after Moses and Elijah disappeared in a cloud, Jesus instructed the disciples *not to tell anyone about what they had just seen*, so apparently there was a need to keep it secret. He may not have been sure how much of the conversation they may have heard before they were put to sleep. Assuming that there was a plan to prevent his actual death, it's possible he was receiving his final instructions about what to do and what to expect during his execution. Such information could be detrimental if it got into the wrong hands, so it is only logical they would want to prevent anyone from hearing the conversation. If that was the case, then the disciples were put to sleep until the information had been passed along to Christ. However, since the Bible states that Moses and Elijah were talking to Christ about his departure (execution) that was about to take place, it suggests that one of the men probably heard part of the conversation. The only thing they remembered after awakening was the appearance of the cloud into which Moses and Elijah disappeared, and the voice of the Lord from inside the cloud telling them that Jesus was his son and that they should listen to him.

Accepting one's life as an expendable commodity for the advancement of a noble cause seemed to be an essential factor in the first experiments, and it appears to have been tested on Isaac and on Samson. Being able to enhance this quality genetically was given priority because Christ had to be willing to accept his fate. If this could not be achieved, then continuing in this direction would have been pointless. Christ's role was critical; if he had backed down, his image would have been tarnished. If he did not initiate the wisdom of his teachings into the minds of men, our system of justice might still be based on "an eye for an eye." Man's progress would have been stifled indefinitely, and the project might have failed.

It appears, however, that Christ was the super hybrid. He had been genetically enhanced with the best of qualities and was fully cooperative in his role of becoming a martyr for his principles. His execution only served to instill in the minds of the men the knowledge that he wholeheartedly believed in the importance of what he preached, and that he was willing to die for it.

During the feast of the Passover, people were flocking into Jerusalem by the thousands. Except for when he was twelve, no one knows if Christ returned during previous Passover celebrations, for he always seemed to avoid the larger cities. Nevertheless, his reputation preceded him, and the news of his arrival with his huge following had the Roman officials on edge—they were afraid of a riot.

When Christ overturned the tables of the moneychangers in the temple, he was setting the stage for the events that would follow by attracting unfavorable attention to himself from both the Roman and Hebrew authorities. And when he claimed to be the Messiah, that pretty much sealed his fate. And he knew this. He was purposely laying the groundwork for his execution—it was part of the plan. In fact, it would appear that he even used Judas Iscariot as an unwitting accomplice. Judas has always been portrayed as a traitor, but I can find nothing in the scriptures to justify that label.

At the Last Supper, Christ announced to his disciples that before the night was over, one of them would betray him. Was this really a prophetic statement of his own doom, or was he simply telling his disciples that the time had come to set the plan in motion? I get the distinct impression that this story became altered in context to make it appear that Judas was conspiring against him. I already pointed out that Christ had explained to them about his execution, even though they may not have understood that he was talking about himself. But I think the plan was to assign one of them the task of turning him in and arranging for his arrest, but he had not yet decided which one it would be. When the disciples queried him as to who it was, Christ said:

> *"It is the one to whom I will give this piece of bread when I have dipped it in the dish."* (Jn 13:26)

As Christ dipped the bread, he made his decision and handed it to Judas. He then told him to go and "quickly do that which you must do" (Jn 13:27). Now Judas did not say, "But, master, what is it that you think I am supposed to do?" This certainly suggest that Judas knew exactly what he was supposed to do, as did the other disciples, had one of them been chosen.

I believe they were all under the impression that Christ would only be arrested and had no idea that he was actually setting up his execution. Had Judas known, he may not have gone along with the plan. Nevertheless, he went to the Hebrew priests and told them that he could identify Christ for them, and they paid him thirty pieces of silver as a reward. Later, when he learned that Christ was going to be put to death, he went back to the priests and tried to return the money in an attempt to turn things around, but by then it was too late; they wouldn't listen to him. And this act certainly does not portray him as a traitor.

I suspect that he (and all the disciples) thought that Christ would only be arrested as part of a plan to make a political statement (probably) against unfair Roman taxation. In everything that is written about Christ, he never once engaged in or condoned antisocial conduct. Overturning the tables of the moneychangers in the temple was extremely radical behavior and completely out of character. So it would appear he was intentionally attracting negative attention to himself in the eyes of the Hebrew and Roman officials.

Judas trying to turn things around by returning the money to the priests, and the fact that he then took his own life, suggests that he felt an overwhelming burden of guilt, believing that if he had not gone along with the plan, Christ would still be alive. So when Christ announced that night that one of them would betray him, he may simply have been telling his disciples that it was time to set the plan in motion—a plan that none suspected would end in his execution.

Christ obviously suffered a great deal during the Crucifixion, and he probably used his powers to help dull the pain. However, if the plan called for him to return to Earth at some future date, then it seems unlikely that the Lord was about to let him die. In fact, the evidence strongly suggests that he did not die. This may sound sacrilegious to some, but when we finish examining all the details, a completely different picture from what we have been led to believe emerges.

In the past few decades, we have gained more knowledge of the old Roman custom of crucifixion. In 1968, archaeologists discovered the heel of a man who had been crucified—the spike still protruding from the bone. Traces of wood revealed that the spike had been pounded through a small wooden block before being pounded into the heel, thereby providing a much firmer hold. And contrary to popular belief, it is more probable that nails were placed through the wrists rather than the hands, as is customarily depicted in religious paintings and statues. Although there have been arguments for and against regarding this issue, experiments have been conducted using cadavers, and most have shown that the hands cannot support the body's weight without eventually tearing apart. So the favored opinion is that nails were placed through the wrists, which provided adequate bone strength to support the body's weight.

Crucifixion was extremely painful, and the person would often suffer for days in prolonged agony before succumbing to death. Sometimes the Romans would even break their legs to speed up the process. Christ's crucifixion was basically no different from any other, which means he should have lived for two or three days. So there is conflict between what we now know to be fact and what the Bible claims to have taken place. According to the Bible, Christ was crucified, died, and sealed in a tomb—all on the same day. This is a significant clue that he may not have been dead but rather in a state of suspended animation.

Suspended animation is defined in the *Merriam-Webster Dictionary* as "temporary suspension of the vital functions." The body's metabolism slows down or appears to cease. Body temperature drops, and breathing becomes practically undetectable, perhaps one heartbeat per minute or less. So it appeared that Christ had stopped breathing, which led one of the soldiers to believe he was dead, so he pierced his side with a spear to see for sure. Since only a little blood seeped from the wound, it seemed to confirm the soldier's belief. But in suspended animation, only a little blood would have seeped from the wound, as opposed to gushing out had he only been unconscious and his heart beating normally. We also have to consider that this wound may have been fatal had Christ not been placed into this state: he could have bled to death.

Just before this, Christ allegedly uttered his last words. According to Matthew 27:46 and Mark 15:34, they were, "My God, My God, why have you forsaken me?" Luke 23:46 claims they were, "Father, into your hands I commit my spirit." John 19:30 claims that Christ said, "It is finished." So which one is correct? Perhaps none, or perhaps they all are; we will never know.

It is not unreasonable to believe that Christ used his own healing power to stifle the pain. Eventually, he would have exhausted his energy and the pain would have been excruciating. At that point, I can understand why he might have asked God (the Lord) why he had forsaken him. The Lord may have been waiting until the last possible moment before placing him into suspended animation in order for those present to register the full impact of what was taking place. Christ's communication with the Lord seems to have always been on a telepathic level, and when the Lord finally told him it was time, and realizing that his mission was finally over, Christ may then have uttered, "It is finished. Father, into your hands I commit my spirit."

Now enters the mysterious Joseph of Arimathea. Nothing is really known about him other than he allegedly was a merchant dealing in metals and seemed to be quite wealthy. Some claim he was a member of the Sanhedrin and a secret disciple of Christ, and others say he was an uncle of Christ's mother, Mary. Somehow, he promptly managed to secure permission from Pontius Pilate to take charge of Christ's body. He wrapped it in fine linen and laid it in a brand-new and unused tomb hewn out of rock in a nearby garden; he had allegedly purchased the tomb for himself. According to John 19:39, he was assisted by a man named Nicodemus, who assisted in taking Christ down from the cross and who brought a mixture of myrrh and aloes to anoint the body. Then, as Christ's mother Mary, Mary Magdalene, and a few others watched, he rolled a large stone across the tomb's entrance and departed. Nothing more is said about him or any other activities in which he may have been involved.

Who was this Joseph of Arimathea? There are a few stories about him in the Apocrypha; however, many scholars view this book with some skepticism because most of the stories read like supermarket tabloids. And where was Arimathea? Although it may have been known by a different name, no one seems to know anything about it.

So here is a man from a distant town who just happens to purchase a new tomb near the site of the crucifixion; he hastily secures Christ's body, wraps it in linen, seals it in the tomb, and then disappears. I can't help but wonder if he and Nicodemus were somehow key players in the plan to prevent Christ's death.

The accounts of the resurrection according to Matthew, Mark, Luke, and John are all different, so in order to understand what really happened, we must examine what each book says about the event. First let's look at the discrepancies.

The Angels at the Tomb

Matthew describes one angel at the tomb. When he appeared, it was like "lightning" and his clothes were as "white as snow."

Mark describes one angel who was dressed in white but nothing about how he arrived at the scene.

Luke describes two men in clothes that "gleamed like lightning" when they appeared.

John only mentions two men who were dressed in white.

Whether it was one or two men/angels, I think we can agree that he/they were wearing white clothing. The lightning appearance and gleaming white clothes were observed the moment they appeared. This would be significant if they had just beamed down, as a bright light seems to be a consistent feature of the teleportation process.

The stories of the men dressed in white only signify their presence at the tomb but make no mention of a lightning appearance, suggesting they were not observed until later, after they had teleported down.

The Women at the Tomb

Matthew tells us that Mary Magdalene arrived at the tomb with two other women, and that there were two men stationed there as guards. Then an angel appeared in a flash of light and rolled the stone away from the entrance. However, according to the other gospel books, the stone had already been rolled away. He instructed them to tell the disciples that Christ had risen, and that he would see them later in Galilee.

In the book of Mark, the conversations between the men/angels with the women are basically the same as in Matthew; the women were to tell the disciples that Christ had risen, and that he would see them later in Galilee.

Luke mentions nothing.

In John's book, during Mary Magdalene's second visit to the tomb, she turned around and saw two men in white sitting in the tomb, and they asked why she was crying and who she was looking for, suggesting she was there alone.

So Matthew and Mark agree that an angel instructed the women to tell the disciples that Christ had risen and would see them later in Galilee. John claims that on her return visit, she turned around and saw two men dressed in white sitting inside the tomb; they asked why she was crying and who she was looking for.

Jesus Appearing to Mary Magdalene

Matthew claims that Jesus met Mary Magdalene and the two other women on the road after they had left the tomb. He repeated the same instructions that the angel had just given them about meeting his disciples in Galilee, which seems rather redundant.

Mark simply states that Jesus appeared to Mary Magdalene on the day he had risen but mentions no conversation between them.

Luke mentions nothing.

John says that right after Mary turned and saw the two men in white sitting in the tomb, Jesus appeared on the scene, and that she did not recognize him. It wasn't until he spoke her name that she realized who he was. Then he warned her not to touch him because he had not yet seen his Father. Why?

Matthew, Mark, and John all agree that Jesus appeared to Mary Magdalene, so we can assume that he did. However, it seems rather doubtful that he met and spoke to her when she was with the two other women after they had left the tomb. Except for when Mary was alone during her second visit to the tomb, his appearances after his resurrection seem to have been restricted to his disciples.

Matthew, Mark, Luke, and John are reporting on the same event, but the details are all different, so which one are we supposed to believe? When we spread all of this information out on the table and carefully sort it out, a little common sense suggests a logical scenario of what probably took place.

The Scenario

Sometime before his side was pierced, Christ had been placed in a state of suspended animation. Due to the excruciating pain he was suffering, it is unlikely that he was relaxed enough to do it himself; it was most likely accomplished by either the Lord or the angels from their ship.

Sometime Friday night, after his body had been sealed in the tomb, it was teleported to a waiting ship right under the noses of two guards who were stationed there. In fact, it may have occurred immediately after he was placed in the tomb—while Joseph of Arimathea and Nicodemus were still there—before the tomb had even been sealed. It's possible they had been assigned the task of expediting Christ's body to a waiting ship for immediate medical attention.

The stab wound in Christ's side was serious and had to be tended to immediately, for had he been conscious, it may have been fatal. The medical team aboard the ship repaired whatever internal damage was caused by the soldier's spear, also tending to the bone and tissue damage to his wrists and his feet, leaving him almost as good as new, except for the open wounds.

They had to leave the wounds open so that when Christ visited his disciples, they would believe it was really him. These open wounds presented a danger of infection, and until they healed sufficiently, his movements had to be restricted. However, with two days of rest, Christ may have been able to replenish enough of his own energy to help dull the pain long enough for a brief visit with his disciples.

He was allowed to make one "trial run" first, just to see how things would go, and that is when he saw Mary Magdalene at the tomb.

Mary had come to the tomb earlier with two other women and found two men guarding it. The angels, whose ship was concealed in the clouds, created sound effects that made the ground shake, giving the effect of an earthquake. This was probably done just to shake up the guards. Then an angel teleported down, appearing in a bright flash of light. This scared the hell out of the guards, who then seem to have fainted.

The angel rolled the stone away from the tomb and showed the women that it was empty. He said that Jesus had risen and to tell his disciples he would see them later in Galilee. At this point, it says that the guards fled in terror. The women then left to find the disciples, and the angel returned to his ship.

Here again is evidence of witnesses being switched off. Just as the angel appeared in a bright light, Matthew 28:4 states, "The guards shook and became like dead men," which could mean they had been put to sleep. Like the disciples who were with Christ at the Transfiguration, they were temporarily switched off to prevent them from hearing the message that the angel delivered to the women. The knowledge that Christ was still alive and going to meet his disciples in Galilee could have resulted in thousands of people going there to see him.

The second appearance of angels occurred when Mary Magdalene returned to the tomb with Simon Peter and another disciple. When the disciples saw that the tomb was empty, they left, leaving Mary standing there alone.

When the disciples were far enough away, two angels teleported down inside the tomb behind Mary, who did not see them until after she turned around. We know she had her back to the tomb, probably watching the two disciples as they were leaving, when she may have heard something. Then she turned around and saw two angels sitting there in their white robes. This would explain the *white robe* description as opposed to the *flash of lightning* appearance, because she did not see them until after they had teleported down.

As they were having their conversation, Jesus teleported down unnoticed behind Mary, and when she turned around and saw him, she thought he was only a caretaker.

The only reason she might not recognize him would be if he wore a long hooded robe that helped shield his face and cover the wounds on his body. It wasn't until he spoke her name that she realized who he was.

We can only imagine the excitement and happiness she must have felt at that moment. Her natural reaction was to embrace him. But he stopped her from touching him by telling her he had not yet seen his Father. Why? We shall see in a moment.

Christ was probably testing his strength and his ability to cope with the pain of his open wounds by walking around at this time. He had plans to come back down later that day and visit with some of his disciples, so this brief appearance may have been a trial run to see how much discomfort he could handle.

After talking with Mary, he returned to the ship so the medical team could check him over and decide whether it was safe to let him return later.

But why wouldn't he let Mary touch him? What difference did it make whether or not he had seen his Father yet? There was a very good reason.

Christ may have had sensors attached to his body to monitor his vital signs, and he wore a long robe that concealed them. If a problem arose, he would immediately be beamed back to the ship.

If anyone were to touch him, it could "short-circuit" his energy and be directed into that person, just as it was in the story of the bleeding woman who came up behind him and touched his robe. This drain, should it ever occur in his weakened state, could have caused him to experience severe pain and put him in danger of passing out. This seems the most logical reason for not letting Mary touch him. And if he did have monitors attached to his body and she felt them underneath his robe and asked what they were, how would he have been able to explain?

Luke 24:13–32 says that Jesus returned later that same day and met two of his disciples on the road to Emmaus, and that they did not recognize him. We might assume that was because he wore a long hooded robe. As they walked along and conversed, they invited Jesus to eat with them and spend the night. It wasn't until during the meal, when Jesus broke bread for them, that they suddenly realized who he was. But then it says he just vanished into thin air—why?

It seems likely that as he was breaking bread, they saw the wounds in his wrists under his sleeves and then realized who he was. The fact that he suddenly vanished is a sign that he had exhausted his healing energy, especially from the long walk along the Emmaus road, and breaking bread would surely have put a strain on his wrists. He probably began to experience severe pain and came close to passing out. That would not look good in front of the disciples, so he was immediately beamed back to the ship.

Later, when the two disciples had returned to Jerusalem, they were telling the others about what had happened, and Jesus suddenly walked in. Apparently, he'd had time to regenerate more of his healing energy by then. They could not believe he was still alive, so he displayed his wounds to prove it was really him and then asked for something to eat. The Bible also tells us that he again had to display his wounds a week later to Thomas, who was not present the first time and did not believe he had come back.

Christ made no public appearances after his resurrection; he only visited his disciples. Had he appeared in public, it certainly would have caused a stir, and surely he would have been prevailed upon to do some healing. In view of his medical condition, that would have been impossible, so until his ascension, he kept a rather low profile. He was around for approximately a month (the Bible says forty days), after which it appears he went with his Father.

According to Acts 1:10, on the day of his ascension, a cloud appeared, covered Christ, and began rising slowly into the sky. As his disciples (now suddenly referred to as apostles) were standing there watching intently as the cloud rose higher and higher, two men dressed in white appeared, standing beside them. They told the apostles that the same Jesus they were watching rise into heaven would return to Earth the same way he was leaving it. Does this mean that when he returns, he will beam down in a cloud?

Since the cloud was used in the teleporting process, we can probably assume that the Lord himself came down personally to escort him up to his ship, or it may have been a member of the medical team.

It was soon after Christ's ascension that one of the Lord's ships came down over the temple where the disciples were gathered and exposed them to beams of light that apparently triggered the brain cells that allowed them to utilize the healing power within them, and it also unlocked their ability to speak in different languages. Then Christ made his presence known for the last time when he converted Saul. He allegedly spoke to Saul on the outskirts of Damascus after he was struck blind by a flash of light that came from the sky. This suggests that Christ was still around and aboard one of the Lord's ships.

Men in White

One thing I noticed is that after the resurrection, all the angels were suddenly wearing white. Why? In their numerous appearances as recorded in the Old Testament, and those who appeared to Zechariah, Mary, and even Christ as described in the New Testament, nothing was ever said about their attire. It would seem that whatever they wore was not significant or worthy of mention. Since their clothes did not seem to attract attention, we might assume that they dressed to blend in with the people. The only exception is in the case of Ezekiel. He did not describe the clothing of the men in the ship per se, but his description of the event suggests that their attire was highly reflective, which could have been uniforms made from a metallic type of fabric.

Since it appears that Ezekiel's visitors did not conform to the normal routine of dressing inconspicuously, it is one of the reasons I believe they were making an unscheduled landing. However, the angels who came on the scene after Christ's resurrection are all described as wearing white. They were never mentioned prior to his crucifixion, nor were any others dressed in normal attire ever said to be following him around. In view of the situation with his open wounds, this suggests that those in white were a medical team that had been assigned to keep an eye on him. We might assume that he was still experiencing discomfort and expending energy to dull the pain from his open wounds. So it was possible that a situation requiring their assistance might arise. In his first appearance in front of the tomb with Mary Magdalene, two of these men in white preceded him—they were not taking any chances; they had to be available when he appeared. And whenever Christ visited his disciples, there were probably two of them nearby at all times. The fact that two were present at his ascension, and possibly another in the cloud that picked him up, suggests they were still not taking any chances.

◆◆◆◆◆

Much publicity has been generated about the Shroud of Turin, what many believe to be Christ's burial shroud. A sample of the cloth acquired by scientists was subjected to carbon dating, and the test dated it to around the thirteenth century. In 1532, the shroud was damaged in a fire, and the scientists suspected that this damage might have caused false readings in the carbon dating test. If true, the test results could be off by as much as thirteen hundred years. However, a new discovery has revealed that the piece of shroud tested was actually part of a patch later woven into the shroud to repair the original fire damage. So it appears that the only way the shroud can be accurately dated is to test a sample of the cloth that was undamaged in the sixteenth-century fire—something that is not likely to happen in the immediate future.

The big mystery is the image of the man on the shroud, which many believe to be that of Christ. It is in reverse color, like a photographic negative, and shows both the front and back image, as would a cloth that had been wrapped completely around a body. The image also reveals wounds in the wrists. If it is Christ's image, then it is further proof that nails were placed through the wrists and not the hands. So far, no one has been able to provide a satisfactory explanation, scientific or otherwise, as to how the image was created, and it continues to mystify scientists.

If—*and it is a big if*—the shroud is ever proven to be authentic, there may be a logical explanation. If Christ was teleported out of the tomb, his molecules would have separated—expanded apart—thereby penetrating the shroud all around his body. It could be that radiation released during this molecular expansion phase is what created the image. Not knowing anything about the technological aspects of a teleporting system or how it might work, this is only speculation. Nevertheless, if the shroud should ever prove to be the real thing, then an investigation along this line might be worth pursuing.

A few scientists have also postulated that the image may have been created by radiation. They are not quite sure of how or why, but they propose that a burst of radiation (possibly gamma) may have occurred at the precise moment of the resurrection.[1] Although the word "teleportation" does not seem to be in their vocabulary, it is a positive sign in that they are beginning to think outside the box. So perhaps they will eventually come up with a logical scientific explanation.

Another item of controversy is *The Da Vinci Code,* a book written by Dan Brown, which was also made into a movie. From what I have been told, I gather that it suggests Christ's relationship with Mary Magdalene was more than platonic, and that she was pregnant with his child at the time of his crucifixion. I have not yet read the book or seen the movie, so I cannot objectively comment on it. However, the idea that Christ and Mary had an intimate relationship or may even have been married and had a child is not so difficult to conceive. There are stories in the Apocrypha describing how Christ frequently kissed Mary. Unfortunately, the original text has missing fragments, such as the section that identifies the part of Mary's body that Christ kissed. So it could be that he kissed her on the cheek, the forehead, the hand, the neck, or on the lips—we will probably never know for sure. If it was on the lips, it might suggest that they had an intimate relationship, and appearing to her at the tomb might tend to reinforce the idea. I suggested that this appearance might have been a trial run to see how much discomfort he could handle before being allowed to visit his disciples, but he could have accomplished that on board the ship. The fact that he came to the tomb when Mary was alone might suggest that it was for the sole purpose of seeing her. What other reason could there have been for him to be there. Because I have not delved into this idea, I will leave it as it is. However, I will keep an open mind to the possibility.

Christ had set the stage for the next phase of the plan—his return. The Bible made it clear that he would come back, which gave mankind something to think about for the future. It was also time for man to begin developing technology if he was to survive, and hopefully he had gained sufficient wisdom to do it without destroying himself in the process. The only major side effect has been the creation of so many different religions and their spin-offs. Some organized religions and the increasing number of cults spouting hollow philosophies have created a wedge of prejudice that separate people instead of bringing them together. This is in total contrast to what Christ was attempting to do.

During the time of the Old Testament, the philosophy was a code of justice based on "an eye for an eye," which was how the people were accustomed to settling their differences. To change things overnight was impossible, so the people had to undergo a gradual conditioning—an indoctrination that would improve their moral and ethical values. This was done with those who had inherited the genes of Isaac, the hybrid from whose seed they had descended. During their period of desert isolation, most had come to accept the new ways while shielded from all other influences, and they established new traditions based on the philosophies that were followed by their descendants. They carried these new values with them into their Promised Land, and although some fell by the wayside, the majority successfully conformed.

When Christ was brought on the scene, his philosophy was to "love your enemy" and "turn the other cheek," which the people were more receptive to by then. The Lord of the Old Testament, who allegedly killed thousands, was in total contrast to Christ's image. Christ was never responsible for, nor advocated, the death of anyone. His mission was to get everyone to discard the old ways of vengeance and killing and bring people together through love and understanding—regardless of their genetic makeup. He was even used as a martyr, which served to impress his philosophy on mankind long after his alleged death. He had set the stage for the next phase of the plan, in which he will return to Earth, and success now hinges on what he will be able to accomplish during the one thousand years that he is predicted to reign.

From the very beginning, suggestions of technology are evident. From Adam's creation to Christ's ascension, the use of such mechanical methods is illogical for a supernatural god. Over the centuries, these events have been portrayed as miracles, but as we progress in science and technology, many of the biblical miracles seem not so miraculous today.

One example is the angel who set Gideon's offering ablaze with the touch of his staff. We can do the same thing with the strike of a match or the "flick of a Bic." And as mentioned previously, turning the waters of the Nile to blood can be compared to the sanitary agent that turns the water blue in toilet tanks; Moses tapping on the rock to produce water can be compared to The Clapper, which turns lights on and off with a clap of the hands. Fire coming out from the Lord might be compared to laser weapons, and flying machines and spaceships are, of course, something we are all familiar with today. Many of the things we considered miracles or science fiction fifty years ago have evolved into technologies that we take for granted today. So it is not unreasonable to expect that that which is deemed impossible today will become commonplace tomorrow—and in someone else's world, may have been commonplace yesterday.

I sincerely believe the decent people in the world today far outnumber the bad. Yet it is no secret that moral decadence is steadily gnawing away at our society. It is inhibiting our progress and deteriorating the respect we have for one another as human beings. If the Lord's project is to be successful, he will probably not let things continue as they are for too much longer. If the prophecies in Revelation are true, he will soon begin taking steps to eliminate this negative influence, just as he did in the time of Noah and Abraham.

As for the Bible, regardless of its discrepancies, nobody should overlook its importance. Many of its stories promote moral and ethical values designed to make the world a better place—if only we would adhere to them. But it also suggests sophisticated technologies. When you study the basic elements of these stories without the religious embellishments, it is hard to ignore the technological aspects staring you in the face. Moreover, when you take a logical look at the progression of events that started with Adam, the scenario certainly suggests that it was an attempt to generate a genetically improved version of mankind and accelerate his technological and moral evolution. The evidence I have provided is based on a logical evaluation of the Bible stories. Whether or not my ideas have merit is something you must decide for yourself.

Notes

1.   Theory that image on shroud created by radiation
"Unraveling the Shroud." *Decoding the Past*. Prod. Lee Schneider.
THC. 2005.

Chapter 20

THE BIBLE FACTS

All the ideas I have proposed in the biblical scenario are based on two things: (1) the possibility that extraterrestrials are engaged in a project to accelerate the evolution of mankind; and (2) a logical and commonsense evaluation of the Bible stories, assuming, of course, that the events described actually occurred and in the sequence in which they are laid out. However, to be completely objective requires presenting all the evidence, even though it may conflict with my ideas.

One contentious point is that some of the Bible stories bear striking similarities to ancient Sumerian texts, suggesting they may have been derived from these earlier writings. One example is *The Epic of Gilgamesh*, which describes details similar to those in Genesis regarding the story of Creation and a beautiful garden. It tells of a man named Utnapishtam, and how he and his family survived a great flood, a story that parallels the account of Noah and the ark. These stories predate the Genesis accounts by one thousand to two thousand years, so if the Genesis stories were borrowed from these earlier writings, then the timeline of biblical history is incorrect and the events could not have occurred as the Bible has them laid out.

Another point is the discrepancies, and there are many, such as the number of animals Noah was to take aboard the ark: Genesis 6:19 says it was two, but Genesis 7:2 claims it was seven of each clean animal.

Exodus 3:2 says an angel of the Lord appeared to Moses in a burning bush, but a few sentences later, the angel suddenly becomes the Lord. This same textual transformation from angel to Lord occurs more than once in the Bible, as does the Lord suddenly being referred to as God.

According to Exodus 34:1, after Moses destroyed the tablets containing the Ten Commandments, the Lord told him to chisel out another set of tablets and bring them up the mountain and he would, again, write them down. But according to Exodus 34:27–28, he told Moses to do it.

In 2 Samuel 24:1, it says that the Lord ordered David to take a census of all the fighting men in Israel, but 1 Chronicles 21:1 says the census was influenced by Satan.

The books of Matthew, Mark, and Luke tell us that immediately after his baptism, Christ went directly into the desert to be tempted for forty days. Yet the book of John tells us he was seen twice in the next two days.

These are only a few of the conflicts, which brings into question not only the credibility of these stories but also the accuracy of the scribes who first put them into writing. However, the Dead Sea Scrolls, discovered in 1947, when compared to many Hebrew scriptures, are quoted almost verbatim, suggesting the scribes were meticulous in their translating, and that the discrepancies in the Torah already existed. We are told that from the time of Moses, the stories had been passed down orally in Aramaic until the first written accounts were transcribed three centuries before Christ. That is an incredibly long time to pass along information by word of mouth without expecting some details to be misinterpreted, altered, or exaggerated in the process.

Now, like the two versions of how many animals Noah was to collect, there are two different stories of the creation, two versions of the covenant that God (the Lord) made with Abraham, two different accounts of Moses obtaining water from a rock, plus many others. Scholars refer to them as *doublets*, and they appear to have been written by different authors, each using a different name for God. The writer in the Hebrew text refers to him as Elohim, and in the other versions, he is called Lord or Yahweh.

It has been suggested that around 922 BCE, two different versions of Moses's books were combined by later writers and editors. This occurred after Solomon took over the throne of Jerusalem, appointed his own high priest, and got rid of the two who had served under David. This created dissension and resulted in a schism in which ten of the twelve tribes allegedly moved south and established their own separate kingdom of Judah. It is theorized that scribes in both camps soon began recording the scriptures, and each referred to God by a different name. Those who settled in Judah called him Yahweh, and those who remained in Jerusalem called him Elohim.

However, some Bible scholars suspect that at least four different authors wrote the five books of Moses. The writer who referred to God as Yahweh was called "J" because supposedly the early Europeans were unfamiliar with the correct pronunciation of Yahweh and called him Jehovah. The writer who referred to God as Elohim was dubbed "E." A third writer, whose style differed from "J" and "E," was called "P" because it was believed he was a priest. In 1807, Wilhelm De Wette, a German theologian, concluded that the book of Deuteronomy was written by a fourth author in a style entirely different from those of "J," "E," and "P," and he is referred to as "D," for Deuteronomist. Each author had a different style of writing and used terms associated with different evolutionary stages of the Hebrew language.

So if the five books of Moses were actually written by him, then the evidence alluding to different authors such as "J," "E," "P," and "D," suggests they were later edited and rewritten, and considering the doublets and other inconsistencies, we seriously have to wonder how many details may have been altered or misrepresented in the process.

We know that the Old Testament documents were first recorded in Ancient Hebrew and Aramaic approximately three hundred years before Christ by scribes whose only reference was from what was passed down in oral tradition. At the time, most of the Old Testament stories were being incorporated into the Hebrew doctrine, so except for the five books of Moses, the Bible, as such, did not yet exist.

It was during the reign of King Ptolemy of Egypt (285–244 BCE) that the Septuagent, the oldest Greek translation of the Torah, was created.

There were many Hebrews living in Alexandria, where the predominant language was Greek. Having been brought up under the influence of Greek culture, many of the Alexandrian Hebrews spoke only Greek, so it became necessary to create a Greek version of the Torah to be used in the temples. Ptolemy also wanted a Greek version for the new library in Alexandria, and it is said that seventy-two elders from Israel were brought in to do the job: six descendants from each of the twelve tribes.

As Christianity became established, so did religious fanaticism. In the tenth through twelfth centuries, when Christian crusaders set out to reclaim Jerusalem from the Muslims, many believed that it was their duty to wipe out all ideologies that did not conform to Christian beliefs. Thus they unleashed a campaign in which there was a mass slaughter of Muslims and those of other religions.

After the Crusades, those seeking religious control of the masses began developing their own individual ideologies. As organized religion grew, more churches appeared, espousing different beliefs, spawning many prejudices. As Christianity gradually gained a stronger foothold, church authorities continued forcing their beliefs on people through intimidation and persecution; anyone who did not go along with what the church believed was considered a heretic. The execution of William Tynedale in the sixteenth century and the religious persecution of Galileo in the seventeenth century are classic examples. However, the roots of religious dissension can be traced back to the fourth century.

Before he became the sole emperor of the Roman Empire, Constantine became a Christian convert, allegedly because he had a religious vision in which Christ spoke to him. There is much doubt among scholars as to whether or not it really happened; they claim the story changed each time he related it to someone else. Constantine was known for being a perspicacious but shrewd statesman, and many believe his conversion was due to the fact that Christian churches were appearing all over the continent and he was simply playing it smart by going with the majority.

Nevertheless, Constantine was faced with the problem of bringing order to the chaos that existed in these early churches with their mixed cultures and varying ideologies. There were those who believed that Jesus was just a man, which didn't sit well with those who believed he was a divine being. In 325 AD, Constantine attempted to resolve the conflict by summoning all of the bishops to Nicea, a seaside town in what is now modern Turkey. He pretty much laid down the law, ordering them to put an end to their bickering and come to an agreement on the humanity and the divinity of Christ. He wanted them to settle on one doctrine that could be understood and practiced by everyone. After much heated debate, they came up with the Nicene Creed, which stated that Christ was a man as well as God. They returned to their own countries, still unimpressed with each other's views, and continued preaching their same old ideas, and the dissension continued for another sixty years.[1]

At the time, Bishop Eusebius of Caesarea had written a history of the church, and he included a list of eighteen books that he felt should be part of the Christian canon. But other bishops had their own ideas of what these books should be, and his choices were ammunition for many heated disputes. However, in 331 AD, Constantine sent Eusebius a letter requesting that he create an official Christian Bible. The letter stated:

I have thought it expedient to instruct your prudence to order fifty copies of the Sacred Scriptures to be written on prepared parchment, in a legible manner and in a convenient portable form, by professional transcribers thoroughly practiced in their art.[2]

Eusebius, of course, used the books from his original list, which included John's book of Revelation—the book most contested by the other bishops: its fire-and-brimstone flavor clashed with the more favorable image of a compassionate God. Nevertheless, as dissension reigned among the churches, Eusebius's Bible eventually became lost. It wasn't until forty years later that twenty-seven New Testament books were finally canonized.

Over the next millennium, the Bible was translated into other languages, but it wasn't until after Guttenburg invented the printing press in the fifteenth century that it became available to the general populace. Until then, all versions had been hand written, and the few that existed were kept in churches and cathedrals and never seen by the public.

So the New Testament was originally written in Greek. Then, about 350 years after Christ, an early church leader named Jerome created a Latin version of the entire Bible, called the *Vulgate*. For over a thousand years, it was the official Bible in Western Europe.

In 1382, John Wycliffe completed an English translation, but because it had not been authorized by the church, it was condemned, and he was branded a heretic.

In 1525, William Tynedale produced another English version from the Greek text. But the church labeled him a heretic and had him executed. However, it is said that over 80 percent of his translations were later incorporated into the King James Version.

In 1534, Martin Luther translated the Bible into German but left out the Apocrypha. At the same time, he became disillusioned by hierarchical corruption in the Catholic Church and nailed a list of grievances to the door of the Wittenberg Cathedral. A revolution followed, and the Protestant Church was created.

In 1535, the first Protestant bishop of Exeter created an English translation of the Bible from Latin and German.

In the sixteenth century, King Henry VIII severed all ties with the Catholic Church, after the pope refused to grant him a divorce from Catherine of Aragon so he could marry the younger Anne Boleyn. He then established the Anglican Church and ordered a new translation of the Bible. It emerged in 1539 and was known as The Great Bible.

In 1557, the Geneva Bible made its appearance under the reign of Elizabeth I and was carried by Pilgrims migrating to the New World. It was also the Bible of Shakespeare.

The most famous English translation came out in 1611. It was commissioned by King James and was known as The King James (Authorized Version).

In the years following, many more versions were published, even one in a Native American language, which was called the Algonquin Bible.

Two thousand years ago—and even after the time of Christ—there were literally hundreds of scrolls and manuscripts in circulation. Many included details of people and events that were more explicit than those contained in the Christian and Hebrew bibles. Many were omitted from the Bible because of similarity, and many were banned because they proposed what the church considered "inappropriate viewpoints."

One of the forbidden books was *The Lives (or The Life) of Adam and Eve*. It tells the story of the temptation based on Eve's perspective, and compared to Genesis, it presents a more detailed account of the Creation.

Among others excluded were the books of Jubilees and Enoch, both of which were found among the Dead Sea Scrolls.

The *Book Of Jubilees* is an attempt to answer the unanswered questions in Genesis, like who Cain's wife really was. It alleges she was one of his sisters, one of the many children subsequently produced by Adam and Eve. But since Cain and his parents were supposed to be the only human beings on Earth at the time, the identity of Cain's wife was a sensitive issue, and the only logical explanation was a sister. That presented a big problem for the church because incest was considered a sin. So unless they wished to refute the Genesis story, the easiest way to avoid the issue was to keep *The Book Of Jubilees* out of the Bible. However, it was included as part of the Old Testament of the Ethiopian Christian Bible.

The Book of Enoch was discovered in Aksum, Ethiopia by James Bruce, a Scottish explorer. It was eventually taken to Europe by later travelers, where it caused quite a stir. One reason proposed as to why it didn't make the Hebrew Bible is that at the time, people were allegedly putting too much emphasis on angel worship. The rabbis may have felt that it was getting out of hand and people were ignoring God. Since it is primarily about the guardians of heaven, which were regarded as angels, they may have thought Enoch's book would only encourage the practice.[3]

Another possible reason for its exclusion was that it was too controversial. It goes into great detail about the angels that became sexually involved with the women of Earth and fathered the mysterious giants referred to in Genesis as the Nephilim.

Then there is a part of the Apocrypha that tells about the childhood of Christ, and some of the stories are rather disturbing. *The Infancy Gospel of Thomas* tells how Jesus caused the death of a playmate by pushing him off the roof of a building. When confronted, Jesus lied and said he didn't do it. Then it says he brought the child back to life and asked him if he pushed him, and the child said that he didn't do it.

Although he appears to have acquired wisdom and compassion as he matured, the young Jesus is portrayed as a spoiled brat in the Apocrypha. But many consider these stories comparable to today's supermarket tabloids, a compilation of falsehoods, exaggerations, and sensationalism.

The Protovangelion of James describes the birth of Christ's mother, Mary, as a miraculous event. It claims her mother was barren, and like Christ, Mary was born from an immaculate conception. It also enforces the idea that she conceived Jesus in a virginal state; a woman named Salome, who inserted her fingers into Mary's vagina to see if it was true, allegedly confirmed this.

In the fourth century, the Roman Catholic Church began promoting the idea that Mary had remained a virgin her entire life. However, in the New Testament, Matthew 1:25 says that Joseph did not have sexual intercourse with Mary until after Jesus was born. Mark 6:3 also brings her celibacy into question by mentioning the brothers and sisters of Jesus. However, according to the Protovangelion, after Mary became pregnant, Joseph was recruited to be her (celibate) husband, and it describes him as a widower with several children. This made it easy for the church to promote Mary's perpetual virginity by claiming that the brothers and sisters of Jesus were really the children of Joseph from a previous marriage.[4] Scholars believe the Protovangelion was omitted from the Bible because it was primarily about Mary; it was stories of Jesus that the church wanted to promote.

Had any of these books been canonized into the Christian Bible, you can see how some of the current doctrines might have been altered.

One of the little-known conflicts of biblical history is the belief that the Lord had a wife known as Ashera, and she is mentioned in the Hebrew Bible at least forty times. Excavations in the Negev Desert south of Jerusalem revealed what appears to have been a cult site in which Yahweh (the Lord) and Ashera were both worshipped. In the 1960s, English archaeologist, Kathleen Kenyon discovered hundreds of broken female figurines in a cave near Solomon's Temple in Jerusalem. Archaeologist William Dever believes the worship of Ashera was a common practice in Jerusalem during the time of Solomon because more artifacts of the goddess have been found in that area than anywhere else in the country. Some speculate that the early Israelites may have borrowed Ashera from their Canaan predecessors, who also are thought to have worshipped her.

However, efforts to promote a monotheistic male deity by the male-dominated religious hierarchy were being hindered by the worship of Ashera, especially the idea that she may have been a consort to the Lord. So using their influence, they managed to suppress and eradicate all references to her.[5] But what if this had not happened? What if the accepted belief today was that the Lord had a wife? Those absorbed by their own religious doctrines might consider it a sacrilege to suggest such a thing, but it could have happened!

Another question raised by some scholars is whether Moses really put his five books into writing, as they have doubts as to whether the art of writing on parchment existed in his time. We know that other civilizations of that era documented information, like the Egyptians, who recorded in hieroglyphs, and the Sumerians, who for over a thousand years created cuneiform tablets, so written records were not uncommon. According to Exodus 17:14, 24:4–7, and 34:27; Numbers 33:2; and Deuteronomy 31:9, 22, and 24, Moses did record his books. Some scholars believe that those familiar with the procedure added these verses later; it provided a convenient explanation as to how the information was passed on. Although it is possible, none of these passages say anything about them being recorded on parchment.

In citing some of the biblical discrepancies, I noted that Moses wrote the second set of commandments on the tablets he had chiseled out, per orders of the Lord. This might lead to speculation that he also wrote his five books on stone tablets. However, it is unlikely, because if they were kept in the Ark of the Covenant, as the Bible claims, it is doubtful it could have held the volume of tablets required to document them.

So there are many questions to deal with concerning the validity of the scriptures. There are clues suggesting that some stories may have been borrowed from earlier Sumerian writings. There is evidence that the scriptures were edited and rewritten later by different scribes, whose expressions and writing style coincided with different evolutionary stages of the Hebrew language. More evidence of altering is apparent by the different names of God, the doublets, and the discrepancies. In the New Testament, the words of Christ are printed in red ink to emphasize the holiness of the text. But how do we know that Christ even spoke these words? Was there a stenographer following him around recording every word he uttered? Doubtful. Then there are the centuries of translations into different languages, which led to eventual dissension among church leaders over how the scriptures should be interpreted, plus the births of many different religions espousing different doctrines.

To top it off, nobody has found either historical or archaeological evidence to corroborate the enslavement of the Hebrews in Egypt for four centuries and the subsequent exodus. Surely hundreds of thousands of people camping in the desert for forty years would have yielded some evidence of their presence, such as broken pottery, discarded personal effects, animal bones, and grave sites. But nothing has ever been found, which means that either no one has looked in the right places—or it never happened. Neither is there any evidence that Moses and Joshua ever existed. Archaeologists involved with excavations in Jericho claim the city had been abandoned centuries before Joshua's time. Some speculate that Moses and Joshua were just fictional characters created as inspirational stories for people coping with the hardships of the time.

David M. Rohl, an Egyptologist and archaeologist, has magnificently researched Egyptian history relating to the Hebrews and the Exodus, and he believes the events did occur—but in a timeline that is inconsistent with biblical chronology.[6] His data is disputed by mainstream historians, but it is impressive. It makes sense and is worthy of consideration.

These are just some of the facts about the Bible. Anyone who believes it is a factual record of history is completely unaware of when and how it actually came into existence, not to mention the numerous changes in editing and translation it has been subjected to over the centuries, sometimes to accommodate political agendas. Except for those thought to have been written by Moses, the authors of all the other scriptures are unknown. They were just books written by people who were simply recording their own views of events that occurred centuries before their own time, and they may have exaggerated and even created a few stories as a way of making a moral statement, with absolutely no idea that their work would one day be canonized and accepted as fact.

Although these facts tend to cast a negative shadow on my ideas, I am still puzzled by what seems like references to sophisticated technologies in the Bible, particularly teleportation and flying craft. However, the Bible is not the only reference alluding to flying craft; they are noted in other ancient texts such as the Mahabharata, the Ramayana, Mesopotamian writings, and so forth. There is the strange aerial craft depicted in medieval paintings—both religious and nonreligious—plus ancient cave drawings and petroglyphs. Even if the Bible turns out to be an invalid reference, how do we explain all the rest?

The events as they are described in the Bible seem to fit much too comfortably into what can easily be construed as an extraterrestrial agenda. There are indications that hybrids were created and situations manipulated as part of a plan to accelerate the evolution of the human race, and even clues to the reason behind it.

From the time of Constantine, it seems that considerable effort was made to establish one solid doctrine and get the stories into the hands of the people. It took centuries to shape the contents of the Bible into what it is today, even though some stories may be out of chronological order, fictitious, or conceived from ancient myths. However, based on the scenario presented in its current form and its numerous technological references, I seriously wonder if it is the result of extraterrestrial influence. Even if the stories are not true, could the Bible be a metaphorical statement meant to enlighten us about what is really going on while at the same time promoting the moral and ethical standards by which we should live? The idea may sound absurd, but after reading the previous nine chapters, one at least has to consider the possibility.

Notes

1. The Council of Nicea
    "Who Wrote the Bible? *Mysteries of the Bible.* Prod. Lionel
    Friedberg. THC. 1998.
    Web link:
    www.bidstrup.com/bible.htm

2. Constantine's letter to Eusebius
    Banned from the Bible. Documentary. Prod. Bram Roos. THC.
    2003.

3. The Book of Enoch
    Web link:
    www.altheim.com/lit/enoch.html

4. Mary's perpetual virginity
    Banned from the Bible. Documentary. Prod. Bram Roos. THC.
    2003.

5. Ashera
    "The Forbidden Goddess." *Archaeology.* Dir. Mimi Edmunds.
    TLC. 1993.

6. The Hebrews in Egypt and the Exodus
    Pharaohs and Kings: A Biblical Quest, parts 1, 2, and 3. *Documentary.*
    Prod./Dir. Timothy Copestake. TLC.

Part 3

FUTURE POSSIBILITIES

Chapter 21

PROPHECY

Prophecy is basically a prediction of something that will happen in the future. A prophet is a person who makes such predictions and is known by various names: augur, diviner, forecaster, foreseer, foreteller, fortune-teller, futurist, prognosticator, prophesier, seer, and soothsayer, and there are many throughout the world preying on people's gullibility, often for profit.

Now, there are psychics (not to be confused with prophets) who seem to possess certain clairvoyant abilities. Of course, there are some crackpots, but there are also many documented cases in which psychics have successfully assisted police agencies in solving kidnappings and murders. And although skeptics are not usually impressed, detectives are frequently amazed at the accuracy in which some psychics described details of a case that were never made public and known only to the investigators involved. On rare occasions, psychics may make a prediction about a case that does come true; however, that does not classify them as prophets—psychics do not go around predicting the future.

Many people believe this is some kind of supernatural power, but I disagree. Just because it cannot be explained by scientific methods does not necessarily mean it is supernatural. It may simply be a dimension of science that incorporates mental abilities that we have not yet learned to recognize and understand. But psychics are not prophets, and it is important that we recognize the distinction between them.

Prophecy is something one should consider with healthy skepticism. Anyone can claim to be a prophet. Anyone can predict that a major flood or earthquake will occur somewhere in the United States within the next year, and because that is such a generalization, they will probably be right. However, I have yet to see any modern-day prophet predict the time, date, and location of an event. When one does dare to be even a little specific, he usually ends up with egg on his face. In many cases, their alleged successful predictions were announced after the fact, with claims that they made the prediction beforehand, something that can rarely be substantiated.

So-called prophets climbing out of the woodwork blowing trumpets of doomsday seem to herald the turn of each new century. The sad thing is that there are gullible people who always believe them. One might wonder if they have taken the works of Nostradamus and the book of Revelation too literally. Not even Nostradamus dared to put dates on his predictions. It is possible that a few of his visions were authentic, but all his so-called prophecies were written in quatrains, which are ambiguous at best and can easily be adapted to fit any number of events that have occurred. And the same goes for Revelation.

From what the Bible tells us about the biblical prophets, we might consider them simply news reporters of their time. They had no precognitive abilities enabling them to see into the future. The Lord or his angels gave them information of future events through mentally induced visions and dreams; it was not something they conjured up by looking into a crystal ball. And this is something one should consider when listening to so-called modern-day prophets and fortune-tellers.

About two thousand years ago, it is alleged the events described in the Book of Revelation were revealed through visions, to a man named John who was exiled on the island of Patmos. He claimed he was told to write them down and send them to the seven churches: Ephesus, Smyrna, Pergamum, Thyatira, Sardis, Philadelphia, and Laodicea. After the Council of Nicea was convened in the fourth century, John's work was included as the last book in the New Testament, much to the chagrin of many bishops. It focuses on periods of tribulation, telling of wars, diseases, severe weather, climatic changes, and seismic activity. The book is downright depressing, and it is understandable why the early bishops were against its inclusion in the Bible.

Many of the predictions are a prelude to Christ's return, and many about what will occur at the end of his one-thousand-year reign. John would not have understood the technologies of future times, so his visions were in the form of symbols that he could recognize. Many of the same prophecies were given to Daniel and other prophets before Christ's time, but with a slight variation in the symbolism, and a few predictions were even made by Christ.

Even if the prophecies are true, what was the point of giving this information to anyone two thousand years ago? What difference would it make if man knew in advance what was going to happen if he was powerless to do anything about it? Granted, he might be able to change a few things on the political or social level, but how could he prevent a volcano from erupting? How could he prevent an earthquake from happening? How could he stop a tornado, hurricane, or a tsunami? If man does not have the power to change these things, then what purpose could they possibly serve other than to exacerbate the fear of God's wrath in the minds of men? But if the book of Revelation is valid, we can only assume the information was made known for a reason.

One thing in Revelation does stand out: Christ's return seems to be conveniently scheduled after this period of chaos, not before. So perhaps it would serve no purpose for him to return during such troubling times. If people are forced to contend with catastrophic problems, the impact of his return would be greatly diminished.

Most of the decadence spawned during Adam's era had been wiped out in the flood. More were taken out in the destruction of Sodom and Gomorrah and possibly a few other cities. Unless these cities were vaporized in an atomic holocaust, we can assume there were survivors. The city of Zoar, which had been slated for elimination, won a last-minute reprieve as a refuge for Abraham's nephew, Lot, and his family; so we can assume the people of that city survived. Over time, these survivors repopulated, and as a result, moral and ethical standards have once again become eroded by the iniquitous winds of depravity. The decline of moral and ethical standards, as it exists today, is probably equal to what prevailed in Sodom and Gomorrah, assuming that the story is even true. So it would seem that once again, it is necessary to purge society of this blemish, and many of the biblical prophecies may pertain to how it will be dealt with.

The prophecies claim that the return of Christ is to be preceded by wars and famine, the likes of which no man has ever seen, and the earth will be overrun with disease. There will be wars and rumors of wars; there will be an increase in the volume and severity of earthquakes and volcanic activity; and weather-related disasters will prevail in the form of tornadoes, hurricanes, and floods. Supposedly, these are the signs that his return is imminent. If the events of the past three decades are any indication, we might very well be witnessing the beginning of the end.

It started in the 1970s, when herpes ran rampant throughout the country. Then, in the mid-1980s, AIDS moved into the spotlight. Ethnic wars erupted in the former Yugoslavia, and there was much starvation and killing in Africa. Since the eruption of Mount St. Helens in May of 1980, volcanic activity and earthquakes have increased in California, Mexico, South America, Japan, China, and Russia. One of the worst occurred on October 17, 1989, when a 7.1 quake caused much devastation in the San Francisco Bay area. But this was just the beginning. There was more to come in weather, seismic, and terrorist activity.

1992:
♦ August: Hurricane Andrew wipes out Homestead, Florida.

1993:
♦ United State: worst blizzards of the century; nation practically divided in half by floods in the Midwest.
♦ February 26: Islamic terrorists exploded truck bomb in underground parking garage in World Trade Center; 6 killed; over 1,000 injured.

♦ California and Australia ravaged by wildfires: millions of acres of land destroyed and thousands lost their homes.

♦ Winter of 1993/1994: fifteen major snowstorms; record amounts of snow across the country.

1994:

♦ Uncontrollable wildfires erupt simultaneously in Idaho, Washington, California, Montana, Wyoming, Utah, Nevada, and Arizona.

♦ Georgia and Texas: severe flooding.

1995:

♦ Nation almost divided in half from severe rains: flooding throughout Mississippi Valley.

♦ Oklahoma City: Alfred P. Murrah Federal Building destroyed by truck bomb; 168 killed, including many children in day care center; 680 injured.

♦ Kobe, Japan: 7.4 magnitude earthquake; massive destruction.

♦ Atlantic/Pacific Oceans: record number of tropical storms, hurricanes, and typhoons.

1996:

♦ Winter of 1995–96: again, record snowfalls across United States; severe January blizzard crippled northeast; airports closed from Boston to Washington, DC, for days; food shortages threaten major cities.

1997:

♦ North Dakota: severe flooding; thousands left homeless; many businesses destroyed.

♦ Iran: 5.5 magnitude earthquake; thousands killed.

♦ Pakistan: 7.2 magnitude earthquake.

1998:

♦ United States: return of El Niño; much destruction along California coast.

♦ Southeastern states ravaged by unprecedented number of tornadoes.

♦ Lockerbie, Scotland: terrorist's bomb explodes on Pan American jetliner; everyone killed.

♦ Flagler County, Florida: Forest fires force evacuation of entire county; nearly half a million acres consumed; major loss of property.

♦ October 26: Hurricane Mitch; massive destruction in Central America; thousands killed in Honduras.

1999:

♦ January, Arkansas and Tennessee: severe tornadoes; more death and destruction.

♦ Colombia, South America: major earthquake; thousands killed; entire villages destroyed.

2000:

♦ February, United States: series of tornados rip through southwestern Georgia.

♦ October 12, Aden Harbor, Yemen: 17 US Navy crewmen killed in terrorist bomb attack on USS *Cole*.

♦ Zimbabwe: 700 people die in floods; 80,000 left homeless, plus 200,000 in Mozambique.

2001:

♦ January, India: 7.9 magnitude earthquake; 19,727 dead, 166,000 injured; and about 600,000 homeless according to official government figures.

♦ September 11: terrorists crash jet airliners into World Trade Center and Pentagon; over 3,000 killed.

2002:

♦ Ascension Islands: region rocked by 7.5 magnitude quake.

♦ October 9–November 5: 108 earthquakes around the world above 5.0 magnitude.

♦ November 4, Ecuador: volcanic eruption; Quito completely covered in ash.

2003:

♦ Drought conditions spawn wildfires: over 7.1 million acres destroyed between Rocky Mountains and West Coast.

2004:

♦ March, Madrid, Spain: terrorists bombs explode on four commuter trains.

♦ August, southwest Florida: Hurricane Charley; damage up into the Carolinas.

♦ September, Florida: Hurricanes Frances, Ivan, and Jeanne; damages up into New York State; 152 known dead.

♦ Indian Ocean Earthquake: deadly tsunami; over 200,000 killed in Indonesia, Sumatra, Thailand, Sri Lanka, and in few countries on west coast of Africa.

2005:

♦ January 11, La Conchita, California: side of a mountain collapses in mudslide; fifteen homes buried; at least sixteen damaged; 10 people killed.

♦ July, London: terrorist bombs explode on three underground trains and bus.

♦ August 29, Gulf of Mexico: Hurricane Katrina; New Orleans devastated and 80 percent of city underwater. Storm also responsible for death and destruction in Gulfport, Biloxi and Pascagoula, Mississippi, and parts of Alabama; hundreds of thousands homeless and without food and water. Worst disaster in US recorded history.

♦ September, again in Gulf of Mexico: Hurricane Rita hits Louisiana/Texas coast; more flooding in New Orleans; city still reeling from Hurricane Katrina.

♦ Gulf of Mexico: Hurricane Wilma; third category 5 storm of season; major destruction on Yucatán Peninsula. Swept back across Gulf into southern Florida as a category 2; millions left homeless; no electric power for weeks.

♦ Two days after official end of hurricane season: Tropical Storm Epsilon turns into hurricane and moves north up the Atlantic; officials revert to Greek alphabet (all available names in Roman alphabet used up); Tropical

Storm Zeta fizzles out in North Atlantic four days later; twenty-seventh named storm of season breaking all records ever recorded.

2006:

♦ May, New Hampshire/Massachusetts: worst flood conditions in seventy years.

♦ October 11, Myanmar (Burma) and Thailand: trail of death and destruction from worst flood conditions in more than decade.

♦ Week of December 18: Malaysia; floods in Johor, Malacca, Pahang and Negeri Sembilan.

♦ October 15, Kohala Coast on island of Hawaii: 6.7 magnitude earthquake followed by over fifty aftershocks.

2007:

♦ July 20, Gloucestershire, United Kingdom: violent rainstorm; hundreds of homes and businesses underwater.

♦ United States: heavy rains; rivers overflow banks; towns and farmland flooded in central Texas, Oklahoma, Kansas, and Missouri.

♦ August 15, central coast of Peru: magnitude 8.0 earthquake.

♦ September 12, southern Sumatra in Indonesia: magnitude 8.5 earthquake.

2008:

♦ Severe flooding in Venice, Italy; Hanoi, Vietnam; Bihar, India; and many other countries around the world.

♦ May 12, southwest China: 7.9 magnitude quake; estimated 80,000 killed; over 10 million homeless; estimated 9,000 children and teachers dead in collapsed school buildings.

♦ June: more flooding in Midwest from overflowing rivers and broken levees in Illinois, Indiana, Iowa, Michigan, Minnesota, Missouri, and Wisconsin.

2009:

♦ January, severe winter ice storm: Arkansas, Kentucky, Missouri, Oklahoma, and Texas crippled by downed power lines; over one million homes without power.

♦ September 29, Samoa: 8.0 earthquake causes tsunami; 116 killed.

♦ September 30, island of Sumatra: 7.6 magnitude earthquake; over 1,000 dead; thousands trapped in rubble of collapsed buildings.

2010:

♦ January 12, Haiti: 7.0 earthquake; estimated 230,000 killed; 300,000 reported injured; and about one million homeless.

♦ March, Iceland: volcanic eruption; air travel throughout Europe disrupted for several days; flights cancelled due to dangerous ash cloud.

♦ May/June: heavy rains; massive flooding throughout Central and Eastern Europe.

♦ December, Washington, DC: city virtually shut down by blizzard dubbed "Snowmageddon"; many highways/airports forced to close in northeast.

2011:

♦ January/early February: massive winter storm stretching from Texas to Maine; record amounts of snow across country; power lines brought down by heavy ice accumulations; cars buried in snow on highways; many airports forced to close.

♦ March 11, Japan: 9.0 magnitude earthquake followed by tsunami approximately thirty feet high; swept inland six miles; over 12,000 dead and thousands missing. Several nuclear power plants seriously damaged, threatening meltdowns; radioactive steam and water released into ocean and atmosphere.

♦ April: unprecedented number of severe tornados wreaked havoc across the central and southern states.

♦ April 27: simultaneous tornado activity in Alabama, Mississippi, Tennessee, Georgia, and Virginia; death toll over 300; entire communities leveled in Tuscaloosa and Birmingham.

This is only a small percentage of weather- and seismic-related disasters and terrorist activity that occurred during this time, and it is still going on. The total amount of destruction, plus the loss of life and property, has far surpassed in both volume and severity anything that occurred prior to the mid-1970s. So it certainly might appear to some that the end times are upon us.

Revelation also predicts the rise of the Antichrist. He is supposed to rise to power in Europe and control a 200-million-man army made up from the different nations in Europe, Asia, and Africa, and when they gather against the Holy Land, the final battle called Armageddon is supposed take place. The prophecies suggest that Armageddon may be comprised of three major conflicts; the first two supposedly will result in much death and destruction in the Holy Land but the enemy will likely be driven back. The third and final conflict is supposed to occur when the armies have assembled along the Euphrates River, near the land of Megiddo. It is then suggested Christ's army will annihilate them as they mount the third assault on Israel. After this, Christ is supposed to return to Jerusalem, appearing in all his glory on the Mount of Olives. They say that he will then begin a one-thousand-year reign, and man will enjoy the greatest era of peace he has ever known.

One rather curious passage is Revelation 20:2–3. It says Christ will banish Satan for one thousand years (which would be during his reign), but then he must be released for a short time. It would appear, in this instance, that Satan is being used symbolically to describe evil: troubles will begin anew at the end of Christ's reign, when people from many lands will gather to attack the camp of Israel, and it says they will be destroyed by fire from heaven. At this time, all of the dead will come back to life to be judged, allegedly in the bodies they occupied when they were alive. Those who are judged unworthy will be cast into eternal damnation, and the righteous will be taken to a place called the "New Jerusalem," or "Holy City," where they will live and reign forever.

Every major war of the twentieth century was thought by someone to be Armageddon, but it was only the armies of man who were involved. So if it really is Christ's army that fights this battle, then the final war has not yet occurred.

Another war described in Revelation 12:7–9 is supposed to occur before Armageddon. It will take place in heaven (space) between the devil's army and an army of angels led by Michael, the archangel. The devil (referred to as the dragon) is supposed to lose this battle, and he and his army will be cast down onto the earth. He will then enter the body of (or exert influence over) someone in high political standing, and it is this person who is supposed to become the Antichrist.

Since this war in heaven is supposed to occur before Christ returns, it suggests that his army will be here ahead of him, as will the devil's army. Could these armies be the UFOs that people are seeing today? Could the alleged UFO crashes possibly be the result of confrontations that have occurred between these two factions?

Since it appears that the Bible is personifying evil by depicting it in a physical form such as the devil, perhaps the antichrist is being personified in the same way. Although it could represent an actual person, a literal translation of Antichrist means "against Christ," which could refer to many things collectively. It could be the violence and perversion expressed in much of today's music and the lewd and obnoxious lyrics to which our children are constantly exposed. It could be the overkill of sex and violence in movies and on television. It could be the growing sexual abuse of children and the exploitation of sexual perversions. It could also be the increase of violence in urban areas, the epidemic proportion of alcohol and drug abuse and the growing number of terrorists and hate groups. I think most will agree that none of these things project a positive influence on any society, nor are they beneficial, productive, moral, or ethical—and they can all be classified as being anti-Christ.

Since I am a practical person, I fail to see how the Lord could know these things in advance—unless he is influencing people and events to conform to these predictions. But what about seismic- and weather-related disasters? How could he predict the vast increase in earthquakes, floods, and hurricanes two thousand years in advance?

If he has the technology to navigate around the galaxy, then he surely would know about tectonics and the effects of shifting continental plates. A geological analysis might have allowed him to predict when major seismic activity would occur—maybe not exact dates but within a window of fifty to one hundred years. And his science was probably fine-tuned to predict changes in weather patterns conducive to creating floods and hurricanes. It is also possible that he was able to control the weather to conform to these predictions. And man's deviant sexual behavior may have been a clue to the diseases that would eventually overtake him. But what I fail to understand is how the Lord could predict a battle between Christ's army and the devil's army. I can see how he might have the wherewithal to influence man, and maybe even the weather, to conform to certain predictions, even war. But how could he know what battles his angels or even Christ might be involved in, especially what the outcome will be—unless it is an allegorical reference to man's own battle against the forces of evil, in which he will control the outcome.

Even so, it does not take someone like Einstein to understand that before further progress can be made, the antisocial elements of criminal behavior, sexual abuse, terrorism, and other forms of declining morality must be eliminated. How far would the second race have progressed if the decadence being spread by Adam's descendants had been allowed to continue? Their perversive influence could have nullified the progress of the new race, so they had to be removed. The darker side of humanity as it exists today will not disappear overnight. Just as it was in biblical times, the negative aspects that currently prevail must be removed, or they will inhibit the positive progress of future generations.

So history may be repeating itself, at least in a biblical perspective. Noah's flood and the destruction of Sodom and Gomorrah wiped out much of the decadence that was caused by Adam's virus, and if we are to believe the scriptures, much of it refers to deviant sexual behavior. If it is the result of a genetic engineering project that went awry, it is still being passed along from the survivors of the first race.

If Christ returns sometime during this millennium or the next, then the end, or whatever it is that is going to happen, will occur after his one-thousand-year reign. The Bible says that many people will be removed from the earth at that time, and if there is any truth to these prophecies, it could be describing an evacuation, possibly because something is going to happen to the earth. The prophecies state that Christ will take his chosen ones to a "city." However, by this time, we will probably have established colonies on the moon and on Mars. There is also a good chance that many will have migrated to another planet that we discover during our exploration of the galaxy. Therefore, even if the earth does suffer some sort of cosmic destruction, confidence is high that the human race will survive.

So what happens after that? If catastrophe does strike, will the earth ever become livable again? Will it rejuvenate itself to where we will someday be able to return? If so, will we find the descendants of those who were left behind that might have survived? They would probably exist in a very primitive state, as all traces of technology would have eroded away. How will they view us, their ancestors, returning from the sky? Will they look upon us as gods? Might it be history repeating itself? That's an interesting thought.

Just before this evacuation takes place, Christ is supposed to bring all the dead back to life to be judged, and in the same bodies they occupied when they were alive, which seems highly unlikely. The judging, it would appear, refers to selecting those that Christ will take with him to this new city, and apparently, it is not for everyone, only those who meet strict moral criteria. Christian doctrine teaches that those who accompany Christ will be transformed into spirits when they go. The rest will be left behind, condemned to burn in hell.

Hell supposedly exists at some lower and undesirable level of the spiritual plane, another superstitious belief invented by man and promoted by religion. If hell really exists, why not just send the evil ones there and let the righteous remain on Earth to live in uninhibited peace? And if the righteous are transformed into spirits, why would spirits need a physical dwelling place like a city?

People will be taken off the earth—that seems to be the gist of what the prophecies are saying—and if true, logic suggests that it is a plan of evacuation. It is doubtful that the ETs (or the Lord or Christ) will be able to evacuate billions of people, and it is unlikely to be their intention. This is where Judgment Day comes in. It is likely that certain standards will have to be met; taking troublemakers along would only rekindle the problems that existed on Earth, so it is only logical that only those of the best moral fiber will be selected.

If, however, the Lord's project has been successful, we should be well on our way into galactic exploration within the next thousand years, and by then we will surely have established bases or colonies on the moon and on Mars and will have a large colony orbiting somewhere in the solar system. It is also possible that by then we will have begun colonizing a planet in some distant solar system.

Now let's examine what the Bible says about Earth's destruction and the migration.

Then I saw a new heaven and a new earth for the first heaven and earth had passed away and there was no longer any sea. (Rev 21:1)

Now, a "new heaven" would seem to suggest a new and different view of the stars—a view you would have on a world in a faraway solar system—and a new earth would seem to suggest a different planet. The first heaven and earth passing away might refer to a cataclysmic event that will leave the earth uninhabitable, and "no longer any sea" would seem to imply that the oceans will disappear. Could it mean that the oceans (and maybe the atmosphere) will be sucked into space by the gravitational effect of a large planet-size body passing close to the earth? The earth would then become a barren world—like Mars. There are clues that Mars once had a lot of water, but what happened to it? Did a similar event transform it into its present state?

The prophecies tend to be a bit confusing because one minute they're talking about a new city, and the next, about a new earth. So which is it, a city or a planet?

I saw the Holy City, the new Jerusalem, coming down out of heaven from God, prepared as a bride beautifully dressed for her husband. (Rev 21:2)

The vision describes a city coming down out of heaven ready to receive its new occupants, suggesting it will be constructed in advance. However, it does not necessarily mean it will land on Earth; coming down from heaven may only signify that it is located somewhere in space. Revelation 21:15–21 describes the city as being laid out in a square within four walls, each wall being two hundred feet thick and 1,400 miles in length, and the city is as wide and high as it is long. Literally, it is describing a cube the size of which would cover a major portion of the United States. It is mind-boggling that anything that big would be constructed by anyone. But if it really is that large, the most logical location would be two hundred feet beneath the surface of some other planet or moon—a world with no breathable atmosphere. And a city that large probably would have several access points. John said it had twelve gates that resembled pearls (Rev 21:12 and 21:21).

The city does not need the sun or the moon to shine on it, for the glory of God gives it light, and the lamb is its lamp. (Rev 21:23)

There will be no more night. They will not need the light of a lamp or the light of the sun, for the Lord God will give them light. And they will reign forever and ever. (Rev 22:5)

This tells us there will be light, but not from the sun or any other star, and if there is no need for lamps, it means the light will be generated. In Revelation 21:19–20, John said there were different colored gems located in the base of the city, which might mean that power would be generated by some form of crystal energy. Revelation 22:1–2 mentions *the river of the water of life* and a *tree of life*, which will bear fruit once a month, standing on each side of the river. It also states that the leaves of those trees will heal the nations and there will no longer be any curse (sickness).

The tree of life contributed to the long lives of Adam and his descendants, and apparently there will be more than one of those trees in the city. So we might assume that those who eat of its fruit will likewise be blessed with unlimited life spans.

So Revelation is telling us that there is a city 1,400 miles long, high, and wide; there are twelve gates to the city; there are various colored gems located at the base of the city; and there are trees producing fruit on both sides of a river in the city. From these descriptions, one might assume the city is a physical dwelling place that will house living, breathing human beings and have absolutely nothing to do with the spirit world.

The size of this city is hard to comprehend, and the technology needed to construct such a wonder is overwhelming. Logic suggests that if it is not on a planet in another star system, it will be an underground location, probably on some small moon—possibly our own—or even Mars.

In his book, *Mysterious Spaceship Moon*, Don Wilson notes that after the astronauts returned to the command ship on each Apollo mission, they sent the landing module crashing back into the lunar surface to take seismic readings by instruments left behind. The readings showed that the moon literally rang like a bell, indicating a large hollow area somewhere beneath the surface. Could this be where the city is located? He also claims that astronomers have seen strange things on the surface of the moon, such as a bridge spanning more than ten miles across a crater. There have also been reports of unexplained lights periodically being observed in some of the craters. On several Apollo moon missions, UFOs were allegedly photographed and even videotaped by astronauts in orbit around the moon as well as on the surface. NASA discredits the photos as being reflections of interior cabin lights of the spacecraft. But the fact that the government has lied before naturally causes one to be suspicious. During one mission, astronauts actually filmed the shadow of a large object moving across the moon's surface.[1] So maybe we should consider the possibility that something is going on up there. However, that is something you will have to decide for yourself.

Exodus II

Unless an unforeseen catastrophe suddenly turns the clock back on our present technology by a millennium or two, we will eventually begin exploring the wonders of the galaxy. We will probably discover at least one planet somewhere that will support human life and begin a gradual migration to colonize this new world. A system of selection will most likely be arranged to decide who will go. Aside from possessing the necessary skills to build and to survive, those selected will most likely be of the best moral fiber and will be most beneficial in building a new world and contributing to its growth and prosperity. This migration will probably proceed in an orderly fashion in the years leading up to the end. But as the final days of Christ's millennial reign draw near, there will be problems. According to Revelation 20:3, that is when Satan must be released from his millennium of banishment for a short time.

This suggests that it may become necessary to move evacuees into well-guarded military facilities that will also serve as departure points. Man's natural instinct for survival will probably mean that many who are unable to go will try gaining access to these camps and maybe even kill others in an attempt to take their place.

They marched across the breadth of the earth and surrounded the camp of God's people, but fire came down from heaven and destroyed them. (Rev 20:9)

This seems to propose that the facilities where Christ's people are waiting will be well protected. Anyone attempting an unauthorized entry or an organized group attack will be eliminated by what sounds like missiles or laser weapons fired from aircraft.

In reference to when the people will be taken (commonly referred to as "the rapture"), 1 Thessalonians 4:17 says they will be caught up (taken up) to meet the Lord "in the air." It states in 1 Corinthians 15:51–54 that they will not sleep (die), but that they will be "changed in a flash, in the twinkling of an eye."

What, exactly, does this mean? Could it mean instantly transported in a beam or flash of light—like the angel who visited Samson's mother ... like the angel who appeared at Christ's tomb ... like the angel who appeared in Peter's prison cell? The ancient Jewish Kabbalah says that "seven thousand people will rise into the air in the form of light." Does this not sound exactly like what people are describing as part of the abduction experience? Are these references to teleportation? It would be the most logical solution for getting people safely aboard ships, as landing might prove too risky with the unrest that is sure to prevail.

I have heard some evangelists preach that the rapture will begin before the period of great tribulation. Whether or not this has some connection to the thousands of people who seem to vanish off the face of the earth every year is something to consider. Of course, there are many who have simply chosen to disappear and start a new life somewhere else for whatever reason. However, the number of people whose disappearances have never been accounted for is legion.

In any event, when the final passengers are beamed aboard and the last ships are on their way, it may be only a matter of months or weeks before whatever is going to happen, happens. All prophecies will then have been fulfilled. Christ will have reigned on Earth for a thousand years and selected those who will go with him; the rest of the decent people will have migrated to their own relocation colonies, and those who cannot go will be left on Earth to fend for themselves.

Now, the allusions to a deity being responsible for all of this may simply signify that it was ETs project of accelerated evolution that enabled man to do it for himself. Fire coming down from heaven could easily pertain to man-made weapons, and the new city might also turn out to be a creation of man.

One detail that would appear to contradict these ideas is that the book of Revelation only mentions those who will go with Christ and says nothing of man making his own way into space and setting up shop on other worlds. This might suggest that planet Earth may experience some kind of technological setback before Christ's return due to global nuclear war or possibly a large asteroid strike. A large asteroid or comet could wipe out a vast amount of the population plus our energy, food, and transportation resources, and we could very well be transformed back into a very primitive existence.

If, however, there is any merit to my ideas about an accelerated evolution project, it presents a logical argument against such a disaster occurring before Christ's return. Assuming there is such a project, why would ETs spend many millennia bringing us to an advanced technological level if we will be wiped out before we have the chance to use it for our survival? It is illogical. Therefore, if we do experience such a disaster, it probably won't be the big one. It may create a few setbacks, but we should rally and continue to move forward in our exploration of space.

The book of Revelation predicts numerous plagues, weather- and seismic-related disasters, the final war, the return of Christ, and possibly the destruction of the earth. It also suggests man's migration to a new world. It would seem that through the scriptures, ET might be giving us advance notice of what is going to happen. Depending on how one chooses to interpret these prophecies, a variety of translations can be postulated. But when you weigh all the evidence that implies sophisticated technologies were at work from the beginning, the application of logic and common sense strongly suggests that we are being prepared for the worst.

◆◆◆◆◆

Genetic manipulation … Accelerated evolution … Alien intervention in the affairs of man … Like chess pieces on the game board of the gods, we have been carefully maneuvered around each obstacle in a timeless game of strategy—or so it seems. If I am right, it is fast approaching the time when we will need to know what is going on. If our survival hinges on migrating to new and undiscovered worlds, then achieving this goal is still centuries away, so we need to start preparing soon. From the information compiled by credible researchers, there are clues that ETs may be using abductees to send us the message.

In one case, an abductee was shown scenes of a large nuclear-type explosion in which the cloud covered one-fifth the diameter of the earth. However, no nuclear device currently in existence would produce a cloud that large, but an asteroid as large as the one that wiped out the dinosaurs could. Being unfamiliar with the cosmic possibilities, he may simply have associated the cloud with a nuclear explosion because he said it was similar to what happened in Japan. He said the aliens seemed surprised that he knew about Japan because it happened some "moments" before he was born, but they told him that this explosion was much greater.

Apparently, these little greys do not, or perhaps cannot, express time as we understand it; they only referred to it as moments in relation to the abductee's life span. The abduction occurred in 1976, when the subject was seventeen, which means he was born around 1959. The bombing of Japan occurred in 1945, so these "moments" would have actually been fourteen years. He was told that the explosion he was shown would not occur until he was a month away from turning forty, which would have been sometime around 1999. Since 1999 has come and gone with no such disaster occurring, I might suspect the story was the product of either an overactive imagination, a false memory that had been implanted in his mind, or possibly that the aliens simply do not understand or are unable to relate to our concept of time. Nevertheless, visions of such disasters seem to be a common factor in many abduction cases—why?

A girl who was sixteen at the time of her abduction said she was shown scenes of planetary destruction and times when people would be starving. She was told that we will have exhausted our resources and energy supplies, and that the earth would blow up. She said the sun would be black, mountains would crumble, and cities would fall. This certainly sounds like the aftermath of a large asteroid or comet impact. And many other abductees shown similar scenes were likewise told that what they were seeing was going to happen. Of course, these visions may simply be false memories. But could it be possible that they are warnings? Are these people being given visions of future events—just as the Lord, in biblical times, gave the prophets visions of future events? If they are warnings, then there seems to be a paradox in that the abductees are forced to forget them along with the rest of their experience, which makes no sense. Why would the aliens alert them about a coming disaster and then block the memory from their conscious minds? If they are warnings, it is illogical that they were meant to be forgotten. So let's examine the situation from a logical perspective.

If you were to wake up in the middle of the night to the smell of smoke and your smoke alarm wailing, what would you do? If you were of average intelligence, you would assume there was a fire and call 911 to report it so they will dispatch the fire department. By simple definition, you would recognize the fact that something was wrong—that there was a problem that required assistance. By the same token, a person who suddenly begins having nightmares, waking up with blood on his pillow and strange marks on his body, suffering from unexplained symptoms of anxiety, or who is unable to account for missing time is likewise being alerted to the fact that something is wrong—that there is a problem. He would eventually, if not sooner, realize that he needs help, and his 911 call would be a visit to a psychiatrist or a psychologist.

Now, if all abductees were returned with complete recall of the physical examinations, anal probing, sperm extraction, insemination, and fetus extraction, how many would actually attempt to go out and tell the world what had just happened to them? When you consider the psychological impact that such an experience would have on most people, there would probably be very few, if any. Let's be realistic—their sanity would be questioned, and their job security would be threatened. But as we already know, the information *is* getting out. How?

The way it seems to be happening is that a certain percentage of these people somehow, for some reason, are *compelled* to seek professional help. It is almost as if they are forced to recognize the aberration in their lives. It is through professional counseling and hypnosis that this information has become known. Over time, the similarities of seemingly unimportant and insignificant little details reported by each abductee have been recognized by well-credentialed professionals as being too numerous to be coincidental. When people like Dr. David Jacobs of Temple University, the late Dr. John Mack, a Pulitzer Prize winner from Harvard University, and a few others began to take a serious interest in the subject, abductions suddenly gained a perspective of credibility.

So perhaps the ETs have a method to their madness. At first, these stories were too incredible to believe, but when those with the proper credentials began to take the subject seriously, others then began to sit up and take notice. It may be through this process that we are being alerted to the fact that something is going to happen. What is the point of showing these catastrophic scenes to abductees and telling them that they are going to occur unless it is a bona fide attempt to enlighten us with the facts? This is something I feel researchers should pay a little more attention to.

Prior to entering the new millennium, the doomsday prophets were having a field day. At the time, most computer software was programmed to store years in two-digit numbers: 91 equaled 1991, 92 equaled 1992, 93 equaled 1993, and so on. This would have caused a problem when the date rolled over to 2000 because systems were unable to distinguish 2000 from 1900. This generated a lot of panic from the doomsday nuts that believed computers controlling the stock market, banking industry, major utilities, large corporations, plus the government, military, and intelligence agencies would crash. Many believed catastrophic problems were imminent, such as the loss of electric power, food shortages, major chaos at airports, and a host of other tumultuous situations. It became known as the Y2K (year 2000) bug. But as it was with previous prophecies of doom, all the wild and catastrophic Y2K predictions failed to occur because steps were taken in plenty of time to correct the situation. Of course, there were a few problems, but nothing serious. The impact it had was relatively insignificant.

However, one positive outcome of the millennial transition was the inundation of movies and documentaries about asteroid and comet disasters that exposed the world to the reality of the threat; we suddenly discovered how many potentially dangerous near-earth-asteroids actually exist.

One controversial item of prophecy I would like to address before ending this chapter is the doomsday predictions of 2012. Many people believe that December 21, 2012—the date the Mayan calendar ends—is a sign that the world will end on that day. Others cite Nostradamus, the book of Revelation, the Hopi prophecies, and certain astronomical events as indicating the same thing. The words of Nostradamus and those in Revelation can be taken many ways, depending on how you choose to interpret them, but the Mayans and Hopis seemed to be more precise in suggesting that something they considered of major importance would occur at that time. We know that certain astronomical events will take place on that date, but how they relate to the prophecy, if at all, is open to debate.

Precession, the wobbling of the earth on its axis, occurs in cycles of twenty-six thousand years and has been going on for probably a few billions years. On December 21, 2012, we will come to the end of the current cycle. Also at this time, the sun will be aligned with the center of the Milky Way, known as the galactic equator. Some doomsday fanatics claim this combination of events will cause cataclysmic disasters marking the end of the world as we know it. But they also predicted the same thing for May 5, 2000, when all the planets were aligned on the same side of the sun. What these nuts failed to consider, or maybe didn't know, is that such alignments occur on a regular basis about every twenty years.

The Mayans, however, had a phenomenal knowledge of astronomy, and their calendar is even more accurate than our own. As for the world coming to an end on December 21, 2012, simply because their calendar ends on that day, I am inclined to think they were simply predicting the end of the current precession cycle and the start of a new one—in other words, the birth of a new age ... not the end of the world. And if Christ is really going to return and reign on Earth for a millennium, then we should have nothing to worry about. Nevertheless, I am sure that as the date draws closer, the doomsday scenario will receive a lot of hype in supermarket tabloids and by modern-day prophets. The unfortunate thing is that there are always gullible people who will believe it.

Notes

1.   Shadow of object passing over moon's surface
       "UFOs Uncovered #2." *Out of This World*. Prod. Peter Lories/
       Bradley Adams. TLC.

Chapter 22

DOOMSDAY

Somehow, I cannot picture an alien scientist sitting around chatting with his colleagues and suddenly saying, "Well, gentlemen, we have nothing to do for the next fifty thousand years, so what do you say we all go to Earth and accelerate their evolution!" I really don't believe aliens would come here and indiscriminately mess with our evolution. It could create an imbalance between wisdom and technology; we could end up causing our own annihilation. The only reason that would make sense is that they deemed it necessary for our survival because they know we are facing a major disaster that will cause our extinction long before we can develop the technology needed to survive. And there is evidence suggesting that this is the case. So what kind of disaster are we facing?

I think we can rule out nuclear war. Unless we actually blew the planet apart, there would probably be survivors. The sun going nova and swallowing up the earth is a possibility, but we have the technology to know that will not happen for another 4.5 billion years. So the most probable threat would seem to be an asteroid or comet strike.

Smaller objects like meteors that usually burn up and disintegrate in the atmosphere continuously bombard the earth, but occasionally, larger ones do impact. A good example is the Barringer Meteor Crater in Arizona; almost a mile wide, it was created by a meteorite impact fifty thousand years ago.[1] A similar strike today would be devastating should it occur in a major populated area, but it would not be large enough to cause extinction; it would take something much bigger.

In 1992, comet Shoemaker-Levy 9 passed very close to Jupiter, and gravitational stress broke it up into twenty-one separate fragments. It was the astronomical highlight of the millennium when they crashed into Jupiter between July 16 and July 22, 1994. A few mountain-size pieces hit the planet and exploded with a force of six million megatons, spewing mushroom clouds of gasses one thousand miles high and leaving cloud scars wider than the earth. What would a similar impact do to Earth? If all the nuclear weapons in existence were stacked together and detonated simultaneously, they would only produce an explosion between thirty and sixty thousand megatons.

During the birth of our solar system, stellar debris was abundant. Heavy meteoric bombardment created impact craters clearly visible on all the planets and moons without an atmosphere to erode them. So we know this was something natural that occurred throughout the entire solar system and probably all others in our galaxy and even the universe. During the next few billion years, much of it fell into the sun or was expelled into deep space. The larger gas giants like Jupiter and Saturn acted like cosmic vacuum cleaners as they orbited through the debris, sucking much of it into their own atmospheres.

However, some of it is still wandering around in our neighborhood. On June 30, 1908, a comet or asteroid exploded in the atmosphere over the Tunguska region of Siberia in a blast that leveled trees for forty miles in all directions. Had it happened over New York, London, or Paris, it would have totally wiped out those cities. In the fall of 1990, at the onset of Desert Storm, a satellite searching for Iraqi troop activity picked up a one-kiloton explosion produced by an asteroid exploding over the Pacific Ocean.[2] On December 9, 1997, a British satellite picked up an asteroid exploding over the southern tip of Greenland. Scientists estimate that it was slightly smaller than the Tunguska explosion.[3] In 2001, another asteroid exploded far above the Pacific with the force of ten Hiroshima bombs, and in 2002, another one blew up over the Mediterranean.[4] Although time has reduced the threat of major impacts, these incidents, especially the Tunguska and Jupiter events, are a sober reminder of the potential danger we face from the debris still floating around in our backyard.

A few scientists have finally begun to take the threat seriously. They are now researching the technology to prevent such a strike, and a number of ideas are being considered. One method that looks good on paper is altering the asteroid's course by detonating one or more nuclear devices near it; the theory is that the shock wave will move it into a nonthreatening orbit. Another is using lasers or reflectors to focus sunlight on its surface. Theoretically, the surface would heat up and release gasses that would act as rocket exhausts and push it into a safer orbit. The least-favored option is blowing it to pieces because, as some astronomers put it, that might be turning a cannonball strike into a shotgun blast. So before they can decide on an appropriate method, they need to send out a probe to analyze its composition. And this would have to be done decades in advance since most asteroids are not discovered until they are too close to allow us time to intercept them.

But if an asteroid is a threat, why can't the aliens alter its course or destroy it instead of interfering with our evolution? If they could part the waters of a sea, you would think they could do something about a rogue comet or asteroid. And wouldn't it seem likely that in another millennium we will have developed the means to prevent it ourselves? Surely by then we will be mining the resources of these nomadic rocks and should have the technology to eliminate the threat of an Earth strike altogether. So why are abductees being shown visions of an apocalyptic disaster and told it is going to happen—why do biblical prophecies suggest an evacuation of earth—unless it is something beyond the control of anyone's technology?

Between the orbits of Mars and Jupiter is a band of rocky debris in orbit around the sun, known as the asteroid belt. Most scientists believe that it is leftover debris from the birth of the solar system—that it never coalesced into a planet. Whenever a comet or asteroid plows through this belt, it occasionally collides with and dislodges other asteroids that could pose a threat to Earth should one of them head our way. Out beyond the orbits of Neptune and Pluto is another band of debris circling the sun, known as the Kuiper Belt, and three light-years out from the sun is a field of debris surrounding our entire solar system, called the Oort cloud. The origins of many comets have been traced to both the Kuiper Belt and the Oort cloud, so innumerable objects that could someday pose a threat to our precious Earth exist in and around our solar system.

While on its way to Jupiter in August of 1993, NASA's *Galileo* spacecraft photographed the asteroid known as 243 Ida. It is approximately thirty-five miles in length, pockmarked with craters, and even has its own mile-wide satellite called Dactyl orbiting around it. Its heavily cratered surface suggests that it may be about 2 billion years old. Because of its orbit and composition, scientists initially thought it belonged to the family of Koronis asteroids that are believed to be the debris from a larger body that was destroyed about 200 million years ago.[5] Fortunately, Ida poses no threat to Earth. But if an asteroid five miles in diameter caused the extinction of the dinosaurs, what amount of devastation would be produced by one like Ida that is thirty-five miles long—or larger? But what if it isn't an asteroid or a comet that is the threat? What if it is something much larger, like a planet? The possibility does exist, and it might explain what the aliens are doing, and why.

The orbit of Pluto, our outermost planet (which has now been demoted to the class of dwarf planet), is elliptical and crosses the orbit of its neighbor, Neptune, twice during its own 248-year trip around the sun. And Pluto's orbit is different; it is tilted at about a 17-degree angle from those of the other planets, which may signify that it is just a large asteroid that was captured by our solar system. Nevertheless, it seems inevitable that at some point in time, the two will simultaneously reach the intersection of their orbital paths and pass very close to each other. Tiny little Pluto could be affected by great big Neptune much like the comet Shoemaker-Levy 9 was affected by Jupiter, possibly resulting in a collision or having its orbit drastically altered. But since it hasn't happened in the 4.5 billion years that our solar system has been around, the odds of it happening anytime soon seem remote.

Astronomers have now discovered the existence of many planet-size bodies out beyond Pluto. There is speculation that one might possibly be a brown dwarf, a star that never ignited, which would mean we live in a binary system, not uncommon in our galaxy. Nevertheless, if one of these planet-size bodies has an elliptical orbit that extends out into the reaches of deep space like the comets, it could pose a potential threat to any of the planets, including Earth. But since there is no record of such a planet in recorded history, it is easy to dismiss its existence. If, however, its orbital year were 125,000 or even 5,000 years, its last approach would have been so long ago that we would have no way of knowing about it today. According to Zechariah Sitchin, ancient Sumerian texts mention a planet called Nibiru, which orbits through our solar system every 3,600 years.[6]

So stellar bodies whose orbital paths intersect are not that unusual. We already know that Pluto's elliptical orbit crosses that of Neptune's, and the orbits of the comets are elliptical and might cross the orbit of any planet as they swing around the sun and return to deep space. When Halley's comet made its last appearance in 1986, it breezed in and out of the inner solar system virtually unnoticed. However, on its previous appearance in 1910, it came close enough so that the earth actually passed through its tail.

Halley's comet appears every 75.8 years, once in the lifetime of most people, but there are other comets that are not seen for hundreds, thousands, or even millions of years. Since we know that comets and at least one planet have elliptical orbits that cross other planetary orbits, it is possible there is an undiscovered planet that also follows an elliptical orbit like the comets and appears every twenty-five millennium or so. Could this be the threat to mankind for which the aliens are preparing us?

There is, of course, no way at this time to verify the existence of such a planet or know that it will collide with the earth. And if a cosmic collision is the fate of the earth, the odds are more in favor of it being with a large asteroid or comet.

What would seem to be the most immediate threat is the asteroid called 99942 Apophis. In 2029, Apophis will pass by Earth below our geosynchronous satellites that orbit at 22,236 miles. On a cosmic scale, that is equivalent to a bullet passing your nose by 1/32 of an inch. Astronomers note that this close approach presents the possibility that it could pass through a gravitational keyhole, a point where the earth's gravity could alter its orbit and set it up for an impact with the earth on April 13, 2036. However, observations made in 2006 suggest that it will *probably* miss the keyhole and reduce the chances of an impact to one in forty-five thousand.[7]

On the other hand, if Apophis does pass through this keyhole and is set up for an Earth strike, it is only about 1,400 feet in diameter and will not be an extinction impact. However, it could create a major tsunami if it hit in the ocean; and if it hit on land, it could kill thousands and maybe millions of people, depending where it comes down. If the threat of impact does turn out to be real, we can only hope that that by then we will have devised a way to prevent it.

The prophecies in Revelation suggesting an evacuation of Earth, and claims made by abductees of being shown images of apocalyptic devastation and told that it is going to occur, suggest that the big one is not Apophis but one that will occur at some other time, possibly in the not-too-distant future. The scary thing is that the number of scientists working on the problem is equivalent to the size of the staff of a fast-food restaurant.

Notes

1.   Barringer Meteor Crater
       Link to image:
       laps.fri.uni-lj.si/~duke/HPpictures/crater.jpg

2.   Asteroid exploding over Pacific in 1990
       Asteroid Impact. Documentary. TLC.

3.   Asteroid exploding over southern tip of Greenland in 1997
       Impact Earth. Documentary. Prod./Dir. Lorne Townend. TLC.

4.   Asteroids exploding over Pacific in 2001 and Mediterranean in
       2002
       Killer Asteroids. Documentary. Prod. Colin Murray. Discovery
       Channel.

5.   Asteroid 243 Ida
       Cosmic Collision, Ultra Science. TLC.
       Links to images:
       www.mhhe.com/physsci/astronomy/fix/student/images/15f12.
       jpg

6.   Nibiru—planet that orbits through solar system every 3,600
       years
       Web link:
       www.crystalinks.com/nibiru.html

7.   Asteroid 99942 Apophis
       Web link:
       en.wikipedia.org/wiki/99942_Apophis

Chapter 23

BABEL: TWENTY-FIRST CENTURY

Mass sightings of UFOs began two years after we dropped atomic bombs on Japan, so our sudden development and use of nuclear weapons may have presented a problem. As the guardians of heaven were left on Earth during the time of Enoch, it suggests that a contingent of ETs may be permanently stationed here keeping watch, and they may have sent word to their leader, who returned with his forces. Of course, this is only hypothetical, but the fact that mass sightings began two years later might be a clue as to how long it took them to make the trip—if only we knew where they came from, that is. Exactly how fast they are capable of traveling through space is anyone's guess. If they have the technology to bend the fabric of the space-time continuum, they may be able to traverse space equivalent to one hundred or even a thousand times the speed of light.

Many believe aliens were attracted to Earth by our atomic testing in the early 1940s; however, it seems highly improbable since the evidence suggests they were already here and have been for many a millennium. Our most advanced technological systems were not developed until after we allegedly acquired a crashed UFO, and it could be that much of our current technology is a result of their being here as opposed to their being here as a result of our technology.

The four millennia separating Adam and Christ had yielded no major technological advancement. Except for those living in coastal areas, who learned how to build boats and navigate the seas, transportation was limited to horses, donkeys, and camels; weapons were the spear, the bow and arrow, and the sword. But sophisticated technologies were looming on the horizon. During the period circa 287–211 BC, upon the scene came men responsible for inventions we seem to have only rediscovered in our own era.

Although a few devices had been invented to record time, none were perfect until Ctesibius of Alexandria came along and invented the first accurate mechanical water clock.

Archimedes, a Greek mathematician, not only discovered pi, but he also invented the pulley, the lever, the odometer, and the Archimedes screw, a device that facilitated the draining of ponds because it could easily be operated by one person. He also invented what might be considered the first laser when he designed a lens to destroy invading Roman warships with concentrated rays of reflected sunlight. Although it was never perfected and used, his idea of using concentrated beams of light is the essence of today's lasers.

Heron (or Hero) of Alexandria invented the catapult, the first coin-operated vending machine, and a surveying device called the dioptra. He also designed an automated theater that would run a twenty-minute performance with light and sound effects. Using the technology of the catapult, he designed a weapon that could rapidly fire a barrage of arrows faster and farther than any archer, what might be considered the earliest version of the Gatling gun.

One of his more impressive designs was an apparatus comprised of pulleys and ropes that would operate on steam power and open the large doors of a temple when the priests lit a fire to the gods. He even designed trumpets to go off at the appropriate time to add to the effect. After the fire went out and the water cooled, the device would automatically close the doors. The public would have been awed into thinking the priests had performed some kind of miracle.

Perhaps his most amazing invention was a miniature steam engine called the aeolipile. It was a ball filled with water, with two exhaust tubes set on an axle, and when heated, the water boiled and steam pressure caused the ball to spin at a phenomenal speed. If he had only followed through with the technical aspects of this idea, might he have created an industrial revolution two thousand years ago?

Then great innovations in medicine were brought about by Galen of Pergamum, who lived circa 129–210 AD. Much of his knowledge was acquired in Alexandria, where he went to study after the death of his father. He made advances in sports medicine while treating Olympic athletes; he was successful in treating the wounds of gladiators; and he even performed eye and brain surgery. Many of the instruments he designed are remarkably similar to those in use today. Unfortunately, the physicians of succeeding generations who studied his notes never took them seriously; his tools and techniques were only reinvented by physicians of our own era.

These men had opened the door to advancement; by thinking outside the box, their ideas were a sign of things that were to come in the not-too-distant future.

It was not until after Christ's time that higher technology slowly began to emerge. As the centuries rolled by, machines were invented that made life a little easier. In the fifteenth century, the printing press appeared on the scene. In the eighteenth century, the steam locomotive made its appearance in England and resulted in a major industrial revolution in the United States in the nineteenth century. As we approached the twentieth century, progress suddenly surged ahead when we learned to harness the power of electricity. The invention of the electric light, the telephone, and the radio were soon followed by the automobile, the airplane, and the atomic bomb. And when compared to the previous six thousand years, the technology achieved since 1940 was again an extraordinary leap forward; it was as though we suddenly shifted into warp drive. We advanced from horse-drawn carriages to spaceships, from the telegraph to satellite communications, from the abacus to multigigabyte computers ... It was also when UFOs became a prominent part of the scene.

When we look at the history of technology, we seriously have to question whether our transition from caveman to spaceman has been an accelerated one. Are we where we are today because of thousands of years of genetic manipulation by extraterrestrials? Assuming that ETs have been juggling our genes, might we wonder where we would be right now had they not done so? Would we still be living in caves? Would we just now be inventing the bow and arrow? How long would it be before we discovered electricity or invented the automobile and the airplane? How long would it be before we put a man on the moon?

It is possible that we have achieved these technologies centuries or even millennia ahead of time. But if things had turned out favorably in the Garden of Eden, might we have reached this plateau much sooner? One thing is certain: if we maintain this rate of advancement, we should be well into galactic exploration by the year 3000, and if it turns out that there is a threat to our planet, we should be able to survive by migrating to new worlds.

Much of what we achieved during the twentieth century was hastily developed because of war. Necessity is the mother of invention, and had it not been for the wars of the twentieth century, we might not yet have put a man on the moon. If the ETs' goal is for us to achieve interstellar travel by 3000, perhaps we should wonder if they were behind this sudden burst of progress as well as the wars that forced us to develop it.

Now it appears our progress is being suppressed, or at least held in check. Since Glasnost, UFO researchers have obtained information on numerous events that occurred in the former Soviet Union. We have learned that on several occasions, UFOs were responsible for completely neutralizing the integrity of their intercontinental ballistic missiles.[1] Coming from Russia, this was rather astonishing news, but the fact is, it also happened in the United States.

In 1964, Robert Jacobs was a lieutenant stationed at Vandenberg Air Force Base in California. He was in charge of a special photographic unit that filmed test flights of Atlas F and Minuteman missiles. It required setting up cameras at thirty or forty different locations to obtain a view from all possible angles; in the event that something went wrong, it would aid in determining the cause of the problem.

In November of 1964, he was assigned to film the launch of an Atlas missile from Big Sur with a new 1,200-inch telescope that was developed at Boston University; the camera was programmed to follow the missile automatically and run for six minutes, until it was out of viewing range. After the film was developed, Jacobs was called to the office of Major F.J. Mansmann, the project director. Two men in grey suits were also in the office and Jacobs was asked to watch the film in their presence. When the projector was turned on, Jacobs said a saucer-shaped object flew up to the warhead, shot four beams at it, then flew away. The warhead then fell into the ocean, way short of its target. When asked what the object was, Jacobs said, *"It looks to me like we got a UFO."* He was then ordered to never mention the incident, that as far as he was concerned, it never happened.[2]

Jacobs remained silent for eighteen years before going public. When producers from the *Sightings* program and the Sci Fi Channel attempted to verify his story, the air force not only denied the incident but also denied that Jacobs was even stationed at Vandenberg. All his military records had disappeared.

Nevertheless, the *Sightings* producers did manage to authenticate his story. They were able to locate Major F. J. Mansmann, Jacobs's direct superior, who confirmed in writing everything that Jacobs said. Jacobs, however, had his own proof. In his archives, he had footage of the telescope being delivered to Big Sur, which clearly shows him and his team assembling it and filming the missile launch.

So it appears that the government is not only covering up the fact that UFOs exist, but to ensure secrecy, they can also undermine the credibility of any witness by making his credentials and records disappear. And it would appear they have done this on more than one occasion. But the issue here is that a UFO zapped an Atlas missile right out of the sky. Why?

A few years later, UFOs paid a visit to two separate missile sites at Malmstrom Air Force Base in Montana. During the early morning hours of March 16, 1967, Robert Salas, deputy crew commander of Oscar Flight Launch Control Center, was on duty in the underground command module when he received a call from security police topside about UFOs flying over the area. He didn't take it seriously at first, but five minutes later, the guard called back saying that a glowing red disc-shaped object was now hovering just outside the front gate. Salas woke his commander, who was on his scheduled sleep period, and began to brief him. Suddenly, all the missiles under their command began to shut down. After the UFO took off, the systems came back online; however, the missiles had been rendered useless. At about eight thirty that morning, it happened again. All the missiles shut down at Echo Flight Launch Control Center, twenty miles to the northwest.

There was no explanation for the missile shutdown because there was absolutely no way to switch them off. Even if there had been a problem with one, it would not have affected others because they operated independently of each other. A complete diagnostic was performed, but nothing was found that could account for what happened. One theory was that a powerful electromagnetic field might have been responsible. However, a thorough investigation turned up no evidence of anything that could possibly be the source of such a field, unless, of course, you wish to consider the UFO.[3] In 1975, UFOs visited other strategic missile sites along the Canadian border: Wurtsmith Air Force Base in Michigan, Loring Air Force Base in Maine, and Minot Air Force Base in North Dakota. So it seems that UFOs have the capability to neutralize our nuclear weapons systems wherever, and whenever, they choose; they have even disabled the weapons systems of military aircraft in pursuit of them.

So what is the reason behind these incidents? Are they trying to tell us something? Are we being warned of the dangerous power we now hold in our hands? Are they telling us to clean up our act before they shut down more than our guided missiles? One message they did convey was the fact that they have the power to render us helpless.

Let us assume they could neutralize every nuclear weapon on the planet. It would be one way to prevent us from annihilating ourselves in a nuclear holocaust. But I would assume that from their perspective, it would be pointless. They cannot develop our wisdom for us; that is something we must do ourselves. We need to learn the futility of war and how stupid it is.

It is up to us to begin trusting each other, to disarm our nuclear weapons, and to learn to live in peace.

Perhaps we are getting the message. We saw the breakup of the Soviet Union and the tearing down of the Berlin Wall; with no more Iron Curtain, we actually began disarming many of our nuclear weapons. This was a positive sign. However, the transition to a democratic Russia has not been easy; it is not a change that can be switched on overnight. Many aspects require a more gradual transition, and hopefully they will make it.

There are, however, other countries seeking to become dominant world powers, and their development of nuclear programs poses a new threat to the world. Is it just a coincidence that at the turn of the millennium, mass UFO sightings suddenly began making the news in China and India? And now we have North Korea and Iran to worry about. How long will it be before ETs provide them with the same sort of demonstration they exhibited in the United States and the Soviet Union, assuming, of course, they haven't done so already.

Nowhere in history is there evidence of a technological boom such as we have experienced in our lifetime. Now it seems that someone has put his foot on our brake pedal; we are rolling to a standstill. NASA has suffered drastic cuts in funding thanks to Congress. Sure, we are sending unmanned spacecraft to Mars and to the outer planets, and the knowledge they have gathered is phenomenal. But when was the last time we went to the moon? Doesn't it stand to reason that the more we go there, the sooner we will develop the means to do it faster and more efficiently? How much longer will it be before we resume such missions? How long will it be before we send a manned mission to Mars?

Not to knock the importance of what robotic probes have accomplished, but they have their limitations. Only man can determine the feasibility of developing a colony on Mars. Given the limitations of the little robotic vehicles that cost many millions of dollars to send there, they can only move so fast, travel so far, and scoop out soil samples close to the surface. Due to space limitation, the onboard system that analyzes the samples can only do so much. It will take human beings to dig deeper into the ground to see what is really there. It will take human beings to perform a more detailed analysis of soil samples and to explore farther into the mountains, valleys, and canyons. It could be centuries before we develop machines capable of doing the job as effectively as man does. Before we can reach the stars, we need to get our feet wet in our own backyard. So why are we restricting funds for NASA? Could the ETs be tightening the reins of progress because our technology has outdistanced our wisdom to use it wisely?

It was important to keep wisdom in balance with technical evolution. The logical thing would have been to let us progress slowly, in small increments, giving us a chance to reflect on our accomplishments. This way, we would have maintained better stability. However, it seems that time is a critical factor. If our survival hinges on achieving interstellar space travel by the year 3000, it will take several centuries for travel among the stars to become routine, so we would have had to begin developing it by the twentieth century.

For almost six thousand years, we progressed socially, but not on a technological level; major advancement did not begin to manifest until the nineteenth century. Our development of technology was beginning to progress, but not fast enough. If we did not reach the moon by the middle of the twentieth century, situations could have arisen to delay or even cripple our progress indefinitely, and we might not achieve the capability to reach the stars in time.

And situations did arise—devastating seismic and weather activity, terrorism, and a worldwide economic crisis! In 2004, the Indian Ocean tsunami made an impact on the economy of many countries. That same year, the United States felt the impact from hurricanes Charley, Frances, Ivan, and Jeanne—and in 2005, from Katrina, Rita, and Wilma. Perhaps the aliens knew these were cyclical situations that occur at regular intervals on our planet. And perhaps they knew that religion would inevitably spawn fanatics that would distort doctrinal teachings to fit their own radical beliefs, such as many extremists are now doing. A good example is the 9/11 attack on the World Trade Center and the Pentagon. This has taxed financial and industrial resources worldwide, and we don't know how long it will continue. The cost of dealing with these situations is bound to have a serious impact on our progress.

So there was no choice but to let us proceed uninhibited for as long as it took to achieve this goal, and it upset the balance. As soon as we learned how to split the atom, the very first thing we did was create a weapon that could cause our own annihilation and use it in war against another nation—even though its effect in ending the war made it seem justifiable.

By the middle of the twentieth century, we made it to the moon. We were beginning to grasp the basics, but the balance between wisdom and technology was completely out of sync—our science had overtaken us. This was never more evident than during the Cold War, when there were enough nuclear weapons stockpiled to destroy the world a hundred times over. Fortunately, it seems we came to our senses in time to prevent total nuclear annihilation, but I suspect there may have been some alien involvement on this issue. We had moved too far too fast, and things were getting out of control. To get a handle on the situation, the ETs may have initiated contact, and the signal for it may have come in 1952, when UFOs invaded the restricted air space over Washington, DC. They may have offered a small bit of technology in return for keeping nuclear weapons in check. Although the United States and Russia continued to stockpile them, they were never used. But to have abandoned them out of the blue would have aroused suspicion among government officials in both countries, who did not know what was going on behind the scenes, and it could have resulted in governmental instability.

The nuclear situation, however, was only part of the problem. During this same period, we succeeded in polluting much of our land, our water supplies, and our atmosphere with carcinogens and toxic chemicals. We have been (and still are) producing nuclear energy with no way to dispose of its waste. Now we are polluting the space around our planet with thousands of pieces of space junk, much of which will be trapped in orbit for decades and even centuries. Whenever a space shuttle or a satellite rocket is launched, NASA carefully has to work out the coordinates to prevent each mission from running into this gauntlet of debris.

For two decades, NASA has been forced to postpone and scrap some major projects due to lack of funding, and things have gotten worse since 9/11. So our progress in space, as far as manned exploration, has been stifled. We have to wonder where we would now be had we not made it to the moon when we did. It has been decades since our last visit, and manned missions are now limited to Earth's orbit.

But the space program has experienced other problems; many Mars missions between the United States and Russia have ended in failure. The only one that NASA could explain was the Mars Climate Orbiter, which crashed into the Red Planet in September of 1999. It was the result of human error: scientists became confused between English and metric measurements. What happened to the others, however, is still somewhat of a mystery.

In 1993, the Mars Observer allegedly disappeared while en route to the Red Planet. NASA believes an explosion occurred aboard the craft. On December 3, 1999, communication was lost with the Mars Polar Lander as it entered the Martian atmosphere. The fate of this craft remains unknown. Many of Russia's Mars missions ended in failure when the rockets exploded on the launch pad or during launch. Five malfunctioned in Earth's orbit, and six failed on their way to or after reaching the Red Planet. What happened to their Phobos 2 mission, however, generated a lot of suspicion among conspiracy freaks who believed aliens destroyed it.

On March 25, 1989, when the spacecraft was photographing the Martian moon Phobos, the last picture transmitted back to Earth showed what appeared to be a huge cylinder-shaped object in front of the craft just moments before the screen went blank. That was the last the Russians heard from their spacecraft.[4] Some claim that the object was an alien mother ship and say that it destroyed the Russian spacecraft, questioning whether NASA is covering up the fact that some of their failed Mars missions met a similar fate.

I suppose it is possible, but I rather doubt it. An article in the October 19, 1989, issue of *Nature* claims that Phobos 2 was spinning, which could have resulted from a computer malfunction or from an impact with an unknown object. It is possible that a small meteoroid struck the spacecraft, knocking the systems off-line and sending it spinning. What looks like a cylindrical object could very well be an anomaly caused by electronics in the system. Other photos taken just prior to the last one showed many similar anomalies. So although it may look suspicious, there is no evidence that aliens are sabotaging our Mars programs. If such subversive activity is in play, it is being covered up very well. If there really is alien involvement, I am more inclined to think it would be related to the cutbacks in funding.

When Congress cut the funds to SETI (the Search for Extraterrestrial Intelligence), the picture they painted was that it was a senseless project. They felt the money could be put to better use on Earth. SETI started out as a NASA project, and I tried to reason why they would be looking for intelligent life in radio signals from space if it were already here in our backyard. Was this the real reason their funding was cut?

There are people who still believe in SETI and keep the project going through donations and private funding. Nevertheless, if they do happen to pick up an intelligent signal, it probably would have originated from normal communications that leaked out into the cosmos from some distant planet, just as our own television and radio signals drift off into space. The idea that a radio signal may have been intentionally directed at us is rather unlikely since it probably would have been sent hundreds or even thousands of years before we even discovered electricity, and they would have had no way of knowing that we were even here.

Radio waves travel at the speed of light, 186,000 miles per second. To send a message to someone in the nearest star system, Alpha Centauri, which is 4.2 light-years distant, the signal would take 4.2 years to get there. However, the probability of an intelligent civilization existing that close seems very remote; it is more likely to be hundreds or thousands of light-years distant. So, any radio signal intentionally directed at us would probably take hundreds or even thousands of years to reach Earth. If we decided to respond, it would require the same amount of time for our signal to reach them, and in all probability, by then, we will have achieved the technology to visit them personally long before our transmission would get there. And the same could be said for them. SETI astronomers are simply hoping to detect a signal that was transmitted by an intelligent civilization as proof that we are not alone in the universe.

Logically, we might expect that any extraterrestrial civilization capable of interstellar travel would have developed an advanced method of communication that would allow them to maintain normal contact over vast cosmic distances. And such methods, whatever they might be, would have to use something other than the standard communication technology we use today. One possibility is light. Like the scientists who accelerated light pulses three hundred times the speed of light, it might eventually prove to be a viable method for interstellar communication. Unless SETI can develop that kind of technology, the odds are that it will probably be a very long time before they ever pick up anything.

If I am right, stifling our progress in space at this point probably would seal our fate. Even if we maintain the level of progress of the past fifty years, it will still take centuries before we develop the technology needed to reach the stars and find other worlds capable of supporting human life. If we are to survive, it is essential that we continue to advance. Had we continued going to the moon, we would be that much closer to developing a faster and more efficient way to do it, and we probably would not be far away from sending a manned expedition to Mars. How long we are held back may make a difference in whether or not we survive. Necessity is the mother of invention, and until we again realize that necessity, our progress will remain stagnant.

There is some evidence that behind the scenes, things may be more optimistic than we think. It is possible that at places like Area 51, we are developing, or maybe already have developed, technologies far advanced from those currently used by NASA. NASA cannot be cut out of the picture because it would be too obvious: the government would need it as a PR vehicle to draw attention away from what is going on behind the scenes. If this is the case, then they are letting it exist on a shoestring budget. The reality check is that space exploration has to happen, and it will happen; the growing population of Earth demands it. There is no place left to go except into space, and once we take the steps, the gains will be forthcoming.

Where would we be if Columbus never left Spain in search of a western approach to India? If it hadn't been Columbus, eventually it would have been someone else—it had to happen. In light of the current situation, it is hard to believe that those in power are really that naive. Surely they realize the importance of space exploration and the future benefits it will yield, so it is difficult to believe that they are sitting on their hands. It may be some time before we learn what they are doing, but the evidence suggests they are doing more than developing stealth aircraft. If the events that occurred in Huffman, Texas, and Rendlesham Forest are any indication, they are experimenting with an entirely new dimension of technology, which could mean that behind the scenes, we are making the necessary advancements to secure our future.

But UFOs disabling missile systems in Russia and the United States and shooting beams that disabled an Atlas missile over the Pacific presents a rather ominous picture. What else might they have done along these lines that we don't know about? What kind of message are they sending us?

The idea that our progress is being stifled by the same beings responsible for accelerating our evolution may seem paradoxical, but it happened when they stifled the progress of Noah's descendants after the flood. Regardless of your perspective, you cannot deny the rapid technological acceleration we experienced during the first half of the twentieth century, at least until we made several trips to the moon. Then, just when we were beginning to make real headway, we were halted in midstream—just like the Tower of Babel.

Notes

1. Russian ICBMs neutralized
    "Report That UFOs Neutralized Soviet Missiles." *Encounters*
    segment. FOX. WPTV. West Palm Beach.

2. UFO zaps guided missile
    "Deliberate Deception", *Sightings* segment, SciFi (now Syfy)

3. US missiles neutralized
    Out of the Blue. Documentary. Dir. James Fox/Tim Coleman. Sci
    Fi (now Syfy).

4. The disappearance of Phobos 2
    Web link:
    www.marsnews.com/news/20020920-phobos2images.html

Chapter 24

THE NEW INDOCTRINATION

D uring NASA's inception, one aspect of space exploration that came under consideration was the possibility of encountering other life-forms. Whether it be microbes found in the soil of another planet or an encounter with intelligent beings, it raised many questions. How would we react to an encounter with an intelligent species? What would be proper protocol in dealing with such a situation? What impact might it have on the cultural values of our civilization? In order to gain a better perspective of these and other issues involving space exploration, NASA commissioned the Brookings Institute in Washington, DC, to do a study in order to determine proper guidelines by which they might proceed. By picking the brains of the best minds in the world, policies could then be determined and established in accordance with their findings.

But if contact had been established in the late 1940s or early 1950s, why conduct a study to learn what to do after the fact—would it not be superfluous? Or was this facet of the study actually done to determine what effect it would have on the public if the truth about UFOs was revealed?

According to the Brookings report, the sudden realization that we were not alone might have a profound impact on our civilization. On page 215 of their report titled "Peaceful Space Activities for Human Affairs," they acknowledge the possibility that other intelligent life may exist in space:

Artifacts left at some point in time by these life forms might possibly be discovered through our space activities on the Moon, Mars, or Venus.

And near the bottom of the page, it reads as follows:

Anthropological files contain many examples of societies, sure of their place in the universe, which have disintegrated when they had to associate with previously unfamiliar societies espousing different ideas and different ways: others that survived such an experience usually did so by paying the price of changes in values and attitudes and behavior.

They are saying that many primitive cultures were ultimately affected through contact with higher levels of civilization, and they cite the impact it had on their traditional values and beliefs, which when narrowed down to the bottom line, means religion. Considering possible consequences on our own civilization, they advise that further study is needed to provide more insight regarding the adjustments we might be required to make.

And on page 216:

How might such information, under what circumstances, be presented to or withheld from the public for what ends? What might be the role of the discovering scientists and other decision makers regarding the fact of discovery?

This suggests that the discovery of extraterrestrial life might be withheld from the public and questions the motives of those associated with making this decision. However, the great minds that compiled this information suggest the greatest impact might be on the scientific community.

Near the bottom of page 225:

It has been speculated that of all groups, scientists and engineers might be the most devastated by the discovery of relatively superior creatures

since these professions are most clearly associated with the mastery of
nature, rather than with the understanding and expression of man.

Now if the same study were conducted today, would they still feel our societal structure would be threatened by the revelation that we are not alone? I think not. It may have been so fifty years ago, but we have since evolved considerably in our expectations regarding space exploration and even contact with ETs. With the discovery of over five hundred extrasolar planets revolving around other stars in the galaxy, we are now focused on finding one like Earth that will support life, and we are more open to the possibility that other intelligent life may be out there.

Remember how much attention was focused on the first Apollo moon landing? People around the world were glued to their television sets, and the event dominated the news for weeks. Media coverage continued in the following missions as viewers watched the astronauts set up experiments, collect rock samples, and ride around in their LEM (lunar excursion module). However, in subsequent years, as it became more routine, live coverage dwindled, as did the public's interest. Even with improved communications and cameras providing sharper color images, fewer people were tuning in. I think that accurately reflects how most people today would be affected by the discovery of intelligent alien life. Of course, the media blitz would be overwhelming at first, but I doubt it would turn the world upside down. Just like the Apollo moon landings, once the novelty wore off, people would continue their normal routine of getting up in the morning, going to work, and earning a living. It seems that the general attitude today is not so much the question of *whether* we discover other intelligent life in space but *when*. The only thing that might have a devastating impact would be a discovery that challenged fundamental religious beliefs; that could create serious problems, and it might be the reason for government silence. If this is the case, as I suspect it is, we will need to make an adjustment in our beliefs before we will be able to accept the truth.

Some may look back to when prayer was first eliminated in public schools as part of this process—a means of conforming the younger generation. But I disagree. Prayer is not religion. I believe prayer or meditation creates a positive influence, beneficial to both mind and body. No. I think the primary goal is to reshape the mental image most people currently have of religion and the deity into a more realistic view. A few bishops are now questioning the validity of certain miracles like the Immaculate Conception. And after eight hundred years, the Catholic Church has eliminated all references to the state of limbo. This could be a sign that logic and common sense are beginning to take root.

The Religion Factor
Most people are prepared to accept the fact that extraterrestrials may be visiting Earth but are unprepared psychologically to deal with the impact it will have on their religious convictions *if the whole truth* were known. This is due to organized religion. Too many religions have divided people with diversified beliefs, many of which conflict with each other, and this may be something the ETs had hoped to avoid. After Christ's time, organized religion experienced rapid growth and expansion, and it has mushroomed out of proportion. The spin-off of so many religions and cults has created problems that can only be resolved by having mankind conform to a more unified and realistic ideology.

No one can deny the fact that religion is the basis of many problems that exist in the world today. The violence that plagued Northern Ireland was nothing more than a war between factions of Protestants and Catholics. And when you take a good close look at what has happened in the former Yugoslavia, it is nothing more than one religious or ethnic group claiming superiority over another. The sectarian violence and killing in Iraq is based on nothing more than a difference of religious beliefs; and in the Holy Land, Jews and Muslims seem unable or unwilling to come to terms with each other. There are extremists who refuse to let any kind of peace process evolve. Then there is the radical Muslim element who considers themselves superior. They believe that anyone who is not a Muslim is an infidel and therefore should be killed. The epitome of this fanatic nonsense is exemplified in Osama bin Laden's disciples who crashed jet airliners into the World Trade Center and the Pentagon. They had been brainwashed into believing that murdering innocent men, women, and children would bring them glory in the eyes of Allah—and the higher the body count, the greater the glory. Their reward in the afterlife would supposedly be seventy-two virgins. These religious nuts have sadistically distorted the teachings of their own religion. They will never rise above their hatred and accept people for who they are and learn to live in peace.

Then there are the cults, many of which are scams to bilk money and property from gullible people. Some cult leaders use God in a manipulative way to brainwash people into accepting a variety of distorted, misguided, radical, militant, and antisocial beliefs, and they are time bombs just waiting to go off. We have seen it in Guyana with Jim Jones. We have seen it in Waco, Texas, with David Koresh and the Branch Davidians. We have seen it with Marshall Applewhite, who convinced his Heaven's Gate cult followers to commit suicide with the belief that their spirits would be transported to a UFO hiding behind the Hale-Bopp Comet. This is all religious-oriented mind control. How could a group of people be persuaded to take their own lives unless they had let themselves become brainwashed with the off-the-wall beliefs of some wacky fanatic?

It is likely that what the aliens revealed (assuming, of course, contact has been made) was shocking, even to the hard-nosed military brass, and they realized the public was not prepared to deal with the facts at that time. To suddenly be told that aliens have been (or were about to begin) abducting people for the purpose of conducting genetic experiments, or that (theoretically) the Lord was really an astronaut from another world, would have had serious repercussions in the religious community and could have led to more serious problems. It had to be kept quiet.

Assuming this is the case, the truth will have to come out eventually. The idea that aliens had manifested themselves as God in biblical times and (theoretically) genetically engineered human beings like Adam, Isaac, and Samson, etc., would have created big problems, especially when it came to Christ. Religious leaders would never have tolerated such claims, for they would have threatened the powers of the religious hierarchy. Schisms would have developed between those willing to accept the truth and those who couldn't, and the resulting chaos could have caused serious world problems. Therefore, it was necessary to formulate a plan to enlighten the public without creating the turmoil.

So it appears that the major problem may not have been UFOs but rather how to handle the public. They had to be educated—and it would take time—a gradual process of indoctrination that could conceivably take up to a century. Just as it was with the Israelites in the desert, it is up to the government to condition the minds of the people into gradually letting go of certain fundamental ideas that have been ingrained into their minds from childhood and accepting the fact that some things might actually be different from what they were taught to believe. If Christ returns in a spaceship, the public will have to be prepared for it. Therefore, it is only logical that their efforts will be directed toward the younger generation.

The aliens actually started the ball rolling. They began building our awareness of them with the frequent appearance of their ships in our skies. In 1952, they visited Washington, DC, and invaded the restricted air space over the US Capitol Building and the White House. That incident seemed to indicate that they were making a statement.

The DC invasion occurred on two consecutive weekends, the nights of July 19 and 26, when UFOs flew over the Capitol and the White House. Airline pilots sighted them visually, and they were tracked by radar at Washington National Airport and at Andrews Air Force Base. Jets were scrambled to intercept the objects, but when they arrived in the area, the objects flew off the radarscopes. When the jets returned to base, the objects returned to DC, and the jets were scrambled again. It was as if they were playing a game of cat and mouse; every time the jets arrived back in the area, the UFOs would take off. However, during one of the intercept missions, the objects did not disappear so quickly; one fighter pilot became a little nervous when some of them actually encircled his plane before streaking off into the night.

This all happened when Bolling Air Force Base, the closest base to DC, was temporarily closed for runway repairs and its jets moved to New Castle Air Force Base in Delaware.[1] This suggests that the ETs knew exactly what they were doing and did it at the most opportune time. They didn't pick any city at random, like London, Paris, Rome, Moscow, Los Angeles, Chicago, or New York City. No. They picked the capital of the most powerful nation on Earth, the city where the most influential and powerful people in the country and the world meet. So it would appear that they knew the significance of Washington, DC. This may very well have been their signal to the government that they needed to talk.

We can theorize that a panel comprised of scientists and high-ranking military and intelligence officials was established to deal with the situation. In fact, if the MJ-12 documents are any indication, such a group may have been created five years earlier because of the Roswell incident. It is likely they would have had almost absolute power and not been answerable to anyone except, maybe, the president. With this power, they could dictate their own policies and literally become a secret government within the government. As presidents came and went, this group would remain, and depending on the political and philosophical views of the president in office, it would be at their discretion what they chose to tell him—or not tell him.

However, they would bear the responsibility of preparing the public to deal with the religious implications. It had to be gradual. A certain degree of influence would have to be exerted on each new generation to become a little more open-minded than the last. People would have to be gently swayed into accepting the UFO reality. The next step would be to break the news that (theoretically) ETs were responsible for creating the deity image, and that religion has greatly distorted our concept of this deity.

Now again, assuming this is the case, it requires channeling the many diversified religions and their perception of God into a global compatibility. Belief systems have to be manipulated to eliminate the prejudice religions have created over the centuries by promoting less-conflicting ideas. Anyone keeping current on world affairs is aware that the European Union is already pushing the idea of a worldwide or unified religion.

So the government is in a difficult situation; they need to tell us the truth, yet they can't tell us anything—at least for the moment. But they do have to prepare us. Desensitizing people to the issues through disinformation is one way. Maintaining the UFO controversy generates publicity from all angles: skeptics, believers, and crackpots. Theories proposing an extraterrestrial link to the deity probably would not be taken seriously at first, but as more information is leaked out, more people will gradually come to realize that there just might be something to it. Many are now beginning to make the connection. The majority, however, will take a little longer. As the older generation dies off, so will old traditions, beliefs, and attitudes. It is the younger generation that will gradually open up to the issues and accept the truth.

After decades of being bombarded with all kinds of stories and theories ranging from scientific evaluations by experts to the most bizarre claims of crackpots, we have gradually gained a better perspective of the issues, and our expectations of encounters with extraterrestrials has, likewise, matured. This is reflected in movies like *Close Encounters of the Third Kind* and *E.T.: The Extra-Terrestrial,* which served to endear us to the extraterrestrial image. The TV series *Star Trek* brought us into the twenty-fourth century without generating the curiosity, the tension, or the apprehension that would likely be involved with making first contact, but rather by working side by side with people of different alien races in the course of daily routine. Unlike the run-of-the-mill sci-fi films and programs filled with their action-packed, high adventure, and horror aspects, we were given a whole new perspective of the alien image besides the slimy bug-eyed green monster. We are gradually becoming less inhibited because now it is science more than science fiction influencing our views. We are beginning to realize that much of yesterday's science fiction is today's science fact, and what is science fiction today may be reality tomorrow. Yet the fact remains that until man sheds the bias created by his many diversified religions, his prospects for both peace and progress remain grim. So it is only logical that the next phase of the plan will be a gradual indoctrination designed to open our eyes and our minds to the real facts.

Notes

1.   UFOs over DC in 1952
      "UFOs: Then and Now? Cause For Alarm." *UFO Files*. Prod.
      Joshua Alper. THC.

Chapter 25

COUNTDOWN

As you can see, the UFO mystery is an extremely complex jigsaw puzzle. It's pieces are varied and many, and the complete picture cannot be seen until all pieces have been fitted into place. I believe that many crucial pieces have been overlooked simply because they have not been recognized as even being a part of the puzzle.

I have presented evidence that the government is well aware of the fact that UFOs exist and is keeping the facts from the public. And I have presented evidence linking the Lord of the Bible directly to the technology of flying machines. The implication is that he and his angels are physical beings from another world, and if the commandments he gave to Moses are any indication, his goal is a noble one. Although the first two commandments tell us we should not worship false gods or take his name in vain, in actuality, they have nothing to do with the others. The other commandments represent solid moral and ethical values and if we all followed them, the world would be a much better place than it is today.

It could be that the first two commandments were simply meant to show man the futility of believing that any image he creates out of wood, stone, or metal has magical, mystical, or supernatural powers. They are what they are: pieces of wood, stone, and metal. But I think they were intended to be a controlling factor over the Hebrews during their forty-years in the desert. Because the Lord was physically present and personally involved at the time, it was important to the project that they accept him as their leader or god figure. However, I don't think he was actually trying to promote himself as God; I think that is a perspective that may have evolved on its own through centuries of oral tradition and probably had its roots in the stories of Moses.

Today, it is difficult for people to associate the Bible with UFOs because it contradicts what organized religion has conditioned them to believe. What they fail to understand is that the scriptures are basically an interpretation of what someone else interpreted of someone else's interpretation of events that occurred long before that person's time, and it is highly likely that much of the original meaning was altered through all these translations. However, when you examine the scriptures with logic and common sense, it is difficult to ignore the many technological implications. In ancient times, such things would have been perceived as miracles because the people had no technology of their own with which to make a comparison. But today we have that advantage. We know about electricity and how it can be used to create light plus its many other applications. We know about machines, computers, and spaceships, and it is easier for us to recognize the technological aspects. In 1950, a UFO was commonly known as a flying saucer; in the Bible, it is described as the "glory of the Lord." In 1950, a laser was depicted as a death ray or a Buck Rogers ray gun; in the Bible, it is described as *fire coming out from the Lord*. Although the descriptions differ according to how they were perceived, the similarities are obvious.

In the Bible, we see suggestions of flying craft, lasers, teleportation, and a host of other technologies. We see situations alluding to genetic engineering, the creation of hybrids, and a project of accelerated evolution. We see that the first attempt to create a new race ended in failure, and that their majority had to be eliminated. We see where a second attempt was successful but necessitated separating them from the remnants of the first race for several centuries to ensure their genetic integrity as they grew into a nation. Then we see how they were isolated for a generation and indoctrinated with improved moral and ethical values before being delivered into their Promised Land, and we see that the Lord had revealed this plan to Abraham five hundred years in advance.

The scenario I have presented is based on the sequence of events as they currently appear in the Bible and the possibility that they actually occurred. Whether the biblical events are truth or fiction is something we may never know for certain. However, organized religion has adapted them to fit supernatural and mystical beliefs in order to control the minds of the masses, and we see how it has created the prejudices responsible for many of the world's problems. Religion has evolved on its own to the point where people have been conditioned in too many diversified beliefs. Every country in the world has its own set of laws, rules, customs, and religious values. In most cases, a conflict of religious beliefs has bred prejudice, contempt, and hatred among the different peoples of the world. It has led to violence and wars over territorial boundaries and cultural differences, many of which are based on religion. It has reached the point where many self-righteous fanatics have gained power and are slaughtering people with different beliefs under the guise of "ethnic cleansing" to justify their actions.

Efforts are currently under way to create a New World Order. One of the first steps (already in progress) is uniting all the European countries into a United States of Europe, and it is a plan designed to encompass the entire world. And the European Union is currently exerting influence on the religious community to join into a worldwide union or a common religion. This will not happen overnight, but the odds are that within the next two or three generations, it could be a reality.

Depending on the ethics and political motives of the world's leaders, or leader, as it may eventually come to be, it could turn out to be a productive move that benefits everyone. Once man has shed the prejudices he created with his religions, he will gain the wisdom needed to deal with his future. On the other hand, if such a world leader turns out to be the Antichrist, he could manipulate religious doctrine to set himself up as God, and if that happens, we are all in trouble.

Meanwhile, the decadence that originated in the first race has steadily regained its strength and has again exceeded the limits of acceptability. It is now being exploited and even flaunted, and the moral decline is obvious. Something must be done before further progress will be realized. Is it just a coincidence that within the last three decades, a plague has been unleashed on the world in the form of the HIV virus, not to mention mad cow disease, Ebola, West Nile virus, bird flu, swine flu, and a host of others?

◆◆◆◆◆

The evidence suggests that some form of communication or dialogue may have been established with at least one alien race, and it is likely that other major powers may also be involved. If aliens are initiating changes in humanity to further their project, they are probably doing it all over the world. If things proceed as I expect, events will occur, possibly in this millennium, that will really open our eyes.

The most significant will be the return of Christ, assuming that he will return. It will probably destroy the illusions people have of their religion, but most will accept the reality of the situation, especially if his army destroys those who rise up against the Holy Land with powerful weapons. Such action will now be recognized for what it really is—a demonstration of firepower, not some kind of miracle.

If what the angel told the apostles at Christ's ascension about his returning is true, we can expect him to beam down in a cloud on the Mount of Olives. But can you imagine the media circus that would create? How will he cope with all the news teams trying to get an interview? I can just picture reporters shoving cameras and microphones in his face: "Mr. Christ ... Mr. Christ ... how long did it take you to make the trip? ... Mr. Christ ... Mr. Christ ... what planet are you from? ... What's it like there? ... Mr. Christ, what are your plans here on Earth?"

Whether he lands in a spaceship or beams down in a cloud or flash of light, the technological aspect of such an entrance is sure to diminish his deity status. So what will people actually think? Will they believe it is really him? Will he have physically aged in two thousand years? How will he be dressed? Will he wear a peasant's robe such as he did two thousand years ago? Will he dress in the style of current times in order to blend in?

Or will he wear clothing more conducive to that of a space traveler? And what language will he speak? Will it be ancient Hebrew or Aramaic, or will he be well versed in English? Although they may be interesting topics to debate, Christ's wardrobe and language are not important issues. The most important issue is how prepared we will be psychologically.

If Christ were to arrive tomorrow, it is doubtful that most people would believe it was really him—they are not prepared mentally to deal with it. The only way they have ever pictured Christ is from the images depicted in religious paintings: long hair, a beard, and clad in the robe of a peasant. However, these are only presumed images; nobody today knows what he looks like. If he were to suddenly step out of a cloud clean-shaven, with short hair and wearing a business suit, how many could psychologically accept that image? If he is to return within this millennium, or the next, it would seem that major psychological preparation is needed—and soon.

It is my belief that if and when he comes, most people will be aware of the fact that it will be in a spaceship. I am not quite certain as to how it will happen, whether it will be through information revealed through abductees, disinformation, documentary films promoting the UFO/deity connection, or maybe a combination of all, but the idea will somehow be promoted so that when the time comes, it will not be too much of a shock.

The Countdown

Should Christ return, the final countdown will begin when he does. Part of his agenda will probably be to reprogram our values. For the project to succeed, we must learn how to live in peace. The wars that were necessary to boost our technology will have to cease, and we will need to reapply our knowledge to more positive and productive pursuits. We will have to be psychologically reprogrammed into adopting new and positive attitudes toward progress and our fellow man.

Our wisdom is still out of sync with our technology, and the abductions may be an indication that genetic experiments are still being conducted in an attempt to bring everything into balance. But what about the hybrid fetuses removed from the wombs of the women they inseminated? For what purpose were they created? Will they play an important role in future events, or are they part of the ongoing process to improve and upgrade our own genetic structure? Until we can learn more about them, this is one piece of the UFO puzzle that is still shrouded in mystery.

One possibility to consider is that there may be hybrids walking among us today. The ETs would surely know enough about us to select women who are married or in a situation where their pregnancies would not come under suspicion. To ensure complete anonymity of the children, these women would most likely be mentally conditioned to block any memory of their abduction experience—even under the most intense regressive hypnosis. There have been many men throughout history who seem to have possessed knowledge and insight far beyond their time, such as Archimedes, Heron, Copernicus, Leonardo da Vinci, and Galileo, to name a few. If aliens have been speeding up our evolution, it is only logical that they would periodically create hybrids with genius qualities necessary to give man a boost over the next hurdle. We should ask ourselves if it is just a coincidence that the technologies we depend on today—electric power, communications, transportation, and aerospace technology—were all introduced by men of the same era: Thomas Edison (1847–1931), Henry Ford (1863–1947), Alexander Graham Bell (1847–1922), and Wilbur and Orville Wright (1867–1955 and 1871–1948, respectively). And what about one of the greatest scientific minds of all time, Albert Einstein (1879–1955)? And let us not forget Nikola Tesla (1856–1943) whose ideas in some ways were far superior to those of Edison. These great men were all alive in 1900, at the dawn of the twentieth century. Might any or all of them have been genetically engineered hybrids created to boost our progress and get us into space *at the precise the time it was needed?* And is it a coincidence that there also were other men involved with these same inventions at the same time? Edison, Ford, Bell, and the Wright brothers just happened to come out on top, but had any of them failed, there were others ready to step in and take their place. Had the development of these technologies not taken place when they did, we would not yet have put a man in space, let alone on the moon.

Now it appears our progress is being stifled. The negative qualities of the first race have again risen to dominance, and we have acquired the technology to cause our own annihilation. Together, these factors are a dangerous combination. I think most will agree that we lack sufficient wisdom to handle the technology we have already developed.

Most of the rivers we swam in as children are now polluted with industrial contaminants; their waters are no longer suitable for swimming, let alone drinking. The illegal burying of chemical waste products over the past three decades has risen up to haunt us. Many of the containers have rotted and rusted away, their contents filtering through the ground and polluting the well water of millions of people throughout the country. We have also come to rely on nuclear power to provide our homes with energy, but we have not yet developed a method to dispose of its waste. Unless we come up with a decent plan soon, it will continue to pile up and present a major problem for our children and grandchildren. From the alien's perspective, our technology has overtaken us, and we have to be slowed down until we put things right.

It has been decades since we went to the moon. Although NASA would like to resume such missions around 2020, as a nation leading the world in technological advancement, our space program should have continued to excel in that direction. We may never live to know the benefits we could have gained if we had only continued moving forward. What would it be like today if, after Edison invented the electric light, after Bell invented the telephone, after Ford built the first horseless carriage, these projects were abandoned because everyone thought they were impractical? In this respect, we can see how the suppression of progress back then would have affected us today. If aliens are responsible for us having reached our current level of achievement, it is likely they are also responsible for our current stagnation. Even if we are developing a completely new dimension of technology at places like Area 51, it doesn't necessarily mean we are out of the woods. As to how long it will be before we shift back into high gear will probably depend on us.

The end will surely come in 4.5 billion years, when the sun swallows up the earth as it runs out of fuel and goes nova. It is also about this time that the Andromeda galaxy will collide with our own Milky Way galaxy. Because of the vast distances between stars, there will be fewer collisions than one might expect, but they will occur. The stellar matter and gasses they release will eventually combine to form new stars and new planets, and the cycle of life will go on. But life on Earth could be wiped out much sooner by a comet or asteroid. Billions of years ago, this same stellar debris built the substance of our world and brought with it the recipe for life. It is ironic that these same things could, in a brief cosmic moment, take it all away. It may not happen in our lifetime, but the chances are that it will happen sometime. We may not be around to face that situation, but our descendants will, and it is important that they develop the technology to survive. Whether they do or not may depend on how much wisdom we acquire collectively, as a race, in this century. If the human race continues to sink into the depths of iniquity, it may not be allowed to develop this knowledge. A race of beings roaming among the stars who are unable to wisely handle the technology at their disposal certainly would not be in anyone's best interest.

In some ways, it appears the ETs regard us in a manner somewhat similar to how we regard animals. There was a time when man had little respect for life. The buffalo nearly became extinct when riders of the first railroads indiscriminately used them for target practice. Today, we are appalled by such deeds, and our compassion for life, be it human or animal, seems to have been greatly enhanced.

Many people are now concerned for endangered species because of man's quest to exploit the resources of their habitats. Therefore, it is necessary on occasion to nurture and promote the breeding of certain species in captivity. Much care is taken not to let these creatures become too familiar with man, as it will only reduce their chances of survival when they are released back into the wild. So it has been the policy to avoid as much direct contact with them as possible—except when absolutely necessary.

Although often perceived as extremists, some environmentalist groups are fighting to preserve the natural habitats of endangered species so that they may continue to exist. It would appear that the alien's involvement with us is pretty much the same thing except that they are unable to prevent the disaster that will eventually destroy our habitat. The only thing they can do is try to prepare us to be able to save ourselves when the time comes. And just as we try to avoid contact with the animals, they have avoided any direct contact with us—except when absolutely necessary. Under normal circumstances, they probably would have ignored us until we began exploring the stars and had evolved to a technological level compatible with their own. However, because of the prevailing situation, it would appear that they have made an exception to the rule—just as we have done in extreme situations dealing with the preservation of endangered species.

Now, being compared to animals may seem like a rather crude analogy, but to the aliens, we may be as primitive to them as animals are to us. Our lack of understanding the messages in the crop circles, assuming of course that they are UFO related, is like the ancient Indians who created glyphs of sine wave patterns; they had no comprehension of their meaning, let alone their technological significance.

There may only be one or two thousand years left, which seems an eternity to us because we won't be around, but to the aliens, it is the final hour and the clock is ticking away. If their project is successful, we will overcome our prejudices and other inadequacies and gain much knowledge and wisdom over the next century. Then we should be released from the backyard of our own solar system, into the wondrous realm of the galaxy.

Until then, we should not ignore what is happening. We need to take a serious look at abductions, crop circles, and the relationship between UFOs and the deity. There is something going on, and the government, I am sure, is aware of what it is. But because of the many religions that man has contrived to fit his own individual beliefs, he has inhibited his ability to recognize the truth. Even if the aliens were to suddenly land and make the truth known, too many people absorbed in a myriad of dogmatic beliefs would still be unable to accept it. Therefore, it is only logical that a process of reprogramming is necessary. Perhaps the more appropriate term is "deprogramming." After all, we must shed the misconceptions and prejudices that we have allowed to influence our minds before we can move forward.

Over the last fifty years, we should have been able to determine whether UFOs are extraterrestrial spacecraft or some yet unknown natural phenomena. The fact that this basic question has not or cannot be answered is evidence that something is going on; surely we have the technological resources to make this determination. Logic and common sense say we have, or at least the government has. But *why* it is being kept secret is the real issue. The only logical reason is that the information would have a chaotic effect on the nation and the world.

I believe people are ready to accept the fact that we are being visited for whatever reason, but most are not prepared to deal with the impact it will have on their religious beliefs. Since religion plays a major role in most people's lives, to discover suddenly that it has all been an extraterrestrial sham could be devastating, and it would seem to be the only logical reason for a cover-up.

However, we are still left with unanswered questions: Why do some UFOs behave in a hostile manner? Why are alien/human hybrids being created? And where do the UFOs come from? Although speculative answers have been proposed regarding the first two questions, there isn't a clue as to the origin of these craft and their occupants. The information does indicate that they are solid metallic vehicles capable of maneuvers and speeds that defy human tolerance and understanding. The fact that our astronauts have also observed them in space tends to indicate they are from another world and possibly even another galaxy.

There also exists the possibility that they are from another dimension—one coexisting alongside our own. Such an idea is rather difficult to comprehend. What would it be like in a different dimension? All kinds of possibilities exist when it comes to the unknown, such as beings existing only in the form of energy, or of time being part of a continuum in which it may not even exist.

Another possibility that has been proposed is that the little greys are from the future and are what we will eventually evolve into. That idea, however, presents a paradox regarding the human-looking aliens; where are they from? Are they from a time less distant in the future than the greys, or are they from yet another world?

It is alleged that many of the first astronauts photographed and videotaped UFOs in space, such as John Glenn during the first Mercury mission and James McDivitt, Frank Borman, and Neil Armstrong during their Gemini missions. Photos of these objects have been plastered all over the Internet by UFO buffs who are absolutely certain they are alien spacecraft. However, NASA claims that they are either reflections of interior cabin lights, nearby satellites, or debris from their spacecraft, claiming that enthusiastic UFO believers are simply exploiting the photos. In this case, I am somewhat inclined to side with NASA. These astronauts have been questioned numerous times about the photos, and although they admit to having seen certain things, they never once suggested they were alien spacecraft.

However, video clips from shuttle missions have been presented in various documentaries of objects that were definitely not reflections, satellites, or spacecraft debris because they performed maneuvers that were obviously under intelligent control. And some of this footage even has NASA scientists baffled. In one clip, a rather large object just seemed to materialize out of nowhere above the earth's atmosphere and drift off into the distance.[1] On August 6, 2005, during Mission STS-114, the shuttle was traveling about eighteen thousand miles an hour when the camera captured an object that suddenly flew into the frame from out of nowhere and stopped. Actually, it appeared to have caught up to the shuttle; after a brief pause, it then reversed course and flew back in the direction from which it came.[2] There is absolutely no way this object can be described as a piece of shuttle debris, a satellite, or a reflection of an interior cabin light.

After seeing these videos, one is inclined to believe that UFOs are space-worthy vehicles and their occupants accomplished space travelers. So the avenue of least resistance would seem to be the interplanetary theory—that they are from another world and not from the future or another dimension, although we cannot completely rule out those possibilities.

Some organization within the government knows the truth, and I have presented a logical and viable reason for their secrecy. I will not be surprised by disinformation released in the near future alluding to the UFO/deity connection. Nor will I be surprised by more reports of abductees being shown scenes of apocalyptic destruction. At the turn of the millennium, I was not surprised by the flood of documentaries and movies about comets and asteroids colliding with the earth. It is a beginning—one way or another, we should eventually get the message.

I wish to reiterate that I am not necessarily denying the existence of God; I am merely presenting evidence suggesting that an alien technology was present in biblical times and operating under the guise of a deity. If anything suggests this, it is Ezekiel's encounter. I have put aside the mystical interpretations and all the supernatural innuendoes and examined the bare facts of the story without the embellished beliefs. I find that if the scriptures are accurate, at least in the context of what they claim took place, then a metallic flying craft did land near Ezekiel; he saw flashing and blinking lights; it had an engine that sounded like "rushing waters"; it had four landing pods; and there were five men on board, one of which presented himself as a deity. Such an event today would likely be considered a close encounter of the third kind.

Other highly credible evidence includes the testimonies of airline and military pilots, military officials, astronauts, and police officers.

Astronaut Gordon Cooper testified that air force personnel filmed a UFO that landed at Edwards Air Force Base. He said the film was immediately whisked off to Washington, DC, never to be seen again.

Police Officer Lonnie Zamora encountered a white egg-shaped craft in Socorro, New Mexico, with two small beings dressed in white standing on the ground beside it.

There is the testimony of the Air Force's Lieutenant Robert Jacobs of a UFO that flew around an Atlas missile he was filming and fired several beams at it, knocking it out of the sky. His direct superior confirmed this in writing.

There is the testimony of Robert Salas, the deputy crew commander of a missile site at Malmstrom Air Force Base; he experienced the shutdown of all guided missiles while a UFO hovered outside the main gate of the compound.

There is the testimony of John Healy, a Cleveland police detective who was a reserve medic on board an army helicopter that was lifted in a beam of green light toward a hovering UFO over Mansfield, Ohio.

There is the incident in Elmwood, Wisconsin, where a UFO fired a blue beam at a police car, completely destroying its electrical system and leaving Officer George Wheeler to suffer in excruciating pain for six months before he died.

There is the four-hundred-foot long object seen by the crew of America West flight 564 over Texas and the recorded communications between the pilot, air traffic control in Albuquerque, Cannon Air Force Base, an F-117A fighter pilot, and NORAD.

But as long as the government continues to keep the lid on the UFO mystery, the same questions that prevailed fifty years ago will continue to go unanswered: *What are they? Where do they come from? Why are they here?*

The facts speak for themselves; some are debatable and some are not. I have tried to present my views in as simple and uncomplicated a way as possible, with logic and with common sense. The events I have detailed regarding prehistoric, biblical, and current times conform to a logical scenario of alien intervention and the genetic manipulation of the human race.

However, what I have proposed is only a theory—a theory based on what I believe to be the most credible information available. I have presented ideas from a simple but logical perspective, a few of which (to the best of my knowledge) have never been considered before. I have raised a few questions regarding biblical scripture, some of which no one has ever thought to ask. I have offered a few opinions and have drawn only a few conclusions, but I do not claim my ideas are the answer to the UFO mystery, just a logical and commonsense evaluation of events as I see them. To some, it may seem like just another UFO theory, and that's exactly what it is. However, it is a theory viewed from a perspective of logic and common sense.

I hope that what I have presented will at least leave some of you thinking. Though not absolute proof, there is an overwhelming amount of evidence supporting my views. However, it is up to you, the reader, to remain objective, weigh the evidence, and decide for yourself.

Notes

1. Object materialized from out of nowhere
   "UFOs Uncovered #2." *Out of This World*. Prod. Peter Lories/
   Bradley Adams. TLC.

2. Object filmed during Shuttle Mission STS-114
   "Black Box UFO Secrets. *UFO Files*. Dir. Jon Alon Walz. THC.
   7 Aug. 2006.

Bibliography

Blum, Howard. *Out There*. Simon and Schuster, New York, 1990.

Blumrich, Josef F., *The Spaceships of Ezekiel*. Bantam, New York, 1974.

"The Peaceful Space Activities for Human Affairs," Brookings Report, Washington, DC, 1961.

Burnham, Robert. "Here's Looking at Ida." *Astronomy Magazine*, April 1994.

Commonwealth of Australia Department of Transport Aircraft Accident Investigation (the Frederich Valentich disappearance)

Cremo, Michael A., and Richard Thompson. *Forbidden Archaeology*. Govardhan Hill Publishing, Alachua, Fl. 1990 and 1996.

Eds., *The Unexplained*. Marshall Cavendish (Research Edition), Freeport, Long Island, NY, 1983.

Eds., *The Wycliffe Bible Commentary*. Moody Press, Chicago, IL. 1962.

Fiore, Edith. *Encounters*. Ballantine, New York, 1990.

Garrett, José Maria de Almeida. *Novos Documentos de Fatima*, Loyala ed., San Paulo, 1984.

Hopkins, Budd. *Missing Time*. Ballantine, New York, 1991 and 1998.

Jacobs, David M., *Secret Life*, Simon & Schuster, Fireside ed., New York, 1993.

Randle, Kevin D., and Donald R. Schmitt. *UFO Crash at Roswell*. Avon Books, New York, 1991.

Rand McNally Cosmopolitan World Atlas. 1979.

Sitchin, Zechariah, *The 12th Planet*. Bear & Co., Rochester, Vt., 1976 and 1991.

Sunday Times, United Kingdom, June 4, 2000.

von Däniken, Eric. *In Search of Ancient Gods*. Souvenir Press,. England. 1970; Corgi, 1976 and 1981.

Webster's Third International Dictionary, Unabridged. G. & C. Merriam Company, 1976. Springfield, MA.

Wilson, Don. *Our Mysterious Spaceship Moon*. Dell, New York, 1975.

Zeidman, Jennie. Helicopter-UFO Encounter over Ohio, Evanston, IL Center for UFO Studies, 1979.